Managing the New Product Development Process

CASES AND NOTES

Robert J. Dolan

HARVARD UNIVERSITY
Graduate School of
Business Administration

▼▼ **Addison-Wesley Publishing Company**
Reading, Massachusetts ■ Menlo Park, California ■ New York
Don Mills, Ontario ■ Wokingham, England ■ Amsterdam ■ Bonn
Sydney ■ Singapore ■ Tokyo ■ Madrid ■ San Juan ■ Milan ■ Paris

Library of Congress Cataloging-in-Publication Data

Dolan, Robert J.
    Managing the new product development process : cases and notes /
  by Robert J. Dolan.
        p.   cm.
    Includes bibliographical references.
    ISBN 0-201-52627-1
    1. New products—Management.   I. Title.
HF5415.153.D65 1993
658.5'75—dc20   92-10721
                                                                                        CIP

ISBN 0-201-52627-1
4 5 6 7 8 9 10-CRS-99 98 97 96 95 94

PREFACE

This book is an outgrowth of my efforts to develop an MBA level course at Harvard Business School entitled "New Product Development: An Analytical Approach." The philosophy of that course, reflected in this book, was that a deep understanding of consumer decision making is key to success at the various stages in the development process and that there is a set of tools which provides managers with the necessary insights. The book's objective is to provide the knowledge necessary for a manager to use and employ these tools effectively in new product decision making.

To this end, the book has four parts. First, Part 1 introduces the concept of the "context" of a new product decision which drives the selection of an appropriate development process. Second, Part 2 considers the decisions to be made prior to the product or service actually coming into being. This section begins by describing the major research tools available for this stage and illustrates their application in case studies. Part 3 has the same structure, except its focus is on the research undertaken between the time a product or service exists and its introduction to the marketplace. Finally, Part 4 concludes with consideration of interfunctional coordination issues and market evolution.

Throughout, we balance the settings across consumer and business-to-business situations. Where research procedures have utility across settings we so describe; if a situation dictates or precludes the effective use of a tool we also recognize that fact. My objective was to provide an opportunity to examine the key product development issues facing businesses and assess the most useful modes of approaching the problem.

The book can be used in two different ways. Coverage of all the case material requires about 12 class sessions of 60–90 minutes each. The notes provide background reading that, depending on exposure to research tools elsewhere, warrant up to 5 lectures/discussion. This was the format at Harvard Business School wherein the materials here were the complete set for a 15-session MBA elective course. For a longer, more comprehensive course on new products, the cases and research tools notes here can be effectively used with a number of the traditional new products texts. In this event, the book provides real-life, organizationally rich new product problems to apply the fruits of learning from these other sources.

Each part contains both notes and cases, which are tightly linked. For example, Part 2 begins with the Concept Testing note describing these research methods that are then heavily utilized in the first case of the section, Techsonic Industries. The other two notes in this part cover Perceptual Mapping and Conjoint Analysis; application of these methods is at the core of the MSA: The Software Company and Emergent Technologies cases completing the part. Throughout, the design is the same: presentation of tool ——➤ discussion of utility ——➤ analysis of actual practical application. In this way, there is a strong linkage between concept and application.

First, I would like to thank my students at Harvard Business School, both in the MBA and Executive programs, who tested a variety of materials. All the materials in this book have passed those managerial utility checks. Some other materials did not and have been excluded. These students helped shape my thinking on new product issues and sharpened the presentation here. Harvard Business School and Dean John McArthur have always been most generous in providing an environment where inquiry into the important problems of firms is encouraged and supported. My colleagues at HBS have been very helpful and stimulating. In particular, I would to thank those who contributed important materials to the book: Pete Clarke (now at Brigham Young University), John Matthews, a doctoral student at HBS; fellow HBS faculty; Melvyn Menezes, Rowland Moriarty, John Quelch, and Ben Shapiro. Beth

Toland, Janice Duff, Patsy DuMoulin, Dave Theisen, Margaret Hanshaw, and others at Addison-Wesley displayed the enthusiasm necessary to keep the project rolling and also asked the right questions at the right time. I had the benefit of critical, constructive review of both the concept and the product itself in various stages from a number of faculty at other institutions. In particular, I wish to thank

Robert T. Davis	Stanford University
Ashok Gupta	Ohio University
Richard T. Hise	Texas A & M University
Thomas Hustad	Indiana University
DiPak Jain	Northwestern University
Michael Johnson	University of Michigan
Robert Smiley	Indiana State University
Dave Wilemon	Syracuse University

Their comments were most helpful in structuring the book and improving the execution of the material.

Thankfully, getting all the material put together and kept in order throughout many revisions was something that I never worried about due to the efforts of Michelle Keith, my secretary, and the Word Processing Operation at HBS.

Finally, I thank and dedicate this book to Kathleen, Hilary and Nicholas, my family.

Boston, Massachusetts   R.J.D.

CONTENTS

PART 3

Formulating the Market Introduction Strategy

PART 4

Managing the Dynamics of Product Line Evolution

PART 1
New Product Development

INTRODUCTION

New products are imperative to long-term success. Customers' wants change; competitive products improve; new entrants appear; and enabling technology develops. The Coca-Colas of the world, holding market share leadership despite a 100-year-old formulation, are indeed rare. Most firms must deal successfully with the issues presented in the Part 1 cases.

NEW YORK LIFE PENSION DEPARTMENT Its "bare-bones" strategy of providing investment vehicles to pension investors but no supporting services seems to be becoming out of touch with the market. The decision-making power in the pension market has shifted apparently in favor of those offering "one-stop shopping." Should New York Life (NYL) adapt its product line strategy to this change in the marketplace? If so, how?

SEALED AIR CORPORATION Its history of technological innovation has generated market share leadership. However, a small competing firm has invented around Sealed Air's patents, introducing a low performance/low price product, capturing significant market share in some regions. Should Sealed Air "trade down" its product line, offering a relatively low performance/low price product to meet this competition?

HENKEL Henkel has two well-established brands in different segments of the adhesives market. In the heavy-duty segment, Pattex is a general-

1

purpose brand under siege from recent technologically driven niche entrants. In the light-duty segment, Pritt is itself a phenomenally success-ful niche player. Can new products be used to capitalize on the brand franchises built up on a worldwide basis?

The examples in Part 1 portray the great variety of stimuli to new product development. As shown in Exhibit 1, a company's efforts can be driven by any combination of the three forces—company assets, cus-tomer wants, and competitive products. The part also presents new product decisions of different forms: for example, product augmentation as new services are added to an unchanged core product (NYL); product substitutes that raise cannibalization concerns (Sealed Air); and product complements that extend into specific segments (Henkel).

The *Matching the Process of Product Development to Its Context* note sets out the major dimensions in which new products differ from one anoth-

Exhibit 1. *Strategic triangle of forces for new product development*

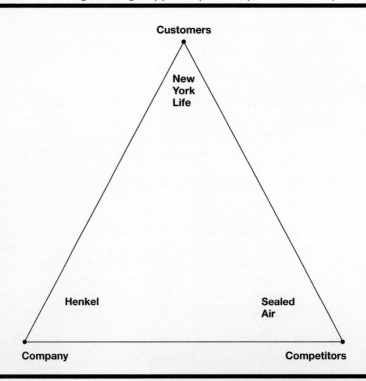

er. In addition to the product type dimension, other contextual factors impact how one ought to consider the development program; for example, the note defines a new product's context based on three factors:

1. The impetus to the introduction;
2. Its position on a "newness map" with the dimensions (a) newness to the company and (b) newness to the market;
3. Its position on a "risk map" with the dimensions (a) opportunity cost and (b) development risk.

Study of the cases allows application of the context mapping framework of the note but also establishes the centrality of understanding consumers to *any* new product decisions. Effective consumer analysis is accomplished in different ways in the Part 1 cases, given the data available; one may find the data wanting in one or more of the cases. Parts 2 and 3 present the research methods that can be used to develop the in-depth understanding of consumers necessary for effective new product management.

1 _NOTE_

Matching the Process of Product Development to Its Context

Robert J. Dolan

INTRODUCTION

The value of an integrated new product development process, i.e., one in which marketing, research and development, and production work together rather than through sequential hand-offs of ideas and blueprints, is well-documented.[1] Each team member brings crucial skills and knowledge to the party; marketing's major job is to bring in the "voice of the market."

---

[1]See, for example, J.L. Bower and T.M. Hout, "Fast-Cycle Capability for Competitive Power," H. Takeuchi and I. Nonaka, "The New New Product Development Game," G. Stalk and T. Hout, _Competing Against Time,_ and K. Clark and T. Fujimoto, _Product Development Performance._

Professor Robert J. Dolan prepared this note as the basis for class discussion.

While marketing's job is clear, its performance overall has led some observers to despair such as in the article "The Decline and Fall of Market Research in Corporate America," viz. "We have lost our energy when it comes to listening to the customer. We are in a state of decompression in that area, and it is killing us in the marketplace." (Hodock [1991])

A major contributor to this lack of vitality in market research is the standardization of research methods across all the company's new product development projects. Rather than a "one-size-fits-all" situation, the market research process must be tailored to context set by three key factors:

1. The impetus to the development activity;
2. The extent of market and company "newness" of the proposed product;
3. The opportunity cost and development risk associated with the project.

This note sets out these three context factors and provides a framework for assessing the specific words to be heard from the voice of the market and the most appropriate means of listening.

CONTEXT DESCRIPTION

The first context descriptor is the impetus to the development activity; i.e., the product's "reason why." Marketing must understand the strategic positioning of the product within the firm to bring the right data to the table. For example, assessing a product's ability to open up new market segments requires different data than assessing its ability to induce current customers to "trade up."

The second key context factor is the product's extent of "newness." A 1982 Booz, Allen and Hamilton survey classified 700 firms' product introductions according to:

1. Newness to the Market.
2. Newness to the Company.

Only 17% had "high" newness to the market comprised of 10% with high company newness and 7% with low company newness. For the vast majority of products, relative comparisons to both currently existing products of the firm and "in-kind" competitors must be considered.

The third key context factor is the product's position on the opportunity cost/development risk map. In his article describing this McKinsey concept, Krubasik [1988] defines opportunity cost as the risk of missing a fast moving market window. Developmental risk is the risk of introducing the wrong product to the market. These variables impact the recommended product development process.

In situations of low development risk and high opportunity cost, getting to the market quickly is the paramount concern and a "crash program" is required. On the other hand, low opportunity cost coupled with high developmental risk makes the time-to-market less important and places emphasis on making sure the product is right once it gets there.

These contextual factors lead to very different optimal product development processes. Rather then relying on a standard set of procedures—in market research, research and development, and engineering—the firm must ask a different set of questions depending upon the context and also utilize a different set of research methods to obtain the necessary market data.

LINKING CONTEXT TO PROCESS

The newness map has the central position in linking context to process. Consider the four examples shown in Fig. A: the Honda Accord Station Wagon, Kodak Filmless Camera, Intecom PBX, and Light Signatures Document Processor. What issues did each face?

The Accord Station Wagon's position is "firm moderate/market low." The executive vice president of Honda's U.S. sales and marketing division explained Honda's choice of a station wagon as opposed to a minivan as "simply a cost efficient way to add a new model. It's an easy way for us to get a vehicle with a certain amount of sales potential, without getting into an area where we have no experience." (Stertz [1990]) Whereas the station wagon was simply a reengineering of the sedan, a minivan would have stretched Honda's capability—in terms of producing the vehicle and entering into intense competition in a segment with well-established competitors. The station wagon was a conservative move presenting little question about the Honda's ability to manufacture effectively. The major issues were: the demand for the station wagon segment overall (registrations had fallen from over 800,000 in 1986 to 450,000 in 1989); to a lesser degree, the extent to which the Accord wagon would take away from sales of the Accord sedan; the fit to the Honda image to the station wagon segment; and the appeal of the Honda wagon relative to currently existing wagons.

Kodak Photo CD in the "firm moderate/market moderate" position is a filmless camera system due out in March 1992 (Rigdon [1991]). The "market moderate" position stems from Sony and Canon filmless sys-

Figure A. *Four product introductions on newness map*

		Intecom: PBX Systems	Light Signatures: Document Processor
	Honda: Accord Station Wagon	Kodak: Filmless Camera	

High — Newness to firm — Low

Low — **Newness to market** — High

tems now available which operate somewhat differently from Kodak's system. These products have had limited success. Sony's MAVICA system captures pictures on a floppy disc which can be instantly shown on a television set but these images are fuzzier than actual film-based photos. Kodak's system will store the photos on a compact disc, shown on either a television or a computer terminal. It is believed the quality of the Kodak system image will be comparable to prints from conventional film systems.

Kodak's situation brings the following to the forefront:

1. What features would be most desired by consumers?
2. Would Kodak's improvement in picture image quality be sufficient to overcome potential consumers' reservations about the available Sony and Canon systems?
3. How should the product be brought to market? i.e., should it be sold through the current camera salesforce or should a new salesforce be set up?
4. How can the cannibalization of its current market-dominating film based system be controlled?

Intecom's voice-and-data PBX is an example of "firm high/market moderate" (see Ghemawat [1991] for details). Intecom was a start-up company which became a successful innovator over industry incumbents AT&T, Rolm and Northern Telecom. The primary product development issues at Intecom were:

1. How likely was it that they would be able to make a commercially viable product?
2. How soon would the incumbents or others match or leapfrog the Intecom technology?
3. How great were switching costs among present users?

An important contrast between Intecom and Kodak is the suppression of cannibalization concerns as one moves from moderate to high on the firm newness dimension. Ghemawat identifies Intecom's freedom from concern about cannibalization as the key driver of the fact that it developed the new technology rather than the industry incumbents.

Finally, Light Signatures Inc.'s Sigma Three Secure Document Processing System (Crane [1988]) is "firm high/market high." This system, designed to reduce stock certificate fraud, operates by passing a light beam through a stock certificate to capture the unique fiber pattern in memory. Issues in product development included:

1. Would the system work?
2. Could potential buyers in the securities and banking industry be convinced to trust it?
3. Could industry standards be set up ensuring compatibility of the system with other necessary in-place parts of a network?

To deal with these risks, Light Signatures entered into Beta Tests with Manufacturers Hanover and Morgan Guaranty. The results of these tests led the Securities Transfer Association and Securities Industry Committee for the American Society of Corporate Secretaries to endorse the Light Signatures system.

Figure B summarizes the key marketing issues as a function of position on the newness map. In each case, the firm must assess consumer likely response to a new offering but the associated key issues differ. Products in the southeast portion of the map raise cannibalization concerns as the low level of market newness limits the potential for expanding the market and low firm newness means competition between the entry and the firm's own existing products.

There are two ways to reduce cannibalization concerns. First, move to the right in Fig. B, retaining low to moderate firm newness but moving to new market segments. New segments ensure sales would be incremental but the cost is an issue of product/market fit. The second alternative is moving directly up in Fig. B, to high firm newness. The cost here

Figure B. *Position on newness map and resulting paramount marketing issues*

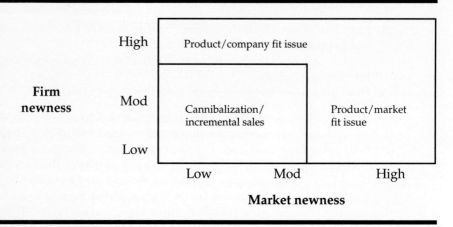

is the question of product/company fit, i.e., how well the firm can deal with development and new manufacturing and marketing requirements. Since the newness to the market is at most moderate, there are established competitors and this potential barrier must be overcome.

Figure C. *Firm positions on risk map*

After consideration of the position on the newness map indicates key area of concern, added insight comes from considering the opportunity cost/development risk position. While these two maps are obviously related, there is not a one-to-one correspondence between them. Figure C shows the four firms on the risk map.

Honda, facing low risk on both dimensions, can proceed with much more latitude than the other firms. Intecom and Light Signatures both face high developmental risk, suggesting a need to "get it right." However, due to the lack of competitors with the same technological aims, Light Signatures has low opportunity cost, permitting lengthy market testing through beta sites. If Intecom utilized a similar market research program, it would probably be beaten to market by a competitor. Kodak represents a lower degree of developmental risk but intermediate position on opportunity cost. This suggests a process to get to market by maintaining flexibility via development of a modular system.

SUMMARY

Figure D presents an overall schematic of how context impacts the proper new product development process. The impetus for a new product program generates a particular purpose for the introduction. This establishes certain evaluation criteria. The position of the idea on the newness map surfaces the key marketing questions and establishes the data requirements. The position on the risk map then helps determine the optimal trade-off of speed vs. accuracy in the research process.

The classic symptoms of poor performance by marketing in the new product development task are:

1. Market research data arriving too late to have an impact on the decision.
2. Market research data not being informative on the key decision issues facing management due to lack of understanding the strategic role of the new product.
3. Market research data documenting the obvious.
4. Market research being designed to confirm an already held view rather than to present possibly disconfirming data.

Understanding of the context and custom tailoring research process to it is key to revitalizing market research and increasing marketing's contribution to the integrated development process.

Figure D. *Context to process model*

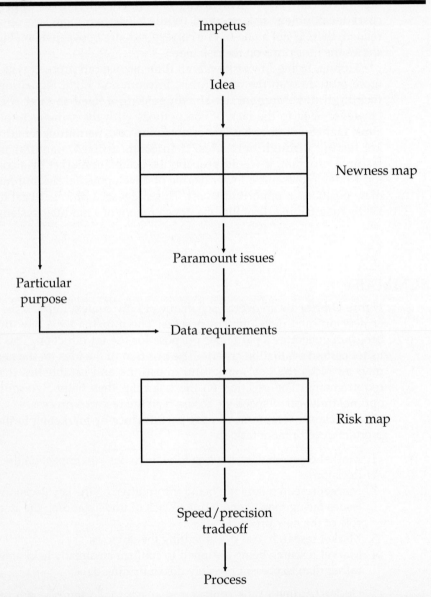

REFERENCES

Booz, Allen and Hamilton, *New Products Management for the 1980s* (New York: Booz, Allen and Hamilton, 1982).

Bower, J. L. and T. M. Hout, "Fast-Cycle Capability for Competitive Power," *Harvard Business Review*, November–December 1988, pp. 110–118.

Clark, K. B. and T. Fujimoto, *Product Development Performance* (Boston: Harvard Business School Press, 1991).

Crane, T. C., "Shedding Light on Security Fraud," *ABA Banking Journal*, May 1988, p. 22ff.

Ghemawat, P., "Market Incumbency and Technological Inertia," *Marketing Science*, Spring 1991, pp. 161–170.

Hodock, C. L. "The Decline and Fall of Marketing Research in Corporate America," *Marketing Research*, June 1991, pp. 12–29.

Krubasik, E. G., "Customize Your Product Development," *Harvard Business Review*, November–December 1988, pp. 46–53.

Rigdon, J. E., "Kodak Tries to Prepare for Filmless Era Without Inviting Demise of Core Business," *Wall Street Journal*, April 18, 1991, p. 131ff.

Stalk, G. and T. Hout, *Competing Against Time* (New York: Free Press, 1990).

Stertz, B. A., "Honda Unveils Wagon, Edging Near Full U.S. Line," *Wall Street Journal*, December 14, 1990, p. 11.

Takeuchi, H. and I. Nonaka, "The New New Product Development Game," *Harvard Business Review*, January–February 1986, pp. 137–146.

1 *CASE*

New York Life Insurance Company: Pension Department

Robert J. Dolan

Charlie Brown, Linus, and three other characters from the Peanuts comic strip had come to the inside front cover of *Pension World* magazine in a Metropolitan Life advertisement. Each was smiling and shaking a neatly wrapped package above ad copy which read:

> **Met Life's packaged 401(k) program has something in it for everyone.**
>
> With the Metropolitan Savings Plan Program, you'll get exactly what you want for your corporate savings plan.

Professor Robert Dolan prepared this case as the basis for class discussion rather than to illustrate either effective or ineffective handling of an administrative situation.

Like daily-valued investment choices, flexible plan design, state-of-the-art record-keeping services, and a well-trained staff of benefit specialists to help you.

We've even packed in additional services you may not find in other 401(a) and 401(k) programs, including our "service guarantee." And since everything's wrapped up in one neat package, Met Life's savings program is more efficient and easier for you and your employees.

In March 1990, this ad was a familiar one to Thomas O'Connor, senior vice president and head of the Pension Department at New York Life (NYL) Insurance Company. Metropolitan and other NYL competitors had been spending heavily in trade journals trumpeting the value of this "bundling" of all necessary services for 401(k)[1] plan management. Their advertisements were directed to corporate managers of defined-contribution plans, the fastest growing type of pension fund. Most of NYL's major competitors followed the same product strategy as Metropolitan, i.e., offer the benefits of "one-stop shopping" by providing not only investment vehicles (such as money market funds and mutual funds), but also all necessary ancillary services—such as record-keeping for all plan participants, education of plan participants about investment options, and filing necessary Internal Revenue Service forms. O'Connor had devised and implemented a different strategy for NYL. He explained:

We are a bare-bones investment house. We have a full-line of investment products: guaranteed investment contracts, bonds, convertibles, equities—and so on. But that's all we offer. We made an explicit decision—don't do individual participant record-keeping or plan administration. We tried a full-service strategy once, about eight years ago, but it turned out to be more expensive than we originally thought and we were not very good at it. So, we said let's get out of this and focus on being successful by restricting ourselves to offering investment products only and having the lowest expense-to-sales ratio in the business. That has worked pretty well for us.

But, it's a different ballgame as you look to the 1990s. It's obvious that the 401(k) market is where the action is. There, you've got Fidelity and the mutual fund companies coming in with lots of advertising dollars, name recognition, and skill in individual record-keeping. They are selling that "full-service" idea heavily. So are Met Life and the other big life insurance companies.

---

[1]A 401(k) plan is a retirement plan which allows individual employees to set aside part of current income on a tax-deferred basis. Employers frequently match part or all of the employee's contribution to encourage use of such a program. Withdrawing plan assets before retirement would result in a 10% tax penalty.

We want to grow. There are some things we can do consistent with our current "bare-bones" investment house strategy, like advertise more and better develop the sales force. But, I'm not sure if that's enough—we have to reassess our basic strategy. Some of our customers seem to want one-stop shopping and our competitors certainly are trying to make it a big deal. So maybe it's time for us to become a full-service provider—even if we think it will cost us a minimum of $10 million to set up the backroom operation to support it.

PENSION FUND INDUSTRY

In 1989, private pension fund assets in the United States were $2 trillion—the bulk of that was in defined benefit plans (DB); however, the $265 billion in defined-contribution (DC) plans in 1989 was expected to grow to $500 billion by 1995. DB and DC plans differed in several important respects:

1. In a DB plan, the employer guaranteed the employee a specified level of benefit from the time of a qualifying retirement until death. In contrast, DCs were essentially tax-exempt savings plans. The employee made a voluntary contribution to his or her individual pension fund. The contribution was exempt from current income taxes. Often, the employer would contribute to the individual's fund on a matching basis, e.g., a typical arrangement was the employer provided $.50 for each dollar contributed to the fund by the employee up to 3% of salary.

2. As a result of #1, DB plans were administered at the company level. Professional managers invested plan assets for the company to minimize the current company expenditure needed to meet future benefit obligations. In a DC plan, the employer selected the investment vehicle options to be made available to individual employees; but, each employee determined his own asset allocation among the options. Thus, a company with 1,000 employees operating under a DB plan would have one professionally allocated portfolio; the same company with a DC plan would have 1,000 amateur allocated portfolios.

3. DC plans were easily portable. An employee leaving a company simply took his pension plan with him. IRS regulations stipulated how the funds were to be invested in order to preserve their tax-exempt status. However, termination of employment before retirement age did not mean loss of all retirement benefits as it would for the nonvested portion of a DB plan.

4. DB plans were significantly more costly for companies to administer due to government regulations intended to protect employees from inadequate funds being available to fund future guaranteed benefits.

While 1989 DC plan assets were small relative to DB plan assets, DC plans had recently become the preferred plan type among both employers and employees. A DC plan relieved an employer of investment risk and shifted it to employees; but, many employees were more than willing to accept the investment risk in return for the portability of DC plans. While the number of companies offering DB plans roughly doubled from 1975 to 1987 (from 100,000 to 210,000), firms offering DC plans nearly tripled (from 210,000 to 610,000). Many companies offered employees both a DB and a DC plan. In 1989, 29 million people were covered by DB plans and 35 million by DC plans.

COMPETITION FOR PENSION FUND MANAGEMENT

Firms managed their pension funds in a number of ways. Some, such as General Electric, set up internally managed subsidiaries or departments. Others relied on some combination of commercial banks, independent investment managers, mutual fund companies, and insurance companies.

Commercial banks typically had lending relationships with their clients which they leveraged off to get into the pension side. Bankers Trust ($79 billion in tax-exempt assets managed) and Wells Fargo ($77 billion) were the two largest in the pension market. Independent investment managers, such as Sanford Bernstein and Miller, Anderson and Sherrerd, were the traditional source of investment vehicles. Mutual fund companies, such as Fidelity ($19 billion) and T. Rowe Price ($9 billion) entered the institutional market from their strength in the retail market. Insurance companies entered via their ability to offer Guaranteed Investment Contracts (GICs). A GIC was similar to a certificate-of-deposit in that it offered a fixed rate of interest. However, the rate was usually higher than a CD-rate and was backed by the entire asset pool of the issuing life insurance company.

An NYL brochure described a GIC and the various types of GICs as follows:

> *Description: A fixed-income investment which guarantees the principal, interest, and expense charges for a specified period of time and which is carried at book value. New York Life offers a wide variety of competitive GICs to meet the differing needs of plan sponsors. These include:*

- Bullet or Compound Interest GICs: *For single deposits. These pay a compounded interest rate at maturity. They can also accommodate benefit withdrawals. Ideal for defined benefit plans.*

- Payback or Simple Interest GICs: *Also for single deposits, but which pay an interest rate annually. The principal is repaid at maturity. Ideal for defined benefit plans.*

- Open Window or Window GICs: *For multiple deposits. These pay a compounded rate and principal at maturity, while providing ongoing benefit withdrawals and investment transfers. Ideal for 401(k), profit-sharing and thrift plans.*

- Floating Rate GICs: *Generally for single deposits. These pay compounded interest at maturity based on a floating spread over an appropriate benchmark such as T-bills. Ideal for defined contribution and defined benefit plans.*

Throughout the second half of the 1980s, the competition for pension fund management centered on DC plans. Many DB plans were "over-funded" as investment performance had exceeded company expectations and no new company investments were required to meet future obligations. DC plan assets grew by 15% per year as contributions were made to existing plans each year and the number of plans increased rapidly. The more conservative nature of the DC plan asset allocation decision maker, i.e., the individual, led to sharply differing investment vehicle utilization rates. Only about 3% of total DB plan assets were invested in GICs. However, it was believed that about 65% of DC plan managers made a GIC option available to firm employees. If the GIC option was available, it attracted about 70% of an employee's assets on average.

A DC plan sponsor at a company needed three types of services: custodial services, record keeping/plan administration, and investment vehicles. Custodial services were typically provided by a bank. Record keeping/plan administration was provided for in one of three ways: done internally, contracted for with a record-keeping firm, or done by one of the providers of investment vehicles. Investment vehicle providers marketed their vehicles to the plan sponsors as appropriate options to include in the firm's DC plan. A DC plan sponsor typically put together a package of three or four investment options to be offered to individual employees. For example, a DC plan might allow an employee to allocate his plan dollars over:

1. a GIC from NYL paying 8.5% interest
2. Fidelity Puritan Fund
3. Own company stock

The most commonly included options along with GICs were money market funds, bond accounts, mutual funds, and the company's own stock. GICs and Money Market Funds were the most conservative form of investments available as the principal was protected and the return known. While GICs were the typical mode of entry for insurance companies into Pension Fund Management, most insurers offered other investment vehicles as well. The largest life insurance companies in terms of total tax-exempt assets managed were Prudential, Equitable, Metropolitan Life, Aetna Life, and The New England. New York Life was the eleventh largest. Its $17 billion in assets managed made it about 1/5 the size of Prudential.

SELLING DC PLAN MANAGEMENT

Mike Harrington, national sales manager for NYL's pension department, explained his approach to the DC business.

The first thing you have to realize is that selling 401(k) plans is not an investment business. Selling defined benefit plans is an investment business. There, you sell to a plan sponsor. His job is to invest money for his company. You sell him ways to do that. It's simple. Selling 401(k) is different. It's a service business. You've got two buyers: the plan sponsor and the individual participants. The plan sponsor is usually the employee benefits director or maybe the CFO in smaller companies. He's got fiduciary responsibility and he wants the employees to get full benefit of what the company is prepared to do for them. He selects the investment vehicles available and provides for plan administration.

Tom O'Connor concurred:

That's right. He's the first gatekeeper; he's trying to provide service to his employees. We concentrate most of our efforts there. But in a DC plan, it really is pretty hazy who your client is. We should take a broad view. Our client is each employee. We would like not only to get their assets in, but keep that person as a client after they retire. We can do this if we manage it right. Since each individual decides whether or not to participate in the plan at all and what to allocate to your particular vehicle, there's a second sell to be made once you get the plan sponsor on board.

Harrington interjected,

That gets back to what I was saying earlier; this is a service business and our customers, the individuals, are bringing over into the tax-exempt arena the set of expectations they have developed in the nontax-exempt investments. They want to be able to get their daily balances; they want to see the funds they are invested in listed in the newspaper; they want to be educated with respect to investment options; they want to be able to switch money from one fund to another. The plan sponsor is going to do what he can to have those service expectations met. That is a real challenge for us.

By March 1990, there was very little significant "new start-up" business in the pension management market. Most new DC plans covered only 10 to 50 people, and hence fell outside the target market of major players such as NYL. Consequently, all major firms focused on "takeover business," i.e., getting a piece of an existing DC plan. The sales process began by identifying prospects from the Money Market Directory. This directory identified the plan sponsor of each company, the number of people participating in the plan, the plan's dollar assets, and the current investment vehicles used. The salesperson would then call the plan sponsor seeking a face-to-face meeting. Plan sponsors reported being solicited at the rates shown in Table A.

Of the plan sponsors, 32% said it was "very likely" or "somewhat likely" that they would establish new relationships with a firm for DC plan management within the next two years. Smaller companies were somewhat less likely than larger ones to establish new relationships.

As Mike Harrington explained,

It's a very long selling process. The Money Market Directory identifies the decisionmaker for you, but it does that for everybody else, too. When we call on someone, we don't expect to sell anything that day. Our objective in making a

TABLE A   Calls received by plan sponsors from pension management firms

Number of calls received per month	Total reported assets of all DB and DC plans combined (in millions)			
	< $10	10–49.9	50–99.9	$100 or more
None	3%	3%	2%	1%
1–4	50%	45%	36%	15%
5–9	26%	17%	28%	26%
10–15	13%	18%	22%	27%
16+	5%	6%	11%	28%
Don't know	3%	1%	1%	3%
Median # of calls received per month	4	4	5	10

sales call is to begin to differentiate ourselves in the plan sponsor's mind from the other 2,700 vendors out there. I want to establish top-of-the-mind awareness of New York Life and what we can do for him so that when an opportunity does come along, he will think of New York Life.

A plan sponsor wishing to include a GIC option in his firm's DC plan at a given time would first estimate the number of participating employees and the dollar amount to be invested. He then would specify the length of the contract, i.e., the term of the deposit. To get the best rate of interest for his firm's employees, the sponsor then asked a number of companies to bid for the business via the rate quoted. This he did by either contacting a number of individual companies directly or by engaging an independent third party who could collect a number of quotes on his behalf. The objective of NYL's selling process was to be on the list of GIC providers asked to quote. The principal and interest on the GIC were guaranteed by the assets of the issuing life insurance company.

NEW YORK LIFE

New York Life Insurance Company with $46 billion in assets and $2.1 billion net worth was one of the largest insurance companies in the United States. Over 140 years old, it enjoyed the highest ratings from Moody's, Standard and Poor's, and A.M. Best. Through its insurance business, NYL had developed good relationships with benefits managers at many corporations. In August 1980, it expanded its product line beyond pure insurance products by offering Guaranteed Investment Contracts.

Initially, NYL sold GICs through its Group Insurance sales force; i.e., a salesperson sold group life insurance, group health insurance, and GICs. In 1981, a dedicated sales force was set up within the Pension Department—drawn from people then in the Group Insurance sales force. Over the years, NYL built up a client base of about 1,000 GIC customers. According to Tom O'Connor, "We did very well with this business. We have pretty steadily maintained a 6%–7% share of the GIC market which is about all we wanted. Metropolitan and Prudential historically have been the leaders in GICs—very aggressive. We have other investment products now, but GICs are still the cornerstone of our current 'investment products only' strategy with no record-keeping at the plan participant level. Historically, our annual return on equity has exceeded 15% after tax. This has allowed the Pension Department to fund its own growth and we can maintain our current GIC share without additional capital.

Our position, though, has been that you don't want too much GIC business—for two reasons. First, because the rate is 'guaranteed' to the client for up to five years, you bear all the investment risk. Sometimes it gets hard to place the money somewhere you know you'll turn a profit. Second, there is an accounting issue. The future GIC payout has to be treated as a liability to the firm. GICs create a surplus strain and for us, the surplus-to-assets ratio is key. So, we try to maintain consistent growth; always being aware of surplus-to-assets ratios. It just would not be good for us as a company overall for me to go all out for market share in GICs."

Given these limitations of GICs, the established client base, and the dedicated sales force for pension products, O'Connor moved to establish "performance products" to broaden the Pension Department's product line. In 1984, NYL purchased MacKay/Shields Financial Corporation for active management of bonds, equities and convertibles. In July 1988, it set up Monitor Capital Advisors for indexed fund management. In September 1988, it entered a joint venture with Credit Commercial de France for Gamma Advisers Limited of London to do active international investment management. The four pieces—GICs, MacKay/Shields, Monitor and Gamma—were brought together in New York Life's MarketMaster Contract as shown in Exhibit 1. NYL positioned MarketMaster as a device for making a broad range of alternatives varying in risk/return available to plan participants. The guiding philosophy was a process-driven investment style with a focus on conservative investments. As suggested by the schematic of the sales brochure shown in Exhibit 1, GICs were the foundation. Other products were to be sold primarily as a cross-sell off the GIC client base. The four different types of investment products allowed NYL to claim no bias to any particular type of asset. NYL's organization structure for these entities is shown in Exhibit 2. 1988 and 1989 performance of the funds as compared to relevant benchmarks are in Table B.

NYL's strategy was to sell the MarketMaster concept primarily to companies in the mid-range of the pension plan market, i.e., corporate pension funds with total assets between $5 million and $100 million. Six thousand five hundred companies fit this description and collectively accounted for $110 billion in DC plan assets.

Harrington's 21 person sales force was organized into three districts: East (10 people), Central (6), and West (5). In each district, one person sold *only* GICs to pension funds with over $100 million in assets. Via this mechanism, NYL could count a number of *Fortune 50* firms among its

Exhibit 1. *NYL's MarketMaster contract*

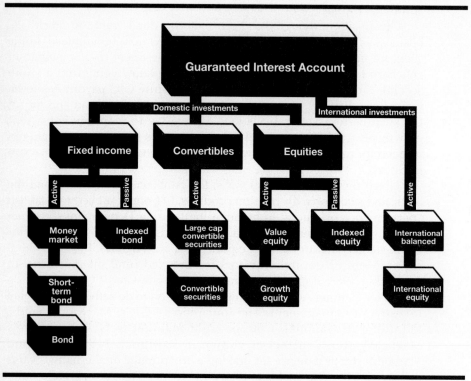

New York Life's MarketMaster contract starts with a competitive and reliable rate of return through its Guaranteed Interest Account—and allows you to diversify among a broad range of domestic and international investments, both actively and passively managed, all at reduced fees and with additional free services.

clients. The other salespeople, however, sold both GICs and performance products to target market firms.

Exhibit 3 gives pension group assets under management and new contribution for both types of products from 1984–1989. There were two types of nonguaranteed accounts: the Money Market account which was quite familiar to DC plan investors and nonmoney market which included the other eight products shown in Table B. Exhibit 4 disaggregates the 1989 statistics by salesperson. GICs and nonguaranteed accounts generated different types of revenue streams for NYL. In a GIC, NYL guaranteed a fixed rate of interest to be paid for a period of time, usually 3–7 years. With the dollars invested in the GIC funds, NYL bought invest-

Exhibit 2. New York Life pension department organizational structure

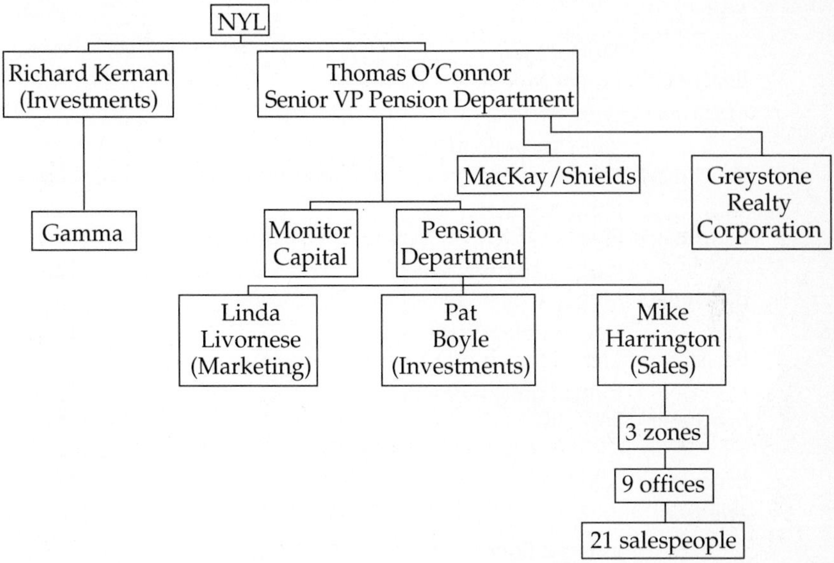

ments to support that rate. NYL's strategy was to invest in high quality instruments to obtain a "spread" of 100 to 110 basis points (i.e., 1.00% to 1.1%) between the return realized on the assets backing the GIC liabilities and the rate paid out. In GICs, NYL bore all the risk and hence the target rate of 100 basis points was higher than in nonguaranteed or "Separate Accounts" area wherein the net profit goal was 40 basis points. In the nonguaranteed area, NYL charged 1% per year for assets in actively managed funds. This was necessary to support the high fixed cost, people-intensive asset management business.

PLANNING FOR THE 1990s

O'Connor considered the 1989 performance numbers in assessing how well the MarketMaster concept was working and what he might do to market his products better in an extremely competitive environment. He had asked his group heads: Linda Livornese—Marketing, Mike

TABLE B   Gross annual return achieved: NYL funds compared to relevant benchmarks

NYL	1988	1989
Money Market Account	7.9%	9.7%
Benchmark: Lipper Money Market Index	7.0	8.8
MacKay-Shields		
Short Term Bond	2.5	10.3
Benchmark: Salomon Brothers 1–3 yr. Treasury Index	2.4	10.9
Bond Account	8.6	13.3
Benchmark: Shearson Lehman Hutton Govt. Corp. Index	7.6	14.2
Large Cap Convertible	12.9	15.1
Benchmark: Merrill Lynch Investment Grade Convertibles	12.3	16.2
Convertible Securities	12.8	13.6
Benchmark: Merrill Lynch All Convertibles Index	12.8	12.5
Value Equity Account	16.8	23.2
Benchmark: S&P 500	16.8	31.5
Growth Equity Account	14.4	21.7
Benchmark: NASDAQ Index	17.7	21.8
Monitor Capital		
Indexed Bond[a]	7.9	14.6
Benchmark: Salomon Brothers B.I.G. Bond Index	8.0	14.4
Indexed Equity[a]	16.2	31.2
Benchmark: S&P 500	16.8	31.5

[a]Funds managed to match performance of benchmark consistently with 25-basis-point tracking error.

Exhibit 3. *New York Life performance, 1984–1989 (all figures in millions of dollars)*

	1984	1985	1986	1987	1988	1989
Assets under management						
Guaranteed	5,805	7,481	8,792	10,217	12,100	12,313
Nonguaranteed	171	261	515	676	814	972
Total	**5,976**	**7,742**	**9,307**	**10,893**	**12,914**	**13,285**
Contributions						
Guaranteed	1,260	1,786	2,288	2,535	2,754	2,485
Nonguaranteed	25	101	296	325	204	243
Total	**1,285**	**1,887**	**2,584**	**2,860**	**2,958**	**2,728**

Exhibit 4. *1989 sales statistics by salesperson (in millions of dollars)*

	Guaranteed investment contracts	Money market	Nonmoney market
Eastern zone			
District Manager	932.12	No Separate Responsibility	
Rep #1	139.41	48.55	3.22
#2	20.46	25.61	5.23
#3	43.26	7.31	4.70
#4	37.48	10.35	.60
#5	27.17	4.90	1.82
#6	30.64	3.40	2.95
#7	18.34	3.81	1.64
#8	50.67	3.27	.51
#9	30.80	1.22	1.58
Central zone			
District Manager	435.90	No Separate Responsibility	
Rep #1	39.11	3.49	7.53
#2	96.65	8.66	2.28
#3	74.32	7.28	4.19
#4	43.04	.70	2.14
#5	33.69	1.55	.14
Western zone			
District Manager	267.37	No Separate Responsibility	
Rep #1	80.55	43.26	3.15
#2	35.44	17.62	6.28
#3	16.98	.75	2.16
#4	31.62	1.02	.04
Total	**2,485.02**	**192.80**	**50.19**

Harrington—Sales, and Pat Boyle—Investments, to make some suggestions about the most profitable growth options for NYL. While the three had somewhat different ideas about the best route, all agreed there were four major possibilities:

1. Target Market Selection—The Pension Department now focused on plans in the $1–$100 million range. Most of the sales force was more com-

fortable in the low end of this range, viz. $1–$15 million. Management felt that improvement was possible in the upper end of the range; some felt the sales force should "move upmarket," as NYL had been successful in selling GICs to some very large pension funds.

The 6,500 firms with pension assets in the $5–$100 million range accounted for $110 billion in pension assets. An additional 500 firms with pension assets in the range $100–$300 million could conceivably be reached by setting up a specialized sales force. These firms collectively represented $90 billion in pension assets.

2. Product Policy—while NYL had a full range of products along the risk/return spectrum with the MarketMaster concept, NYL still was basically an investment products provider. Full service vendors in the pension field supplied accounts with "one-stop shopping" by providing:

a. Plan Design and Filing of Initial forms with Internal Revenue.
b. Compliance Testing—to make sure the plan was in compliance with regulations on tax-exempt funds. Since laws were constantly changing, this compliance testing was an on-going process.
c. Record Keeping and Reporting—both at the company level and individual level; i.e., the vendor provided all information to the company and sent each individual periodic reports on his or her holdings by type of investment.
d. IRS Reports on an Annual Basis.
e. Investment Products.

NYL provided only the last of these. Most major insurance companies were full-service, including Prudential, Metropolitan, Equitable, Aetna, CIGNA, John Hancock, and Travelers. Like Metropolitan (ad quoted on first page of case), several featured this "one-stop shopping" in their ads as a key benefit. CIGNA and Mutual of New York ads are in Exhibit 5. For a mutual fund company, ongoing record keeping at the individual investor level was nothing new and consequently a relative strength in the pension market which they emphasized. (See Dreyfus, T. Rowe Price, and Fidelity ad copy in Exhibit 6.)

If an investment product provider did not supply the other services, the plan sponsor could do it in house or acquire the necessary services from a network of pension plan consultants or independent record keeping organizations. Some pension consulting firms such as William M. Mercer–Meidingor–Hansen, Inc. of New York, and National FSI in Dallas, were quite well-known and well-regarded. National FSI, for

Exhibit 5. *"One-stop shopping" advertisements of two representative insurance companies* Source: Excerpt from ad in Pension World, *March 1990*

Mutual of New York

Here are the services Societe Generale gets with their 401(k) plan from MONY. And the services you can have, too.

- Six investment alternatives. That's more diversification than most of our competition offers. (Plus, all investments cover the anticipated 404(c) fiduciary requirements.)
- A personalized communications program to introduce the plan to your employees.
- STRATEGIES, a quarterly asset allocation newsletter for your employees.
- Electronic mail, tape-to-tape, disk-to-disk transmission of data. We eliminate the paper in 401(k) administration.
- Complete record keeping. That's a service we've furnished our clients for over 25 years.
- Your own personal manager who services your account.

Call us about a 401(k) plan. No matter what your size, we'll treat you like one of the biggest companies in the world.

Cigna

At the CIGNA companies, our job is to make your job easier. We not only have everything you need to operate a 401(k) or retirement plan. We simplify the entire process.

---

example, consulted to over 200 plans and 180,000 participants. In NYL's target market, most recordkeepers were regional firms. Some at NYL felt that the presence of these providers obviated the need for NYL to be "full-service."

NYL had to decide whether to continue as it has as an investment house or to go full service. There were a number of ways to execute the full-service option. First, they could set up their own operation. This would require a large infrastructure. The data processing investment would be substantial—a minimum of $10 million. Then a facility to service in-coming and outgoing calls would have to be set up. NYL would have to become expert at handling large databases with lots of customized programming.

A second option was to acquire a record-keeping firm. Based on several investigations, it appeared the initial cost of this would be about the

Exhibit 6.   *Representative advertisements of mutual fund companies*
Source: *Excerpt from ad in* Pension World, *February 1990*

Dreyfus Services

With all the requirements that have to be met to make a 401(k) plan successful, you might think there's no way it could be simple. Yet "simple" is exactly the way you'd describe the Lion's Share 401(k). For one thing, Dreyfus is already a symbol of quality and reliability to your employees and key executives. What's more, we provide a full range of administrative support services for plan administrators—everything from our full investment menu (including a GIC fund), to state-of-the-art record keeping, trustee services and employee education.

T. Rowe Price

When it comes to 401(k) plans, nobody has more expertise than T. Rowe Price. So whatever your company's size—from 500 employees to 50,000 or more—we have what it takes to cover all your 401(k) plan needs. Because we've been administering defined contribution plans longer than any other mutual fund firm, we've learned how to do it better. Our PAS (Plan Administrative Service) offers state-of-the-art automated record-keeping reporting, benefit payments and more. We do it all.

Fidelity Institutional Retirement Services Company
Is there any such thing as a hassle-free 401(k)?

One with single-source capability? From investment management, to record-keeping, to employee communications support? One that gives you 30-day statements that are punctual as well as accurate? To learn more about Fidelity's 401(k) and other defined contribution plan services, please call Jeffrey Paster, Vice President, at 1-800-345-5033, extension 5692.

---

same as the first option. Finally, it was possible to explore an alliance with a record-keeping firm under which that firm would provide record keeping under the "NYL brand name." As far as the customer was concerned, the record keepers could just as well be NYL employees.

3. Sales force—75% of the Pension Department sales force was made up of previous GIC salespeople. The compensation system had been redesigned to motivate them to sell Separate Accounts. Commission income on GICs was capped at a level many salespeople reached. There was no maximum on the compensation which could be obtained from selling Separate Accounts. There was question about what other steps might be taken to improve sales force productivity.

4. Advertising—NYL's Pension Department did essentially no advertising and NYL's corporate level advertising was significantly less than Metropolitan Life's, for example. Also, with competition in the 401(k) market against a firm with the name recognition of a Fidelity, there was concern about whether NYL could afford not to allocate dollars to an advertising campaign. If there were major dollars to be committed, should it be spent to communicate with plan sponsors in trade journals or individual participants in broader media?

Faced with these questions, O'Connor asked the head of Marketing, Linda Livornese, to develop some data on the market to assist in the decision-making task. Livornese purchased syndicated reports on Defined Contribution Plans from Pension Management Associates (PMA) and the Gallup Organization. She also commissioned a large scale custom survey from the Gallup Organization to focus on NYL's target market, the $5 million–$100 million corporate pension market.

The PMA Report applied to the entire pension market of firms with plans over $5 million. The Gallup Syndicated Study restricted its sample to U.S. firms with between $5 million and $300 million in total pension assets. Gallup's data were collected from 820 company executives who were "responsible for selecting the outside financial institutions used to manage pension and retirement plan assets." The follow-up study done on a custom basis by Gallup for New York Life collected data from 400 similar company executives, except the sample was restricted to firms in the $5 million to $100 million total pension asset range.

RESEARCH FINDINGS

As Linda Livornese went back over the three research reports, representing a five-inch high pile on her desk, she thought the most relevant data for her colleagues' consideration were on customer buying behavior and current awareness and perception of various firms. These data seemed to have implications for each of the four growth options being considered.

CUSTOMER BUYING BEHAVIOR

Both syndicated surveys probed why pension managers selected the investment managers which they did. In the PMA survey, respondents rated a

TABLE C   Ranking of selection factors in order of importance

Investment performance
Reputation among employees
Record keeping and administrative services
Full product line of investment products
Fees charged
Availability of literature for employees
Geographical location

number of factors in terms of importance in the selection process. Table C shows the ranking of these factors, from most important to least important.

In the Gallup Syndicated Study, respondents were read a list of factors and asked, "Were any of the following an influence on your company's most recent selection of an outside investment manager?" See Table D.

The custom Gallup survey followed up by probing the importance of certain aspects of service (see Table E) and record-keeping in particular (see Table F).

Finally, Livornese believed that about 35% to 40% of firms in New York Life's target market used one firm for record keeping and asset management. The Gallup syndicated data provided data on this broken down by size of pension fund (see Table G).

KNOWLEDGE AND PERCEPTIONS OF COMPANIES

The Gallup Syndicated Report probed respondents' awareness of various firms by asking if they were familiar enough with the company to provide an assessment of the quality of its investment performance relative to risk. Twenty companies were included in this phase of the question. Table H reports the "able to rate" percentage for each company in descending order. Also, the average quality rating for return given risk is reported. The average is based on Excellent=4, Good=3, Fair=2, Poor=1.

There was significant variation in the "ability to rate" percentage across the asset size of respondents. Fidelity Investments, for example, while in eighth place in Table H on familiarity across the whole sample was in first place among plans with over $100 million in assets—a 66% "ability to rate" percentage. For most of the insurance companies, famil-

TABLE D   Gallup results on selection influences   Factors influencing the most recent selection of an outside investment manager, by total reported assets

Influence	Total %	Total reported assets of all defined benefit and defined contribution plans combined (in millions)			
		Less than $10 %	$10 to $49.9 %	$50 to $99.9 %	$100 or more %
Stated investment performance record	74	71	74	81	86
Investment philosophy/style of management	72	67	73	80	86
Formal sales presentations	57	49	59	62	66
The advice of consultants or selection specialists	38	31	40	48	43
The fact that their representative was accessible via a local office	35	43	37	21	21
A prior relationship for any business related service (net)	33	44	33	23	20
A prior relationship as a provider of credit services	19	26	18	12	14
A prior relationship for other business financial services	18	25	16	15	8
Their ability to also provide administrative and record-keeping services for plan sponsors	30	36	33	22	8
The recommendation of a friend or colleague	23	18	27	15	26
A prior relationship for personal financial services	6	10	6	3	1
Total	a	a	a	a	a
Number of interviews	(820)	(174)	(345)	(127)	(158)

Note: Base = Total

[a]Total exceeds 100% due to multiple responses

From the 1987 Gallup Study of Mid-Sized Pension Funds and Defined Contribution Plans–Analysis of Results–Vol. IV. ©1988. Reprinted by permission of the Gallup Organization.

iarity drops with asset size. In particular, New York Life's familiarity rating as a function of asset size was as follows:

	<$10 million	$10–49.9 million	$50–99.9 million	+$100 million
New York Life "ability to rate" score	67	55	51	36

TABLE E   Rating of importance of various other specific aspects of service

Other contact/communication services	Importance				
	Not too important %	Important but not essential %	Essential %	Don't know / doesn't apply %	Total %
Ability to provide other non-pension services	78	18	4	[a]	100
Providing financial planning services for company's officers	80	14	4	2	100
Providing financial planning services for employees	81	16	3	[a]	100
Providing a performance evaluation service (rating a fund's performance against that of other managers or an index)	20	36	42	2	100
Ability to provide a formal asset allocation analysis for company's plan	15	36	46	3	100
Ability to offer ongoing individual discretionary management	30	38	26	6	100
Ability to offer participants actively-managed investment options beyond a guaranteed vehicle/money market vehicle (for defined contribution plans)	33	21	28	18	100
Ability to offer a wide range of investment choices/ styles, so that the portfolio is adjustable	21	27	32	20	100
Number of interviews: 400					

[a]Less than 0.5%

TABLE F   Rating of importance of various record-keeping and administrative services

Other contact/communication services	Not too important %	Important but not essential %	Essential %	Don't know/doesn't apply %	Total %
			Importance		
Ability to provide record-keeping and administrative services, in addition to investment management	24	26	47	3	100
Providing accurate and comprehensive statements for company (the plan sponsor)	3	16	80	1	100
Providing accurate and clear statements to company plan participants (for defined contribution plans)	21	16	38	25	100
Providing company plan participants with investment information/economic reports (for defined contribution plans)	37	22	16	25	100
Ability to provide payment checks to retirees	23	16	57	4	100

Number of interviews: 400

TABLE G   Preference for obtaining record-keeping and administrative services from the same source as that which manages DC plan assets

| | | Total reported assets of all defined benefit and defined contribution plans combined (in millions) | | | |
	Total %	Less than $10 %	$10 to $49.9 %	$50 to $99.9 %	$100 or more %
From same source	35	37	37	22	24
From different sources	33	29	32	43	39
Not particularly important	29	34	27	32	34
Don't know	3	a	4	3	3
Total	100	100	100	100	100
Number of interviews	(658)	(129)	(267)	(105)	(142)

Note: Base = Companies which offer any defined contribution plans
[a]Less than 0.5%
From the 1987 Gallup Study of Mid-Sized Pension Funds and Defined Contribution Plans–
Analysis of Results–Vol. IV. ©1988. Reprinted by permission of the Gallup Organization.

The Custom Gallup study also obtained respondent's overall impressions of institutions they employed by type of firm on the dimensions of rate of return achieved and general quality of service (Table I).

O'Connor considered the data carefully. He also thought again about the headaches of efficient record-keeping and how trying to do it at NYL's current location in New York City probably did not make sense. On the other hand, the fundamental rule of marketing was being "close-to-the-customer." It would be a real advantage to keep that customer's records—to know how much money he had and when it started to go out rather than in. Forging a lifetime relationship was clearly facilitated by being the record keeper.

Mike Harrington focused on the other key in the marketing picture:

We want to be able to go to that plan sponsor in the mid-range market and say, "Look, whatever the issue, we can handle it for you. You're important to us." We have to build that trust in us and have him see that a relationship with us is the solution to his problems. Now, can we do that without offering him plan administration and record-keeping? That's the key question.

TABLE H   General familiarity with and rating of quality of investment performance relative to risk

	Ability to rate (%)	Average rating
Merrill Lynch	72	2.83
Aetna Life	62	2.90
E.F. Hutton	61	2.51
Prudential Asset Management	59	2.91
John Hancock	58	2.69
Paine Webber	58	2.69
New York Life	55	2.58
Fidelity Investment Institutional	54	3.13
Travelers	54	2.77
Metropolitan Life	50	2.82
Citicorp Investment	48	2.77
I.D.S. Trust	48	2.56
Bankers Trust	47	2.87
T. Rowe Price	47	2.79
State Street	46	2.85
Equitable Capital Management	40	2.77
Northern Trust	31	2.97
Wilmington Trust	21	2.71
Norwest Bank/Minneapolis	21	2.52
Supreme Bank	10	2.70

TABLE I   Perceptions by company type

	Insurance company		Commercial bank		Independent investment manager	
	Rate of return	Quality of service	Rate of return	Quality of service	Rate of return	Quality of service
Excellent	25	14	20	31	35	36
Good	66	63	58	53	52	58
Fair	8	17	14	12	8	4
Poor	–	6	2	2	2	–
Don't know	1	–	6	2	3	2

2 *CASE*

Sealed Air Corporation

Robert J. Dolan

The president and chief executive officer of Sealed Air Corporation, T. J. Dermot Dunphy, explained the firm's 25% average annual growth in net sales and net earnings from 1971 to 1980:

> *The company's history has been characterized by technical accomplishment and market leadership. During the last 10 years we built on our development of the first closed-cell, lightweight cushioning material, introduced the first foam-in-place packaging system, and engineered the first complete solar heating system for swimming pools. We intend to follow the same management guidelines in*

Professor Robert J. Dolan prepared this case as the basis for class discussion rather than to illustrate either effective or ineffective handling of an administrative situation. Certain nonpublic data have been disguised.

the 1980s. We intend to seek market leadership because leadership optimizes profit, and foster technological leadership because it is the only long-term guarantee of market leadership.

In July 1981, Barrett Hauser, product manager of Sealed Air's Air Cellular Products, was reflecting on Dunphy's management philosophy as he considered how Sealed Air should respond to some unanticipated competition in the protective packaging market. As product manager, Hauser was responsible for the closed-cell, light-weight cushioning material that Dunphy had mentioned. Sealed Air's registered trademark name for this product was AirCap.[1] AirCap cushioning materials had always faced a variety of competitors in the protective packaging market. More recently, however, several small regional producers had invented around Sealed Air's manufacturing process patents and begun to market cheap imitations of AirCap in the United States.

AIRCAP CUSHIONING AND ITS COMPETITORS

AirCap cushioning was a clear, laminated plastic sheet containing air bubbles of uniform size (see Exhibit 1). The feature that differentiated AirCap cushioning from all other bubble products was its "barrier-coating": Each AirCap bubble was coated on the inside with saran. This greatly increased air retention, meaning less compression of the material during shipment and, consequently, better protection. Barrier-coating and its customer benefits had been the central theme of Sealed Air's AirCap cushioning selling effort for 10 years.

Between 1971 and 1980, Sealed Air and Astro Packaging of Hawthorne, New Jersey, were the only air bubble packaging material producers in the United States. Sealed Air licensed Astro to use Sealed Air's patented technology. Astro produced two types of bubbles: a barrier bubble similar to AirCap,[2] and an uncoated bubble. Its sales were split about evenly between the two. In 1980, Astro's total U.S. sales were approximately $10.5 million, compared with $25.35 million in U.S. sales for AirCap cushioning. Sealed Air's market education had made customers aware of the advantages of coated bubbles; consequently, uncoated

---

[1]Sealed Air, AirCap, and Instapak are registered ® trademarks of Sealed Air Corporation. Solar Pool Blanket is a TM trademark of the same corporation.

[2]Astro's barrier bubble and the AirCap bubble differed in both manufacturing process and coating material. Astro used nylon rather than saran. The basic idea of reinforcing the polyethylene bubbles to improve air retention was, however, the same.

Exhibit 1. *AirCap® product and uses*

Cushioning

AirCap® air bubble cushioning protects products against shock and vibration during handling and shipping by literally floating them on a cushion of air. This material offers consistent performance because our unique *barrier-coating* guarantees air retention. AirCap withstands repeated impact since it will not fatigue or take a compression set. Cushioning applications include a range of products from lightweight retail items to delicate power supplies weighing several hundred pounds. Choose the grade that best fits *your* cushioning application!

SC-120   ST-120/ST-240   SD-120/SD-240/SD-480

Regular Duty   Regular, Heavy Duty   Regular, Heavy, Super Duty

Protective Wrap/Interleaving

AirCap is an excellent "protective wrap" material and ideal for "interleaving" between similarly shaped items. It is clean, non-abrasive, easy to use and provides superior surface protection. Lay your product on AirCap sheeting, fold it over and your product is fully protected! Typical protective wrap/interleaving applications include china, glassware, printed circuit boards, and spare parts.

SB-110   SC-120/SC-240   ST-120

Light Duty   Regular, Heavy Duty   Regular Duty

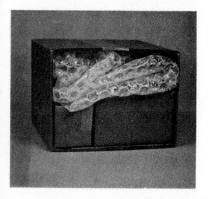

Void Fill

When a void in a package is not completely filled, the cushioned product may migrate within the shipping container. This movement is a major cause of damage in transit. Since large *regular-duty* AirCap bubbles do not compress, they fill voids effectively and eliminate product movement. Simply stuff AirCap sheeting into the carton, (left) or use an economical rolled "log". It's easy, clean, lightweight and cost efficient!

ST-120   SD-120

Regular Duty   Regular Duty

bubbles had never achieved greater than a 15% dollar share of the U.S. market before 1980.

In July 1981, uncoated bubble operations were being set up in Ohio, California, and New York. GAFCEL, which served the metropolitan New York market, was the only competitor yet to achieve significant sales volume. Two GAFCEL salespeople—one full time, the other about half time—had reached a $1 million annual sales rate. Several of AirCap's distributors had taken on the GAFCEL line.

Hauser was preparing to recommend Sealed Air's reaction to these somewhat unanticipated competitors. The firm could produce an uncoated bubble as cheaply as GAFCEL within a month with no major capital investment; it could run on machines used for another Sealed Air product. If Hauser were to recommend that the historic champion of barrier-coating offer an uncoated bubble, he would have to specify timing, the marketing program for the new product, and any adjustments in policies for AirCap cushioning and Sealed Air's other products. As Hauser thought about his options, he again flipped through the training manual recently distributed to Sealed Air's sales force: "How to Sell Against Uncoated Bubbles."

THE PROTECTIVE PACKAGING MARKET

The three major use segments of the protective packaging market were:

1. Positioning, blocking, and bracing: These protective materials had to secure large, heavy, usually semirugged items in a container. Typical applications included shipment of motors and computer peripherals.
2. Flexible wraps: These materials came under less pressure per square foot. Applications included glassware, small spare parts, and light medical instruments.
3. Void fill: These materials were added to prevent movement during shipping when an item and its protective wrap (if any) did not fill its carton.

The positioning, blocking, and bracing market was unique because of the heavier weights of items shipped. Flexible wrap and void fill were sometimes hard to separate because it was convenient to use the same product for both functions. The key distinction was that loose fills (for instance, polystyrene beads) dominated the void fill market but provided no cushioning protection and, hence, did not qualify as flexible wrap.

Until 1970, most materials used for protective packaging were produced primarily for other purposes. Heavy, paper-based products had dominated the market. Sealed Air was one of the first companies to approach the market with a customer orientation, i.e., it began product development with an assessment of packagers' needs. Since then, a variety of products specifically designed for protective packaging had appeared.

Sealed Air served these markets with two products:

1. Instapak© foam-in-place systems (1980 worldwide sales of $38.8 million) could accommodate any application, though their most advantageous use was for heavy items. In this process, two liquid chemicals were pumped into a shipping container. The chemicals rapidly expanded to form a foam cushion around the product. Instapak's comparative advantage resulted in a majority of applications in positioning, blocking, and bracing.
2. AirCap bubbles (1980 worldwide sales of $34.3 million) primarily served the flexible wrap and void fill markets.

In addition to coated and uncoated polyethylene air bubbles, there were two major competitors in these markets: paper-based products (cellulose wadding, single-face corrugated, and indented kraft), and foams (polyurethane, polypropylene, and polyethylene).

An excerpt from an AirCap promotional brochure in Exhibit 2 shows how Sealed Air positioned AirCap as a cost-effective substitute for these competitive products and loose fills. The brochure first pointed out the cost savings from AirCap cushioning, then presented results of "fatigue" and "original thickness retention" tests to demonstrate AirCap's protective superiority. Exhibit 3 compares products competitive with AirCap cushioning and Exhibit 4 gives their U.S. list prices, which represent relative costs for any order size from an end-user. Quantity discounts were offered on all materials.

BUYING INFLUENCES

The proliferation of packaging products and the lack of easily demonstrable universal superiority caused confusion among end-users. For example, products such as pewter mugs were shipped around the United States in AirCap cushioning, Astro coated bubbles, or even old newspapers.

Users were a varied lot. Some bought on a scientific price/performance basis. They understood "cushioning curves" such as those in Exhibit 5. Sealed Air could provide independently measured cushioning curves for competitive products as well as its own. Regardless, many firms did their own testing.

Exhibit 2. Sealed Air presents AirCap as cost-effective substitute

Typical Cost-Savings Comparisons

AirCap Vs. Corrugated Inserts

A manufacturer using corrugated inserts, cellulose wadding and polyethylene foam eliminated the need to inventory many packaging components (right), and reduced labor 84% by switching to AirCap (left).

Item	Corrugated Package	AirCap Package
Carton	$ .55	$ .55
Inner packaging	.80	1.05
Labor	.83	.13
Freight	2.60	2.40
Total cost	$4.78	$4.13
Savings using AirCap		$ .65

AirCap Vs. Thin-Grade Foams

An electronic service center employing the use of a thin-grade foam (right) required many layers of wrapping to protect against shock and vibration. Large AirCap bubbles (left) provided superior performance and lower packaging costs.

Item	Foam Package	AirCap Package
Carton	$ .46	$ .38
Inner packaging	1.33	.87
Labor	.66	.33
Freight	4.09	3.94
Total cost	$6.54	$5.52
Savings using AirCap		$1.02

AirCap Vs. Loose Fills

A distributing firm found that it needed an excessive amount of flowable loose fill to prevent product migration. A new AirCap package (left) using a simple criss-cross technique resulted in reduced material, shipping, labor and carton costs.

Item	Loose Fill Package	AirCap Package
Carton	$ .73	$ 47
Inner packaging	.75	.54
Labor	.42	.25
Freight	3.02	2.72
Total cost	$4.92	$3.98
Savings using AirCap		$ .94

AirCap Vs. Cellulose Wadding

A metering firm discovered it needed only half as much AirCap to achieve the same performance that cellulose wadding provided (right). In addition to lowering material costs, AirCap (left) is clean, lint free, non-abrasive and lightweight.

Item	Cellulose Wadding Package	AirCap Package
Carton	$ .30	$ .22
Inner packaging	.22	.12
Labor	.25	.08
Freight	1.35	1.20
Total cost	$2.12	$1.62
Savings using AirCap		$ .50

Resists Fatigue

In the transportation environment, packages are subjected to many jolts, bumps and shocks that can potentially cause damage. To function effectively, a cushioning material must retain its ability to protect over a series of repeated impacts. The loss of protective ability during repeated impact is termed "material fatigue".

This graph (left) indicates the increased shock an average product (0.25 psi) will receive during a ten-drop sequence from 24 inches. Test results show barrier-coated AirCap outperforms all materials tested.

BARRIER-COATING
Each individual AirCap bubble is barrier-coated to retain the air.

Retains Original Thickness

When a load is placed on a cushioning material two things occur that may contribute to a deterioration in its performance. First, is the immediate compression of the material, termed "creep". Generally, excessive thickness loss of a material results in increased material usage in cushioning and dunnage applications. Creep may contribute to product damage as the loss of thickness creates a void in a package, allowing the product to move, shift or rotate.

This chart (left) demonstrates how barrier-coated AirCap retains its original thickness better than all materials tested and provides product protection throughout the entire packaging, shipping, handling and storage cycle.

Material Tested	Initial Thickness Loss Upon 0.4 psi Load	Gradual Thickness Loss After 30 Days	Total Thickness Loss
AirCap SD240	7%	7%	14%
Polypropylene Foam	19%	11%	30%
Polyethylene Foam	16%	24%	40%
Cellulose Wadding	26%	12%	38%
Rubberized Hair IV	24%	27%	51%
Uncoated Bubbles (Large)	14%	50%	64%
Urethane Foam (1.25 pcf.)	53%		•
Embossed Polyethylene (Hex)	54%		•

*30 day evaluation not conducted due to excessive initial thickness loss.

IMMEDIATE THICKNESS LOSS

AirCap retains its original thickness upon the immediate application of a load. (See Below).

UNLOADED	LOADED	UNLOADED	LOADED
BARRIER-COATED AirCap (0.4 psi)		CONVENTIONAL CELLULOSE MATERIAL (0.4 psi)	

GRADUAL THICKNESS LOSS (CREEP)

AirCap's unique barrier-coating retains the air more effectively than uncoated bubbles, eliminating creep.

DAY 1	DAY 30	DAY 1	DAY 30
BARRIER-COATED AirCap (0.4 psi)		UNCOATED BUBBLES (0.4 psi)	

Exhibit 3. *Competitive product information*

1. Cellulose wadding (a paper-based product which tries to trap air between piles of sheeting)
   - Major suppliers:
     Jiffy Packaging, Hillside, N.J.
     CelluProducts Co., Patterson, N.C.
   - Sizes available:
     Thickness of 0.17 in., 0.25 in., 0.37 in., 0.50 in.
   - Advantages/disadvantages:
     Much cheaper than AirCap in thin grades; will not mark item wrapped; heavier than AirCap (3–4 lbs. per cu. ft. versus less than 1 lb. for AirCap) meaning higher shipping cost; excessive compression under heavy loads (see test results, Exhibit 2)
2. Corrugated products (sheets of ribbed cardboard, often cut and perforated to specific sizes)
   - Major suppliers:
     About 800 firms manufacturing in 47 states, including larger paper companies.
   - Advantages/disadvantages:
     Single face (cardboard with ribs on one side) appreciably cheaper than AirCap on square-foot basis; labor cost of using corrugated usually very high; poor cushioning.
3. Polyethylene foam (thin, smooth, rigid sheets of low-density foam)
   - Major suppliers:
     Sentinel Foam Products, Hyannis, Mass.
     CelluProducts Co., Patterson, N.C.
     Jiffy Packaging, Hillside, N.J.
   - Sizes available:
     48 or 68 in. wide rolls of thickness 1/16, 3/32, 3/16, 1/4 inch.
   - Advantages/disadvantages:
     Appreciably cheaper than AirCap in thin grades on square-foot basis; does not mark item wrapped; rigid product means hard to work with; tendency to tear; cushioning inferior to AirCap; more expensive than AirCap in thicker grades.
4. Polypropylene foam (thin, coarse, rigid sheets of low-density foam)
   - Major supplier:
     Du Pont Microfoam
   - Sizes available:
     Standard 72 in. wide rolls of thickness 1/16, 3/32, 1/8, 3/16, 1/4, 3/8 inches.
   - Advantages/disadvantages:
     Basically the same as for polyethylene foam.
5. Loose fills (expanded polystyrene beads, peanuts, etc.)
   - Major suppliers:
     Many small firms

(continued)

Exhibit 3 (continued)

- Advantages/disadvantages:
  50% cheaper than AirCap on cubic foot basis; messy; poor cushioning.
6. Uncoated bubbles (sheets of small air bubbles made of polyethylene film)
   - Major producer:
     Astro, Hawthorne, N.J. (Sealed Air licensee)
   - Sizes available:
     48 in. wide roll standard, bubble heights 3/16, 1/4, 1/2 inches. Bubbles also varied in the thickness of the films used. Generally, thicknesses were 1, 2, 3 or 4 mils with increasing film thickness giving greater strength.
   - Advantages/disadvantages:
     Cheaper than comparable height coated bubble; excessive air loss over time (about 65% height loss under 50 lbs. per sq. ft. pressure over 30 days versus 15% for AirCap).
7. Competitive coated bubble (essentially the same as uncoated bubble except nylon film coating added)
   - Major supplier:
     Astro, Hawthorne, N.J. (Sealed Air licensee)
   - Sizes available:
     48 in. wide roll standard, bubble heights 1/8, 3/16, 1/4, 1/2, 1 in.
   - Advantages/disadvantages:
     Under heavy loading, nylon barrier holds up better than Sealed Air's saran barrier; poor quality control (bubble heights generally 13% less than specified).

At the other end of the spectrum were firms with "a purchasing-department mentality," as some packaging materials suppliers put it. Price per square foot was their first consideration, delivery their second. As one Sealed Air executive commented, "To these people, cushioning curves are like accounting numbers. They think you can make them say anything you want."

There were no systematically collected data on the buying process or the extent to which price dominated performance in the purchase decision. Based on his experience as a district sales manager and now product manager, Hauser guessed that a packaging engineer influenced about 40% of the material purchase decisions.

Exhibit 4. *Suggested end user prices (in dollars) for major competitive products*

1. Paper-based cellulose wadding (Jiffy Packaging)

Thickness (in.)	Price	Single-face Corrugated
0.17	$27.70	$22.75
0.25	37.40	
0.37	50.60	
0.50	65.00	

2. Foams

Thickness (in.)	Jiffy Packaging (polyethylene)	Sentinel Products (polyethylene)	Du Pont Microfoam (polypropylene)
1/16	$20.30	$18.20	$17.20
3/32	25.90	24.00	25.17
1/8	34.15	32.70	34.90
3/16	53.35	49.40	53.86
3/8	na	na	109.72

3. Competitive bubbles (Astro)

Coated Nylon			Uncoated—Polyethylene		
Bubble height (in.)	Film thickness[a] (mils)	Price	Bubble height (in.)	Film thickness (mils)	Price
1/8	1 and 1	$35.25			
3/16	1 and 2	49.50	3/16	2 and 3	$47.00
1/4	1 and 2	57.00	1/4	2 and 3	54.50
1/2	1 and 2	71.75	1/2	2 and 4	65.75
1/2	2 and 4	87.75			
1	1 and 2	90.00			
1	2 and 4	110.00			

Note: Prices are per 1,000 sq. ft. based on a 50,000-sq.-ft. order.
[a]Each bubble is made of two layers of film. Thicknesses shown are for individual layers in mils. Thicker film produces a stronger product.

Exhibit 5. *Comparative cushioning performance by grade*
Source: AirCap brochure

Engineered To Provide Superior Cushioning

The test data on the graph below was developed by the Lansmont Corporation, an independent testing laboratory. The test method used closely simulates actual shipping conditions, and employs the use of an enclosed test block and shock machine. Five bottom drops were executed from 24 inches at each static stress. The last four drops were averaged to arrive at data points used to develop each cushioning effectiveness curve. This data illustrates AirCap's superior performance over a wide range of loadings, and may be used for comparison and to specify the best AirCap grade and thickness for your cushioning requirements. (SD-240 curves taken from data provided in Military Handbook 304-A.)

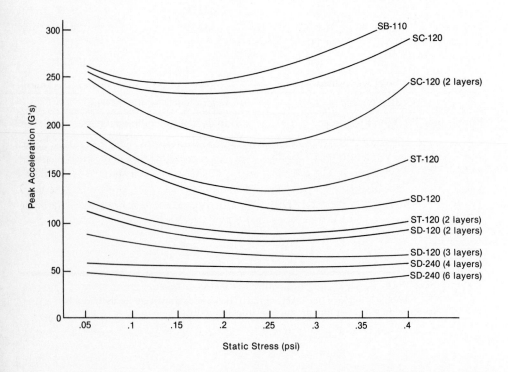

Note: To be read: For a product exerting 0.25 lbs. per sq. in. of pressure on the packaging material while at rest, the peak acceleration (a measure of shock to the product) when dropped from 2 ft. is 118 g. if SD-120 is used, 260 g. if SB-110 is used.

THE U.S. MARKET

In 1980, dollar sales by segment in the U.S. protective packaging market were:

- Positioning, blocking, and bracing: $585 million
- Flexible wrap: $126 million
- Void fill: $15.6 million

Exhibit 6 breaks down total sales for the flexible wrap market by product type for 1975, 1978, and 1980.

AirCap cushioning annual sales in the United States since 1972 were:

Year	Gross sales (in millions)	Year	Gross sales (in millions)
1972	$7.7	1977	$16.4
1973	10.0	1978	18.4
1974	13.0	1979	21.2
1975	12.8	1980	25.3
1976	14.6		

Despite the high cost of coated bubbles relative to the uncoated product, Sealed Air had kept most of the U.S. air bubble market. Key factors were Sealed Air's patent protection and licensing of only one competitor, extensive market education, and the packaging mentality in the United States. Packaging engineers enjoyed a status in U.S. organizations not accorded them elsewhere. Packaging supplies were viewed as a productive, cost-saving resource. In contrast, recent research by Sealed Air indicated that many European firms viewed packaging supplies as "expendable commodities."

THE EUROPEAN MARKET

Sealed Air had manufacturing operations in England and France and a sales organization in Germany.[3] It was the only company selling a coated

---

[3]The firm also had a manufacturing facility in Canada and a sales organization in Japan. Sealed Air licensees operated manufacturing facilities in Australia, Mexico, South Africa, and Spain.

product in these countries. Sales figures for 1980 were:

Germany	Total bubble sales	AirCap sales
England	$3,649,000	$2,488,500
France	4,480,000	592,200
Germany	7,688,000	404,600

ENGLAND   Sealed Air had developed the protective packaging market here and had good distribution. Later on, Sansetsu, a Japanese firm, began marketing a high-quality uncoated product made in Germany. Prices for the uncoated bubble were 50% less than the cost of comparably-sized AirCap cushioning. Sansetsu and other uncoated bubble manufacturers had chipped away at Sealed Air's one-time 90% market share. The most pessimistic Sealed Air distributors estimated that the firm would lose 50% of its current market share to uncoated bubbles within three years.

Exhibit 6. U.S. market—flexible wraps by product type (in millions of manufacturers' dollars) Source: Company records

	1975	1978	1980
Paper-based			
Cellulose wadding	20	23	23
Single-face corrugated	20	25	27
Indented kraft	1	1	1
	41	49	51
Foams[a]			
Polyurethane	10	11	12
Polypropylene	4	5	7
Polyethylene	1	6	25
	15	22	44
Polyethylene air bubbles[b]			
Coated and uncoated (combined)	15	22	31
Total	71	93	126

[a]Sales figures exclude nonpackaging uses, such as construction and furniture industries.
[b]Figures are for flexible wrap market only and are therefore less than AirCap's and Astro's total U.S. sales.

FRANCE   Here, Sealed Air owned an uncoated bubble manufacturer, SIBCO, with sales of $750,000 in 1980. In 1972, SIBCO was the only marketer of uncoated bubbles in France. Two major competitors, one with superior production facilities, had entered the market. Uncoated bubbles were priced about 40% lower than AirCap, and price was the key buying determinant. The major French distributor of AirCap cushioning had a 50-50 mix of coated and uncoated sales in 1978. In 1980, the mix had changed to 70-30 (uncoated over coated), with 90% of new bubble applications being uncoated.

GERMANY   AirCap cushioning was a late entrant (1973) to the German market and never held commanding share. Moreover, from 1978 to 1980, it had lost share at a rate of 20% to 30% per year. Sansetsu had an efficient manufacturing facility in Germany and sold approximately $6 million of uncoated product in 1980. (The price for uncoated was about 35% less than for coated.)

AIRCAP CUSHIONING

GRADES AND SALES

AirCap cushioning grades differed in bubble height and thickness of the plastic films. Bubble heights were designated by a letter code, and the plastic films came in four thicknesses (see Table A). Sealed Air produced eight different height/thickness combinations (see Table B). Some of the known end uses for each grade are shown in Exhibit 7.

Sales by grade for the last six months of 1979 and the first six months of 1980 are shown in Table C.

PRICING

All AirCap cushioning was sold through distributors. Prices reflected Sealed Air's costs and the prices of competitive products. Variable costs and prices to the distributor are shown in Table D.

Sealed Air's suggested resale price list is shown in Exhibit 8. Largely because of its selective distribution policy, distributors generally followed this list. The price schedule entailed quantity discounts for end users. Thus, distributor margins varied with the size of the customer's individual order. (Quantity price was determined by the total square footage of a single order, combining all grades, ordered for shipment at one time to a single destination.) In some major metropolitan areas, up to

TABLE A   Differing grades of AirCap cushioning

Bubble heights

SB: 1/8 in. high, used for surface protection when cushioning requirements were minimal.

SC: 3/16 in. high, used primarily for wrapping small, intricate items, possibly for larger items if not very fragile.

ST: 5/16 in. high, used in same kinds of applications as SC grade, except with slightly greater cushioning requirements. Also used as a void fill.

SD: 1/2 in. high, used for large, heavy, or fragile items or as a void fill.

Plastic film thicknesses

Light duty (110): each layer of film was 1 mil (1/1,000 of an inch) thick; used for light loads.

Regular duty (120): one layer of 1 mil and one layer of 2 mils; for loads up to 50 lbs. per sq. ft.

Heavy duty (240): one layer of 2 mils and one of 4 mils; for loads up to 100 lbs. per sq. ft.

Super duty (480): one layer of 4 mils and one of 8; for loads over 100 lbs per sq. ft.

50% of AirCap business was truckload/railcar orders by end users. In this event, Sealed Air shipped the material from its plant directly to the end user; the distributor received a 10% margin and handled user credit and technical service. In some markets the percentage of direct shipments was as low as 10%.

TABLE B   Eight different height/thicknesses by Sealed Air

Height (inches)	Thickness			
	110	120	240	480
SB-1/8	X			
SC-3/16		X	X	
ST-5/16		X	X	
SD-1/2		X	X	X

Exhibit 7. AirCap applications by grade

Grade	Package contents	Packaging material displaced (if known)
SB-110	Furnace thermostats	
	Shorthand machines	
	Taco shells	Corrugated
	Tempered glass sheets	1/16-in. polypropylene foam
SC-120	Clocks	Shredded paper
SC-240	Wooden picture frames	Corrugated
ST-120	Light fixtures	Corrugated
	Overhead projector lenses	
	Computer components	
	Telephone bell ringers	Corrugated
	Amplifiers	3/32-in. polyethylene foam
	Saucepans	Corrugated
	Two-way radios	Urethane foam pads
ST-240	Exit alarms	
	Mixers	
	Fryers	
	Carbonless paper rolls	
SD-120	Oven burners	
	Pharmaceutical bottles	Shredded paper
	Candleholders	
	Recorders	
	Carburetors	Polypropylene foam
SD-240	Lamps	
	Gallon jugs	
	Computer terminals	Corrugated
	Printed circuit boards	Foam pads and corrugated
	Foil wallpaper	
	Blood coagulation timers	Corrugated
SD-480	Leaded glass windows	
	Custom motorcycle seats	Astro uncoated bubble LP-24
	Motor controls	

TABLE C   AirCap sales by grade

Grade	Sales in 1,000 square feet	
	July–December 1979	January–June 1980
1/8 in.		
SB-110	59,128	48,513
3/16 in.		
SC-120	76,349	81,014
SC-240	5,036	4,426
5/16 in.		
ST-120	31,912	42,234
ST-240	4,369	3,914
1/2 in.		
SD-120	44,252	43,624
SD-240	25,202	21,799
SD-480	3,138	1,358
Total sales	249,386	246,882

Note: In addition, because SB-110 could not compete in price against foams for many surface protection applications, Sealed Air introduced an A-100 grade in January 1980. The A-100 bubble was 3/32 in. high—the shortest coated bubble Sealed Air could make with available technology. January to June 1980 sales of A-100 were 17,802,000 sq. ft.

SELLING EFFORT

Sealed Air's U.S. operation consisted of 7 regional manufacturing operations, 62 salespeople (each selling AirCap cushioning, Instapak, and other Sealed Air products), and 370 distributors. To control the shipping cost of its bulky product, Sealed Air had regional manufacturing operations in three eastern states, plus Ohio, Illinois, Texas, and California. The regional presence, however, had proven to be an effective sales promotion device as well.

Before Instapak was acquired in 1976, 28 salespeople devoted 90% of their time to AirCap cushioning products. In 1981, the 62-person force was expected to allocate time as follows: 60% to Instapak systems, 35% to AirCap cushioning, and 5% to other Sealed Air products. (Exhibit 9 shows Sealed Air sales by product line and other financial data.)

Part of Sealed Air's market share leadership philosophy was a consultative selling approach. Salespeople spent about half their time making cost studies at end user locations. With the help of Sealed Air's pack-

TABLE D   AirCap variable costs and distributor prices (in dollars per 1,000 sq. ft.)

Grade	Manufacturing	Freight	(1) Total variable cost	(2) Price to distributor for truckload delivery[a]	(2) – (1) Sealed Air dollar margin
A-100 (3/32 in.)	$12.46	$1.32	$13.78	$20.60	$6.82
SB-110 (1/8 in.)	14.02	1.99	16.01	30.25	14.24
SC-120 (3/16 in.)	17.92	2.64	20.56	43.50	22.94
SC-240 (3/16 in.)	29.83	2.64	32.47	56.30	23.83
ST-120 (5/16 in.)	25.36	5.29	30.65	51.40	20.75
ST-240 (5/16 in.)	32.83	5.29	38.12	65.35	27.23
SD-120 (1/2 in.)	28.38	7.93	36.31	65.35	29.04
SD-240 (1/2 in.)	36.52	7.93	44.45	78.60	34.15
SD-480 (1/2 in.)	62.88	7.93	70.81	140.90	70.09

[a]Less than truckload shipments were priced 15% to 20% higher. Consequently, distributors almost always ordered in truckload quantities. They were allowed to mix grades within an order. Depending on the grade ordered, a truckload could contain 70,000 sq. ft. (all SD-480) to 420,000 sq. ft. (all A-100).

aging labs, salespeople attempted to show how their products could save on material and labor cost and reduce damage in the end user's particular situation. Distributors' salespeople took orders on AirCap cushioning but did little to demonstrate AirCap use and application to customers. If a distributor's salesperson identified a potential AirCap account, he or she would inform the Sealed Air salesperson and a joint call would be arranged. In this way, the potential account learned about the product and ordering procedures simultaneously.

Distributors sometimes complained to Sealed Air about the level of AirCap selling effort. Since distributor's margins on AirCap cushioning were generally higher than the 10% to 12% for Instapak sales, distributors were not happy with Sealed Air's greater allocation of salesperson time to Instapak. Some distributors said they would be content if the salesperson in their area really allocated 35% to AirCap; some claimed the actual AirCap selling effort amounted to only 20%. Instapak's sales growth had been impressive, but some Sealed Air executives felt this had cost them some distributor satisfaction.

Both distributors and end users regarded Sealed Air's salespeople as among the best trained and most knowledgeable in the packaging industry. Sales force salaries were above average. They were composed of a

Exhibit 8. *Suggested U.S. resale price list, effective March 1980*

Item (thickness in inches)	Sq. ft. per order per single destination	Price per 1,000 sq. ft.
A-100 (3/32)	1,000 or more	$34.30
	5,000 or more	30.85
	10,000 or more	27.45
	30,000 or more	25.70
	50,000 or more	24.75
	Truckload/railcar	22.80
SB-110 (1/8)	1,000 or more	50.00
	5,000 or more	45.40
	10,000 or more	40.90
	30,000 or more	38.10
	50,000 or more	37.05
	Truckload/railcar	33.50
SC-120 (3/16)	1,000 or more	71.70
	5,000 or more	64.55
	10,000 or more	57.40
	30,000 or more	53.75
	50,000 or more	52.60
	Truckload/railcar	47.65
SC-240 (3/16)	1,000 or more	93.40
	5,000 or more	84.40
	10,000 or more	74.95
	30,000 or more	70.20
	50,000 or more	68.60
	Truckload/railcar	62.25
ST-120 (5/16)	1,000 or more	85.30
	5,000 or more	77.10
	10,000 or more	68.50
	30,000 or more	64.25
	50,000 or more	62.75
	Truckload/railcar	$57.25
ST-240 (5/16)	Same price per 1,000 sq. ft. as SD-120	
SD-120 (1/2)	1,000 or more	$107.85
	5,000 or more	97.70
	10,000 or more	87.55
	30,000 or more	81.40
	50,000 or more	79.35
	Truckload/railcar	72.40

(continued)

Exhibit 8 *(continued)*

Item (thickness in inches)	Sq. ft. per order per single destination	Price per 1,000 sq. ft.
SD-240 (1/2)	1,000 or more	130.75
	5,000 or more	118.30
	10,000 or more	105.95
	30,000 or more	98.55
	50,000 or more	95.70
	Truckload/railcar	87.25
SD-480 (1/2)	1,000 or more	232.75
	5,000 or more	210.55
	10,000 or more	188.35
	30,000 or more	175.5
	50,000 or more	171.25
	Truckload/railcar	$155.60

Exhibit 9. *Selected financial data ($ thousands)* Source: Sealed Air Annual Reports 1979, 1980.

	1976	1977	1978	1979	1980
Net sales by class of product					
Air cellular packaging	$18,872	$21,422	$25,028	$29,996	$34,330
Foam-in-place packaging	3,049	15,489	21,133	29,056	38,802
Other packaging	4,553	3,595	3,453	3,432	3,688
Recreational and energy product		2,682	4,644	7,951	11,777
Total worldwide	$26,474	$43,188	$54,258	$70,435	$88,597
United States	—	35,765	43,410	54,325	67,344
Costs and expenses					
Cost of sales	$16,451	$24,270	$31,111	$43,199	$54,125
Marketing, administration, development	6,696	12,093	14,527	16,855	21,485
Other income (expense)	32	(816)	(738)	(278)	(119)
Earnings before income tax	3,359	6,009	7,882	10,103	12,868

base salary plus commissions of 2% on net AirCap sales and 1% on net sales of all other products, including Instapak. (As an added incentive, Sealed Air gave salespeople $75 for each Instapak dispenser placed. It took back $75 for each one removed.) In a typical week a salesperson called on 20 end users and checked in with two or three distributors.

U.S. DISTRIBUTORS

During the 1970s, Sealed Air invested heavily in developing a selected distributor network. The firm had 370 distributors by 1980. Sealed Air considered 135 of these their "first-line distributors" because they collectively handled over 80% of its business. The 20 largest AirCap distributors handled about 35% of the business. Larger distributors typically carried both Instapak foam-in-place and AirCap cushioning. The largest distributor of Sealed Air products had 1980 Sealed Air sales of approximately $2 million, just about half of which were AirCap.

Distributors traditionally tried to be full-line houses—capable of meeting each customer's complete packaging needs—so they carried a broad range of products. A survey of Sealed Air's first-line distributors showed that 83% carried loose fills, 65% carried polyethylene foam, and 29% carried Du Pont's polypropylene foam. Although most carried competitive products, distributors had displayed loyalty to Sealed Air and AirCap cushioning. Sealed Air, in turn, had kept to its selective distribution policy.

COMPETING UNCOATED BUBBLE CUSHIONING

Sealed Air considered both types of bubbles made by Astro as inferior products. GAFCEL, the new regional producer, made a "decent product" in Hauser's estimation; he felt that its success to date came largely at Astro's expense.

The New York metropolitan market was ideal for the new producer. It was not customer- or distributor-loyal, and price was a key variable. Sealed Air's estimate of GAFCEL sales rates was $750,000 per year for the 1/2-in.-high uncoated bubble and $250,000 per year for the 3/16-in. bubble. Both had two layers of film 2 mils each.

GAFCEL's distributor prices for truckload shipments and suggested resale prices to end users for the metropolitan New York market are shown in Table E. (Astro's uncoated bubble prices are in Exhibit 4.)

Sealed Air had not yet extensively tested the GAFCEL uncoated bubble. Although it was better than Astro's uncoated, its performance would not be dramatically different from that found in previous uncoated test-

TABLE E   GAFCEL's distributor prices per 1,000 sq. ft.

	SO-22 (3/16 in.)	LO-22 (1/2 in.)
Distributor-truckload	$31.63	$36.03
Suggested resale by order size:		
1,000 sq. ft.	$56.54	$75.24
20,000 sq. ft.	47.12	62.70
40,000 sq. ft.	42.84	57.07
100,000 sq. ft,	39.40	44.68
Truckload	34.79	39.63

ing (see Exhibit 2). In terms of cushioning curves, the 1/2-in. GAFCEL bubble was comparable to Sealed Air's ST-120 or SD-120 for very light loads, not greater than 0.15 lbs./sq. in. pressure. At greater loads, however, the acceleration curve would increase rapidly, moving above even the SB-110 by pressures of 0.25 lbs./sq. in. (see Exhibit 5).

SEALED AIR DECISIONS

Sealed Air had conducted a good deal of research on manufacturing uncoated bubble products. It knew the best production process would be similar to that currently used for its Solar Pool Blankets™. Thus, the firm could begin manufacture of an uncoated product quickly in its New Jersey plant. Likely distributor response to a Sealed Air uncoated product was difficult to predict. Some distributors had requested it, but others regularly complained that there were already too many coated grades.

Preliminary estimates of the variable costs for producing Sealed Air uncoated bubbles were $19 per 1,000 sq. ft. for 3/16 in. height, $20 per 1,000 sq. ft. for 5/16 in., and $21 per 1,000 sq. ft. for 1/2 inch. Freight cost depended on bubble height and distance shipped. Although GAFCEL's production process was completely different, its production costs were believed to be comparable.

Hauser now had to decide whether to recommend that Sealed Air enter the uncoated bubble market (with an about-face on its previous exclusive emphasis on coated bubbles), or whether to suggest some other reaction to its new competitors.

3 *CASE*

Henkel Group: Umbrella Branding and Global Decisions

Robert J. Dolan

At Henkel Group, headquartered in Dusseldorf, West Germany, brand names were a highly valued asset. For example, the company's Persil brand detergent, introduced in 1907, was one of the most widely known and respected brand names in Europe. As marketing director of Henkel's Chemical Technical Products for Craftsmen and Do-It-Yourselfers (HD/BC), Gunther von Briskorn was custodian of two of Henkel's most important brands: Pritt and Pattex. In early 1981, von Briskorn was con-

This case was prepared by Associate Professor Robert J. Dolan as the basis for class discussion rather than to illustrate either effective or ineffective handling of an administrative situation.

61

cerned about the performance of these household adhesives on an international basis. He was considering a radical change in brand strategy. As
he discussed with Wolfgang Heck, his group product manager for
Craftsmen/DIY/Household Adhesives, and Mr. Heck's assistant for
Household Adhesives, Herbert Tossing:

> *Mr. Heck, if we are to be successful in Germany and the rest of the world, we
> must find an innovative approach. These adhesive markets are small to begin
> with and now we are seeing increased fragmentation and specialization. Our
> friends in the detergent group do not face the same issues. Every country market
> they go into has a large, not strongly segmented detergent market. They can
> afford a policy of one brand for one product. The brand philosophy which has been
> successful for them has not been successful for us—we must develop greater coor-
> dination between the individual products we sell and the individual country mar-
> kets we sell them in. Please get together with Mr. Printz (the HD/BC advertising
> manager assigned to von Briskorn's group) to develop some ideas on how we can
> move in the direction of greater coordination across products and markets.*

In July 1981, six months of work researching and thinking about the
problem had resulted in a proposed strategy which would fundamentally change HD/BC marketing practices. The strategy embodied two
major concepts: umbrella branding (i.e., developing an integrated strategy for the marketing of a variety of products under each of the two
brand names) and global standardization of the umbrella. As von
Briskorn considered the proposal he had developed, he recognized that
both concepts underlying the strategy were counter to the traditional
"each product/each country profit center on its own" philosophy of the
Henkel Group. Second, Dr. Roman Dohr, head of the Adhesives and
Chemical Auxiliaries Division, had expressed concern about the umbrella branding aspects. In his own mind, von Briskorn knew the strategy
was not without risk. Both Tossing (who became product manager when
Heck was given a U.S. assignment in connection with Henkel's acquisition of Ross Chemical in Detroit) and Printz had raised quite valid concerns in laying out the "pros and cons" of the strategy. In view of the
importance of the decision, von Briskorn resolved to consider all the evidence once again in resolving the issues he faced:

- Does the umbrella branding concept make sense for the household
  adhesives markets?
- Does it make sense specifically for the two brand names? Which
  products could be put under each umbrella?
- Is it possible to globalize an umbrella strategy?
- How could a global/umbrella strategy be implemented?
- What are the alternatives if we decide not to follow this strategy?

HENKEL GROUP

In 1980, the over 8000 products sold by the Henkel Group yielded sales revenues of DM 6.9 billion. The family-owned company, founded by Fritz Henkel as a bleaching powder company in 1876, had grown to over 100 operating companies in more than 40 countries. The international scope of the company resulted in 60% of sales being outside Germany.

The diverse product line was sold by eight groups:

1. Detergents and Cleaning Agents
2. Personal Care Products and Cosmetics
3. Household Care Products
4. Adhesives
5. Inorganic Chemicals
6. Organic Chemicals
7. Foodstuffs
8. Packaging

The common element through the groups was a reliance on "chemistry in production." Top management considered Henkel to be "specialists in applying chemistry to the needs of the consumer, of institutions, of industry, and of craftsmen."

Adhesives represented a major growth opportunity for Henkel. In 1980, the adhesives product line contained over 800 products and generated sales of approximately DM 1.2 billion. As shown in Exhibit 1, the Adhesives Division had three groups:

1. Industrial Adhesives
2. Leather and Textile Auxiliaries
3. HD/BC: Chemical Technical Products for Craftsmen and Do-It-Yourself Markets/Building Chemical (in German, Handwerk/DIY/Bauchemie, hence the HD/BC abbreviation)

The pattern of new product development in the Adhesives group was typically to develop a product for industrial and craftsman use and then adapt it to the household market if possible. Despite the focus on industrial sectors for new product development, the HD/BC group accounted for 57% of Henkel's adhesives sales. The 15 items in the HD/BC product line are shown in Exhibit 2. These products were targeted to a variety of users, representing very different levels of product performance requirements and product knowledge. Main target groups included:

Craftsmen	Households	Other
Painter	DIY-ers	Office
Decorator	Hobbyists	School

Exhibit 1. *Organization chart*

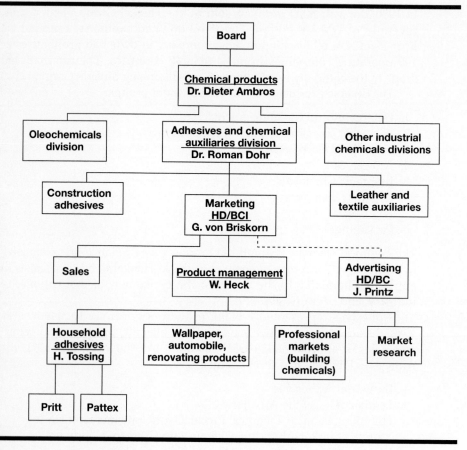

Craftsmen	Households	Other
Paperhanger	"Moonlighters"	Kindergartens
Carpenter		
Shoemaker		
Floor coverer		
Bricklayer		
Metalworker		
Plumber		

As a consequence, HD/BC employed a broad array of distribution channels (see Exhibit 3) ranging from lumberyards to supermarkets.

Exhibit 2. HD/BC product line

HD/BC Product Line

Pattex contact cement

Ponal wood glue

Metylan wallpaper paste

Pritt Stick/all purpose glue

Saxit tile adhesives

Polifac car care products

Assil structural adhesives

Thomsit floorlaying adhesives

Ovalit wallcovering adhesives

Tangit PVC pipe adhesives

Dufix home decorating products

Gori wood preservatives

Sista sealants + PU foam (Insulating foam)

Kieselit silicate paints

Randamit construction products

Exhibit 3. HD/BC distribution channels

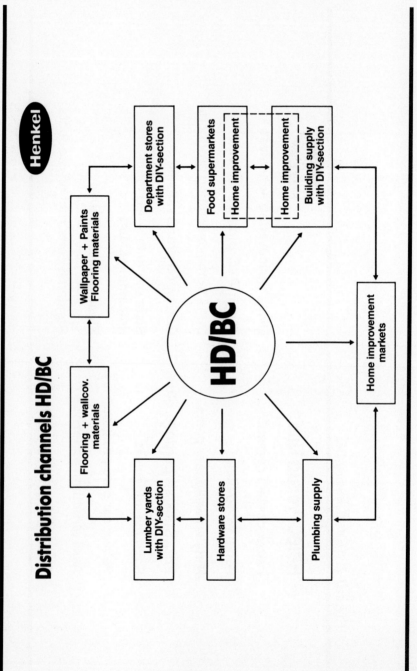

Gunther von Briskorn explained the major marketing problems facing HD/BC:

> As you can see from the number of products we sell and the channels we use, we face selling into very deeply segmented markets. Some of our users are very sophisticated—the craftsman usually has a very specific need, so we have to have the product out there to meet that need. For example, take our SISTA sealants product line. We have four different types of sealant: bathtub, glass, joints and cracks, and "multipurpose" because of differing needs. Then, you need different colors and package sizes—all told, we have 47 different type/color/package combinations. So, the craftsman coming into the store knows what he's looking for and we have it. But look what this does to our other market—households. This poor fellow probably buys sealants once a year, does not know anything about sealants. He comes into the store knowing he needs something to fix a drafty window—but he doesn't know if he should use tape or an adhesive or what. He may not even know what sealants are. And we give him four different types to choose from! So, first we have to educate him what to buy and then how to apply it—and all this on a small communications budget because it's a low expenditure per capita item.

> Of course, our international strategy adds a second dimension to the problem. We sell the Pritt line in 15 European countries and 50 outside Europe. So, the "small markets" problem we see due to the low purchase frequency and deep segmentation in Germany is really compounded when we go into a market like Finland, where there just are not that many people. That's why I think we have to get multiple use out of our own resources—by umbrella branding and global standardization where possible.

> We face strong competition from Uhu, now owned by Beecham. Historically, there were two main segments of the craftsman/DIY market: contact adhesives for heavy jobs and "all-purpose" adhesives for jobs not requiring great bonding strength. We dominated the contact adhesive segment with our Pattex brand originally oriented to the craftsman and Uhu dominated the all-purpose segment with its more consumer-oriented products. In 1969, we attacked their light duty market by offering the Pritt Glue Stick. Uhu was not yet offering a contact adhesive although they did come after us in that segment four years later with Uhu Greenit adhesive. Ever since then there has been brand proliferation and greater segmentation of the market.

PATTEX BRAND

Pattex held the "strength adhesive" positioning within HD/BC. Launched in 1956 as a contact adhesive for the professional, Pattex penetrated the household and DIY segments as well and became the leading contact adhesive in West Germany. The bonding strength required for the professional market, e.g., furniture and leather workers, necessitated a somewhat messy, drippy-with-strings formulation. By 1973, HD/BC was able to serve the DIY market better with a nondripping formulation, which sacrificed bonding strength to convenience. Pattex Compact, as the brand was called, was positioned as "The Clean and Powerful Adhesive." It was supported by an introductory advertising campaign of DM 2 million on television. It proved to be a good extension to the line, allowing Henkel to penetrate new segments rather than cannibalizing the original Pattex.

In 1980, Henkel held 80% of the contact adhesive market in West Germany (with sales split equally between Pattex and Pattex Compact). Brand awareness in West Germany topped 80% and trade support was excellent. Over 65% of Pattex sales came from outside Germany as Pattex was distributed in more than 50 countries worldwide. Total Pattex sales were approximately DM 66 million worldwide.

While worldwide sales increased during the late 1970s, sales in the West German market had stagnated (see Exhibit 4). Since Pattex was probably the second most important brand name within Henkel (next to Persil), Gunther von Briskorn was concerned about the performance as he assumed the HD/BC marketing director position in April 1979. Von Briskorn explained the situation:

> We were basically experiencing product life cycle problems. We had a pretty traditional technology—while we were holding our share of the contact adhesive market based on the Pattex technology, we were being attacked by alternative technologies. Probably the most important of these was the cyanoacrylates or CAs, the "Superglues" as people called them. In some respects they were super—offering a one-minute curing time as compared to Pattex's ten minutes plus they were being offered by strong companies like Uhu and Loctite. At this time, we were selling lots of CAs to industrial users, but we were really concerned about offering it as a consumer product for health reasons. Anyway, these more modern technologies really hurt us—we had a great brand name in Pattex, but the product/technology attached to it was weakening.

Exhibit 4. *Sales and advertising in Germany*

	Pritt		Pattex	
Year	Sales (DM in millions)	Advertising (DM in millions)	Sales (DM in millions)	Advertising (DM in millions)
1970	4.0	1.0	16.0	.3
1973	7.0	0.5	22.0	2.0
1976	9.0	2.0	22.0	1.0
1980	8.5	.5	21.0	1.5
1981 (est.)	8.0	.5	24.0	1.5

During 1980, Henkel responded to Uhu and Loctite's CA progress by introducing their own CA brand: Stabilit Rasant. However, the brand was given very little advertising support since it was a late entrant and some health concerns still remained within Henkel. Von Briskorn described the situation in early 1981:

> *It was pretty clear where the contact adhesive market was going—there were new, innovative growth segments popping up and attacking the "general purpose" contact adhesives like Pattex. First there were the Superglues, then the Two Component Glues. Also, we saw some potential for moving the hot melt technology from the industrial sphere to the consumer end. We already saw this occur in the U.S. and some small companies were offering it in Europe—but with no clear brand profile yet emerging.*

PRITT BRAND

Through the 1960s, the dominant company in the consumer adhesive market in Germany was Uhu. Introduced in 1932, Uhu's "Alleskleber" (i.e., all-purpose glue) held 80% market share and had easily fended off several competitive "all-purpose" strategies. The Pritt Glue Stick was an innovation developed as a segmentation strategy in the market. In 1969, Henkel introduced the Glue Stick to serve a special purpose: paper-sticking. This segment represented roughly 40% of the total consumer "all-purpose" adhesive market. The nationwide launch in 1969 (managed by von Briskorn as his first assignment with Henkel Corporation) was supported by a DM 3 million television, print, promotion, and point-of-purchase campaign.

The Pritt Glue Stick was a patentable innovation in formulation and convenience-oriented packaging. The density of the glue stick allowed it to be packaged in a twist-up tube, similar to lipstick. The user simply took off the top, twisted the bottom of the tube to push up the glue stick, and then applied a small amount of glue on the paper—the same way one would write with a crayon. Main user groups were households, offices, and schools. Schools were important because research in the adhesive market had shown that adults tended to use the brand they used as children. Thus, having the "no-mess" Pritt stick in kindergartens was important for future Pritt sales, as well as current revenues.

Henkel licensed the Glue Stick technology to a few selected licensees including Uhu. However, because of cannibalization problems and its commitment to the "general purpose" concept, Uhu did not aggressively pursue the stick market. The introduction of the Glue Stick was not easy for Henkel. Positioned as the "clean, easy-to-use paper glue," the primary markets would be schools and offices. Serving these markets effectively required stationery store distribution rather than the wallpaper and paint stores where Henkel was established selling the contact adhesive. Pelikan was the market share leader in products such as carbon paper, ink, stamps, etc. in the stationery store channel. Henkel and Pelikan reached an agreement for Pelikan to handle Pritt Glue Stick distribution in the paper/office/stationery (PBS) sector in Germany. The price of the Pritt Glue Stick was DM 1.2 for the German introduction. Production capacity for 1969 was strained at this price level.

In 1970, the international expansion of Pritt Glue Stick began. The introduction was standardized globally and by 1980, the Pritt Glue Stick was Henkel's most successful brand internationally. Distributed in 15 countries in Europe and 50 outside of Europe, annual sales totaled more than 50 million units with sales revenue of DM 80 million.

From 1972–1981, five additional products were introduced under the Pritt brand name. As shown in Exhibit 5, these products were:

1. *Pritt Alleskleber:* The Pritt All-Purpose Adhesive was introduced in 1972 with DM 2 million advertising support. Essentially a "me-too" product to Uhu's all-purpose product, it received good sell-in to the trade because of the Pritt name and advertising support, but poor customer takeaway because of lack of any advantage over Uhu. Reformulated to have a "no-drip" feature, the product was relaunched in 1975, but was unable to achieve even sell-in to the trade because of the 1972 failure. These two failures led to adoption of a "no more me-too's" policy within HD/BC.

2. *Pritt Allesklebe Creme:* The Pritt All-Purpose Creme glue was launched in 1976 with a unique selling proposition. Other adhesives were solvent-based, which created health issues and concern about "glue sniffing." The All-Purpose Creme glue was not solvent-based and was therefore harmless. Supported by a DM 3 million advertising budget, the product received good sell-in but, as with the first Pritt all-purpose product, poor takeaway. Reasons for the lackluster performance seemed to be two: (i) the product performance was not very good on paper and cardboard, and (ii) this was the first time an adhesive product used "creme" in the product name. The brand positioning was "strong bonding" and there was some concern about the compatibility of the positioning and the name. "Creme" did not seem to imply strength.

3. *Pritt Hafties:* Pritt Buddies (as they were referred to in English) were introduced in 1976. Small wads of adhesive, these Buddies were to be used to stick notes on a door temporarily, hold an item in place on a desk, and hopefully a wide variety of other uses which consumers would discover. Initially

Exhibit 5. The Pritt product line

supported by a DM 2 million advertising budget, the Buddies did well but sales dropped quickly as soon as the advertising support was dropped.

4. *Pritt Alleskleber (bottle):* In 1977, the Pritt all-purpose adhesive was put out in bottle form. Sales were poor due to inferiority in dispensing technology as compared to the Uhu bottled adhesive, the Uhu Flinke Flasche, introduced in 1976.

5. *Pritt Klebepads:* Introduced in 1978, Pritt Adhesive Pads (double-sided foam pads) were very similar in concept to the Pritt Buddies; the physical difference was that the adhesive pads were flat and used for permanent sticking. Not given any special support, the product never did very well. Consumers never seemed to figure out the best applications for these pads or Buddies.

Von Briskorn had been product manager for the Pritt Glue Stick launch in 1969, but had not presided over the product line extension activities of the 1970s, having left Dusseldorf for Henkel assignments in Italy and France. In April 1979, he returned to Dusseldorf to assume the role of marketing director HD/BC, responsible for 15 brands including his first assigned brand, Pritt. In early 1981, he addressed Wolfgang Heck, the present group product manager for Craftsmen/DIY Products:

> The Pritt Glue Stick has been great. It was a real innovation and allowed us to capture the clean, easy-bonding positioning. It is an international success story. But these flankers, the all-purpose product and the creme product and so on—they have really hurt us. We have created so many flops; we are losing money on them and everybody is mad at us. The retail trade is not giving us the sell-in and Pelikan, our key distributor, is angry too. We jeopardized our relationship with Kokuyo in Japan—the all-purpose products and the Buddies flopped there too. Maybe it's the products, they are really average in performance. There has been no real significant innovation since the Glue Stick. But we have not really developed any coordinated marketing strategy for these products either—the product line has no visual harmony (see Exhibit 5), all advertising has been for a single brand at a time. We face a real challenge in a few years when the Glue Stick formula patent expires. By that time, we have to be executing a coordinated strategy for the Pritt family or have cleared the scenery of these products which are pulling us down.

UMBRELLA BRANDING POSSIBILITIES

With Wolfgang Heck's departure from Dusseldorf to a Henkel assignment in the United States, Herbert Tossing assumed the position of product manager Household Adhesives. Along with Joachim Printz, advertising manager, Tossing had the primary responsibility of developing the marketing strategy responsive to von Briskorn's declaration that "if we are to be successful in Germany and the rest of the world, we must find an innovative approach." Exhibit 6 gives the HD/BC organizational structure through which Herbert Tossing would have to work in developing and implementing the strategy. Basically, HD/BC integrated sales and product management in the same organization. As shown in Exhibit 6, profit center responsibility was given to the three sales organizations serving Germany, and the affiliated companies in Europe and the affiliated companies overseas. Product management had no regional profit center responsibility, but rather global consolidated responsibility. It had an international role developing the central brand strategy, coordinating the individual market strategies and monitoring progress. The advertising function was similar in its international orientation. Printz would be responsible for developing the basic advertising concept and then coordinating with advertising agencies across the markets to ensure international implementation of the advertising strategy. Regional autonomy and profit center responsibility for affiliated companies were a strong part of the Henkel culture. Tossing began his strategy formulation with the Pattex brand.

PATTEX UMBRELLA POTENTIAL

In the case of Pattex, the umbrella question was easy to state: could a very highly regarded brand name (Pattex) tied to a product in a no-growth segment (contact adhesives) be transferred to new products to be positioned in higher growth segments of the market? In particular, Tossing saw three possibilities:

1. Remarket Stabilit Rasant, Henkel's recent but unsupported entry into the fast-growing CA market, under the name Pattex Super Glue.
2. Develop a Pattex entry into the emerging "hot melt" market.
3. Market a Pattex No-Mix product which would be a new generation two component glue, a special purpose item.

The first step in assessing the viability of these steps was to determine consumers' current perception of the Pattex brand name. Research in West Germany, Benelux and Austria showed the Pattex name to be associated with "strong bonding" and "technical uses." Researching the potential for stretching the Pattex name in the three directions noted above, Tossing found that:

1. *CAs* had a very popular, not at all technical, image. Consequently, the fit with Pattex's image on this dimension was not strong. However,

Exhibit 6. HD/BC organization structure

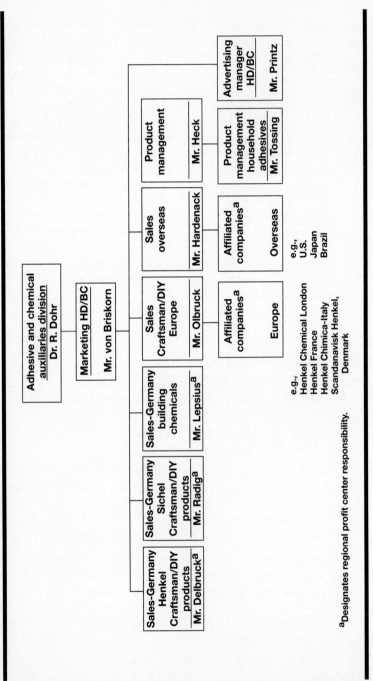

Adhesive and chemical auxiliaries division
Dr. R. Dohr

Marketing HD/BC
Mr. von Briskorn

Sales-Germany Henkel Craftsman/DIY products
Mr. Delbruck[a]

Sales-Germany Sichel Craftsman/DIY products
Mr. Radig[a]

Sales-Germany building chemicals
Mr. Lepsius[a]

Sales Craftsman/DIY Europe
Mr. Olbruck

Sales overseas
Mr. Hardenack

Product management
Mr. Heck

Advertising manager HD/BC
Mr. Printz

Product management household adhesives
Mr. Tossing

Affiliated companies[a]
Europe

e.g.,
Henkel Chemical London
Henkel France
Henkel Chimica-Italy
Scandanavisk Henkel, Denmark

Affiliated companies[a]
Overseas

e.g.,
U.S.
Japan
Brazil

[a]Designates regional profit center responsibility.

Stabilit Rasant was not doing well because of its late entry into the market after Uhu and Loctite.

2. The *Hot Melt* market (with the dispensing guns) had a technical image. This could enhance the Pattex name. Henkel possessed the production know-how from industrial experience. Consequently, Henkel could probably produce a high quality product for most applications. Consumer research showed that DIY-ers viewed Henkel as a credible source for hot melt products. Unlike other Pattex products, it would be a seasonal, gift-oriented item because of the cost of the dispensing gun. It was also felt that the market may be a price-oriented one.

3. Serving the *Two Compound Glue* segment with Pattex No Mix would definitely enhance the Pattex technical image as it required no dosing or mixing. The product would, however, be a niche product generating low turnover for the trade. Historically, Pattex had been viewed as a "fast mover" by the trade. A second problem with No Mix was consumers perceived it to smell very bad—would this "bad smell" perception hurt other Pattex brands if No Mix were brought under the Pattex umbrella?

In general, the research finding was that a line extension would not degrade consumers' perception of the Pattex name as long as the umbrella products were compatible with Pattex's high-bonding strength image. The research results in Exhibit 7 show the mean score on a 1–10 scale of 100 respondents exposed to just the Pattex name (control group) and a test group exposed to the line extension through seeing product package mock-ups and product descriptions. The second research finding was that the new brands would benefit greatly from the power and authority of the Pattex name.

PRITT UMBRELLA POTENTIAL

The Pritt situation was quite different from Pattex. The Pattex name was currently positioned in a no-growth category and the extension under consideration was to new products or to a very recent introduction (Stabilit Rasant). The question for the Pattex situation was can the new products save the brand? In Pritt, the question was can the brand save the products (i.e., the flankers to the Glue Stick) if more actively promoted? Printz played a key role in reviewing packaging design, proposing a new line design, and testing the consumers' reaction to the new line.

The first step was to review the Glue Stick design for consumer acceptance and conveyance of a "modern image." Based on research in Benelux and West Germany, the red, white and black Pritt stick design

Exhibit 7.   *Research results—Pattex brand*

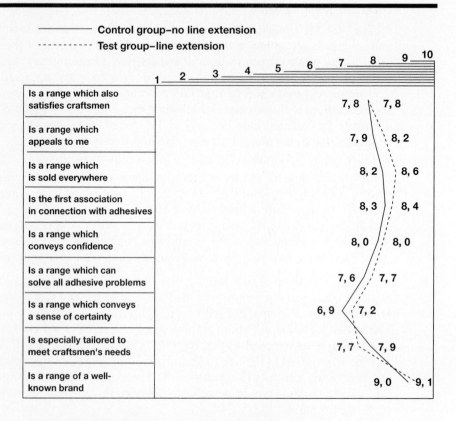

Note: One hundred people in each of the test and control groups were asked
to indicate agreement/disagreement with the statement "Pattex is..."
1 indicates "strongly disagree" and 10 indicates "strongly agree."

was deemed acceptable and "modern." Based on this, Printz proposed a visual harmonization of the line, all oriented toward the leader product. The proposed design is shown in Exhibit 8. This design introduced the chevron to all packages and extended the red background, black lettering on white color scheme of the Glue Stick to all elements in the line.

Printz proposed a similar visual harmonization as recently created for Pattex line where the chevron was used but with yellow as the primary background color. Tests of the nonharmonized vs. harmonized design for the Pritt product line were conducted. Results are shown in Exhibit 9.

Exhibit 8. Proposed visual harmonization of the Pritt product line

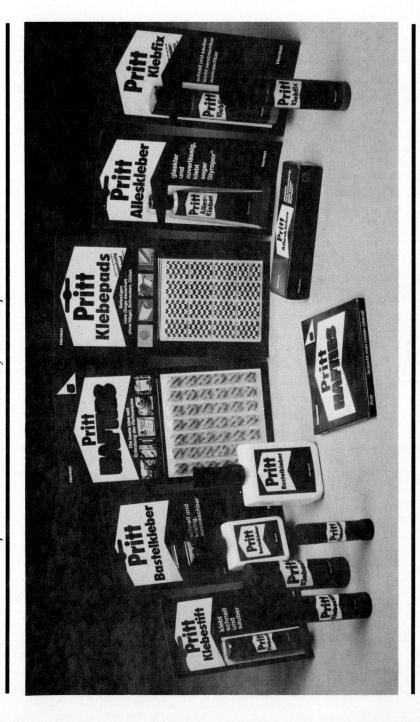

Exhibit 9.   Research results on perceptions of Pritt current line, Pritt harmonized line, and Uhu

	Pritt current (see Exhibit 5) N = 100		Pritt harmonized (see Exhibit 8) N = 100	
	Pritt	Uhu	Pritt	Uhu
conveys confidence	6,8	8,5	7,5	8,3
is of high quality	7,2	8,4	7,5	8,4
is for special uses only	6,5	5,5	5,6	5,6
is only for sticking paper	5,7	4,3	4,8	3,9
is somehow likeable	6,4	7,2	6,6	7,2
glues reliably	7,1	8,4	7,5	8,5
is of great strength	6,9	8,3	7,1	8,4
is a well-known brand	7,9	9,7	8,0	9,6
is for general purposes	6,5	8,1	7,0	8,1
is usually reasonably priced	6,5	6,7	5,9	6,4
is sold everywhere	7,4	8,9	7,9	9,0
offers all adhesives you need	7,1	8,3	7,2	7,9
is more for children	4,9	4,5	4,9	4,6
is more known from the office	6,3	5,6	5,9	5,5
offers useful adhesives	8,0	8,7	8,1	8,7
has a well-structured range	6,9	7,9	7,8	8,1
is something for experts	2,4	3,0	3,3	3,5
is clean in use	7,6	7,7	8,0	7,7

Note: One hundred people in each group were exposed to simulated store settings showing either the current Pritt or proposed harmonized packaging design. They were then asked to indicate agreement/disagreement with the statements shown for Pritt and Uhu (1 = strongly disagree, 10 = agree).

Respondents were exposed to either the harmonized or nonharmonized lines and asked to rate both Pritt and Uhu on the dimensions shown.

DECISIONS AND IMPLEMENTATION

Whatever strategy decisions he made, von Briskorn had to be concerned about how he could get the strategy sold within Henkel. He knew that Dr. Roman Dohr, head of Adhesives and Chemical auxiliaries, would have questions on all aspects of the strategy. He had previously expressed concerns about the risks inherent in an umbrella strategy. The recent problems with the Pritt flankers and the declining fortunes of Pattex had made these two products highly visible in the Adhesives group. Von Briskorn and his product management team would also have to convince those with profit center responsibility in the affiliated foreign companies to implement the plan. His problems only began with the decision of which products to put under the umbrellas. He would have to make suggestions as well on Henkel advertising strategy, e.g., should they advertise the whole umbrella as a group, concentrate on one brand and hope others got pulled along somehow, or divide dollars and advertise each on its own? What should be the timing of the expansion of the strategy to worldwide markets—what kind of markets should be tried first? Should he advocate standardization of the strategy across markets or be yielding on individual adaptation? Last, he had to consider how to sell the ideas to the trade. Distributors and retailers were vital to Henkel success; however, with the recent record of HD/BC, trade receptivity to another HD/BC venture was not overwhelming.

Von Briskorn believed very strongly in the brand philosophy he had developed over the past few years—"Concentrate on a few, but really strong umbrellas and, as far as possible, have an internationally standardized strategy." In the abstract, the philosophy seemed to fit the adhesives market well, but now was the time to implement rather than philosophize.

PART 2

Market-based Guidelines for Product Design and Positioning

INTRODUCTION

The consumer research available to support the decision-making in the cases of Part 1 was limited. In Sealed Air, there was "no systematically collected data on the buying process on the extent to which price dominated performance in the purchase decision." Henkel's consumer research consisted of test and control groups of 100 people each answering questions on the Pattex and Pritt lines (case Exhibits 7 and 9). The consumer data were more extensive at New York Life as the head of marketing obtained "three research reports, representing a five-inch high pile on her desk." Relevant data from the five-inch pile were presented in seven case Tables (C through I). All of these data were of the simple "check-the-box" variety; for example, Is this service:

- not too important;
- important but not essential;
- essential;
- don't know.

or simple rate scale judgments.

In many situations, a more extensive data collection effort is warranted before resources are committed to product development. The first two cases in Part 2 each feature $100,000 pre-product development research programs. Techsonic Industries calls market research its "secret weapon" over competitors. In the words of the vice president of marketing, "We're about the only ones who actually ask and listen." MSA: The Software Company commissioned a leading, state-of-the-art research company to get data which "could get beyond the superficial in a timely way and be of real value."

This part presents the most useful research tools which can be employed at this stage in the development process. The three notes present the fundamentals of concept testing, perceptual mapping, and conjoint analysis. The cases then present applications of these methods. Specifically, Techsonics heavily uses concept testing. MSA's testing is similar in spirit but uses the advanced form of concept testing, conjoint analysis. Finally, the Strategic Industry Model exercise provides the actual perceptual mapping and conjoint analysis from a computer model to provide experience in analyzing these outputs. The notes, cases, and exercise:

1. Provide intuitive understanding of the major research procedures supporting pre-development decision making.
2. Develop skill in integrating the research findings with other key factors bearing on the decision.
3. Reveal the critical points of interaction between a research supplier in an effective research process.
4. Provide an appreciation of the scope of applicability of research procedures at the phase.
5. Show possible organizational barriers to the utilization of market research and illustrate how they can be overcome.

The focus of Part 2 is pre-product development testing (e.g., MSA is faced with a decision of whether or not to invest the $3 million necessary to develop a fully-featured product). Part 3 turns to consideration of research which can further guide the strategy development once the physical product exists.

2 *NOTE*

Concept Testing

Robert J. Dolan

CONCEPT TESTING: DEFINITION AND PURPOSE

Managers often screen new product ideas first with respect to internal considerations, e.g., can we efficiently manufacture the product, does it fit our existing channels of distribution, does it fit with the general corporate image, etc. If the internal checks are met, attention turns to assessing the market viability of the *idea* prior to incurring the development expense of actually fabricating a product. Research on the concept may begin with qualitative research procedures such as a focus group in which consumers react to the idea in a moderated, but free-form discus-

Professor Robert Dolan prepared this note as the basis for class discussion.

Copyright © 1989 by the President and Fellows of Harvard College. Harvard Business School case 590-063.

sion. A *quantitative* research phase follows measuring consumers' reaction to a proposed product on multiple dimensions, e.g., likelihood of purchase, perceived importance of product, and perceived quality of product. This phase produces both a sales volume forecast and diagnostic information to guide the positioning in the marketplace. We refer to this phase as a concept testing.

Most firms follow a similar procedure for all of their concept tests—utilizing many of the same measurements—in order to build a data base of benchmarks useful in interpreting test results.

EXECUTING A CONCEPT TEST

In addition to the usual sample selection issue,[1] the major executional considerations in a concept test are the concept communication method and the consumer response measured.

Communication can be in a factual, nonemotional way or in the context of persuasive communications as would surround the product in a typical market situation. Crawford (1987) offers a good illustration of the alternatives. In General Mills' consideration of a new low-calorie peanut butter consumer reaction to which concept would be more useful:

> *Concept A: "A low-calorie form of peanut butter that can be used in most diets."*

OR

> *Concept B: "A marvelous new way to chase the blahs from your diet has been discovered by General Mills scientists—a low-calorie version of ever-popular peanut butter. As tasty as ever and produced by a natural process, our new Light Peanut Butter will fit every weight-control diet in use today virtually without restriction."*

Concept statement A has the advantage of eliciting evaluation of the concept rather than the concept plus communication strategy. The disadvantage is that the consumer is reacting to something quite unlike that which he/she will "see" in the marketplace. Generally, concept statements such as B (referred to as a "positioning concept" as opposed to the "core idea" concept of A) yield better behavioral predictions from consumers since there is a greater similarity to the actual purchase situation.

---

[1]The issue of sample selection is not discussed here since it is the same as for any market research survey. This issue is covered in most market research texts and in the Note on Survey Research Methods, HBS Case Services No. 582-055.

The second communication issue is whether to use words only or add illustration, e.g., a rough sketch, photograph, or film. There is no general rule as to which is better. For example, testing alternative new course electives among MBA students is better done with words only; whereas a designer clothing item would be difficult to communicate in words.

Figure A shows the six possible combinations of concept communication mode and tone. No one cell of Fig. A inherently dominates the others. However, it is important to recognize the impact of concept type on respondents' reactions—in particular, the purchase intent scores. Generally, a move from factual to persuasive tone increases purchase intent scores. Similarly, words plus visual generally produces scores greater than either alone. Comparing concepts with executions from different cells of Fig. A is invalid. In "Do Concept Scores Measure The Message or The Method?", Lewis (1984) documents the impact of context in consumer products research, via data from three situations, two at Pfizer and one at Clairol. Identical concepts were tested first in a words-only form and then in a words-plus visual form. In particular, the visual was a mock-up of the product for consumers to see and hold. Table A shows the percentage of respondents who declared "positive interest" in the concept. On average, the addition of the visual drove up the positive interest score by 20 percentage points. Table A illustrates the danger of naively comparing concept scores across types. Suppose Pfizer A concept had been tested only in the Words Plus Visual form while Pfizer B had been tested only in the Words Only form. Without recognition of the mode effect, one would say that A "outscored" B by 46% to 35% when, in fact, B dominates A in both modes.

Figure A. *Six types of concepts*

		Tone	
		Factual	Persuasive
M	Words only		
O			
D	Visual only		
E	Words plus visual		

TABLE A   **Purchase interest percentage for concepts with different executions**

	Pfizer A	Pfizer B	Clairol
1. Words only	20%	35%	33%
2. Words plus visual	46	52	50
3. Difference (Row 2 minus Row 1)	26	17	17

The second major execution issue is determining the data to collect. Typically, the data fall into four classes:

1. Intended Purchase Measures
2. Overall Product Diagnostics
3. Special Attribute Diagnostics
4. Respondent Profiling Variables

DATA TYPE #1: PURCHASE MEASURES

Purchase measures cover purchase intention and expected frequency. Purchase intention is included in virtually all concept tests. The form is typically: "Based on this product description, how likely would you be to buy this product if it were available at a store in your area?"; check one:

- Definitely would buy
- Probably would buy
- Might or might not buy
- Probably would not buy
- Definitely would not buy

While this five-point scale is most common, six-, seven-, and eleven-point scales are also regularly used.

For nondurable goods, the frequency of purchase is also key. Purchase intent is a good indicator of trial, but forecasting volume requires knowing whether the product is part of someone's everyday consumption habit or a special occasion item. The expected purchase incidence question adds this dimension. Again, there is a variety of ways to specify this question but generally it takes a form such as: "Which statement best describes how often you think you would buy this product if it were available to you?"

- Once a week or more often
- Once every two or three weeks

- Once a month
- Once every two to three months
- Once every four to six months
- Once or twice a year
- Less often
- Never

In cases where the product may come in different sizes or is such that multiple units might be purchased at one time, these issues are also addressed.

In summary, given:

Sales volume per household in time period = % households in market who try

- expected # purchases in the period for triers
- expected # units per purchase

the purchase measures from a concept test typically are designed to measure the three variables on the right-hand side.

DATA TYPE #2: OVERALL PRODUCT DIAGNOSTICS

Managers want to obtain data to understand why the purchase measures turn out the way they do. Concept diagnostics are of two types: (i) a set devoted to the overall idea and (ii) a set on specific attributes. With respect to overall product judgments, there is a standard battery of questions addressing the concept's:

1. uniqueness or differentiation from other products
2. believability
3. importance in solving a consumer's problem
4. inherent interest
5. value for the money

Uniqueness and believability are the two most widely used diagnostic measures. Since it is possible that a high uniqueness, high believability concept could still generate low purchase interest, firms usually assess how salient the product is to solving a consumer's problem and its overall interest. For example, while a respondent may rate a television permitting the viewing of two channels at once as both unique and believable, purchase interest may be low because the respondent does not view the current constraint of one channel at a time as a problem.

Finally, if the concept statement includes the price at which the product will be offered, a measure is usually taken on the relative size of the benefits (which all the above has been related to) versus the cost. This is usually done in a "value-for-the-money" question measured on a five-point scale.

DATA TYPE #3: SPECIFIC ATTRIBUTE DIAGNOSTICS

When a concept has a number of attributes or benefits offered, it is useful to probe which attributes/benefits contribute to the purchase intention. In some cases, this probing is achieved through the use of open-ended questions such as "you said that you [state respondent's answer to purchase intention question]. What is it specifically about the product which makes you feel this way?"

Second, it is often useful to collect data on perceptions of specific attributes and their importance to the consumer. For example, a new food item might be rated on the perception and important scales as follows:

	Perception				
	Excellent				Poor
Ease of preparation	☐	☐	☐	☐	☐
For serving guests	☐	☐	☐	☐	☐
Calorie level	☐	☐	☐	☐	☐
	Attribute Importance				
	Very important				Not at all important
Ease of preparation	☐	☐	☐	☐	☐
For serving guests	☐	☐	☐	☐	☐
Calorie level	☐	☐	☐	☐	☐

Schwartz (1989) suggests using these data in "quadrant analysis" which shows each attribute as falling in one of the quadrants as shown in Fig. B.

Quadrants 1 and 3 contain attributes which the consumer does not care about. In one sense, they are "no problem" areas but if many of the attribute scores are in Quadrant 1, it suggests the concept is good on the wrong things. Quadrant 2 is the set of key communication attributes—both important and the product does well on them. Quadrant 4 is the problem quadrant where one should focus product improvement efforts as they are salient to the consumer and the concept currently is viewed poorly on them.

Figure B. *Quadrant analysis*

```
                            Rating
                            | Excellent

              1             |             2


    ─────────────────────────────────────────────  Very
                            |                    Hi  important
      Not at all            |
      important             |
                   3        |             4

                            | Poor
```

DATA TYPE #4: RESPONDENT PROFILING VARIABLES

The final set of variables useful in analyzing concepts is the type of consumers who respond in different ways. The most obvious of these is demographics which help in targeting efforts but other more innovative data collection can be useful as well, e.g., data on:

■ current purchase behavior
■ perception of the category
■ barriers to changing brands
■ influence in actual purchase decision

For example, it might be important to understand how satisfied those with high purchase intent scores are with their current brand. High satisfaction with the current brand makes a switch to a new brand less likely.

INTERPRETING THE PURCHASE INTENT DATA

Of all the data, the PI score is at the heart of a concept test. How best does one interpret these data? Suppose the concept test on low-calorie peanut butter yields PI data:

Definitely will buy	15%
Probably will buy	45

Might/might not buy	20
Probably not buy	10
Definitely not buy	9

Is this a good or bad set of scores? If the product was introduced, what sales volume would you expect? These are two important, logical questions which cannot be answered just by looking at the five numbers.

General rules of thumb on "good" PI scores exist. For example, Taylor, Houlahan, and Gabriel (1975) claim that based on their experience with over 100 brands in many product categories ". . . a concept statement should receive 80% to 90% favorable answers ["definitely will buy" or "probably will buy"] to encourage subsequent development work." Thus with its 60% favorable answer score, our low-cal peanut butter falls short of this published norm. Schwartz (1987) states the following average scores across all product categories:

Definitely will buy	19%
Probably will buy	64%

for an average 83% favorable rating score—a number not inconsistent with the rule-of-thumb of Taylor, Houlahan, and Gabriel. However, Schwartz also makes the important point that average scores vary appreciably across product categories. For example, he presents data on four categories' average "definitely will buy" scores as shown in Fig. C.

Thus, while Taylor et al.'s "rule-of-thumb" may be a useful first cut in assessing the "goodness" of the PI scores, it is only that. The variation in scores across categories shows the need to have category specific norms. These can come from three places: (i) published sources (such as Schwartz), (ii) the company's own files, or (iii) the files of the research company hired to do the concept test. Helpful information from pub-

Figure C. *Average "definitely will buy" percent—Across all categories and in four specific categories*

Fragrances	Detergents		Food	Cleaning products
9	12	19%	20	28

Across all categories

lished sources is very limited. The second source may suffice for an active company regularly introducing products into the same categories. Generally, however, there is important value in the benchmarks established by research firms with a broad array of clients participating in many product categories. In fact, one of the major concept testing research firms uses its extensive data base built up from its past tests as its primary competitive advantage.

RELATIONSHIP BETWEEN INTENT AND ACTUAL PURCHASE

With respect to sales volume estimation, research shows that there is a strong correlation between PI and trial, i.e., concepts with higher PI scores than benchmarks tend to have higher trial rates. For consumer packaged goods, the rule-of-thumb is that the "top-box" (i.e., "definitely intend to buy") is a good indicator of the likely trial rate. Anecdotal evidence for this is in Taylor, Houlahan, and Gabriel (1975). Their test involves a finished product in a finished package rather than a concept statement. But the PI scores were collected in the same way. Consumers in certain neighborhoods of a city were given three samples of a product. Ten days later they were called to obtain purchase intention ratings. At the end of the interview, they were told that the product would be available in a specific store in their neighborhood. The PI scores were:

Definitely would buy	18%
Probably would buy	29
Might/Might not buy	28
Probably would not buy	17
Definitely would not buy	15

Using the "Top-Box" rule, 18% trial would be expected. After six weeks, people were called back and it was found that 19% of those exposed to the product in supermarkets had bought it at least once. Nobody in the "bottom-three" boxes had tried the product. Trial among those in the "Top-2" boxes were 35% of those exposed to the product. The advertising agency, BBDO, uses the Top Box score from a standard concept test as an estimate of the trial rate in its New Product Early Warning System forecasting model (Pringle, Wilson, and Brody [1982]) and apparently has had good success with it.

Note that PI is a predictor only of trial and not repeat purchase. Tauber (1981) provides compelling data on this. For six new food products which went to test market or national introduction, he tracked awareness, trial rate and repeat purchase rates by stated purchase intention in a standard concept test. The results were as follows:

Stated intention	Became aware of product	Tried given aware	Repeat given trial
Definitely buy	71	31	52
Probably	60	16	43
Might/might not	54	17	56
Probably not	52	8	50
Definitely not	38	10	40

The last column shows that while intenders are more likely to become aware and try, purchase intention at the concept stage does not differentiate those who are repeaters. This is because product satisfaction drives repeat and satisfaction is not a factor in a concept test.

The centrality of PI scores in new product development and the lack of apparent grounding for the different rules of thumb have prompted academic investigation of the PI/purchase behavior relationship by Morrison (1979) and Kalwani and Silk (1982). Kalwani and Silk show PI scores do correlate with actual purchase behavior for a broad array of products. However, the relationship between PI scores and purchase behavior does vary by product category. For consumer packaged goods, their data support the current emphasis on the "top-box." On the other hand, for durables, they show that a weighted average of all box scores leads to better estimates of purchase.

SUMMARY

Concept testing is a staple of the research process for new products. It is a key tool for setting development priorities, prior to major investments to create the product or service. Key guidelines to the execution and interpretation of concept tests are:

a. select the tone/mode appropriate to the situation
b. interpret PI scores in light of the tone/mode selection and appropriate benchmarks.
c. design the test to afford diagnostic as well as predictive information.

REFERENCES

Crawford, M.C. *New Products Management*, (Homewood, Ill.: Irwin, 1987).

Kalwani, M. and A. Silk. "On the Reliability and Predictive Validity of Purchase Intention Measures," *Marketing Science*, Summer 1982, pp. 243–287.

Lewis, I. "Do Concept Scores Measure the Message or the Method?," *Journal of Advertising Research*, February–March 1984, pp. 54–56.

Morrison, D. "Purchase Intentions and Purchase Behavior," *Journal of Marketing*, Spring 1979, pp. 65–74.

Pringle, L., R. Wilson, and E. Brody. "News: A Decision-Oriented Model for New Product Analysis and Forecasting," *Marketing Science*, Winter 1982, pp. 1–30.

Schwartz, D. *Concept Testing*, AMACOM, 1987.

Taylor, J., J. Houlahan, and A. Gabriel. "The Purchase Intention Question in New Product Development: A Field Test," *Journal of Marketing*, January 1975, pp. 90–92.

Tauber, E. "Utilization of Concept Testing for New Product Forecasting: Traditional vs. Multiattribute Approaches," in *New Product Forecasting*, Wind, Mahajan, and Cardozo (editors), (Lexington, Mass.: Lexington Books, 1981).

Tauber, E. "Predictive Validity in Consumer Research," *Journal of Advertising Research*, October 1975, pp. 59–64.

3 *NOTE*

Perceptual Mapping: A Manager's Guide

Robert J. Dolan

INTRODUCTION

Pictures are often more effective than words, e.g., basketball coaches map out plays on mini-blackboards during time-outs; a company's annual reports set out sales figures in a bar graph; and executives study maps of sales regions to identify account concentration and territory development. Similar pictures often play a role in new product development as evidenced by the common usage of terms like "product positioning" and "market structure." These terms seem to indicate that the manager is visualizing a map of the marketplace in which brands are positioned

Professor Robert J. Dolan prepared this note as the basis for class discussion.

against one another vying for the spot which consumers most desire. In strategic planning sessions, it is not unusual for a participant to pick up a marker and make his vision explicit on a flip chart. For example, a V.P. of marketing for a men's tailored clothing company might think of the dimensions of competition as mainly two: price and youthfulness of appeal and thus sketch out the "map" in Fig. A.

Products range from the very expensive Hickey Freeman for the mature person to Austin Reed as branded low-price alternative for the younger set, to private label clothing. The strategic planners use this map as the focal point of a discussion on where the firm's new suit line should be placed.

Implicitly, the group makes two assumptions in using the map in this way: (i) potential customers use these same two dimensions in differentiating brands, i.e., price and youthfulness of appeal are key to customers and (ii) the placement of a brand on the two dimensions reflects the beliefs of customers. If it is a reliable representation of the views of customers in the marketplace, this type of map can illuminate discussions on target market selection, product design and product communications strategy.

Figure A. **Map of competitors in suit business**

Since the perceptions of customers are key, a set of market research tools has been developed to produce maps based on hard consumer perception data. These data replace perhaps informed, but somewhat subjective, judgment of managers. This note discusses these "Perceptual Mapping" tools. Having given some rationale for the construction of maps, Section 2 discusses construction procedures and Section 3 presents some illustrative applications and details the uses of the maps.

DEVELOPING THE MAP

One obvious way to develop the map of a product category is to ask a consumer to name the two most important differentiating characteristics and then rate each product on these characteristics. This might work reasonably well in some situations. However, in general, it places too great a burden on respondents to result in reliable maps.

There are two major alternatives for constructing maps, differing in what is asked of consumers: (i) attribute rating method (AR) and (ii) overall similarity method (OS). The AR method is similar to the one proposed above except consumers are presented a full list of possible relevant attributes and rate each item on each attribute. For example, Siemer (1989) uses the AR method to map the competition among vendors of specialty plastics. Potential customers rated Dow Chemical and three competitors on the eight attributes which Dow believed important:

1. meets scheduled delivery dates
2. practices innovation and development
3. has fair pricing
4. has consistent product
5. provides support in solving processing problems
6. has custom color capability
7. provides adequate technical literature
8. withstands high heat distortion temperatures

The data collection phase of the AR approach results in a "data cube" as shown in Fig. B.

Each respondent provides 32 numbers, i.e., the ratings of each vendor on each of eight attributes. As shown in Fig. B, for N respondents, one can think of the data from each being stacked up together in the data cube of 32 x N numbers. Now the question is how to extract some infor-

Figure B. The "data cube" of the AR method

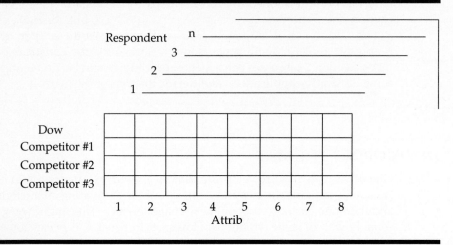

mation from these data. This is the role of statistical analysis. The process is:

The statistical analysis (either "factor analysis" or "multiple discriminant analysis") essentially works on one set of vendor attribute ratings. This one set can be obtained by averaging the ratings across all respondents to obtain an aggregate market view or the analysis can be done sequentially for smaller groups of respondents to examine whether segments exist which vary in their perceptions of products. The philosophy behind the analysis is to find the two axes for the perceptual map which will convey the most information in the data cube.

The statistical analysis defines the axes by including the original attributes with different weights.[1] Intuitively, what the procedures do is "look" at situations such as shown in Fig. C. In Fig. Ca, we see all vendors are rated identically for attribute #1, so that is not a very interesting

---

[1]For details and a comparison of the statistical methods, see Hauser and Koppelman (1979).

Figure C. *Attribute analysis*

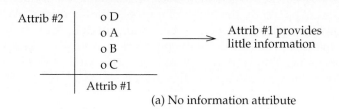

(a) No information attribute

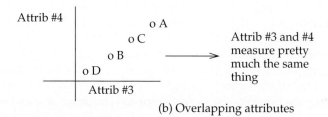

(b) Overlapping attributes

feature. Once the statistical analysis reveals this, it does not give attribute #1 much importance in portraying the situation. Attribute #2 on the other hand varies across products and would have a place in the final map. Figure Cb is a situation in what attributes #3 and #4 are highly correlated, i.e., the vendors rated high on #3 are also rated high on #4. The statistical analysis would thus treat #3 and #4 as measurements of the same underlying construct.

The analysis collapses down from the original set of attributes to a two-dimensional map with the four vendors positioned on the axes. Since the original data are in eight dimensions (attributes) and the perceptual map is reduced down to two, the map cannot capture all the variation among the vendors given in the data matrix. However, essentially it does the best it can, i.e., retains the most important information from the full data matrix and reports it in two dimensions to provide visual impact. For some representative maps using the AR method, see:

Siemer (1989)	—	p. 112	—	Vendors of Specialty Plastics
Johnson (1987)	—	p. 144	—	Presidential Candidates
Block (1989)	—	p. 122	—	Channels of Distribution Alternatives
Stannard (1989)	—	p. 133	—	Automobiles

The AR method has a key limitation for some product types, i.e., it requires the researcher to articulate and the respondent to think in terms of attributes. Apparently this was not a problem for specialty plastics at Dow. However, imagine executing the AR approach in the soft drink or perfume market. In categories with competition driven by tastes, odors, or aesthetics—i.e., things we do not verbalize very well—the AR method breaks down. In such situations, the overall similarity (OS) method is preferred.

The OS method produces a map similar to that of AR. However, the input data are quite different. In OS, we do not specify any attributes of the products. We simply ask the respondent to make judgments about the overall similarity of pairs of items. Specifically, for n items, we require the respondent to rank the $(n)(n-1)/2$ possible pairs of items from most similar to least similar. For example, mapping the movie market we might consider 6 items: *Henry V, A Fish Called Wanda, Nuns on the Run, The Little Mermaid, Field of Dreams,* and *Teenage Mutant Ninja Turtles.* (Note: we limit this to six for simplicity in showing how the procedure works. Ordinarily, one would want to consider all relevant competition.) With 6 items, there are 15 pairs. A convenient way to represent the required input is in matrix form with a 1 = most similar pair and a 15 = least similar pair. Suppose one respondent gave the judgments as shown in Table A.

"Eyeballing" the data, we might notice a couple of things. First, *Field of Dreams* is seen as pretty similar to all the movies (obviously this hypothetical respondent never threw a baseball with his hypothetical father). Also, the *Mermaid-Ninja* pair is rated ninth—less similar than the average pair. This might seem odd as they are two children's movies in the set. In order to sort these things out, we submit the data to a statistical proce-

TABLE A   Respondent ranking of similarity of six movies

	Wanda	Nuns	Mermaid	Field	Ninja
Henry	11	12	10	6	13
Wanda	–	1	14	2	5
Nuns		–	15	3	6
Mermaid			–	8	9
Field				–	4
Ninja					–

dure (Multidimensional Scaling), to develop a map to permit us to "see" the data and get the information from it.

The statistical analysis attempts to find a map such that the distance between the movies as shown on the map match up (i.e., be in the same order) as the rank numbers in the input data matrix of Table A. The map in Fig. D fits this bill. The output of multidimensional scaling is a plot like Fig. D and a statistic which tells how closely the distances on the map match up with the original input data. Note that we do not know what the axes are—but our knowledge of the category can help us to name them. On the vertical axis, it's *Henry V*, *A Fish Called Wanda*, and *Nuns on the Run* on one end versus *Teenage Mutant Ninja Turtles* and *The Little Mermaid* on the other. This strongly suggests an adult versus kids audience vertical dimension. Second, the horizontal axis has *Henry V* and *The Little Mermaid* versus *Nuns on the Run*, *A Fish Called Wanda* and *Teenage Mutant Ninja Turtles*—strongly suggesting a humor dimension. *Field of Dreams* is the middle position—with broad audience appeal and a mix of serious and humorous. The map helps explain what might seem odd to us from "eyeballing" the data. While *The Little Mermaid* and *Teenage Mutant Ninja Turtles* are seen as similar in their target audience, this respondent differentiates them on the basis of their relative use of humor.

The OS method thus allows us not only to map products but also infer the attributes used by the respondent in making distinctions. Note, however, that these inferences were somewhat subjective (e.g., one might say the horizontal axis is quality of the musical score) and

Figure D. *Perceptual map of movie market*

required knowledge of the objects by the analyst. The OS procedure has been used in the mapping of:

- Retail stores by Arora (1982), Singson (1975)
- Desserts by Jain (1978)
- Food Products by Lautman, Percy and Kordish (1978)
- Ethical Drugs by Neidell (1969)
- Cigarette Brands by Smith and Lusch (1976)

Table B summarizes the major differences between the AR and OS methods.

The major difference is in the input data required. While OS does require specialized software, a number of packages are available at no great cost. However, because of issues relating to statistical power, OS is inappropriate for applications with less than 8 brands to be mapped. Because the nature of the different product category determines which method is more appropriate, AR and OS should be viewed as complements to one another, rather than substitutes.

TABLE B   Comparison of AR and OS methods

AR	OS
Input data	
■ brand ratings on attributes ■ attributes prespecified by analyst	■ overall similarity ranking ■ definition of similarity left to respondent
Statistical technique	
■ factor analysis or multiple discriminant analysis (software generally available)	■ multidimensional scaling (special-purpose software required; however, efficient packages available at low cost)
Output	
■ product positions on axes defined as combination of original values	■ relative product positions; axes must be interpreted by analyst
Best suited for	
■ applications with hard attributes which can be verbalized	■ categories dominated by not easily articulated attributes

APPLYING THE MAPS IN NEW PRODUCT DEVELOPMENT

There are three major ways in which perceptual maps are used in the new product development process:

   i. to obtain a better understanding of market structure
  ii. to test where a new product being considered for introduction would be perceived
 iii. to provide direction to R&D efforts to satisfy the wants of consumers better.

In many studies, perceptual maps are used for all three of these purposes simultaneously. The third is somewhat different from the others in that it requires representation of consumers' preferred positions (their "ideal points") as well as competitors' positions on the map. The procedure for achieving this will be discussed below. We will now cover the three purposes in turn.

PURPOSE #1: UNDERSTANDING MARKET STRUCTURE

At the idea generation stage of the new product development process, perceptual maps can be a useful stimulus to opportunity identification. Our vice president of marketing for the suit manufacturer was putting maps to this use in the example above. Specifically, the map of Fig. A can indicate "holes" in the product space which might be exploited. These "holes" may represent niches of the market which current competitors have overlooked and could be developed. Second, the maps indicate the vulnerability of competitors by showing how consumers perceive them. For example, there are cases where a dominant share brand seems impossible to attack. However, a deeper understanding of customers' attitudes and perceptions can show the means of attacking this seemingly impregnable incumbent. Consider Fig. E, a hypothetical map of eight vendors. Suppose using the AR or OS method generated the map with the axes interpreted as shown in the figure. Market shares in the category are:

    A— 58%   E— 8%
    B— 8%   F— 1%
    C— 9%   G— 5%
    D— 7%   H— 4%

These market shares are compatible with the map positions and the notion that a large proportion of the customers in the category are quite quality sensitive and hence buy from firm A even though it is perceived as "unfair."

Figure E. Map of competitive positions of eight firms

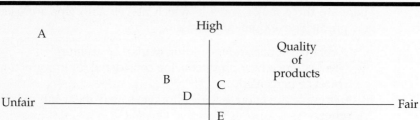

The market share numbers suggest a difficult job in attacking A. However, the map indicates A's vulnerability. A's differentiation on quality, i.e., even firms B, C, D, and E are significantly lower in quality, grants it some power which it has exercised to the point of being negatively perceived by customers. If A were positioned in the map in the upper right hand quadrant, (say at A's quality and H's fairness), there would be no basis for attacking A. However, its poor position on fairness indicates A's market share can be taken away if a firm is able to produce product near A's quality level and treat customers well simultaneously.

PURPOSE #2: PERCEPTIONS OF A PRODUCT CONCEPT

Once a general opportunity has been identified (either with or without perceptual maps) the process usually moves forward to concept development and testing and, in consumer packaged goods, some form of product use test or laboratory test market. In either of these phases, perceptual maps can be used to test if the concept or product would be perceived as the firm intended by consumers. The ASSESSOR pretest market system (see Silk and Urban (1978) for details) regularly uses perceptual mapping (an AR version) to provide diagnostic information to complement its prediction of the market share a proposed new product would attain.

For this use, respondents must be informed about the new concept or product, either through a concept statement or, if possible, product use. Once they are able to form their own image and judgments about the brand, the method proceeds as usual.

For example, suppose a firm in the computer business already participates in the market and the key attributes are ease of use, flexibility, and price. A Perceptual Map of the market is shown in Fig. F.

The map shows a group of competitors in the middle of the map; firms G and H offer less flexibility and convenience (presumably at lower prices). Our Firm X has been able to differentiate itself from the group via innovation on flexibility, taking point X on the map. Although not depicted on the map, this is at a slight price premium over the offerings of A, B, C, D, E, and F. Firm I has been able to differentiate itself by offering both greater flexibility and greater ease of use, but its offering is at a significant price premium.

Our firm is considering expanding its product line to bring out a machine which is very easy to use, but with average flexibility, i.e., a product in the area of the circle drawn on the map. Such a product would sell at the same price level as X, but would (it was hoped) not cannibalize X but rather appeal to a market segment now buying F or I. The question is whether the product could take on this position in customers' eyes even if, in a technical performance sense, it provided average flexibility but was quite easy to use. Perceptual mapping can provide an answer to the advisability of the strategy. Once consumers understand the proposed product, a mapping study could be done to see where the new product falls. Figure G shows the four zones.

If the new product takes on a position in consumer's eyes in Zone 1, the basic positioning is viable. The product is positioned strongly on the ease-of-use dimension and the trade-off for ease-of-use for flexibility is communicated. All other zones are problematic. Zone 2 puts the firm "in the bunch" with firms A, B, C, D, E, and F—not differentiated enough to make a prod-

Figure F. **Perceptual map of personal computer market**

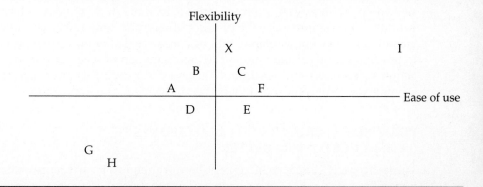

Figure G. Possible product positionings

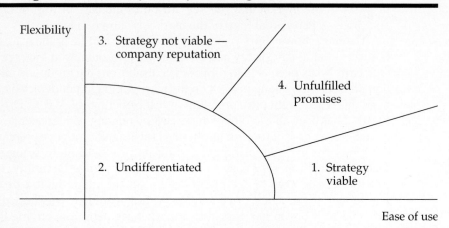

uct line extension worthwhile. Zone 3 is a basic failure to capture the desired position. The firm's reputation for flexibility overwhelms the new product features and the new product is seen to have the same basic strengths and weaknesses as the firm's current offering. Finally, Zone 4 may initially look like a good place to be—offering both improved ease-of-use and flexibility over the "bunch," but the product cannot deliver against those expectations and hence in the long term this would be a disaster.

Similarly, a map can be used after a product introduction to track the positioning. For example, suppose the study at this stage showed the new product to be on the border between Zones 1 and 4. One might then argue that the respondents had limited communication about the new product and that an actual introduction would be accompanied by extensive company-managed communication and trade press reviews which would be sufficient to place the product squarely in Zone 1, the "strategy viable" zone. Perceptual maps could be constructed after the introduction to test this hypothesis and aid in the determination of whether remedial action was necessary. Smith and Lusch (1976) used this approach to examine the effectiveness of a Liggett and Myers repositioning effort.

PURPOSE #3: DIRECTION TO R&D EFFORTS TO SATISFY CUSTOMERS BETTER

This purpose is similar to #2, except here we require formal representation of the "ideal point" of a customer, i.e., what point on the map represents the ideal combination of attributes for different customer groups.

Our example in #2 was chosen to sidestep this issue by choosing two attributes which almost everybody would like as much of as he could get for a given price. Consequently, we could think of the "ideal" being as far to the northeast on Fig. F as possible.

When we have attributes for which more is not necessarily better, we will want to represent explicitly these ideals. There are two methods for doing this, both of which are applicable in either the AR or OS procedure. The first method is to alter the input data collection phase to include the respondent's "ideal" in the set of things to be rated on each attribute (AR method) or to be considered in forming all possible pairs for similarity ranking (OS method). The second method is to augment the data collection on perceptions with a preference phase. Statistical analysis, called preference mapping or "unfolding," is then used to position a respondent "ideal point" on the map following the principle that the ideal should be "close to" the brands at the top of the preference ranking and "far from" those at the bottom of the preference ranking (see Jain (1978) for example).

The examples in the literature point out the value of doing this because the ideal points of individuals while usually clustered, are spread out across the map of brands. For example, Johnson's work (1987) on presidential candidates identified eight clusters with significantly varied ideals on the two key dimensions of candidate differentiation:

- liberal versus conservative
- reduce government involvement versus increase government involvement.

Often the intent is to use perceptual maps to serve each of these three purposes. The potential for managerial utility is hopefully clear from the description of the technique; however, added testimony comes from the number of firms regularly using the method and the reaction of some of those users. For example, in discussing Dow Chemical's application in the specialty plastics market, Siemer (1989) notes the following contributions of the perceptual mapping study:

> Some of the facts we learned from this study shocked us. . . . We had focused on physical product benefits as a basis for competitive advantage. Instead, we found a market more interested in service issues. [The study provided] greater understanding of the market structure . . . an understanding of the unique needs of industry segments [and] . . . competitors' vulnerabilities from the point of view of our customers.

The impact of this improved understanding was a change in Dow's basic approach to the market and spending plans, viz. "We were able to develop a strategic positioning for Dow that focused and prioritized our resources where they would have the greatest competitive advantage, and then were able to abandon issues and priorities that had low potential return because of customer indifference."

SUMMARY

Perceptual mapping has proven a useful tool. It does have a number of limitations, however, which should be noted. First, it presents a static view, i.e., it is a snapshot of consumers' current perceptions. If a series of studies of the same market is done over time, some trends can be monitored. Second, while it may help a firm determine what it would like to do vis-à-vis the market, it provides no indication of the cost or likelihood of being able to achieve the desired positioning.

In short, it in no way substitutes for management judgment but often provides valuable input and serves as a very useful focal point in strategic planning discussions.

REFERENCES

Arora, R. "Consumer Involvement in Retail Store Positioning," *Journal of Academy of Marketing Science*, Spring 1982, vol. 10, No. 2, pp. 109–124.

Block, R. A. "Evaluating Distribution Channels with Perceptual Mapping," *1989 Sawtooth Software Conference Proceedings*, 1989, pp. 115–124.

Hauser, J. and F. Koppelman. "Alternative Perceptual Mapping Techniques: Relative Accuracy and Usefulness," *Journal of Marketing Research*, Vol. XVI, November 1979, pp. 495–506.

Jain, A. "A Predictive Study in Perceptual and Evaluative Mapping," *Journal of Academy of Marketing Science*, Fall 1978, Vol. 6, No. 4, pp. 300–313.

Johnson, R. M. "Adaptive Perceptual Mapping," *Sawtooth Software Conference on Perceptual Mapping, Conjoint Analysis, and Computer Interviewing*, 1987, pp. 143–158.

Lautman, M. R., L. M. Percy, and G.R. Kordish. "Campaigns from Multidimensional Scaling," *Journal of Advertising Research*, Vol. 18, No. 3, June 1978, pp. 35–40.

Neidell, C. A. "The Use of Nonmetric Multidimensional Scaling in Marketing Analysis," *Journal of Marketing*, Vol. 33, October 1969, pp. 37–43.

Siemer, R. H. "Using Perceptual Mapping for Market-Entry Decisions," *1989 Sawtooth Software Conference Proceedings*, 1989, pp. 107–114.

Silk, A. and G. Urban. "Pre-Test-Market Evaluation of New Packaged Goods: A Model and Measurement Methodology," *Journal of Marketing Research*, Vol. XV, May 1978, pp. 171–191.

Singson, R. L. "Multidimensional Scaling Analysis of Store Image and Shopping Behavior," *Journal of Retailing*, Vol. 51, No. 2, Summer 1975.

Smith, R. E. and R. F. Lusch. "How Advertising Can Position a Brand," *Journal of Advertising Research*, Vol. 16, February 1976, pp. 37–43.

Stannard, C. I. "Perceptual Mapping and Cluster Analysis: Some Problems and Solutions," *1989 Sawtooth Software Conference Proceedings*, 1989, pp. 133–142.

4 *NOTE*

Conjoint Analysis: A Manager's Guide

Robert J. Dolan

INTRODUCTION

Conjoint analysis has been widely used in the new product development process—for selecting among alternative product designs, targeting, and pricing. Cattin and Wittink's two surveys (Cattin and Wittink (1982) and Wittink and Cattin (1989)) document over 1,000 applications from 1981 to 1985. They estimate 400 commercial studies per year in the mid-1980s. Applications cover a broad range of industries with extensive use noted at Boston Consulting Group (Prensky (1987)), Procter & Gamble (Tumbusch (1987)), Smith, Kline and French (Marshall (1987)), and Xerox

Professor Robert J. Dolan prepared this note as the basis for class discussion.

Copyright © 1990 by the President and Fellows of Harvard College. Harvard Business School case 590-059.

(Vaccarelli (1987)). Some other companies using conjoint are:

- Ashton-Tate—computer software (Eisenhart (1988))
- Fujitsu America—cellular telephones (Eisenhart (1988))
- ISU International—insurance distribution systems (Eisenhart (1988))
- Levi Strauss—blue jeans (Tyner and Weiner (1990))
- Marriott Corporation—hotels (Wind, Green, Shifflet and Scarbrough (1989))
- Sunbeam—food processors (Page and Rosenbaum (1987))

Applications have also been reported for a variety of types of products/services.

- **Consumer durables**:
  condominium design and pricing (Fiedler (1988))
  snowmobiles (Huber (1987))
- **Consumer nondurables**:
  rug cleaner (Green and Wind (1975))
  clothing (Ettenson, Gaeth, and Wagner (1988))
- **Consumer services**:
  credit cards (Stahl (1988))
  rural health care systems (Parker and Srinivasan (1976))
  energy conservation systems (Bennett and Moore (1981))
  performing art series (Currim, Weinberg and Wittink (1981))
- **Business products**:
  aircraft (Green and Wind (1975))
  lift trucks (Clarke (1981))
  computer software (Dolan (1990))
- **Business services**:
  technical information services (Wind, Grashof and Goldhar (1978))

This note provides a nontechnical introduction to the procedure. Section 2 explains the basic idea, i.e., the decomposition of a product into its attributes and subsequent valuation of the utility of each individual attribute. Section 3 covers the analysis of conjoint results to derive managerial implications. Section 4 discusses the accuracy of the method and Section 5 provides guidelines on when it should and should not be used.

HOW CONJOINT WORKS

DEFINING A PRODUCT

Conjoint analysis requires that a product can be broken down into a set of relevant attributes. For example, Parker and Srinivasan (1976) describe a rural health care facility by five attributes:

1. residence to facility travel time
2. time lag in obtaining an appointment
3. waiting time at the facility
4. hours of operation
5. facility type (nurse practitioner, doctor's office or health care center)

Finding the right combination of attributes to offer depends on the cost of various aspects and the value of each attribute to a consumer. However, consumers are not very good at directly stating attribute importance. In recognition of this, conjoint was designed to take overall preference judgments and infer from them the underlying values of the consumer.

As an example, consider a fitness facility interested in optimal design of its locker rooms. For simplicity, let's assume there are just two attributes which are potentially important to users: (i) whether or not there is a sauna and (ii) the size of available lockers. There are two alternative "levels" for the sauna ("yes" and "no") and three levels for lockers:

A. *Small* (20" x 20" x 20") storage lockers permanently assigned plus large hanging ones (72" x 20" x 20") for daily use.
B. *Medium* (36" x 20" x 20") only permanently assigned.
C. No permanently assigned locker; *large* locker (72" x 20" x 20") available on daily basis with mirror inside door.

There are thus 2 x 3 = 6 different sauna/locker combinations or products. The respondent ranks the six possible combinations from most to least preferred. The individual might respond as follows:

		Sauna	
		Yes	No
	Small	Rank 2	Rank 4
Locker	Medium	Rank 1	Rank 3
	Large	Rank 5	Rank 6

With these ranks, we can give utility points (where higher is better) to the options to capture these expressed preferences. For example, we might code the best as five points and then go down from there, so the least desired alternative gets a zero. That would yield:

Sauna

		Yes	No	
	S	4	2	Average = 3
Locker	M	5	3	Average = 4
	L	1	0	Average = 0.5

Average = 3.33   Average = 1.67

Since each locker size is rated with both levels of the sauna attribute, we can calculate the utility of an attribute level as the average of the score across all choices where it appears. Following this, we would have:

Sauna:
Yes = 3.33
No = 1.67

Locker:
M = 4
S = 3
L = 0.5

This is the individual's "value system." Note that it recaptures the stated original ranking data:

Product	Value system score	Value system score rank	Stated original rank
Medium + Sauna	4 + 3.33 = 7.33	1	1
Small + Sauna	3 + 3.33 = 6.33	2	2
Medium + No Sauna	4 + 1.67 = 5.67	3	3
Small + No Sauna	3 + 1.67 = 4.67	4	4
Large + Sauna	.5 + 3.33 = 3.83	5	5
Large + No Sauna	.5 + 1.67 = 2.17	6	6

This is the objective of the procedure, i.e., to have an individual provide *overall* preference judgments for various products and then use mathematical analysis to tease out the individual's underlying "value system," i.e., the value of each level of each attribute. The procedure allows us to assess a consumer's willingness to trade off one feature for another. The value system shows that this individual is averse to the idea of not having a storage locker (L = 0.5) and would be unwilling to trade in a storage locker on a daily basis (since at minimum this decreases his utility by $3 - .5 = 2.5$ points) in order to get a sauna (since this increases his utility by only $3.33 - 1.67 = 1.66$).

This simple example is meant only to provide some intuition for how the procedure works. Although not demonstrated in our example, a key point is that the respondent need not rank all possible products in order to be able to derive the value system. For example, Green and Wind's (1975) respondents ranking 18 products allowed estimation of the value system for a product of five attributes (3 attributes with 3 levels and 2 attributes with 2). With the value system, one can predict relative preference for all $3 \times 3 \times 3 \times 2 \times 2 = 108$ possible products.

The term "conjoint analysis" applies to a variety of procedures developed to estimate individual value systems from overall product judgments. The remainder of this section covers input data and data analysis alternatives.

STUDY DESIGN

A conjoint study has five design stages as shown in Fig. A. The first two decisions relate to what a respondent is asked about; the second two to how the respondent replies; the last to how the respondent's data are analyzed.

We now discuss each step in turn.

DETERMINING RELEVANT ATTRIBUTES   The burden is on the analyst to prespecify the attributes impacting a consumer's purchase decision. If an attribute of no real importance is included in the study, the value system will indicate this attribute's limited role. However, conjoint analysis will not directly indicate the absence of an important attribute. Consequently, one must be confident that the right attributes have been included. In practice, the preliminary attribute list is usually developed in-house via contact with company people from a variety of functions— new product development, advertising, manufacturing, etc. Tumbusch (1987) advocates using all attributes that are known to consumers and feasible for change. He notes three kinds of attributes considered in conjoint studies at Procter & Gamble:

1. Physical attributes—refers to product itself, e.g., legcuffs on disposable diapers.
2. Performance benefit—refers to outcome, e.g., dryness of baby.
3. Psychological positioning—refers to user, e.g., assurance.

MacLachlan, Mulhern and Shocker (1988) present a similar list, and note "the stimuli descriptions must convey all the information that respon-

Figure A. *Decision stages in conjoint study*

1. Determine relevant attributes

2. Choose: stimulus representations
   (i.e., how products are described
   to respondents)

3. Choose: response type
   (i.e., judgments respondents give:
   choice among alternatives, rankings,
   ratings)

4. Choose: criterion
   (i.e., the standard to be used by
   respondents: liking, preference,
   likelihood of purchasing)

5. Choose: method of data analysis

dents feel they need to make their decisions." Consequently, for unfamiliar product categories, a small scale consumer research project may be needed prior to the conjoint phase.

STIMULUS REPRESENTATION   The second design question is how to present products to the respondent: partial or full profile method. In the full profile approach, each product is described on all the relevant attributes. An example of this is Ettenson, Gaeth and Wagner's 1988 study of the impact of made-in-the-U.S.A. labeling on clothing. Female respondents in the study rated 40 profiles of blouses which were described to them on all six attributes in the study. For example, a sample rating task is:

   Blouse XYZ
   1. The style of the blouse is *classic*.
   2. The quality of the blouse is *better than average*.
   3. The fiber content of the blouse is *65% cotton/35% polyester*.

4. The price is *several dollars more than the average.*
5. The blouse is *made in the U.S.A.*
6. The label on the blouse is a *designer label.*

Based on the information above, how likely is it that you would purchase this blouse?

|——|

Not at   Very
all likely   likely

This "full profile" approach is utilized by many analysts because it is felt to be the most realistic representation of a consumer's actual decision process. The alternative "partial profile" approach describes concepts on only a subset of the full attribute list. The argument for this is that while the full list is in some sense the reality, its use may render the rating task too complex and confusing for respondents. By using partial profiles, the analyst gets a better understanding of the desired level and relative importance of secondary attributes. In the partial profile method, the attributes which are specified vary systematically from one judgment to the next, so that in the end, the value system for the full set of attributes can be estimated.

RESPONSE TYPE   Design decision three is the manner in which respondents express their judgments, viz. as ratings or ranks. The made-in-the-U.S.A. study noted above is a ratings scale application, i.e., without explicitly considering other options, consumers were asked to state how likely they would be to purchase an item.

In ranking methods, respondents are asked to consider explicitly the relevant options. Preferences are expressed in one of two ways—a "paired comparison" task or a top-to-bottom ranking. In paired comparisons, the respondent is presented with a number of pairs of products and is asked to *choose* one or the other. For example, execution of the made-in-the-U.S.A. study in this format would replace the purchase likelihood rating with a series of questions such as:

Which blouse do you prefer?

Classic style
65% cotton/35% polyester
Made in U.S.A.
Private label
Quality is average
Price is several dollars
    more than average
	OR	Trendy style
		100% cotton
		Made in China
		Designer label
		Quality is below average
		Price is several dollars
		    less than average

The second type of ranking method is to rank order a set of concepts from most to least desirable. To facilitate this task, the respondent usually is first asked to sort the product descriptions into three piles, e.g., those which he or she

1. Likes very much
2. Likes moderately
3. Likes little or not at all

and then rank within the piles. This produces the full ranking from most desired to least. Ranking n concepts is equivalent to making $n(n-1)/2$ paired comparisons, the number of distinct pairs which can be formed by taking two items at a time from a set of n items. This approach requires the concepts to be stated in full profile form.

Ranking and rating data generally produce very similar final results (Green and Srinivasan (1978)). Traditionally, ranking methods were preferred because providing a quantitative measurement of the "degree of liking" or "degree of intention to buy" was felt to be straining the capabilities of respondents. However, Wittink and Cattin (1989) report that rating scales increased from 34% frequency of use in 1971–1980 to 49% in 1981–1985. The choice of one method or the other is largely situation-specific and relates to via which form a respondent is able to provide more reliable input.

CRITERION   Whatever the stage 3 decision, there is the related but distinct issue of the standard to be used in the judgments. The two major types of standards are:

■ preference
■ likelihood or intention to purchase

This is not a trivial task since the answer to a choice between:

Mercedes		Ford Taurus
5-year warranty	*OR*	3-year warranty
$35,000		$15,000

might be different depending on the question being

Which do you prefer?
vs.
Which are you more likely to buy?

I may in some sense "prefer" the Mercedes option (even if it does involve parting with $35,000) but because I don't have the $35,000 in the first place I may be more likely to purchase the Ford.

These two different standards are used about equally often in practice (Cattin and Wittink (1982)). The choice depends largely on whether the focus of the study is market share or unit sales where the market size is to be estimated. If the latter, then intention to purchase is necessary to gauge the likely market size.

METHODS OF DATA ANALYSIS   The data analysis depends on the previous decisions made with respect to the input data collected. Most commonly, the following are used:

Form of judgment about alternatives	Data analysis
Rating Scores	Simple Regression
Probability of Purchase	Logit Model
Rankings	MONANOVA

If rating scores have been collected, e.g. "indicate how much you like this product on a scale from 1 to 10," the value system is derived through regression analysis. If the respondent has expressed a probability of purchase, a logit model (an adaptation of regression) is used to accommodate the fact that probabilities are between 0 and 1. Finally, if ranks are used, it is appropriate to recognize that we really do not know *by how much* one alternative is preferred over another. We analyze only the ordering by a monotone analysis of variance (MONANOVA).

Each procedure yields an estimate of the value system of the respondent. For example, Montgomery and Wittink (1979) report the value system of Stanford MBAs (on average) with respect to job choice (we report only three of the eight attributes here):

Business travel per month
≤1 night	.163
2–5 nights	.109
≥6 nights	−.273

Geographic location of job
East	.070
Midwest	−.198
South	−.321
West	.449

Opportunity for advancement
Rapid	.216
Moderate	−.216

From this value system, one can estimate the utility of any given job offer. Hence, one could predict which job the MBA would take. (Note: the other attributes in the study were company growth rate, functional activity emphasized, desirability of job location, salary, and competitiveness of co-workers). The following section more completely describes the type of analyses one can do with these data.

ANALYZING THE OUTPUTS

In conjoint, each individual provides a set of judgments and his value system is computed separately. There is no assumption that all consumers have the same value system. The three major types of analysis are:

1. Aggregate analysis of attribute importance and desirability.
2. Segmentation analysis.
3. Competitive scenario simulations to predict sales levels.

AGGREGATE ANALYSIS

Although one of the virtues of conjoint is its separate treatment of each individual, the most common first interpretation step is to average the utilities of each attribute level across the entire sample of respondents to give the analyst an overall feeling for which attributes are generally important and the most desired level of each. Consider again the average value system for Stanford MBAs regarding job choice:

Business travel		Geographic area		Opportunity for advancement	
≤1 night	.163	East	.070	Rapid	.216
2–5 nights	.109	Midwest	−.198	Moderate	−.216
≥6 nights	−.273	South	−.321		
		West	.449		

First, the scores indicate the relative desirability of alternative levels of each attribute. Not surprisingly, Stanford MBAs prefer jobs which have rapid advancement opportunities and are in the West. With respect to business travel, they prefer one night or less per month. The fact that this is preferable to two to five nights may be surprising.

Second, the difference among the scores for levels for a given attribute gives a rough measure of that attribute's importance. In general, the relative importance is proportional to the range covered by the levels. The business travel attribute levels range from −.273 to .163, a range of .436. Geographic area levels range from −.321 to .449, a range of .770. Opportunity for advancement levels range from −.216 to .216, a range of .432. Dividing each of these ranges by the sum of the three ranges gives a set of relative importance numbers which sum to one:

$$\text{Business Travel} = \frac{.436}{.436 + .770 + .432} = 26.6\%$$

$$\text{Geographic Area} = \frac{.770}{.436 + .770 + .432} = 47.0\%$$

$$\text{Opportunity for Advancement} = \frac{.432}{.436 + .770 + .432} = 26.4\%$$

We say that this is a rough indicator of importance, because the percentages are dependent on the specific levels of the attribute used in the study. For example, suppose the business travel variable levels were:

$\leq$1 night
2-15 nights
$\geq$15 nights

This would increase the importance of the business travel attribute given this method of calculation because $\geq$15 nights would have a large negative utility. This must be kept in mind when interpreting the results. It is a good estimate of importance only if the variable levels specified cover the range of relevant options.

SEGMENTATION ANALYSIS

While the averages provide a convenient, easy-to-comprehend summary measure, in most marketing situations one courts disaster by not investigating the variation across customers. The data matrix containing the value system of each individual can be analyzed (most often via a procedure called cluster analysis) to produce "benefit segments" wherein segments are defined so values are similar within a segment but quite different across.

Wind, Grashof and Goldhar (1978) performed this type of analysis in their technical information delivery service study. They identified five segments which displayed different values from one another. At the overall market level, price was the most important variable of the 12 considered (with a relative importance of 26.6%). However, when a segmentation analysis was done, the largest segment identified (48% of consumers) was a performance-oriented segment wherein price played only an 8.9% role. The second largest segment was price oriented. For this segment's members, price accounted for 34.8% of their decision.

Understanding this variation of attribute importance and desired levels across consumers is crucial for target market selection. As Wind, Grashof and Goldhar conclude, "An examination of these utilities suggests quite clearly that there is no universally desirable STI system. . . . The managerial question, therefore, is which of these segments should management select as their target market?"

SCENARIO SIMULATIONS

The third major use of conjoint analysis is in predicting market shares or unit sales in various scenarios. Given the value system of a consumer and a description of alternative available products, one can calculate the value of alternative products. These values permit prediction of the choice the consumer would make if confronted with these products in the marketplace.

The process works as shown in Fig. B. Consumer judgments are made about alternative products and these are analyzed to produce the value system. Given this value system, one can derive the value of *any* product which can be described by the set of attributes included in the analysis. Note that the value system expresses consumer preferences and is independent of the competitive products available in the marketplace.

Consider an example of the personal computer and, to keep things simple, let's say there are four attributes of importance: weight, battery life, quality of resolution of screen, and price. A standard conjoint analysis produces the following value system for an individual.

Weight	Battery life	Quality of resolution	Price
≤2 lbs.: 1.2	1 hour: 0.0	Below Average: 0.0	$1,000: 1.0
2–5 lbs.: .9	2 hours: .2	Average: .4	2,000: .5
≥5 lbs.: 0.0	4 hours: 1.5	Above Average: .5	3,000: 0.0
	8 hours: 1.5		

Given a set of product descriptions on these attributes, one can calculate the value of each alternative and make a prediction about which

Figure B. *Scenario process*

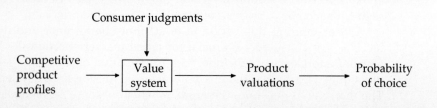

system would be purchased. For example, if the three products available are:

Product	Weight	Battery life	Resolution quality	Price
A	2 lbs.	1 hour	Below Average	$2,000
B	5 lbs.	4 hours	Average	3,000
C	≥5 lbs.	8 hours	Average	1,000

We can calculate the value of each product as follows:

$$\begin{aligned}
\text{Value of Product A} &= \text{Value of 2 lbs. weight} \\
&\quad + \text{Value of 1-hour battery life} \\
&\quad + \text{Value of below-average resolution} \\
&\quad + \text{Value of \$2,000 price} \\
&= 1.2 + 0 + 0 + .5 = 1.7
\end{aligned}$$

Similarly, the value of products B and C for this individual are 1.9 and 3.0, respectively.

There are two common rules used to translate these values into choice predictions: the "first choice" rule and the "share of preference" rule. In the first choice rule, we simply say the person will buy the product that has the highest value. In this case, we predict this individual would purchase product C. Its low price and eight-hour battery life more than make up for its disadvantage on weight compared to the other two products. We do this for each individual in the sample. A product's market share is simply the percentage of consumers for whom that product "wins," i.e., has the highest value.

The second rule used is the "share of preference" rule which in effect gives a probability estimate that a consumer will buy a brand. In our example, the values are:

Value	
Product A –	1.7
Product B –	1.9
Product C –	3.0
Sum	6.6

In the "share of preference" approach, we say that the probability that this individual chooses the "best" product, C, is 3.0/6.6 = 45%. The probability of choosing A or B is 26% (1.7/6.6) and 29% (1.9/6.6), respectively. The market share for a product is the average purchase probability across all subjects in the study. The rationale behind the share of preference method is that consumers do not always buy their most preferred brand (e.g., due to availability which is not considered in the conjoint analysis) and the value system estimates are in fact *estimates*, not the truth. Many conjoint users report that the first choice rule tends to overpredict for high share brands. Most commercial conjoint packages offer the analyst the option of choosing which of these two rules to use. Further discussion of these issues are in Finkbeiner (1988) and Elrod and Kumar (1989).

The scenario simulation capability is a powerful tool with respect to assessing new product introduction strategy. By describing a prospective new product on the salient attributes, one can obtain not only a market share estimate, but also an indication of which competitive products will be hurt most. This is achieved by first simulating the scenario of only the current competitive products being available and then the environment of current competitive products plus the prospective new product.

ACCURACY OF CONJOINT METHODS

As noted in the introduction, conjoint analysis has been used for a wide variety of applications. Many firms are "repeat buyers" of the methodology, suggesting satisfaction with the accuracy of the results and their utility.

There are, however, very few published studies which examine the validity of the conjoint results (see Montgomery and Wittink (1979) as one of the few). Therefore, it is important in an individual situation to be able to check the validity of the findings before implementing actions based on the result. The three primary checks are: (i) red-face test, (ii) holdout prediction, and (iii) actual vs. predicted market share.

In the "red-face" test, one simply asks if the results make sense given everything else we know. For example, we may have a prior, strongly held belief, that price is the most important attribute in a category. If we run a conjoint and price does not come up as key, we should question the appropriateness of using conjoint. A second possible check of this type is to see if the parameter estimates vary across individuals in a reasonable way. Going back to our computer example, battery life is one of the key attributes. If we also collected data from students on whether or not they planned to use their PCs in four-hour examination situations, those who indicated "yes" would logically place more value on a battery life that can make it through four hours than those who do not plan to use the computer in such a way. We could check to see if this holds up across our sample.

The second possible test is a holdout prediction. This was used by Wind, Grashof and Goldhar (1978), for example. In this test, a small number of the original products rated by the respondent are "held out" from the calculation of the value system. (Wind et al. held out 4 of 22 rated concepts.) Once the value system is computed, the value of all concepts (those held out and those not) is calculated. The test can be made if the value system-based calculations rate the held-out concepts correctly with respect to the other concepts. In their study, Wind et al. report 84% of the held-out concepts being correctly classified, "suggesting a high level of validity" (p. 36).

Finally, in some cases it is possible to simulate the current market situation and compare the market share estimates from the conjoint model with those observed in the marketplace. Also, if it is possible to observe what an individual respondent's "current brand" is, a check can be made to see if that brand has the highest value of all products currently available. Parker and Srinivasan (1976) used this test in their study of rural health care facilities.

The ultimate test, of course, is whether the predicted results "come true" in the marketplace when certain actions are taken. While there is little documentation of such comparisons, the regular use of conjoint suggests it meets the market test on this dimension.

GUIDELINES FOR USE

Necessary assumptions underlying conjoint have been mentioned throughout this discussion. We collect them here to summarize situations wherein conjoint would be most applicable.

Product as a bundle of attributes The product must be able to be specified as a collection of attributes. There are some largely image products, e.g., a perfume, for which this is just not possible.

Must know important attributes Conjoint requires that we either know or find out by another method what attributes are salient in the product category. We need to specify a set of attributes which consumers view independently, i.e., the value of one attribute should not be dependent on the level of another.

Respondents can reasonably rate products The input data we require from respondents are overall preference or purchase likelihood judgments. This requires a level of respondent familiarity with the product category. Consequently, conjoint is not appropriate for situations where the category is totally revolutionary.

Attributes should be actionable The firm should, in most cases, be able to act upon the output of the conjoint by constructing products which deliver the attribute levels used in the analysis.

This note has tried only to communicate the basic principles of conjoint analysis. Many researchers are currently at work expanding the domain of applicability and accuracy of conjoint. For example, hybrid conjoint analysis merges the individual's own articulation of the value system with classic conjoint output. No doubt these efforts are resulting in better results from conjoint and we expect to see increased application of conjoint-type methods in the future.

REFERENCES

Bennett, P. and N. Moore. "Consumers' Preferences for Alternative Energy Conservation Policies: A Trade-Off Analysis," *Journal of Consumer Research,* Vol. 8 (December 1981), pp. 313–321.

Cattin, P. and R. Wittink. "Commercial Use of Conjoint Analysis: A Survey," *Journal of Marketing,* Vol. 46 (Summer 1982), pp. 44–53.

Clarke, D. "Clark Material Handling Group—Overseas: Brazilian Product Strategy (A)," (Boston, Mass.: Harvard Business School Case Services, Case No. 581-091, 1981).

Currim, I., C. Weinberg, and R. Wittink, "Design of Subscription Programs for a Performing Arts Series," *Journal of Consumer Research,* Vol. 8 (June 1981), pp. 67–75.

Dolan, R. "MSA: The Software Company," (Boston, Mass.: Harvard Business School Case No. 590-069, 1990).

Eisenhart, T. "Marketers Trade Off for Research Productivity," *Business Marketing* (February 1988), p. 101ff.

Elrod, T. and S. K. Kumar. "Bias in the First Choice Rule for Predicting Share," *Proceedings,* "Gaining a Competitive Advantage Through PC-based Interviewing and Analysis," Vol. I, Sawtooth Software, 1989, pp. 259–271.

Ettenson, R., G. Gaeth, and J. Wagner. "Evaluating the Effect of Country of Origin and the 'Made in the U.S.A.' Campaign: A Conjoint Approach," *Journal of Retailing,* Vol. 64, No. 1 (Spring 1988), pp. 85–100.

Fiedler, J. "Conjoint Predictions 15 Years Later," *Proceedings,* Sawtooth Software Conference on Perceptual Mapping, Conjoint Analysis and Computer Interviewing, 1988, pp. 25–36.

Finkbeiner, C. "Comparison of Conjoint Choice Simulators," *Proceedings,* Sawtooth Conference on Perceptual Mapping, Conjoint Analysis and Computer Interviewing, 1988, pp. 75–104.

Green, P. and V. Srinivasan. "Conjoint Analysis in Consumer Research: Issue and Outlook," *Journal of Consumer Research,* Vol. 5 (September 1978), pp. 103–123.

Green, P. and Y. Wind. "New Way to Measure Consumers' Judgments," *Harvard Business Review,* Vol. 53 (1975), pp. 107–117.

Huber, J. "Conjoint Analysis: How We Got Here and Where We Are," *Proceedings,* Sawtooth Conference on Perceptual Mapping, Conjoint Analysis and Computer Interviewing, 1987, pp. 237–251.

MacLachlan, D., M. Mulhern, and A. Shocker. "Reliability Issues in Attribute Selection," *Proceedings,* Sawtooth Conference on Perceptual Mapping, Conjoint Analysis and Computer Interviewing, 1988, pp. 37–50.

Marshall, D. "Analysis and Interpretation of Conjoint Results," *Proceedings,* Sawtooth Conference on Perceptual Mapping, Conjoint Analysis and Computer Interviewing, 1987, pp. 307–316.

Montgomery, D. and R. Wittink. "Predictive Validity of Conjoint Analysis for Alternative Aggregation Schemes," *Proceedings,* Marketing Measurement Conference, 1979, pp. 298–309.

Page, A. and H. Rosenbaum. "Redesigning Product Lines with Conjoint Analysis: How Sunbeam Does It," *Journal of Product Innovation Management,* Vol. 4 (1987), pp. 120–137.

Parker, B. and V. Srinivasan. "A Consumer Preference Approach to the Planning of Rural Primary Health-Care Facilities," *Operations Research,* Vol. 24, No. 5 (September–October 1976), pp. 991–1025.

Prensky, M. "Presenting Results," *Proceedings,* Sawtooth Software Conference on Perceptual Mapping, Conjoint Analysis and Computer Interviewing, 1987, pp. 327–334.

Tumbusch, J. "How to Design a Conjoint Study," *Proceedings,* Sawtooth Software Conference on Perceptual Mapping, Conjoint Analysis and Computer Interviewing, 1987, pp. 283–288.

Tyner, M. J. and J. Weiner. "Optimal Pricing Strategies Through Conjoint Analysis," *Proceedings,* "Gaining a Competitive Advantage Through PC-based Interviewing and Analysis," Vol. 1, Sawtooth Software, 1989, pp. 45–52.

Vaccarelli, V. "How to Sell Conjoint Analysis," *Proceedings,* Sawtooth Software Conference on Perceptual Mapping, Conjoint Analysis and Computer Interviewing, 1987, pp. 275–282.

Wind, J., P. Green, D. Shifflet, and M. Scarbrough. "Courtyard by Marriott: Designing a Hotel Facility with Consumer-based Marketing Models," *Interfaces,* 19:1 (January–February 1989), pp. 25–47.

Wind, Y., J. Grashof, and J. Goldhar. "Market-based Guidelines for Design of Industrial Products," *Journal of Marketing* (July 1978), pp. 27–37.

Wittink, R. and P. Cattin. "Commercial Use of Conjoint Analysis: An Update," *Journal of Marketing,* Vol. 53 (July 1989), pp. 91–96.

Wittink, R. and J. Walsh. "Conjoint Analysis: Its Reliability, Validity and Usefulness," *Proceedings,* Sawtooth Conference on Perceptual Mapping, Conjoint Analysis and Computer Interviewing, 1988, pp. 1–24.

4 CASE

Techsonic Industries, Inc.:
Humminbird—New Products

Melvyn A. Menezes
Eric D. Beinhocker

In July of 1989, the top management of Techsonic Industries, Inc. of Eufaula, Alabama, met to make plans for an important industry trade show coming up in October. Techsonic, a privately held company, was the leading manufacturer of depth sounders, devices that used sonar to help sports fishers measure the depth of the water beneath their boats and locate fish. Techsonic sold its products under its well-known "Humminbird" brand name. The upcoming annual trade show was often used to introduce new products to the market and it was a company

This case was prepared by Eric D. Beinhocker, research associate, under the supervision of Professor Melvyn A. J. Menezes as the basis for class discussion rather than to illustrate either effective or ineffective handling of an administrative situation. Certain data have been disguised.

tradition to have something at the show each year to excite its customers and the industry.

The company had three new products in various stages of development: a new depth sounder—the "901", a VHF (very high frequency) marine radio, and a navigation device based on newly available satellite technology. Whereas the 901 would be an extension of Techsonic's existing line of depth sounders, the radio and the navigation device would be the start of two new product lines. The company had completed substantial market research on all three of these products and had to decide which ones it would proceed with and the priorities it would attach to each. In addition, Techsonic's Chairman Jim Balkcom and President Tom Dyer wanted to see marketing plans for the new products before the trade show.

COMPANY BACKGROUND[1]

In 1989, Eufaula, Alabama, was a small southern town with stately old homes, beautiful dogwood trees, and numerous bass boats on trailers headed toward the town's lake. Techsonic Industries, located on the shores of Lake Eufaula, was founded in 1971 by Yank Dean IV, an inventor, Eufaula native, and bass fisher. During the early 1970s, bass anglers began using sonar depth sounders to measure the depth of the lake bottom beneath their boats. The depth sounder would also display the depth of objects such as logs, sea grass, and, anglers hoped, fish. The type of depth sounder most commonly used was called a "flasher" because it indicated the depth of objects with flashing lights on a circular display. Dean's and his fishing friends' dissatisfaction with existing flashers spurred Dean to develop one that they themselves would like to use. The "Humminbird Super 60" was introduced with a waterproof case, an easy to read display, sturdy components, and a three-day repair guarantee (see Exhibit 1 for product photos). Although incremental, these improvements struck a chord with anglers, and the Super 60 became a legendary product in the bass fishing community.

Though pleased with the Super 60's success, the company's very profitable $2 million a year in revenues, and the regional customer base, Dean knew that the company had greater potential. In 1976, he recruited Jim Balkcom, an Atlanta banker, West Point graduate, and Harvard Business School MBA, to join Techsonic as a vice president. Although

---

[1]In addition to field interviews, the first two sections draw on material from Joshua Hyatt, "Ask and You Shall Receive," *Inc.*, September 1989, pp. 90–97.

Exhibit 1. *Product photographs*

Super 60 Flasher:
(1989 net dealer price:

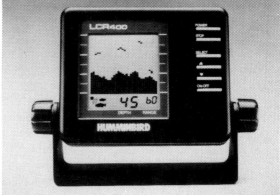

LCR:
(two LCR models: $163 and $426)

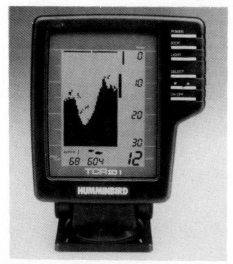

TCR:
(four TCR models: $214, $349, $369, and $979)

Balkcom was an Atlanta native and a non-fisher, Dean convinced him of the opportunity to build a business in Eufaula. Eleven months after Balkcom joined, Dean died of a heart attack while jogging. In 1977, Balkcom found himself president of a company that needed new products but had just lost its only inventor, engineer, and source of market knowledge.

Despite these difficulties, Balkcom had ambitious plans for Techsonic. His long-range vision focused on growth through new products and customer loyalty through outstanding service. He poured money into efforts to enhance the existing product line and enter the market for a different type of depth sounder known as a chart recorder.[2] During the six-year period 1977 to 1982, Techsonic introduced nine new products, all of which turned out to be, as one executive put it, "half-dead dogs." The new flashers did not offer any new features that were truly useful, and the chart recorders were too expensive, complicated, and unreliable for Humminbird's customer base.

Fortunately for Techsonic, the Super 60's reputation for quality and the company's high standards of service kept customers loyal. When Yank Dean was alive, customer service often consisted of his crawling under customers' boats on a Saturday morning to get their Super 60s working. Techsonic developed a reputation for standing behind its products. After Dean's death Balkcom worked to develop an organization and culture that could build on that image in the market as the company grew.

In 1978, while Techsonic was still struggling to develop new products, Balkcom hired his West Point classmate, Tom Dyer, to head sales and marketing. Over the next several years, Balkcom and Dyer greatly expanded distribution from local sporting goods and fishing shops to mass market retailers such as Wal-Mart and Kmart, catalogers such as Bass Pro, and marine and sporting goods stores nationwide. Although revenues increased to $19.6 million in the fiscal year ended June 30, 1983, the Super 60 still accounted for 97% of the company's sales (a summary of Techsonic's financial history from 1985 appears in Exhibit 2).

NEW PRODUCT DEVELOPMENT

In early 1984, Techsonic's management took a step that was unprecedented in their $55-million-a-year industry. They began a deliberate effort to research their customer base—both existing and potential.

---

[2]Instead of flashing lights on a depth scale, chart recorders trace an image showing the location of fish with a pen on paper moving between two rollers.

Exhibit 2. *Summary financial statements*

Income (Year Ended June 30) ($000)	1985	1986	1987	1988	1989
Net Sales	52,063	94,792	106,155	122,534	107,089
Gross Profit	23,975	45,546	47,602	46,968	32,001
Sales & Marketing	8,146	12,949	14,125	17,272	19,239
Engineering	1,345	1,949	2,289	3,590	3,851
General & Administration	4,452	5,953	5,678	5,742	5,076
Other Expenses	3,652	6,217	6,742	0	0
Interest Expense	0	0	0	9,591	16,240
Refinance Expense	0	0	0	12,415	0
Pretax Profit	6,380	18,478	18,768	(1,642)	(12,405)
Income Tax	2,210	8,016	8,371	850	(5,253)
ESOP Contribution	340	510	510	0	0
Discontinued Operations	1,387	184	(26)	0	0
Net Income	2,443	9,768	9,913	(2,492)	(7,152)

The company's balance sheet as of June 30, 1990, showed $798,000 cash, current assets of $33.3 million, current liabilities of $16.8 million, long-term debt of $29.7 million, subordinated debt of $33.1 million, and stockholders' equity of $3.7 million.

Although concerned about spending $20,000 for "a folder with some stuff in it," they commissioned a market research firm (MRF) to perform market research using focus groups[3] and telephone interviews. MRF ran focus groups in nine cities across the country and oversaw 2,500 phone interviews. They found that Techsonic's customers wanted a product that was easier to read in sunlight and that had a graphic representation like that of a chart recorder, but was as reliable and inexpensive as a flasher. Techsonic's management was surprised to learn that most of their customers really did not know how to use their flashers and wanted a simpler product. They had always assumed that their customers liked lots of buttons and features.

---

[3]In a focus group, an interviewer spends time with a group of customers to gauge reactions to new product or advertising concepts.

Techsonic's management soon realized that the solution to these customer needs lay in a new technology, liquid crystal displays (LCDs). LCDs, which in 1983 were found mostly in digital watch and calculator displays, would allow a graphic representation of the bottom, fish, and other objects. But, unlike a chart recorder, there would be no moving parts to break down or paper that could get wet. The unit could be waterproof, sturdy, and, with its large display, easy to read in sunlight. In addition, the product could be easy to use with an "automatic mode," allowing anglers simply to turn the unit on and use it, but still have the option of changing settings if they wanted to.

By the fall of 1984, Techsonic began to build prototypes and, consistent with its new philosophy of listening to its customers, returned to focus groups to test reactions to the product. The reactions were positive, though not exactly what management expected. The majority of the participants said they would not remove their old flashers and replace them with this new product. Instead they would mount the two side by side on their boats.

In June 1984, a month before the new product's introduction, the company began to build interest and demand in the distribution channel through heavy advertising in the top fishing magazines. Rather than positioning the product as competing with flashers, the advertising copy, with the slogan "Bridging the Gap—between flashers and charts," was based on data from the focus groups. Each point that had emerged as important in the focus groups—for example, ability to view in sunlight—was addressed in the ads. Techsonic introduced the product in July 1984 as the "Humminbird LCR" (liquid crystal recorder) (photo in Ex. 1) at the American Fishing and Tackle Manufacturers Association trade show, with the largest booth it had ever had.

By the end of fiscal year 1985, eleven months after the introduction, the company had sold 238,000 LCR units. The most Super 60s it had ever sold in a year was 163,780. Revenues increased more than two and a half times, to $52.7 million, with the Super 60 accounting for only 25% of unit sales. Management was surprised to learn that almost half of the LCR's sales were to first-time buyers. The LCR product had not only increased Humminbird's market share, but had also brought new buyers into the market, increasing the total market size.

The LCR's success helped make listening to the customer the foundation of the company's culture. Balkcom and a group of employees developed a "corporate values" card for every employee to carry which featured the company motto, "The Quality of any Product or Service is what the Customer says it is." "The Customer" was placed at the top of the organizational chart in Techsonic's lobby, and management began to believe that its lack of fishing experience was actually an advantage in an industry in which most executives were avid anglers. As Al Nunley, vice president of marketing, described it, "We don't have any preconceived ideas, and our emotions about our own likes and dislikes in fishing don't get in the way. Others in this industry think they know what the customer wants. We're about the only ones who actually ask and listen."

According to Dyer, "Now we had a secret weapon. We were stupid enough to think that if it worked for us once, it could work for us again." In the spring of 1985, MRF returned to focus groups to start the product development cycle again, this time using warranty cards from LCR purchasers to select the groups. With these groups, a single theme repeatedly appeared. Claiming that it was too difficult to distinguish fish from rocks and other objects, participants suggested displaying the "fish in red." The LCD supplier developed a new black and red LCD, and Techsonic quickly built a series of prototypes.

Focus groups were held for the new products, trying different symbols and mixes of red and black to depict different sizes of fish and varying bottom hardness. Their message was "Keep it simple. Show fish in red and the bottom in black."

Techsonic introduced its new "4-ID" product in July 1986 with the slogan, "If it's red, it's fish. It's that simple." Data from focus groups and telephone interviews showed a very positive response to the new product. However, the company could not believe that it would repeat the LCR's success. For one, at $350 the new 4-ID was significantly more expensive than the LCR, which in 1986 sold for $200. Techsonic shipped 163,000 4-ID units from January to June. By December end it had shipped 230,000 4-ID units, with total company sales growing to $95 million. Once again, the company had both increased its market share and brought new buyers into the market by introducing an easier-to-use, more functional product.

As new Humminbird products expanded the market, competitors began to enter, mimicking Humminbird features. Prices began to erode and product life cycles shortened.

During 1987, the product development cycle at Techsonic was repeated. But this time the focus groups and interviews with Humminbird users revealed fewer and less substantial problems to be solved. Customers were pretty satisfied with their LCRs, 4-IDs or their imitators.

Thus, the next product in the Humminbird line, the TCR, was much the same as the 4-ID, but with some incremental improvements to the resolution of the sonar, the mounting system, and the product's ease of use. Although the improvements were useful, none had the impact of the first

LCR or "fish in red." The positioning statement for the TCR was "The Next Generation," and the product line was introduced in August 1988.

In addition to its middle- and low-end TCR products, Techsonic introduced a high-end product, the TCR Color-1, which used a new eight-color LCD technology. However, anglers were not sufficiently interested in color to justify the product's higher price and it failed to become a mainstream hit.

The TCR line sold at a rate just under its target until April of 1989, when the entire marine market went into a nosedive. As Balkcom described it, "everything stopped." A large portion of Techsonic's sales were to new-boat buyers, so that when new-boat sales diminished, its sales were strongly affected, causing a build-up of inventory in the company's sales channels. Because most of Techsonic's competitors were similarly affected, significant price reductions occurred as manufacturers and dealers attempted to clear the excess inventory from the channel.

DEPTH SOUNDER MARKET

The total depth sounder market in 1989 was approximately $286 million, up from $20 million in 1976 and $55 million in 1983. The productwise breakup was: LCDs–$264 million, 1,050,000 units; flashers–$17 million, 110,000 units; chart recorders–$5 million, 10,000 units. In 1989, the depth sounder market and the entire U.S. fishing electronics industry experienced a sharp downturn, with sales and profits dropping an average of 15%. A slowdown in the new-boat market and increased competition led to a significant erosion in depth sounder prices.

COMPETITION   Competition in the depth sounder market increased from a handful of companies to more than 30 in 1989, with Humminbird and MorPal the dominant ones. There were seven others that competed directly with Humminbird (see Exhibit 3).

In the low-end of the market (below $135 retail price), a number of smaller companies had come out with products copying Humminbird features. As Balkcom described it, depth sounders in the low-end were about as differentiated as "jellybeans." Meanwhile, the high-end of the market was involved in a "feature war," with new technologies and features being added to products at a rapid pace and vendors unable to increase their prices to reflect the additional functionality. Some of the features Techsonic's competitors were adding in 1989 included split screens that showed both an LCR-like graph and a flasher-like display, touch screens replacing buttons for function selection, and digital water temperature, speed, and depth indicators.

Exhibit 3. *U.S. market share and industry advertising expenditures,*
1989   Source: Techsonic Industries, Inc.

Company	Total (% $)	LCDs (% units)		Flashers (% units)		Chart (% units)		Advertising expenditure ($)
		F	S	F	S	F	S	
Techsonic Industries	38	31	16	22	12	6	4	$1,700
MorPal	26	12	10	29	18	35	25	674
Hammertech Electronics	9	na	na	na	na	na	na	721
PAR Digital	6	4	5	5	5	—	14	383
Marmen	6	na	na	na	na	na	na	374
Lisotech	4	10	22	1	2	—	—	199
Navsonic	4	na	na	na	na	na	na	753
FindFish Electronics	na	8	1	7	9	—	8	346
Jules Marine Technology	na	1	0	3	0	1	0	1,020
All Others	7	34	46	33	54	58	49	3,256
	100	100	100	100	100	100	100	$9,426

F   freshwater market   S   saltwater market
na   not available   —   Company does not manufacture a product in this category

END-USERS   In early 1987, Techsonic commissioned a market research firm (MRF) to gather information on the end-users of depth sounders. It conducted telephone interviews of 605 noncommercial power boat owners. A summary of that survey's findings is presented in Exhibit 4.

Exhibit 4. *End-user telephone survey, 1987: Summary results*
Source: Company records

- Noncommercial power boat owners were predominantly male (94%), average age 45, and average annual income $40,000. Their occupations were professional or managerial (50%), blue collar (24%), or retired (18%).

(continued)

Exhibit 4 (continued)

- Noncommercial power boat owners used their boats primarily for sports fishing (89%). They fished primarily in freshwater (95%), and to a much lesser extent in saltwater (14%) or in the Great Lakes (14%). On average, they spent $900 a year on boating and fishing equipment, not including major purchases such as boats and trailers.
- Most of the respondents watched boating- and fishing-related TV programs (72%) and attended boat shows (59%).
- Unaided brand awareness and brand preference for depth sounders were as follows:

	Unaided awareness	Most preferred	Also considered
Humminbird	70%	28%	37%
MorPal	73	40	28
Jules Marine Tech.	32	5	34
PAR Digital	20	2	15
FindFish Electronics	17	1	12

- Seventy-seven percent of the respondents owned depth sounders, and the average number of depth sounders owned was two. Of those who owned a depth sounder, 75% owned a flasher, 28% an LCD, and 26% a chart.
- Among depth sounder owners, Humminbird was owned by 47%, MorPal by 41%, and Jules Marine Tech. by 12%. Humminbird was popular in LCDs (57% share) and flashers (41%), but was weak in charts (15%). On the other hand, MorPal was strong in charts (54%) and flashers (42%), but not so strong in LCDs (25%).
- Respondents purchased their depth sounders from a variety of outlets: marine stores (28%), sporting goods stores (16%), mass merchants (15%), catalogs (15%), OEM as part of the boat (13%), and another fisher (5%).

MARKETING

DISTRIBUTION   Techsonic sold its products through multiple sales channels. To reach these channels, it used a sales force of 29 people in the United States, including three regional managers. Most of Techsonic sales were through mass merchants and catalogers. Other channels used by Techsonic included marine distributors, marine dealers, sporting goods distributors and dealers and OEM.

Mass merchants and catalogers operated with lower gross margins (1%–15%) than did the other channels (20%–40%). Consequently, the volume of Humminbird product sold through mass merchants and catalogers resulted in heavy discounting of the products in the marketplace. As a result, many marine dealers and distributors were unable to make an adequate return on Humminbird. Although a few marine dealers made 20% margins on Humminbird, most of them broke even or lost money. They wanted to make 30%–40% margin on the products they stocked, but believed that a margin of at least 20% was necessary for survival. In 1989, many marine dealers were dropping the Humminbird line and stocking competing brands that were not sold by mass merchants, even though they often had to put in greater efforts to sell them.

Most distribution channel members viewed Humminbird as a mid-level product, both in technology and price. Although Techsonic had pioneered many of the innovations in the industry, many of its dealers perceived MorPal as the technological leader, and some considered Humminbird's "fish in red" a sales gimmick that seemed to work well with customers. They considered the Humminbird brand to be a good value with high customer acceptance, believing it most appropriate for first-time buyers and weekend fishers.

COMMUNICATIONS Techsonic spent approximately $1.7 million on print advertising in 1989, the highest in the industry. Humminbird products were advertised regularly in fishing and outdoor magazines such as *Bass Masters, Field & Stream, Fins and Feathers,* and *Bassin'* and occasionally in publications such as *USA Today* and *Sports Illustrated.* Favorable product reviews in trade magazines were important, and Techsonic had a public relations firm assist it in communicating with the press.

Boat shows and industry trade shows also played an important role in promoting Humminbird products. Techsonic used them to demonstrate its products to dealers and customers, as well as to introduce new products, assess the competition, and get feedback from the market.

Techsonic also sponsored the "Humminbird Sports Team," a group of well-known professional bass fishers and other athletes. In addition, it sponsored a number of sporting events carried on cable television, including: "Humminbird Bass & Golf" (fishing and golf competition), "Humminbird Bass & Race" (fishing and car racing), and an annual celebrity bass-fishing tournament.

NEW PRODUCT OPTIONS

PROJECT 901

In 1989, to reassert its position as the market and technological leader, Techsonic's R&D team developed a revolutionary new fish-finding system. The product, referred to internally as Project 901, had taken years to develop and was aimed at satisfying two important benefits that Techsonic believed anglers sought in a depth sounder: to find fish faster and to see fish better. The product provided the first truly three-dimensional view of the water ever available in a depth sounder, allowing anglers to distinguish more easily between fish and other objects, as well as to more precisely locate the fish.

MARKET STUDY   Techsonic commissioned a market research firm at a cost of $50,000 to conduct a market study on the 901. The objectives were to determine the customer's intention to buy and the perceived uniqueness of the product, the market and sales potential for the first three years, and a profile of the potential customer, and to provide guidelines for product positioning, features to be included in the standard and deluxe models, and the best price for each model.

METHODOLOGY   MRF conducted 375 interviews in three key markets: freshwater, saltwater, and Great Lakes. The respondents were boat owners who planned to buy a depth sounder during the next three years. The interviews, lasting 15 minutes, were conducted at the boat owners' homes by experienced interviewers. Respondents were paid $15 for their participation and were not informed that the research was being conducted for Humminbird.

After a few questions obtaining demographic information and the brand of depth sounder they would consider buying, participants were shown a short video of the 901. They were then asked about (a) their likelihood of buying the 901 if it were available at a reasonable price (no price was stated); (b) the perceived uniqueness of the 901; (c) pricing; and (d) their likelihood of buying the 901 within the next year if it were available at $449.

Next, participants were shown another short video explaining some additional or optional features of the 901. For each feature, participants were asked whether they believed that (a) it was essential to the product and had to be included for them to purchase the product; (b) it increased the value of the product, for which they would pay more if it were included; or (c) it had no effect on whether or not they would buy the product. They were then asked questions about pricing the deluxe model (which had all the features they wanted), and how likely they were to buy it within the next year if it were available at $629.

ANALYSIS AND RECOMMENDATIONS

Customer Interest   The market research firm concluded that the 901 was a clear winner because it scored high on the dimensions of uniqueness and purchase likelihood (see Exhibit 5). In addition, the 901 results compared very favorably with those of past new products from Techsonic. It earned the highest uniqueness score of any Techsonic product and the highest intention-to-buy score since the original LCR in 1984.

Freshwater fishers and mid-sized boat owners were the most likely to buy the product. Those who did not own a depth sounder and those who currently owned an LCD or chart recorder indicated they were most likely to buy the 901.

Market and Sales Potential   MRF estimated the total market potential for the first three years to be 320,000 units and Humminbird's sales potential at 139,871 units (including 93,030 standard units and 46,841 deluxe units) during that period (see Exhibit 6). Based on Techsonic's retail pricing plans of $449 for the standard unit and $629 for the deluxe unit, the 901 would represent retail sales of $71.2 million over three years.

Exhibit 5. *Project 901 product test: Customer interest*
Source: Company records

The average respondent was 45 years old, most likely a professional, executive or manager and had an average annual income of $50,000, a profile which was similar to the general population of boat owners.

Participants were asked the following two questions:

"You said you were considering buying a depth sounder. If this new product were available to you at a reasonable price, how likely would you be to *buy it* during the *next year*? Would you be: *very likely to buy; somewhat likely to buy; not very likely to buy; or not at all likely to buy* it during the next year?"

"How different or *unique* would you say this product is compared to what is now available to you to buy? Would you say it is: *Very unique, somewhat unique; not very unique; or not at all unique* or different from what is available now?"

(continued)

Exhibit 5 (continued)

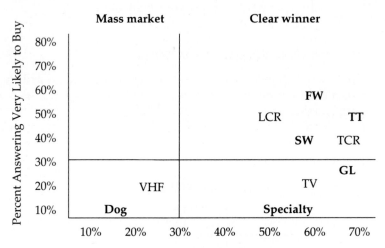

901 Test Results:
TT	=	Total market
FW	=	Freshwater
GL	=	Great Lakes
SW	=	Saltwater

Past Results:
LCR	=	Where LCR scored when tested
TCR	=	Where TCR scored when tested

Test Controls (other products used to gauge reaction):
TV	=	A random LCD television
VHF	=	A random saltwater VHF marine radio

Important assumptions in the calculation of the market and sales potential given in Exhibit 6 were:

(1) All respondents who said that they were "very likely to buy" the 901 at a reasonable price were considered potential customers for year one. Respondents who indicated they were "somewhat likely" to buy the 901 at a reasonable price were considered potential customers for years two to three.

(2) For participants for whom Humminbird was not the first-choice vendor for the next depth sounder purchased, for each manufacturer the proportion of respondents who said they would consider Humminbird was applied to that manufacturer's potential market share to estimate Humminbird's potential sales.

Exhibit 6. *Project 901 test: U.S. market potential* Source: *Company records*

Total market potential for Humminbird 901:

	Number of boats	%	Basis
A. Boats whose use makes them eligible to own depth sounders	4,000,000		Past experience
B. Boats likely to purchase depth sounders in next 1–3 years	320,000	8% of A	Past experience
Total Market Potential	**320,000 units**		

First-year sales potential for Humminbird 901:

Stated first choice	"Very likely" first year	"Would buy" Humminbird	Total units	
(31%) Humminbird = 99,200	X 49%	X 100%	48,608	(Humminbird share)
(20%) MorPal = 64,000	X 27%	X 38%	6,566	(MorPal, but would buy Humminbird)
(14%) Jules Marine = 44,800	X 48%	X 71%	15,268	(Jules Marine, but would buy Humminbird)
Humminbird sales potential in first year:			70,442	

Based on responses, sales of standard units at $449 each were estimated to be 47,530 units and sales of deluxe units at $629 each were estimated to be 22,912 units.

Second- and third-year sales potential for Humminbird 901:

Stated first choice	"Somewhat likely"	"Would buy" Humminbird	Total units	
(31%) Humminbird = 99,200	X 45%	X 100%	44,640	(Humminbird share)
(20%) MorPal = 64,000	X 47%	X 38%	11,430	(MorPal, but would buy Humminbird)
(14%) Jules Marine = 44,800	X 42%	X 71%	13,359	(Jules Marine, but would buy Humminbird)
Humminbird sales potential in second and third years:			69,429	

Based on responses, sales of standard units at $449 each were estimated to be 45,500 and sales of deluxe units at $629 were estimated to be 23,929.

Product Positioning   Based on the responses to the product description, MRF concluded that despite the 901's technological wizardry, its most important perceived benefit was that it helped customers find fish faster and see them better. Respondents' comments indicated that although technology played an important role in the 901's perceived uniqueness, they had come to expect technology and were no longer amazed by it. MRF felt that although people responded to the 901's novelty and many considered it their next great toy, these considerations were secondary to the ease factor (see Exhibit 7). They recommended emphasizing that the 901 made fishing easier, and thus more fun.

Product Features   Customer evaluations of the various 901 features are shown in Exhibit 8. Based on these responses, MRF recommended that the standard 901 model should include: 3-D view to 240 feet, a video operator's manual, a temperature gauge, and ability to match display speed and boat speed. They recommended that the following additional features be included in the deluxe model: bottom hardness indicator, ability to program the display to show different fish sizes, three simultaneous views of the bottom from different angles, marine plotter connection, and a speedometer.

Exhibit 7. *Project 901 study: Product positioning*
Source: Company records

The interviewer read the following: "I now will read you four different ways this new product could be described. Please listen carefully and choose the *one* description which *best* matches *your perception* of this new product." Questions were read in order. Cards with questions written on them were placed on the table for the respondents to study.

Question	Response
a. It's the next hot item for fishermen. Anyone who values having the very latest equipment would just have to have it.	15%
b. It's much easier to understand what's on the screen. It looks as though it would be easy to use, and it would make catching fish easier.	48%
c. It's fascinating to watch the bottom and fish move across the screen. It would be fun to have this product on a boat.	12%
d. It's the next generation of fish-finding technology. It's obviously light years ahead of anything else on the market.	25%

Pricing Before seeing or hearing about the 901, the amount of money people said they planned to spend on their next depth sounder ranged from $219 to $560. The suggested "best prices" for the 901 indicated that Techsonic was on target with the $629 price for the deluxe model, but that they could charge substantially more than the previously considered $449 for the standard model. Considering all this, MRF suggested retail prices of $529 and $629 for the standard and deluxe models, respectively.

Margins Techsonic management expected dealer margins to be anywhere from 15% to 40%, depending on the channel. In planning for the product, they decided to use a net price to dealers of $390 for the standard model and $440 for the deluxe model, and unit sales levels of 120,000 and 36,000, respectively over the next three years (see Exhibit 9).

At a similar stage, the company's last two products to be introduced, the TCR ID-1 and TCR ID-10, had been projected to sell approximately 21,600 units each over three years. The average price over the same period for both products was forecast at about $260, with gross margins of 42% and 46%, respectively. The total capital expenditures for both prod-

Exhibit 8. Project 901 study: Product features Source: Company records

	Available with competitive products	Essential for purchase (%)	Would pay more for feature (%)	No effect on purchase (%)
1. View three different angles	No	39	22	39
2. Instructions on videotape	No	38	23	39
3. Temperature gauge	On some	36	46	18
4. Display speed matches boat speed	No	28	39	39
5. Show fish size	On some	29	50	21
6. Bottom hardness indicator	No	29	39	32
7. Distance display from back to front	On some	28	31	41
8. 3-D View to 240 feet	No	28	47	25
9. Speedometer	On some	22	26	52
10. 6" X 4" screen	On some	18	37	45
11. Regular view 240–600 ft.	On some	18	19	63
12. Bottom alarm	Yes	13	28	59
13. Marine plotter connection	On some	11	40	49

Exhibit 9. *Project 901: Profit and loss forecast*   Source: Company records

(Year Ending June 30)	1991	1992	1993	Total
Standard model				
Unit Sales	28,000	32,000	60,000	120,000
Net Price per Unit	390.00	$330.00	$280.00	$319.00 avg.
Net Sales	10,920,000	10,560,000	16,800,000	38,280,000
Gross Profit	4,914,000	4,224,000	5,880,000	15,018,000
%	45.00%	40.00%	35.00%	39.23%
SG&A (25%)	2,730,000	2,640,000	4,200,000	9,570,000
Other	933,000	426,000	271,000	1,630,000
EBI&T	$1,251,000	$1,158,000	$1,409,000	$3,818,000
Deluxe model				
Unit Sales	4,000	12,000	20,000	36,000
Net Price per Unit	$440.00	$375.00	$320.00	$351.67 avg.
Net Sales	1,760,000	4,500,000	6,400,000	12,660,000
Gross Profit	792,000	1,800,000	2,240,000	4,832,000
%	45.00%	40.00%	35.00%	38.17%
SG&A (25%)	440,000	1,125,000	1,600,000	3,165,000
Other	217,000	146,000	101,000	464,000
EBI&T	$135,000	$529,000	$ 539,000	$1,203,000

Capital expenditures for both products combined:				
Packaging	$36,000			
Tooling	136,000			
Equipment	38,000			
R&D	400,000			
Total	$610,000			

ucts was $151,643, and the total projected earnings before interest and taxes was $2.08 million.

THE VHF MARINE RADIO

In 1988, Techsonic's board of directors decided that it would be in the company's interest to move beyond its dependence on depth sounders and to make additional use of its powerful brand name and distribution network. The board believed that marine communications, in particular VHF radios, presented an opportunity because of the relatively small degree of penetration in Humminbird's customer base. The VHF radio market was fragmented, with no dominant competitor, and weakly represented in Humminbird's distribution channels. Finally, Techsonic felt it could build a differentiated product using its brand name and reputation for waterproofing, durability, and service.

MARKET STUDY AND METHODOLOGY Techsonic commissioned MRF at a cost of $26,000 to do a market study to determine the market potential for a Humminbird radio and to define an appropriate product. MRF interviewed three groups of potential buyers: recreational boaters, sports fishers, and Humminbird customers.

VHF MARKET VHF radios were used primarily for safety: to communicate for help in an emergency and to find out the weather. However, in addition to providing a "lifeline for survival," VHFs provided a "social pipeline." A popular method of communication among boaters, they were used to talk to friends on the shore, to contact other boaters, and to find out where fish were, what bait was working, and who was catching what. Although fishing was often characterized as a solitary sport, most fishers appreciated the opportunity to interact with others (see Exhibit 10).

The study confirmed the fragmented nature of the market. FindFish Electronics was owned by 17% of the respondents, STEBOB Radio by 7%, IGM Communications by 5%, and various other brands (none of which had more than 3% market share) by 45%. The remaining 26% did not know the brand of their VHF radio.

END-USERS More than two-thirds of the respondents had a VHF and about one third had a CB (Citizens Band) radio. MRF concluded that most boaters would therefore be purchasing a VHF radio as a replacement for an older unit. Although the demographic profile of VHF owners was very similar to that of depth sounders, only 7% of Humminbird's customers owned a VHF, and 42% owned a CB radio.

A majority (56%) of the respondents purchased their VHF radios from marine dealers. The other major channels of distribution included mail order catalogs (14%), department stores (6%), sporting goods stores (6%), and catalog showrooms (5%). About two-thirds of the respondents installed the radios themselves.

Nearly two-thirds of the respondents attended a boat show within the previous year. About 25% participated or watched fishing tournaments, and about as many belonged to a fishing or boating club that held regular meetings.

Exhibit 10. *VHF/marine radio market study: What would you like to do?/What would you use a radio for?* Source: Company records

	Recreational boaters		Fishermen		Humminbird customers	
	A %	B %	A %	B %	A %	B %
Get the weather	62	56	67	66	42	33
Radio for help in emergency	56	56	56	57	33	39
Find out where the fish are biting	27	23	38	34	26	23
Know what bait is working	25	21	36	33	27	23
Talk to friends on shore	19	21	36	29	20	13
Know who's catching what	18	14	34	26	23	14
Talk with other boaters	24	11	24	15	18	8
Touch base with home	19	24	26	27	11	15
Schedule meeting with other boaters	21	17	13	13	11	8
Order supplies from offshore	8	8	13	8	4	4

A. = Would like to be able to do often
B. = Would use a marine/VHF radio to do

PRODUCT FEATURES A vast majority (88%) of the respondents purchased fixed-mount radios, as opposed to hand-held radios, and bought an antenna at the same time (90%), though in most cases (57%) not as a package.

The major problems VHF owners faced concerned the radio's durability, the battery's dying, and the absence of waterproofing. However, it was not clear exactly what impact solving these problems would have on brand choice.

CONCERNS Techsonic management was concerned about a few problems regarding the distribution channels. First, radios were typically purchased through marine dealers, a channel in which Techsonic was quite weak, accounting for only 11% of Humminbird depth sounder sales. The trend for depth sounders was moving away from marine dealers as price competition from the mass merchants and catalogers was driving dealers away from the Humminbird line. Techsonic's management had in the past encouraged this trend because research had indicated that product availability was a major sales bottleneck, a problem that the mass merchants could solve.

Techsonic management believed that there was an opportunity to increase the number of radios sold in the mass merchant channels and that it had the right product to do so. At the same time, the MRF research indicated that a strong presence in marine dealers would be critical for success. However, there was some expectation that marine dealers would be quite wary about being "burned" by Humminbird again, especially if they saw Techsonic pushing the radios through the mass merchants.

The second problem centered around the mass merchants. A small number of mass merchants that moved significant amounts of Humminbird product traditionally allocated three SKUs (stock keeping units) to Humminbird. They had communicated strong resistance to increasing this number of SKUs, leading MRF to believe that a Humminbird radio would potentially force the removal of another Humminbird product from these retailers' shelves.

The third problem centered around pricing through the mass merchant channel. Pricing was not addressed in the MRF survey, but Techsonic had decided to set $269 as the expected retail price, based on a competitive analysis of similarly featured radios (though some Humminbird features such as waterproofing were unique) and Techsonic's internal profit targets. Management expected dealers to make 15% to 35% on the product and used a net dealer price of $195 in their internal profit forecast (see Exhibit 11).

Early discussions with Humminbird dealers revealed a potential problem with these prices. Mass merchants traditionally viewed Humminbird as the mid-point in their lines, and wanted to sell the radio at $199. At $269, a Humminbird radio would be at the high-end of the radios they were selling. Although they felt that the Humminbird VHF was an attractive product with some differentiating features, they were skeptical as to the value of its brand name at the high-end of the radio market.

Finally, there was some concern among Techsonic managers that the radio would be the first Humminbird product manufactured outside the company. At least initially, the radio's electronics would be manufactured in the Philippines by an experienced, low-cost producer. Final assembly, testing, and packaging would be done in Eufaula.

NAVIGATION PRODUCTS

In addition to radios, Balkcom and Dyer were considering expanding into marine navigation electronics, in which they believed there was significant opportunity because of a new technology that would be introduced to the market in late 1990.

Exhibit 11. *VHF/marine radio: Profit and loss forecast*
Source: Company records

(Year Ending June 30)	1991	1992	1993	Total
Unit Sales	5,600	20,000	24,000	49,600
Net Price per Unit	$195.00	$175.00	$157.00	$168.55 avg.
Net Sales	1,092,000	3,500,000	3,768,000	8,360,000
Gross Profit	218,400	1,225,000	1,507,200	2,950,600
%	20.00%	35.00%	40.00%	35.29%
SG&A (25%)	273,000	875,000	942,000	2,090,000
Other	240,000	48,000	0	288,000
EBI&T	($294,600)	$302,000	$565,200	$572,600
Capital Expenditures:				
Packaging	$ 18,000			
Tooling	318,000			
Equipment	60,000			
R&D	180,000			
Total	$576,000			

NAVIGATION MARKET   In 1989, the most commonly used navigation system for recreational boating and sports fishing was LOCATOR. Boats equipped for LOCATOR had a device that received LOCATOR signals and displayed an estimate of the boat's position. By timing the differences in the reception of signals transmitted from three or more of the LOCATOR network's ground-based stations, the receiving unit on the boat could estimate the boat's position.

The LOCATOR market was small (estimated 1989 sales of 80,000 units) and very fragmented. Only two brands (PAR Digital and Onkar Marine) held more than a 10% market share. LOCATOR products had a retail price beginning at about $300 and required a considerable amount of skill to operate. Most LOCATOR receivers were not user friendly, and owners complained of having to refer to the manual constantly. Some of the problems LOCATOR users faced were performance-related: accuracy tended to degrade in bad weather, signals were subject to interference, it was often unusable because a transmitter was not operating, and the transmitters were concentrated along the coasts, leaving most inland lakes and waterways with poor or no coverage.

GPS (Global Positioning System) was a new satellite-based navigation system sold in the commercial market and priced between $3,000 and $5,000. A GPS receiver in a boat used time differences in its reception of signals from a group of satellites to determine the boat's location. The major advantages of GPS over LOCATOR were that its readings were more accurate, its signals were much less susceptible to interference or weather problems, and it would cover the entire world. Although limited in 1989 to approximately 10 hours per day, GPS was expected to become 24-hour effective by late 1990, with worldwide coverage expected to be completed in late 1991.

Balkcom and Dyer believed that the shift in navigation technology from LOCATOR to GPS presented Techsonic with two opportunities. The first was to enter the navigation market by introducing a product based on GPS technology. Techsonic hoped to introduce GPS to the recreational boating and sports fishing market by developing a user-friendly version priced to consumers at about $1000.

The second opportunity was to attempt to expand the LOCATOR market significantly by introducing a more user-friendly version of LOCATOR and selling it at $50 less than competitively priced products. They believed that the LOCATOR market had been limited by operational complexity and price. They felt they could take advantage of Humminbird's reputation among freshwater fishers and smaller-boat owners, where LOCATOR had a low level of penetration.

MARKET STUDY Balkcom and Dyer commissioned a market research firm (MRF) at a cost of $33,000 to study the market for navigation devices and help identify appropriate market opportunities. Specifically, the study sought (a) to examine whether the LOCATOR and/or GPS markets were worth pursuing, and (b) to determine for the LOCATOR and GPS systems appropriate product positioning, desired features and configurations, comparative ratings and purchase intentions, and price expectations and sensitivities.

METHODOLOGY The study was conducted using 308 mailed questionnaires to noncommercial powerboat owners, of whom 205 owned LOCATORs and 103 owned no navigation system. Both groups contained saltwater and freshwater boat owners.

ANALYSIS AND RECOMMENDATIONS

Navigational Problems LOCATORs were purchased primarily for navigational purposes, especially for navigating in bad weather, for determining the boat's exact position, and for returning to favorite fishing or diving spots. The problems frequently mentioned by LOCATOR owners were "having to refer to the manual all the time" (62%), "not being able to use the LOCATOR because a transmitter was not operating" (43%), "forgetting which waypoint number identifies a particular position" (39%), "taking a long time to warm up and lock on to a signal" (38%), "not being able to use it because of interference or bad weather" (37%), and "getting incorrect readings" (37%).

The predominant reasons for not purchasing a LOCATOR were price (50%) and the lack of a need (32%). The problems faced by LOCATOR nonowners are summarized in Exhibit 12.

Brand Preferences and Product Design   There was considerable lack of involvement with the product category. Half the respondents were unable to give a specific answer when asked which brand of LOCATOR they would purchase. Among LOCATOR owners, PAR Digital (14%) and Onkar Marine (12%) had the highest market shares. Other popular brands were Global Navigation (9%), Navsonic (8%) and Marmen (7%). LOCATOR units were purchased either as stand-alone units (79%), or as combinations: LOCATOR/depth sounder (13%) or LOCATOR/plotter (8%). However, regarding what they would like to buy, respondents' preferences were: stand-alone units (40%), LOCATOR/depth sounder (26%), LOCATOR/marine plotter (23%), and LOCATOR/GPS (8%).

Exhibit 12. *Global Positioning System: Problems faced by LOCATOR non-owners* Source: Company records

	Frequent problem	If occurs, major problem
Not being able to determine your exact position	67%	30%
Not being able to navigate in the fog	67	72
Not being able to tell how much time it will take to get to a particular destination	62	16
Not being able to tell someone your position, or find someone according to their position	60	39
Not being able to return to favorite fishing/diving spot	58	33
Not being able to find your way in strange/new waters	49	48
Not being able to navigate through difficult channels	40	54
Not being able to determine your course heading	40	39
Not being able to find your way back to harbor in bad weather	34	54
Not being able to find your way back to harbor at night	32%	67%

Nonowners were significantly more interested in a depth sounder combination, whereas LOCATOR owners significantly preferred a marine plotter combination.

Respondents were asked to evaluate various attribute and benefit statements in terms of both desirability and impact on the selection of a system. MRF then combined impact and desirability ratings to come up with a "Motivating Power" score for each product feature or benefit. Comparing the motivating power score with desirability (see Exhibit 13),

Exhibit 13. *Global Positioning System: Purchase motivators and feature desirability* Source: Company records

	Rankings					
	Total sample		LOCATOR owners		Non-owners	
Features	*MP*	*D*	*MP*	*D*	*MP*	*D*
Works in all weather	1	1	1	1	1	1
Provides the highest level of accuracy	2	4	2	3	3	9
Not affected by interference	3	7	3	6	5	6
Won't become obsolete	4	6	6	7	2	3
Provides total coverage	5	3	4	2	6	11
Locks on to weak signals	6	12	5	9	11	15
Best value	7	2	11	4	4	2
Most technologically advanced	8	13	8	13	10	14
Clearly displaying all information at the same time	9	11	9	11	9	12
Being the easiest to learn how to operate	10	8	7	8	14	5
Being serviced and returned within three days	11	9	12	10	8	7
Quickly installed by you, yourself	12	10	14	12	7	4
Being priced appropriately for needs	13	5	10	5	15	8
Saltwater proof, submersible	14	14	13	14	16	13
Showing the shoreline, position, and course	15	16	15	16	12	10
Allowing for software update	16	15	16	15	13	16

MP = Motivating power of feature in purchase decision
D = Desirability of feature

MRF concluded that although performance characteristics emerged as the most critical, respondents sometimes tended to understate the importance of not being affected by interference, being able to lock on to weak signals, and being the most technologically advanced system. They also concluded that respondents overestimated the importance of price dimensions such as best value and being priced appropriately for navigation needs.

LOCATOR vs. GPS   The awareness of LOCATOR (90% unaided, 98% aided) was substantially higher than that of other navigation systems: SATNAV (27% and 65%), Compass (20% and 88%), and GPS (12% and 76%). Nearly half the respondents who were aware of GPS did not know how it worked. Respondents rated LOCATOR and GPS systems on various attributes and benefits. The two systems were then compared along the continuum of motivating power. On many of the most motivating performance characteristics, GPS was judged superior to LOCATOR. LOCATOR had a big advantage over GPS on price, which, according to MRF's analysis, played only a relatively modest role in selecting a navigation system.

The purchase intentions of respondents in terms of the percentage who said that they would definitely or probably purchase during the next three years is given in Table A.

Respondents who indicated a greater purchase interest in GPS tended to have higher incomes.

Pricing   To provide guidelines on the optimal price for a LOCATOR or GPS system, respondents were asked a series of questions such as: At what price does a LOCATOR/GPS begin to be expensive? To be cheap?

TABLE A   Purchase intention for LOCATOR and GPS

Time period	LOCATOR Owners	LOCATOR Nonowners	Total
Next Year:			
LOCATOR	11%	34%	19%
GPS	7%	14%	9%
Years 2–3:			
LOCATOR	19%	37%	25%
GPS	24%	30%	26%

To be so expensive that you would never consider using it? To be so cheap that you would question its quality? Responses to these questions indicated that for LOCATOR owners, the optimal price for a LOCATOR ranged from $780 to $915, and for a GPS system, it ranged from $910 to $1,399. For nonowners the corresponding optimal price ranges were $480 to $580 and $580 to $960.

RECOMMENDATIONS   Based on the results of this study, MRF recommended that Techsonic immediately pursue the development of a GPS system rather than a LOCATOR system. According to them, the GPS system represented the best solution to many of the problems experienced by boat owners regarding navigation and positioning. MRF also noted that both LOCATOR owners and nonowners were concerned with LOCATOR obsolescence.

MRF concluded that they expected interest to build in GPS as it became fully operational and as costs declined. The Humminbird GPS system should be positioned as the most state-of-the-art and user-friendly system available, and, MRF believed, it could be priced at $1,000 or more.

Margins   Management expected dealers to realize margins of anywhere from 15% to 40% on GPS products and estimated its net sales price to dealers at $800 during the first year of sales. The expected retail price for a LOCATOR product was $630 with a net dealer price of $450. An analysis of Techsonic's expected margins on the GPS and LOCATOR products appear in Exhibit 14.

Joint Venture   To facilitate entry into the GPS market, Balkcom and Dyer had discussed the possibility of a joint venture with Standard Telecommunications, Inc. (STel) of Palo Alto, California. STel, which had worked on GPS-based navigation systems as a U.S. Department of Defense contractor, was interested in diversifying into civilian applications of GPS and agreed to develop low cost GPS products for Techsonic for a $1,000,000 "development fee." If the joint venture went through, STel would be responsible for the GPS electronics and Techsonic would specify features and develop the user interfaces, displays, and casings for the products. Techsonic would have exclusive rights to manufacture and market all STel GPS products for the consumer market. Such exclusivity would not extend to commercial or military markets.

Balkcom and Dyer believed that this joint venture would put Techsonic in a unique position for entering the GPS market. None of STel's competitors that were experienced in working with GPS, such as

Exhibit 14. *Navigation systems: Profit and loss forecast*
Source: *Company records*

Global Positioning System

(Year ending June 30)	1991	1992	1993	Total	
Unit Sales	400	6,000	16,800	23,200	
Net Price per Unit	$800.00	$704.00	$620.00	$644.83	avg.
Net Sales	320,000	4,224,000	10,416,000	14,960,000	
Gross Profit	114,688	2,407,680	4,999,680	7,522,048	
%	35.84%	57.00%	48.00%	50.28%	
SG&A (25%)	80,000	1,056,000	1,249,920	2,385,920	
EBI&T	$34,688	$1,351,680	$3,749,760	$5,136,128	

Capital Expenditures:	
Packaging	$ 28,000
Tooling	80,000
Equipment	36,000
R & D	220,000
Joint Venture Investment	400,000
Total	$764,000

LOCATOR

(Year ending June 30)	1991	1992	1993	Total	
Unit sales	4,000	12,000	5,600	21,600	
Net price per unit	$450.00	$375.00	$300.00	$369.44	avg.
Net sales	1,800,000	4,500,000	1,680,000	7,980,000	
Gross profit	630,000	1,440,000	470,400	2,540,400	
%	35.00%	32.00%	28.00%	31.83%	
SG&A (25%)	450,000	1,125,000	420,000	1,995,000	
EBI&T	180,000	315,000	50,400	545,400	

Capital Expenditures:	
Packaging	$ 21,600
Tooling	88,000
Equipment	72,000
R & D	120,000
Total	$301,600

Trimble, Magellan, or Sony, had any presence in the consumer market for marine electronics. Similarly, none of Humminbird's competitors that were considering GPS, such as MorPal, Onkar Marine, ESTAP-Sonic, or PAR Digital, had any expertise with the technology.

THE DECISION

On July 30, Techsonic's senior management met to decide the fates of the three new products. Al Nunley, vice president of marketing, was scheduled to make a presentation of his recommendations and marketing plans. He had asked his marketing manager, Mike Centers, to assist him in the preparation as well as in the presentation at the meeting.

Centers, a 1989 graduate of Harvard Business School, had joined Techsonic in June after spending the previous summer there. Although Centers was a relative newcomer to Techsonic, he had become steeped in its culture of listening to and serving the customer. He was very impressed with how well that strategy had served the company.

Centers thought about how these new products fit into that tradition of listening. He also wondered whether an almost single-minded devotion to listening to the customer could lead to problems, and whether listening to the customer was really the major reason behind Techsonic's success.

As they prepared for the presentation Nunley and Centers wondered which of the products Techsonic ought to introduce and the priorities they ought to recommend.

5 *CASE*

MSA: The Software Company: Planning the AMAPS Product Line

Robert J. Dolan

We'll spend about $150 million this year developing and marketing our products. With this $150 million, we have to do three things. First, we maintain, sell, and support the customers using our old technology. Second, we enhance some of our old technologies. Finally, we better be developing new technology or we'll be in trouble down the road. Deciding on which projects you'll pursue—which bets you want to make—is really the key to being a leader in the software business.

Casewriter's note: As deemed necessary, explanations are added to bottom of an exhibit slide and are attributed to the casewriter.

Professor Robert J. Dolan prepared this case as the basis for class discussion rather than to illustrate either effective or ineffective handling of an administrative situation. For confidentiality, certain data and names in the case have been disguised.

So commented William Rodgers vice president and director of Development at Management Science America (MSA).

On October 9, 1988, Robert Neal, president of MSA's Advanced Manufacturing Division, went to the thirteenth-floor conference room to meet with Mr. Rodgers and Thomas Franklin, his vice president of marketing, to determine the investment they would make in their AMAPS/G software package. AMAPS/G was MSA's Manufacturing Resource Planning package designed specifically for government contractors. Recent actions by the Department of Defense (DOD) had caused a major disruption in this market overall. Because of these unusual events, MSA had commissioned a market research study of potential demand for 1989 and beyond. John Morton Company of Chicago had completed the study, and Jeff Perelman, the project manager from John Morton, had flown to Atlanta to present the study findings to Neal and his people. Neal would rely heavily on input from Rodgers and Franklin since they had worked on the AMAPS product line for some time. Both had come to MSA in February 1987 when MSA acquired Comserv, the developer of AMAPS. Rodgers had worked on AMAPS development at Comserv since 1974 and Franklin, as vice president of marketing and sales, was instrumental in growing Comserv's 1985 revenues to $28 million.

Not everyone at MSA had endorsed the idea of spending about $100,000 on a study by an outside agency. Some questioned if any research could get beyond the superficial in a timely way and be of real value. Michael Whalen, MSA's Product Planning manager, had worked closely with John Morton throughout the study to make this study useful to MSA management. John Morton had completed the study in the agreed-upon time frame and now the question was what impact the findings would have on the AMAPS/G decision. Neal and his associates had to answer two questions. Should they spend the $1.5 million per year necessary to field a dedicated AMAPS/G selling and support organization which would make MSA a significant player in the governmental supplier market? Second, should they invest $3 million in adding the cost-tracking feature which current AMAPS/G users were asking for? The value of the JM study would derive largely from the extent to which it helped to answer these questions.

MSA BACKGROUND

Management Science America (MSA) was founded in 1963 as a computer service bureau and custom software house. It went public in 1981 and its 1985 revenues of $150 million made it the largest independent (in the sense that it did not sell hardware) supplier of mainframe applications software. Financial data for the years 1984-1987 are in Exhibit 1. MSA's first major success was in finance and human resources packages used in administrative offices.

As part of an expansion and diversification strategy, MSA made three acquisitions in 1986: (i) Information Associates, Inc., was the leading software vendor in the higher education market. Over 400 colleges and universities used the software for functions such as student record keeping and class scheduling; (ii) RTS Ltd., based in Ireland, sold manufacturing and financial software incorporating multicurrency and multilingual capabilities; (iii) by the end of 1986, MSA had acquired 63% of Comserv's stock. The remaining 37% was purchased in February 1987. Comserv's AMAPS product line was the leader among independents in the manufacturing sector.

While MSA had once produced generic software to cut across a number of market segments, its strategy had evolved over time to be one more focused on vertical markets, viz. five were key: (1) manufacturing, (2) government, (3) financial services, (4) higher education, and (5) health care. With the Comserv acquisition, MSA set up a separate organization, MSA Advanced Manufacturing, Inc., to develop, sell, and support a full line of products for manufacturers. However, as CEO, John Imlay, Jr., later reflected: "The price paid in absorbing the acquisition was greater than anticipated." MSA Advanced Manufacturing, Inc. posted a loss for 1987. Robert Neal became president of the division in 1988. Generally, MSA's overall company performance was disappointing in 1987 and through the first three quarters of 1988. While revenues increased 34%

Exhibit 1. MSA financials *(in thousands of dollars)*

Revenues	1984	1985	1986	1987
Software license fees	$ 93,320	$ 87,333	$120,601	$125,982
Support revenues	47,622	62,751	71,742	130,577
Other	874	1,077	1,106	1,984
Total	141,816	151,661	193,449	258,543
Expense				
Selling and marketing	47,598	53,812	63,808	93,207
Product development	32,060	36,941	29,749	52,702
Customer support	28,670	41,065	51,046	85,067
G&A	16,827	17,675	19,191	(221)

from 1986 to 1987, special charges (not shown in Exhibit 1) resulted in a $70 million loss. In August 1988, MSA's president resigned. He had been president for nine years and an MSA employee since the company's birth in 1963. CEO and chairman of the board, John Imlay, Jr., took over control of day-to-day operations.

In addition, Computer Associates attempted to take over MSA during the summer of 1988. Computer Associates was fended off, but all these events contributed to the atmosphere at MSA headquarters in Atlanta. The board of directors had been promised a rethinking of MSA's product line strategy. It was against this backdrop that Neal and his team met to consider funding of product development for the AMAPS/G product.

COMSERV AND AMAPS

Comserv was founded in 1968 and by 1982, sales revenues were $20 million. The vision of 1968, to produce a "manufacturing management information system," came to fruition in 1976 with the release of AMAPS—Advanced Manufacturing, Accounting, and Production System. Systems such as AMAPS were known as MRP or MRPII systems. MRP originally signified "Material Requirements Planning." However, as system capability expanded to cover not only material but also labor and other inputs, the more general Manufacturing Resource Planning term became prevalent. Some people referred to these more advanced systems as MRPII, others just used MRP. (In this case, we will use just the term MRP.)

The basic idea of an MRP system as shown in Fig. A is quite simple. Complexity comes from the sheer volume of data to be handled efficiently. The firm receives customer orders with required due dates.

From this, it develops a master production schedule. The master production schedule is bumped against two files: (i) the bill of material file defines the product structure, i.e., it breaks an item down into its component parts which are either fabricated, purchased, or drawn from on-hand inventory. It also contains purchasing lead-time information. (ii) the Engineering and Manufacturing database contains capital equipment and labor requirements. This is bumped against the capacity file showing availability of resources by time. The system produces order release notices and inventory status reports.

The challenge to software designers for such a system is that it must be a dynamic system capable of efficiently handling changes, e.g., in product due dates, product design, the bill of material file, and the variance of actual capacity utilization to what is specified in the Engineering

Figure A. *A simple MRP system*

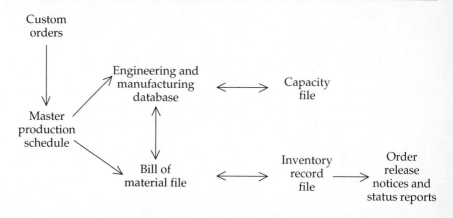

and Manufacturing Database. The AMAPS system was modular in design. It had ten modules; and the system implementer chose the subset best suited to the needs of the customer. An idea of the sophistication of the AMAPS system was suggested by the typical license fee of approximately $300,000. On average, a system contained seven modules. The target customer for AMAPS was a manufacturer with annual sales of over $60 million. Each customer was encouraged to subscribe to Comserv's product enhancement program. Subscribers paid an annual fee of about 12% of the system cost entitling them to updates of the product and a voice in the direction of product development efforts. Ninety percent of customers became subscribers. The AMAPS user group met twice a year for a formal conference and interchange of ideas among one another and with Comserv. By 1983, 3,000 AMAPS modules had been installed at over 400 manufacturing locations.

AMAPS was thought to be as good as any available MRP but Comserv faced formidable competition from IBM and Arthur Andersen. To help resolve some short-term cash flow problems, Comserv had facilitated Arthur Andersen's participation in the market by selling it the source code for AMAPS in 1980. While Arthur Andersen apparently made additional investment in developing its competitive product MAC-PAC, Comserv executives felt "MACPAC had its roots in AMAPS." Xerox had competed in the market with ARISTA, which it eventually sold to MSA in 1982. Other competitors were Rath and Strong, McCormick and Dodge, and Western Data Systems.

In 1982, two important events occurred. First, Comserv recognized a basic flaw in its design philosophy. Each AMAPS module was an entity unto itself. Modules passed information back and forth from one another but incoming data often had to be entered into several modules. Hence, there was duplicate computer code in the system. Given the possibility of significant efficiency gains, Comserv funded a project to establish a new architecture for AMAPS to eliminate this redundancy. The second major event was recognition of an opportunity to penetrate a niche of the market via a product modification. This led to the development of AMAPS/G for government contractors. As Bill Rodgers put it:

> *Some of the big A&D [aerospace and defense] people came to us and said, "Look, AMAPS is nice but you guys really do not understand what we need. Doing business with the government is a whole different ballgame. We have to keep track of things on an individual contract basis and our reporting requirements are incredible. These MRPs developed for commercial users just don't cut it for us. You can help us. We've got money. We'll fund the development. We'll work with you. And, we need this help quick. If you can't do it, we'll go somewhere else or get together and do it ourselves."*

> *Now this presented us some problems. We could see that what they were saying was right. Trying to take AMAPS and somehow fit it into their environment was too big a job for any one customer to foot the bill for—even though we are talking about guys like General Dynamics, AVCO Defense, and McDonnell Douglas. We had dabbled some in the government contract marketplace, so we had some idea of what would be required but we had never focused on it because it wasn't really clear that the market was big enough to bring out a special system for—even if we could get a price premium over the basic AMAPS product.*

> *We had just committed big bucks to change from the AMAPS to what we eventually called the AMAPS/Q architecture. But it would be a while until AMAPS/Q was ready and we got convinced that the window of opportunity was not very wide with these guys. It sounds like a good deal. You have some high-quality companies come along and say, "We'll help you design it, test it, and fund it"—so what do you say to these guys with the money—wait? So, we were building a new platform—AMAPS/Q which it would have been fairly easy to add /G functionality to, but it seemed that waiting for /Q to be ready would not be responsive. So, we made a decision—build /G off the old architecture so we could get going right away. This had some big implications—now we had two separate architectures, two separate design teams—nothing we did on /Q could be incorporated into /G. To move either forward would be a big investment. In retrospect, the window of opportunity was probably a little wider than we thought at the time but that's what we did and we set up three separate groups under three different vice presidents to sell our mainframe product to commercial users (AMAPS/Q), our mid-range product to people*

with Hewlett-Packard equipment (AMAPS/3000) and our special market product (AMAPS/G).

Rodgers also explained the vision Comserv had for AMAPS/G in the aerospace and defense contractor market.

We figured it would cost us about $3 million to get a first release on AMAPS/G. So, we said we would go forward if we got 10 people to sign up. To "sign up" cost you $300,000 and a commitment to be a member of the "guide group" for the development of /G. The guide group members provide information on their requirements, do early module testing, help you understand training requirements and so on. Within six months, we got five sign-ups—half of the $3 million we really needed to get first release. But, again because of the time pressure, we decided to go ahead. So /G really started out with two strikes against it—we were undercapitalized and we were building it on the old AMAPS release. But we still thought we had a reasonable chance to sell 35 systems at maybe $600,000—so off we went.

AMAPS/G

From a government contractor's point of view, the major shortcoming of MRP systems designed for commercial firms (such as AMAPS/Q) was the inability to track at the individual contract level. Commercial MRP systems drove off customer orders; the identity of the customer was transparent to the system. Government contractors, however, were required to track everything individually by contract. This presented particular problems when it was desirable to reallocate a component purchased for use in contract A to contract B. Such swaps had to leave an extensive "audit trail" in government systems to permit proper costing.

Comserv achieved first release of AMAPS/G in 1984. A sale of a system generated approximately $500,000 in initial fees. Annual maintenance averaged $70,000 per user but ranged from $40,000–$100,000 depending on the sophistication of the system involved. AMAPS/G had an installed base of 18 users by the end of 1985. (In contrast, Arthur Andersen's MACPAC/D product was believed to be installed with about 30 users and was the leader in this segment.) MSA's "flagship product" AMAPS/Q had an installed base of 500. /Q sold for about $300,000 and annual maintenance per user averaged $40,000.

According to Tom Franklin,

/G never sold a lot because the purchase process for these government contractors was so long. They would kick tires for two years looking at every material requirements planning vendor out there and, then, more often than not go to

"no decision." It was phenomenally expensive to go through a sales cycle with these guys. First, you went to them and did a presentation. Then, they came to Minnesota [Comserv headquarters] for the product demo. You fly four or five guys in—for a week, because it's pretty complicated to demo. Maybe you do this twice. Then they have to go visit current users to see the system in operation. You have a rep and three sales consultants going through this with them. Then they go to no decision—you've spent $150,000. Then, management changes at the company and the new guys want to start the thing all over again!

After first release, development on /G was largely limited to what members of the guide group were willing to pay for. Two factors contributed to this. First, Comserv was having financial difficulties. Second, because there were different architectures for /G and /Q, the two were always competing for available product development dollars. As Rodgers put it: "You've got this product with an installed base of 500 customers and you think there are hundreds more possible. Then, you've got this product with an installed base of 18, and you think maybe there is another 18 possible. Which one would you put the R&D dollars into?"

DEPARTMENT OF DEFENSE

In 1985, the Department of Defense (DOD) dealt a severe blow to the MRP market for government contractors. DOD audited 12 major suppliers using MRP systems and all failed the audit. Although none of these were Comserv customers, ensuing events effectively shut down the entire market for government contractor MRP systems. The DOD audit resulted in a 50% reduction in progress payments to one contractor. The Defense Contract Audit Agency (DCAA) formally established an audit program of MRP systems in June 1986. DCAA promoted reports of Pentagon auditors funding "hundreds of millions of dollars" in unwarranted profits generated by the MRP systems of eight firms. William Reed, director of DCAA, testified to the House Armed Services Subcommittee on Readiness that "MRP/MRPII systems have contributed to double-billing for spare parts, inflated prices, caused improper progress payments, and resulted in inaccurate costs being charged and billed to the government." The DCAA developed a list of 10 common deficiencies in MRP systems and sent the list to major defense contractors. In May 1987, the *Wall Street Journal* quoted a Pentagon official as saying, "If we can't rely on computerized systems, I don't know of any alternative but to require a manual system." The impact on AMAPS/G was stated by Michael Whalen:

> *Make a sale? We did not even see a prospect for two years from 1985–1987. It is a little hard to sell something that the DCAA is telling your customers is nothing more than an automated way to cheat the public and that we are going to be coming around to see if you are using one.*

MSA acquired Comserv and the AMAPS product line in the midst of these activities. AMAPS/Q was unaffected by the government market uproar. With the acquisition and attention to devote to AMAPS/Q, Comserv/MSA played a limited role in the MRP industry's response to the DOD/DCAA allegations. However, an MSA representative testified before the Readiness Subcommittee of the House Armed Services Committee along with representatives from Cullinet, McCormick and Dodge, and Western Data. Principally working through the Aerospace Industries Association, the MRP suppliers tried to make the government aware of the potential gains in contractor efficiency from a properly implemented MRP system. In 1986, the Packard Commission had recommended that defense contractors adopt more of the production techniques of the commercial sector to achieve lower costs. However, many of the efficiency gains possible with MRP seemed to conflict with DCAA desires. The most prominent example of this was commingling of inventories, i.e., maintenance of a pooled collection of supplies rather than separate supplies for each contract. DOD, with its focus on contract reporting, limited commingling while it was widely recognized the efficient inventory management at the manufacturer level required commingling.

A process of discussions and six congressional hearings through the summer of 1987 resulted in the "Spector Memorandum" of December 10, 1987. Eleanor Spector was Deputy Assistant Secretary for Defense for Procurement and issued "DOD's Final Policy Guidance on Contractors' MRP Systems." The Spector memorandum recognized the potential benefits of an MRP system but also the potential conflict with government regulations, viz. "problems identified by DCAA indicated that the full benefits of these systems are not being realized nor are government contract costing requirements being appropriately considered in some cases." The memo then went on to define 10 key elements of a "Material Management and Accounting System." The "Implementation Guidance" section of the memorandum stated that contractors must demonstrate compliance with these 10 key criteria and empowered government officers to "reduce payments" to those suppliers not in compliance. The ten criteria fell into three basic categories as follows:

Department of Defense: List of key elements

- Cost Management
    1. Cost assurance of purchased and fabricated material
    2. Documentation of consistent, equitable, and unbiased logic for costing of material transactions
- Inventory Management
    3. Established record keeping on recorded inventory versus physical inventory
    4. Documentation of transfer of parts
    5. Documentation of allocations and reallocation process
    6. Controls for physical commingling of inventory
- Management Practices
    7. Published documentation describing prices, procedures, and operating instruction of all MRPII system areas
    8. Documentation mechanisms to resolve MRPII system weaknesses
    9. Audit trails and records maintenance to evaluate and verify the desired performance of MRPII system
    10. Periodic internal audits to ensure compliance

Some MRP software vendors predicted a great sales boost due to the whole DOD process and the resulting Spector Memorandum. While MRP suppliers once feared a government ban on MRPs, the Spector memorandum promoted MRPs—if properly implemented. Chuck Nedell, director of aerospace and defense products for Cullinet, was quoted in the March 1988 issue of *Software Magazine*: "We felt good about it. I think it will increase the market opportunity for software vendors who understand the business and are willing to invest the necessary resources."

The AMAPS/G guide group had been requesting a cost management system which would perform similarly to the cost system in AMAPS/Q. This seemed an important feature in light of the DOD memorandum. With no prospects of sales in the past two years, however, the /G development team and sales support organization had been disbanded. MSA had effectively moved /G to "stabilization" status, i.e., /G would be maintained, but not enriched through developmental efforts. Two or three of the current /G users seemed willing to pay $300,000 each for development of a cost management system but others felt they were "owed" this feature already.

In addition to the DOD regulations and the AMAPS/G guide group requests, investing in AMAPS/G would be influenced by MSA's tight cash situation and imminent changes in its strategic direction as the mainframe market peaked. Franklin estimated that it would cost $3 million to add a cost management system to AMAPS/G and about $1.5 million per year to field a first-rate sales organization. While the market might indeed take off, given the DOD boost, an investment of almost $5 million in the next year was hardly warranted given the currently available information and other activities at MSA. Consequently, in May 1988, MSA hired John Morton Company of Chicago to do a market study as input to the funding decision. Morton was highly recommended by an MSA employee based on his experience with the firm at a previous employer. The report was to be completed in October 1988.

JOHN MORTON STUDY

PURPOSE AND STUDY DESIGN

The market research was to help answer two questions:

1. Was AMAPS/G a viable product with its current functionality? More specifically, the research was to estimate the size of the MRP market for government contractors to see if the DOD activity had boosted potential as some were suggesting.
2. Was it worth the development expense to add a Cost Management Module to the basic MRP system? AMAPS/G users were requesting this and it could be a key to the market overall.

In the course of providing input to these questions, the John Morton (JM) study would also provide input on a third frequently debated question at MSA, viz. could market research done by an outside firm be useful in an industry like computer software and in an entrepreneurial firm like MSA?

Jeff Perelman was the manager of the MSA project. Because of the time pressure to execute the study, a second company officer, Robert Block, was assigned to develop the analysis plan. A Northwestern MBA, Perelman had worked with JM for seven years and had managed a number of similar projects, but he noted the special challenges of MSA's situation:

> *Our research methodology is based on getting consumers to react to alternative product configurations. So, we always face the challenge of first identifying the real decision maker in a product category so we know whom to interview. In many studies, consumer package goods, for example, this is pretty easy. For AMAPS though, it was pretty complex because the AMAPS product was designed to provide benefits to a number of different kinds of people within the*

organization. At John Morton, we have developed some ways to cope with these complex decision-making units, but these methods take a little time and MSA was really on a tight time schedule. The study was commissioned in May and we had to have a full presentation of results ready by October. It was tight, but we knew that we had to do it if we were to have any impact.

The study had three major phases:

1. Qualitative Research
2. Quantitative Research
3. Analysis and Presentation of Results

The qualitative phase consisted of three focus groups conducted in mid-July. The core of the quantitative phase was a conjoint analysis study of the market. Respondents evaluated a number of possible MRP system configurations. This permitted JM to calculate the value respondents placed on various system features. From this, JM could then develop estimates of market potential given various product configurations. Don Greenberg of JM was responsible for the execution of most of the analysis. The JM study team of Perelman, Block, and Greenberg then analyzed the data to develop strategy recommendations. Michael Whalen, MSA's manager of the JM effort, worked with JM on a regular basis throughout the project to help assure the data analysis was relevant to the needs of the decision makers at MSA. Perelman and Whalen recognized that the time frame and environment at MSA would make this a project in which oral presentation would play a major role over a formal written report.

QUALITATIVE RESEARCH PHASE

The qualitative research phase consisted of three focus groups—two with potential customers and one with current AMAPS/G users. Because of the greater density of potential customers in California than elsewhere, those focus groups were run in Los Angeles (5 participants) and San Diego (7 participants) to facilitate recruitment of participants. The AMAPS/G user focus group was held in Minneapolis for the convenience of the 12 companies who would be represented. Telephone interviews were conducted with the six AMAPS/G user companies not represented at the Minneapolis focus groups.

JM hired a California-based research firm to recruit focus group participants who were to be "the person most involved or significantly involved in evaluating and purchasing manufacturing software." The sessions lasted about two hours. Participants received dinner and a $100 contribution was made to the charity of their choice. A JM moderator led each of the three sessions according to the "Moderator's Guide" in Appendix A.

The most important findings from the qualitative stage were as follows:

- *"Spector Memo on 10 Points of MRP"*
  - These requirements were not seen as a new set of rules, but did suggest a greater stringency with regard to already existing rules. Contractors did see the rules as a threat to their progress payments: "You used to be able to get paid by the government as you paid your bills. They ain't going to do that anymore."
- *Decision Making for MRP Software*
  - Decisions involve many people at each company. A common situation was to have a committee with a representative from finance, manufacturing, and information systems with an outside consultant, frequently from one of the Big 8.
  - No vendor had established itself as *the* source for manufacturing software.
- *Expectations of MRP Software*
  - No package was expected to meet 100% of a company's needs; if a package met 80% of a company's needs and the other 20% had to be custom developed somehow, that seemed acceptable. There was great variance among participants with respect to whether "home-grown/do-it-yourself" or "vendor-supplied" customization was preferable.
- *Price*
  - Initial price of the software was seen as "peanuts" compared to the implementation costs and potential benefits. "If I could prove that a canned vendor package is going to be the best thing in the whole world, money would be no object."
  - AMAPS/G users, however, were adamant about not paying in advance for new modules, nor paying at all for modules which they felt had already been financed through yearly product enhancement fees.
- *MRP System Capabilities*
  - Primary deficiency across all currently available packages was in the area of cost tracking. "Collect accurate costs, apply the right ownership to those costs, be able to track them, be able to use those costs for monitoring contract performance and manufacturing performance."
  - The second most important deficiency was "serial number effectivity," the ability to track a change which is to be implemented not

as of a certain date but as of the production of a certain number of parts.
- Other deficiencies mentioned were in real-time shop-floor control (being able to track labor usage as it is happening rather than on an overnight basis) and archival data (the storage of records which may be needed in the event of a government audit).
- These deficiencies were seen to exist across all vendors.

These focus group results were presented to MSA management and used by JM to design the quantitative phase of the study.

QUANTITATIVE RESEARCH PHASE

Based on the results from the qualitative phase, JM developed a microcomputer-based interview to be administered to a large sample of decision makers in the government contracting market. Pretesting of the questionnaire in July resulted in some minor adjustments. Simultaneous with questionnaire pretesting, JM and Mike Whalen jointly developed the sampling plan. Whalen located two major sources of names of government contractors: (i) the *Congressional Record* listing of 450 prime contractors (defined as contractors doing over $25 million in revenue with the government and the majority as a prime [rather than sub] contractor), and (ii) DOD's list of 5,000 firms doing business with the government.

The second major aspect of the sampling plan was to determine who in a given company to interview. The focus groups provided some input on this. However, Whalen supplemented this by a series of telephone interviews with potential customers "scoping the DMU" (decision-making unit) and by input from MSA's salespeople. In many cases, JM interviewed more than one individual in a company to permit comparison of results.

In August, the study went to the field using 17 sites in the United States; 219 completed interviews were obtained, representing 139 companies. The companies were a random sample from MSA's supplied list. Industries prominently represented in the sample were: aircraft (28% of sample), navigation (18%), communications (16%), electronics (14%), and missiles (11%). The interview took about one and a half hours to complete. Respondents sat at a computer terminal and typed in their answers. The interview was interactive in the sense that the answer to one question could impact the nature of the future questions. A JM person was present to assist the respondent as needed, but the computerized questionnaire was designed to minimize the need for such intervention.

Two types of questions were posed during the interview: (i) traditional multiple choice and short open-ended questions (e.g., when was your Manufacturing Information Management System implemented?) and (ii) a conjoint analysis task to provide data for a market-size projection.

CONJOINT ANALYSIS

For this phase, the product concept was decomposed into six attributes.

Attribute #1: MRP System Features
- This attribute described the functionality of the basic MRP system. It had five levels:
  1. No functionality
  2. MRP by Contract Reporting (Base)
  3. Base plus a Serial Number Effectivity Feature
  4. Base plus a Real-Time Shop Floor Control Feature
  5. Base plus both Serial Number and Real-Time Features

  The added features of Serial Number Effectivity and Real-Time Shop Floor Control were identified in the focus groups as potentially important.

Attribute #2: Time of Availability
- When would the system be available to the purchaser? It had five levels:
  1. Now
  2. In 6 months
  3. In 12 months
  4. In 24 months
  5. In 36 months

Attribute #3: Price
- This took on 10 different levels between $200,000 and $1,900,000.

Attribute #4: Platform
- Specified whether the product would run on the firm's current computer system or not. These were two levels: yes and no.

The remaining two attributes specified whether the system incorporated major features which theoretically could be stand-alone systems or included in an integrated Manufacturing Information Management System. Since these two could operate without a base MRP system, these were different from Serial Number Effectivity and Real-Time Shop-Floor Control which were only add-ons to a base MRP system and thus, for the survey, had to be implemented as a level of Attribute #1. These two features were:

Attribute #5: Cost Management System
- This was the attribute sought by AMAPS/G users and its development was a major question of the study. It was incorporated as two levels: present or not.

Attribute #6: Shop-Floor Management and Execution System—incorporated as two levels: present or not.

After a number of background questions on such issues as familiarity with DOD regulations, the firm's manufacturing environment and the like, the respondent reached the conjoint part of the survey. For this part of the survey, consumers were instructed to answer "under the assumption that you are, in fact, intending to make a purchase to improve your system." The JM interviewer handed the respondents a stack of 20 cards. Each card contained a description of a potential product on four attributes, e.g., one card read:

- MRPII by Contract with Serial Number Effectivity
- Generally Available in Six Months
- Runs on Same Computer as Your Current System
- Price $400,000

Subjects were told to evaluate the product description on each of the 20 cards "on its own merits; not relative to any other products. You will be given an opportunity to state your preference for individual products later."

Respondents manually sorted the cards into three piles according to:

Stack 1: Products you would be 50%–99% likely to purchase (somewhat likely to purchase)

Stack 2: Products you would be 1% to 49% likely to purchase (somewhat less likely to purchase)

Stack 3: Products you would be 0% likely to purchase (definitely would not purchase)

After the subjects hit a key indicating that they had completed the manual sort, the computer screen showed the full list of 20 card numbers. Respondents were instructed to enter in the identification numbers of all cards in Stack 1. When this was done, the program selected the first card entered by the respondent and asked:

"How likely would you be to purchase this product?"

Respondents input a number from a six-point scale: 50%, 60%, 70%, 80%, 90%, 99%. This question was asked for all cards in Stack 1. Then, the program asked for entry of the identification numbers of the cards sorted into Stack 2. The same question was then asked for each of these product descriptions; the six-point scale was adjusted to 1%, 10%, 20%, 30%, 40%, 49% to reflect the range specified originally for Stack 2. Since Stack 3 was "definitely not purchase" cards, there were no further questions asked of these products. These likelihood numbers were then transformed into market size estimates via the conjoint methodology specified in *Appendix B.*

After the conjoint task, the questionnaire went on with a number of additional standard survey questions.

JOHN MORTON RESULTS

Jeff Perelman checked his slides one more time as the MSA management team got settled in the conference room. Robert Neal, president of MSA Advanced Manufacturing, had asked MSA's vice president of Quality and vice president of Marketing to sit in on the presentation. Also present were those most intimately involved with AMAPS and AMAPS/G: Franklin, Rodgers, and Whalen. Pulling the blinds on the floor-to-ceiling conference room windows, Neal told Perelman the floor was his.

Perelman's presentation had three major sections.

1. Description of Current Environment
2. Impact of DOD Activity
3. Predicted Market Potential

The major slides from the Current Environment section are in Exhibits 2-7.

Exhibit 2: Market Profile

Exhibit 3: When Do You Think You Will Make a Decision to Modify Present or Purchase a New MRP System?

Exhibit 4: Was Your MRP System Internally Developed, Purchased, or Some of Each?

Exhibit 5: Age of Current MRP Systems in Use

Exhibit 6: Origin of Current MRP System

Exhibit 7: Degree of Modification of Purchased System to Make Fit Requirements

Major slides from the DOD Influence section are in Exhibits 8–11.

Exhibit 8: Familiarity with DOD Memorandum on Key Elements of MRP System

Exhibit 9: Perceived Status of Compliance with DOD Regulations Regarding: (1) Cost Management, (2) Inventory Management, and (3) Management Practices

Exhibit 10: Beliefs Regarding Compliance

Exhibit 11: Beliefs Regarding Anticipated Enforcement

Major slides from the Predicted Market Potential section are in Exhibits 12–17.

Exhibit 12: Definition of Prediction

Exhibit 13: Prediction Assumptions

Exhibit 14: Predicted Market Potential for Selling Base MRPII Systems to IBM Environment at Various Prices

Exhibit 15: Predicted Market Potential If Both Base MRPII and MRPII with Cost Module Are Offered to Market

Exhibit 16: Impact of Price Variation for MRPII with Cost

Exhibit 17: Impact of Serial Number Effectivity and Real-Time Shop-Floor Control on Market Potential

MSA DECISION MAKING

Perelman gathered up his presentation material and once again thanked MSA for the opportunity to work on the project and Whalen for his help throughout. In return, Robert Neal thanked Perelman. As Perelman left the conference room, Neal turned to his AMAPS experts: "So, what should we do?"

Exhibit 2. *Market profile*

Manufacturing Environment

- On average, companies
  - manufacture products at six sites
  - manufacture products at five sites under government contract
  - derive 67% of revenues from projects under government contract
  - have 4,300 employees

Typical Contract

- On average, contractors under government contract are currently running 43 different projects. Shipbuilding and R&D industry groups run fewer.
- These contracts represent, on average, 47 different manufactured items. There is obviously great variation by industry.
- The average government contract lasts two and a half years.

Exhibit 3. *When do you think you will make a decision to modify present or purchase a new MRP system?*

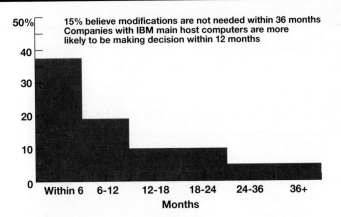

15% believe modifications are not needed within 36 months
Companies with IBM main host computers are more likely to be making decision within 12 months

Two thirds believe a satisfactory MRPII will be ready within their decision time frame

Exhibit 4. Was your MRP system internally developed, purchased, or some of each?

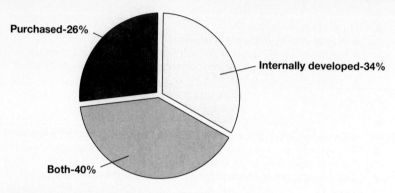

Purchased-26%

Internally developed-34%

Both-40%

Systems designed for government are much more likely to be developed internally only [51% vs. 22% of commercial]

Exhibit 5. Age of current MRP systems in use

- Time since implementation

  Industry average   2.4 years
  IBM mainframe   3.7 years

- Over 50% of IBM mainframe systems are at least five years old

Exhibit 6. Origin of current MRP system

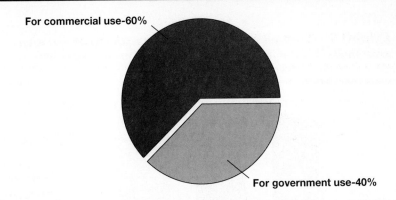

For commercial use-60%

For government use-40%

Exhibit 7. Degree of modification

Asked of those who purchased systems:

What was the extent of the modifications required to make your purchased system fit your needs?

- *none*
- *minor*
- *major*

Answers:

no modification	*4%*
minor modifications	*23%*
major modifications	*73%*

Exhibit 8. Familiarity with DOD memorandum on key elements of MRP system

Extremely familiar	6%
Very familiar	19%
Somewhat familiar	39%
Not very familiar	22%
Not at all familiar	14%

Casewriter's note: The question referred to the recent "10 points" of the Spector Memorandum issued by the Department of Defense and asked respondents to state their familiarity with these points. Larger company representatives stated more familiarity than others.

Exhibit 9. *Perceived status of compliance with DOD regulations regarding: (1) cost management, (2) inventory management, and (3) management practices*

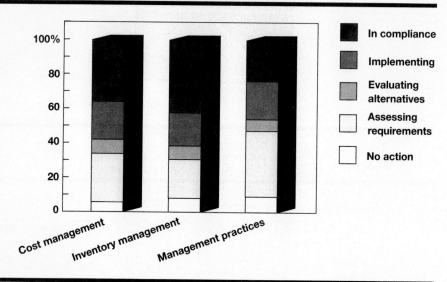

Casewriter's note: This question asked people to say what they were doing with respect to complying with the three key topics of the 10 points: cost management, inventory management, and management practices. Respondents chose from five options.

1. *Implementing* procedures
2. *Evaluating* identified *alternatives*
3. *Assessing requirements* for compliance
4. We do not feel compliance is relevant; *no action planned*
5. Presently *in compliance;* no action planned

Exhibit 10. *Beliefs regarding compliance*

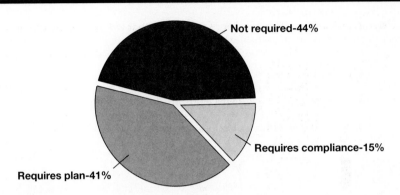

Not required-44%

Requires compliance-15%

Requires plan-41%

Larger companies and IBM mainframe group are more likely to feel actual compliance or plan is required

Casewriter's note: Question asked was "Does DOD require being in compliance or having a plan to be in compliance by a certain date?" In fact, DOD requires compliance and suspends payments otherwise but "the percentage of the suspension will be impacted by the quality of the contractor's self-assessment and corrective action plan."

Exhibit 11. *Beliefs regarding anticipated enforcement*

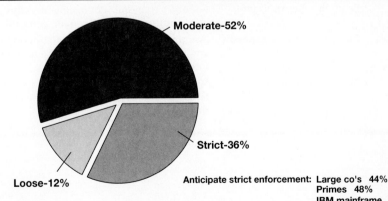

Moderate-52%

Strict-36%

Loose-12%

Anticipate strict enforcement: Large co's 44%
Primes 48%
IBM mainframe 46%
Fully integr. 45%
Government 43%

Exhibit 12. **Definition of prediction**

- A prediction of the number of companies that will purchase variously configured systems in the next three to five years, defined in terms of specific product attributes/levels, based on a predetermined set of assumptions.

  - Predictions are based on actual decision maker value systems, needs, and likelihoods of purchase.
  - Decision makers were selected from a valid random sample of actual A&D market.
  - The universe upon which these predictions are based is:

Prime Contractors	420
Sub Contractors	4,000[a]
Total	4,420

- Results are for total market potential, not potential by vendor.

[a]Most conservative estimate used.

Exhibit 13. **Prediction assumptions**

Regulatory Environment:	Based upon regulatory environment and knowledge of regulations prevailing during summer of 1988
Economic Environment:	Assumes economic environment in this sector as of summer 1988 will remain constant
Competitive Environment:	Assumes competitors are operating in today's competitive environment and have equal and fair access to that market
Methodological:	Assumes full diffusion of knowledge and equal availability of products and features modeled

Exhibit 14. *Predicted market potential for selling base MRPII systems to IBM environment at various prices*

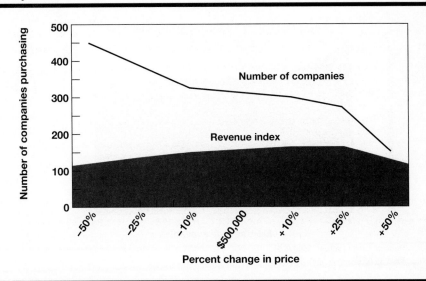

Casewriter's note: Assumes that only a base MRPII system is available (similar in functionality to AMAPS/G current version) and no cost management system is available. Levels of other attributes are:
- Time: available now
- No serial number effectivity feature
- No real-time shop-floor control
- Runs on IBM and this market potential estimate is based only on selling to current IBM-installed base
- No shop-floor management and execution system

Exhibit 15. *Predicted market potential if both base MRPII and MRPII with cost module are offered to market*

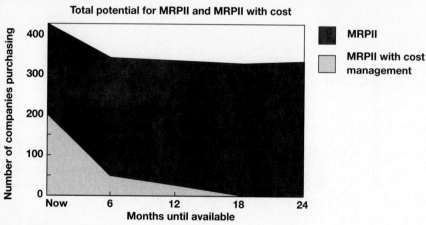

Price of MRPII system: $500,000
Price of MRPII with cost: $800,000

Casewriter's note: This scenario has two products offered: Base MRPII and Base MRPII with a cost management module. The base MRPII is available now at $500,000. The base MRPII with cost management module is priced at $800,000 and is available at varying times as shown on the horizontal axis. All other assumptions are as in the previous exhibit.

Exhibit 16. *Impact of price variation for MRPII with cost*

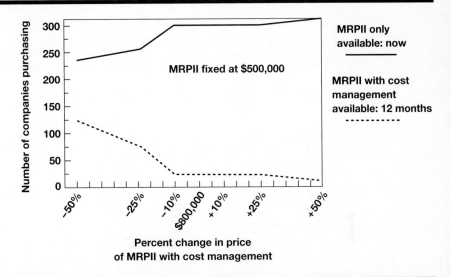

Casewriter's note: This scenario fixes the time of availability of MRPII with cost at 12 months and varies the price. As in previous scenarios, base MRPII is available now for $500,000.

Exhibit 17. *Impact of serial number effectivity and real-time shop-floor control on market potential*

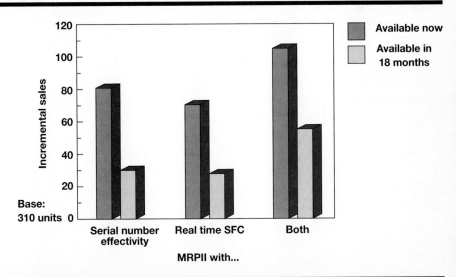

Casewriter's note: This scenario assumes only the base MRPII is offered at $500,000. Serial number effectivity and real-time shop-floor control are implicitly offered "for free" and this scenario shows incremental units sold for varying times of availability.

APPENDIX A FOCUS GROUP OUTLINE

I. **INTRODUCTION**
   - A. Moderator
   - B. Purpose
   - C. Respondents

II. **BACKGROUND**
   - A. Platform
     1. IBM mainframe or other
     2. Plans to downsize to mini or other
     3. Relationship of these plans to government regulations, if any
   - B. Database software
     1. Purchased or home-grown; hierarchical or relational (show of hands)
     2. Plans to switch
     3. Relation to use of MRPII—which drives decisions
     4. Relation to government regulations

III. **COMPANY CULTURE**
   - A. How are needs in this area identified, evaluated, solved
   - B. Who would we need to talk to to get the whole picture
   - C. Who has final say

IV. **GOVERNMENT COMPLIANCE**
   - A. In general, how different from nongovernment work
   - B. Evaluation of how systems have been meeting needs up to now

V. **FUTURE GOVERNMENT COMPLIANCE**
   - A. What has changed, if anything
   - B. What further developments will take place
   - C. What impact does this have—suspension of progress payments; fear of decertification
   - D. What action, in general, is now being taken or contemplated

VI. **EFFECT OF CHANGES ON MRPII NEEDS**
   - A. Functions/features—necessary or *desirable*
     1. Costing
     2. Model unit effectivity
     3. Real-time shop-floor control
     4. Other
   - B. Service and support
     1. Implementation, maintenance
     2. Consulting—inside, outside, or from vendor
   - C. Options
     1. MSA and other vendors
     2. In-house resources
     3. Other

187

VII. PROCESS TO ACHIEVE COMPLIANCE
    A. Evaluation of solutions
       1. Internal
       2. Interaction with vendor
       3. Cost—purchasing, development, maintenance; vendor's contribution vs. users, trade-off with priority of need
       4. External factors (political/economical)
       5. Acceptability of PC-base for costing
    B. Time frame

VIII. OTHER DEVELOPMENTS
    A. CIM
    B. JIT
    C. Shop-floor management
    D. GT, CAD/CAM, FMS, A1, simulation, etc.

IX. SUMMARY
    A. Break; questions from behind mirror
    B. What, ultimately, is needed
    C. What is next step
    D. Other comments

APPENDIX B CONJOINT ANALYSIS METHODOLOGY

The input to the conjoint analysis is the individual's rating of 20 different products on a "likelihood of purchase" scale. These ratings and the product profiles, i.e., the attributes present in the given product, are used in a regression-type analysis to produce the individual's "value system." The value system shows how each attribute impacts probability of choice, e.g., the time of availability scores for an individual's value system might be:

Now:	+16
in 6 months:	+16
in 12 months:	+3
in 24 months:	+1
in 36 months:	0

This would reflect that the individual is indifferent about having the product now or in 6 months, but is 16% more likely to buy if it is available within 6 months as compared to having to wait three years.

The importance of value system is that it enables the analyst to calculate the individual's "likelihood of purchase" for any product, not just the 20 which the individual provided data for.

In sum, Step 1 of the procedure is:

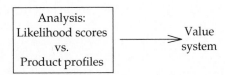

This permits the value system to be used in Step 2 to simulate any market environment. Step 2 works as follows. Suppose a firm is offering products X and Y. These descriptions are input to the value system to yield "likelihood of purchase" scores for both product X and product Y.

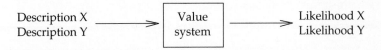

Since a consumer will buy only one product in this category, only the product with the maximum likelihood score is considered further.

For example if:

$$\text{Likelihood Buy X} = .7$$
$$\text{Likelihood Buy Y} = .5$$

The analysis assumes the individual does not buy Y and there is a 70% chance that he will buy X.

At this stage, John Morton makes an additional adjustment. If the likelihood score for the most desired product is less than .25 (a number judgmentally set), it was felt that the product was unlikely to generate sufficient enthusiasm to induce the firm to go through a purchase cycle. Consequently, the probability was set to zero if likelihood <.25.

The result to this point is, for each individual in the sample, an estimate of the probability they would buy a given product in a particular market situation.

The last step in the analysis is to go from these probabilities for individuals in the sample to a market estimate. This calculation is most easily explained by example. Consider three individuals and a situation with two products available on the market, A and B. Probabilities of purchase are:

Product	1	2	3
A	.8	.4	0
B	0	0	.5

Note that each column can have only one positive entry since Step 2 gives positive probability only to the product with the greatest likelihood score.

Without any adjustment, the expected demand for A would be 1.2 units (.8 + .4) and for B .5 units from these three individuals. However, if one knew that individual 1 only had half the decision making authority at his or her company, while individuals 2 and 3 had complete authority, the .8 in individual 1's column should not be counted as heavily. To reflect this, John Morton multiplies the numbers in each column by the percentage of the decision making authority the person holds in their company. (These data have been self-reported by the person in the questionnaire.) If authority levels for 1, 2, and 3 were .5, 1, and 1 respectively, the adjusted matrix would be:

	1	2	3
A	.4	.4	0
B	0	0	.5

So, demand now would be .8 for A and .5 for B per every three people. If there were 300 potential buyers, we would estimate demand for A at 80 units and B at 50 units—if we believed the potential buyer population to have 1/3 people like our individual #1, 1/3 like #2, and 1/3 like #3. If on the other hand, we believed 1/2 the population to be like #1, and 1/4 like each #2 and 3, then we would want our estimation to reflect this, viz:

$$\text{Potential for A} = 150\,(.4) + 75\,(4) + 75\,(0) = 90$$
$$\text{Potential for B} = 150\,(0) + 0\,(0) + 75\,(.5) \;= 37.5$$

This "reweighting" of the sample is the last step of the procedure. In particular, John Morton reweighted the sample to reflect better the buying potential population in terms of prime versus sub contractors and type of computer system installed.

6 _CASE_

Strategic Industry Model:
Emergent Technologies

Robert J. Dolan

In Spring 1990, Emergent Technologies was considering entry into the Desktop Computer Market. At issue for Emergent was the question of whether it would gain sufficient market share to warrant entry and what an optimal entry strategy would be. The primary focus was the Reseller Market, i.e., firms who would buy Emergent's product and integrate it with other hardware or software to serve a specific user need.

Competition in this market was conducted on a worldwide basis. Of the nine major firms (representing 96% of unit sales in the market), four

Professor Robert J. Dolan prepared this note as the basis for class discussion.

Copyright © 1992 by the President and Fellows of Harvard College. Harvard Business School case 592-086.

were from the United States, three from Europe, and two from Asia. Their approximate market shares were:

United States	European	Asian
Alliance–15%	Attwood Associates–10%	Cheong–6%
Beta Technologies–12%	Penucchini Processors–9%	Kojima–7%
Computer Process Systems–14%	Stobart Systems–11%	
Developmental Integration Systems–11%		

John Morton Company of Chicago conducted a consulting assignment resulting in a "Strategic Industry Model" to let Emergent examine strategic alternatives.

THE RESEARCH

The "Strategic Industry Model" was the result of a three stage research process. In Stage 1, qualitative interviews were done with 30 firms to locate the decision making authority in the firm and to elicit the product attributes used in making purchase decisions. These interviews and Emergent input led to specification of 14 potentially important attributes of four types:

   I. Vendor Descriptions
      1. Brand Name/Reputation
      2. Breadth of Vendor's Product Line
      3. Time to Market Reputation
  II. Product Price and Terms
      4. Price
      5. Payment Terms
      6. Financing Available
      7. Warranty Length
 III. Support
      8. Response Time for Support
      9. Installation and Maintenance
    10. Response Time for Hardware Service
    11. Training
    12. Marketing Support
 IV. Product Features
    13. Software Compatibility
    14. Processor Speed

See Exhibit 1 for formal definition of the attributes and specification of how they were measured in the study. Exhibit 2 shows each vendor's score on the 14 attributes. Some of these are "average perceptions" of the market—perceptions were not found to vary much across customers. Others, such as price, are simply facts. In addition to ratings for all ten

Exhibit 1. *Attribute definitions*

1. **Brand**   self-explanatory; this attribute cannot be changed.
2. **Computer Breadth**   a measure of the breadth of supplier's computer line. Continuous variable; scored on a scale of 1–3 with:
   1. single product only
   2. limited product only
   3. broad range of products
3. **Time to Market**   measures whether the manufacturer tends to offer new products before, at the same time, or after competitor's similarly advanced technology. Measured in months on a scale ranging from −12 to +6 where:

   $$-12:\ \text{usually 12 months late}$$
   $$+6:\ \text{usually 6 months ahead}$$

4. **Price**   self-explanatory continuous variable: ranges from $2,000 to $5,000.
5. **Payment Terms**   the number of days after invoice date in which full payment is due; measured in days on a continuous scale ranging from 30 days to 120 days.
6. **Financing Available**   designates the financing available; measured on a discrete scale where:
   1. no financing
   2. only end user financing
   3. only reseller inventory financing
   4. both end user and reseller inventory
7. **Warranty**   designates length of warranty period; measured on a continuous scale in months ranges from 6 to 36.
8. **Support Response**   designates manufacturer's speed of response to queries; measured on a continuous scale from 1 to 3, where:
   1. immediately
   2. same day
   3. next day
9. **Installation and Maintenance**   designates support of manufacturer on installation and maintenance; measured on a discrete scale with:

(continued)

Exhibit 1 (continued)

    1. not available
    2. installation only
    3. maintenance only
    4. both installation and maintenance

10. **Hardware Service**   designates the speed on manufacturer's response to hardware problems; measured on a continuous scale from 1 to 4 where:
    1. within four days
    2. same day
    3. next day
    4. within a week

11. **Training**   describes the type of training offered by the manufacturer; measured on a discrete scale with:
    1. none
    2. instructor-based training
    3. computer-based training

12. **Marketing Support**   describes support provided by manufacturer to resellers in their marketing efforts; measured on a discrete scale with:
    1. none
    2. lead generation only
    3. cooperative advertising only
    4. both lead generation and cooperative advertising

13. **Software Compatibility**   describes the range of compatibility of firm's software; measured on a continuous scale ranging from 1 to 3 where:
    1. only the reseller's software
    2. some software
    3. a wide range of software

14. **Processor Speed**   describes the speed of the vendor's offering relative to the average speed of competitors; measured on a continuous scale from 1 to 5 where:
    1. 50% slower
    2. 25% slower
    3. as fast
    4. 25% faster
    5. 50% faster

Exhibit 2. Attribute/supplier offering matrix[a]

Attributes	United States					European			Asian		
	Alliance	Beta	CPS	DIFS	Proposed Emergent	Attwood	Penucchini	Stobart	Cheong	Kojima	Clones
Brand	6	4	5	9	7	8	1	3	10	2	11
Computer Line Breadth	2.8	2.9	2.8	2.1	1.4	1.8	1.9	1.7	1.8	1.5	1.8
Time to Market	-7	-3	-2	+4	-1	5	2	2	-5	-3	-5
Price	3,700	3,800	3,500	3,300	3,800	3,500	3,900	3,600	3,800	2,400	2,300
Payment Terms	38	42	41	33	36	45	43	33	42	37	38
Financing Available	4	4	4	1	2	1	4	1	1	1	1
Warranty	12	9	9	9	9	12	12	12	12	6	12
Support Response	2	2.4	1.9	1.9	1.6	2	1.9	1.5	2.2	2.1	2.0
Installation and Maintenance	4	4	4	4	4	4	1	1	1	1	1
Hardware Service	1.7	1.9	2.0	2.3	3.2	2.6	3.4	2.2	3.4	2.9	3.3
Training	2	2	2	2	3	2	3	2	1	1	1
Marketing Support	4	4	4	2	2	3	4	4	1	1	2
Software Compatibility	2.3	2.2	2.1	2.3	2.0	2.6	2.6	3.0	2.4	2.9	2.8
Processor Speed	3.3	2.9	3.2	3.2	3.2	3.8	3.1	3.6	3.2	2.9	2.9

[a] See Exhibit 1 for detailed explanation of the attributes and the scale on which they are measured.

major players, Exhibit 2 shows ratings for a group of clones and a possible set of attributes for Emergent's entry.

In Stage 2, approximately 225 individual decision makers in prospect firms performed a computerized interviewing session to provide data for a conjoint analysis. Respondents were asked a series of questions such as: Which of the following would you prefer, A or B?

A: Alliance Brand, priced at $4,000, with a 12-month warranty

or

B: Penucchini Brand, priced at $3,700, with a 6-month warranty

Based on many questions like this, i.e., overall preference judgements, conjoint analysis teases out the "value system" underlying the choices. (See "Conjoint Analysis: A Manager's Guide" note for details.)

In Stage 3, John Morton validated the model finding it to be an adequate representation of the marketplace. In the end, the "Strategic Model" allowed Emergent to specify any competitive scenario, i.e., description of suppliers on the 14 attributes, and assess the expected market shares. The process is:

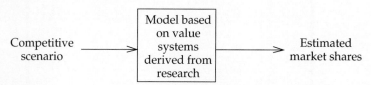

DEVELOPING A STRATEGY RECOMMENDATION FOR EMERGENT

The Strategic Industry Model provides two kinds of data which can be useful in developing a strategy recommendation: (i) perceptual maps; and (ii) outputs from competitive scenario simulations.

First, consider the perceptual data. How do potential customers see the competition among suppliers? A perceptual mapping algorithm applied to the data of Exhibit 2 produced the map in Fig. 1. The length of the vectors in Fig. 1 represent the extent of variation among competitors on that dimension.

Question 1.   Based on the perceptual map, define the bases for competition in the market. Are there any "strategic groups?"

Question 2.   How "well-positioned" is Emergent with its proposed attribute levels?

Question 3.   In general, assess the utility of perceptual mapping by comparing the insights available from examining Fig. 1 to those obtainable from examining the raw data of Exhibit 2.

The second major part of the Strategic Industry Model is competitive scenario simulations. Exhibit 3 contains the results of the "Base Case" simulation, i.e., the result of simulating the scenario of the competitive data given in Exhibit 2. This shows a 7.5% market share for Emergent.

Figure 1. *Strategic industry model, plot map example*

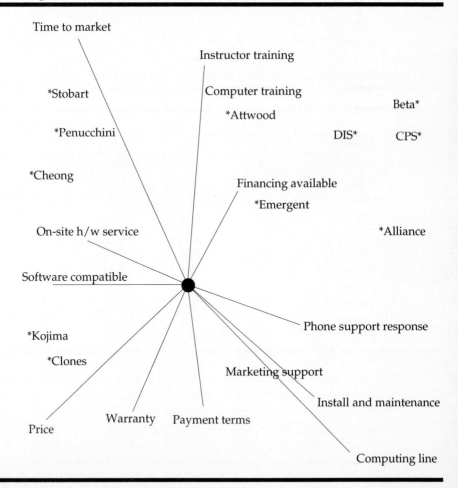

Exhibit 3. *Base case results*

Report:	Demand Share	Sorted by:	Order of Base Case
Title:	base case		
Date:	Friday 10/25/91 - 15:07:35		

Run description

Customer selected

All segments included

Resulting number of customers: 225

Product market changes

Added products:

Deleted products:

Changed products:

Key

CUR RUN	Calculated Demand Share, Current Run
BASE	Base Case Demand Share, Market Unchanged
DIF	Difference between RUN and BASE

Name	Cur Run	Base	Dif
Alliance	12.9	12.9	0.0
Beta	11.1	11.1	0.0
CPS	12.5	12.5	0.0
DIS	10.4	10.4	0.0
Emergent	7.5	7.5	0.0
Attwood	8.9	8.9	0.0
Penucchini	8.0	8.0	0.0
Stobart	9.6	9.6	0.0
Cheong	4.7	4.7	0.0
Kojima	7.1	7.1	0.0
Clones	7.2	7.2	0.0

This share prediction is based on Emergent achieving comparable levels of awareness and distribution to that of incumbent firms.

Exhibit 4 is the output of the Factor Sensitivity feature of the Strategic Industry Model. Starting from the base case with the 7.5% share achieved by Emergent based on the attribute values of Exhibit 2, the Factor Sensitivity Model examines the impact of Emergent changing its positioning. Specifically, it takes each of the 14 attributes; changes

Exhibit 4. *Factor level sensitivity*

Report: Factor Level Sensitivity
Title: Factor Sensitivity
Date: Friday 10/25/91 - 15:40:00

Run description

Customer selected
All segments included
Resulting number of customers: 225

Product market changes
Added products:
Deleted products:
Changed products:

Key

Run Share	Calculated Demand Share, Current Market
SHARE	Calculated Demand Share, Current Market, New Level
DIF, %DIF	Absolute, Percent change between Run Share and SHARE
Current Level	Current Factor Specification

Product: Emergent	Run Share: 7.5		
Name	Share	Dif	%Dif
Manufacturer			
Current Level: 7.00			
Penucchini	7.9	0.4	4.7
Kojima	8.1	0.6	7.5
Stobart	8.7	1.2	15.7
Beta	8.5	0.9	12.3
CPS	8.6	1.0	13.3
Alliance	9.1	1.5	20.3
Emergent	7.5	−0.0	−0.0
Attwood	7.4	−0.1	−1.5
DIS	8.6	1.1	14.4
Cheong	7.9	0.3	4.6
Clones	7.8	0.3	3.9

(continued)

Exhibit 4 (continued)

Product: US mfr 4		Run Share: 7.5	
Name	Share	Dif	%Dif
Compute breadth			
Current level: 1.40			
1. Single prod only	7.3	−0.2	−3.3
2. Limited prods	7.9	0.4	5.2
3. Broad range prod	8.6	1.0	13.6
Time to market			
Current level: −1.00			
−12. (−) 12 months late	6.7	−0.8	−11.0
(−) 6 months late	7.2	−0.4	−4.9
On time	7.6	0.1	1.0
6. (+) 6 months ahead	8.1	0.6	7.3
Price			
Current level: 3800.00			
2000. $2,000	10.7	3.2	42.0
$2,500	9.4	1.8	24.0
$3,000	8.4	0.9	11.4
$4,000	7.4	−0.2	−2.5
5000. $5,000	6.4	−1.1	−14.8
Paymt term (days)			
Current level: 36.00			
1. within 30 days	7.4	−0.1	−1.4
within 60 days	8.0	0.5	6.2
120. within 120 days	8.5	0.9	12.2
Financing avail			
Current level: 2.00			
1. None	6.9	−0.6	−8.4
2. End user	7.5	−0.0	−0.0
3. Inventory	7.5	−0.1	−0.8
4. Both	7.9	0.3	4.2
Warranty (months)			
Current level: 9.00			
6 months	7.4	−0.1	−1.7
12 months	8.1	0.6	7.4
36 months	8.7	1.1	14.9

(continued)

Exhibit 4 (continued)

Name	Share	Dif	%Dif
Support response			
Current level: 1.60			
1. Immediately	7.9	0.4	4.8
2. Same day	7.3	−0.2	−3.0
3. Next day	6.6	−0.9	−12.1
Install and maint			
Current level: 4.00			
1. Not available	6.2	−1.3	−17.5
2. Installation	6.7	−0.8	−11.0
3. Maintenance	7.2	−0.3	−4.4
4. Both	7.5	−0.0	−0.0
Hardware service			
Current level: 3.20			
1. Within 4 hours	8.9	1.4	18.2
2. Same day	8.4	0.8	11.2
3. Next day	7.7	0.2	2.2
4. Within a week	6.9	−0.6	−8.3
Training			
Current level: 3.00			
1. None	6.8	−0.7	−9.9
2. Instructor-base	7.5	−0.0	−0.4
3. Computer-based	7.5	−0.0	−0.0
Marketing support			
Current level: 2.00			
1. None	6.7	−0.8	−10.8
2. Lead generation	7.5	−0.0	−0.0
3. Co-op advertising	7.3	−0.3	−3.4
4. Lead gen/coop adv	8.0	0.5	6.0
Software compatability			
Current level: 2.00			
1. Only your sftwr	6.8	−0.7	−9.3
2. Some software	7.5	−0.0	−0.0
3. Wide range sftwr	8.2	0.7	9.2

(continued)

Exhibit 4 (continued)

Product: US mfr 4	Run Share: 7.5		
Name	Share	Dif	%Dif
Processor speed *Current level: 3.20*			
1. 50% slower	6.3	−1.2	−16.0
2. 25% slower	6.8	−0.7	−9.2
3. As fast	7.4	−0.1	−1.3
4. 25% faster	8.0	0.4	5.4
5. 50% faster	8.5	0.9	12.2

Emergent's level to the ones shown and simulates this new competitive environment. For example, consider "Computer Breadth," the second attribute which is "a measure of the breadth of supplier's computer line." It is measured on a continuous scale from 1 to 3 (see Exhibit 1) with 1 = single product, 2 = limited product, and 3 = broad range. Emergent's proposed strategy has a 1.4 level—which represents a level of more than one product but still fewer than necessary to reach "limited." In contrast, Alliance, Beta, and CPS all have pretty broad product lines at levels 2.8, 2.9, and 2.8 respectively (see Exhibit 2). The output of the Factor Level Sensitivity says that if Emergent changed from 1.4 to:

- A 1 rating, i.e., dropping to single product, its share would decrease by .2 share points to 7.3% share representing a 3.3% drop in Emergent volume, i.e., (7.5–7.3)/7.5 = 3.3%
- A 2 rating, i.e., expanding to reach "limited," yields an improvement from 7.5% to 7.9% share, up 5.2%.
- A 3 rating, i.e., expand to reach "broad," yields an improvement to 8.6% share, up 13.6%.

Other variables are interpreted in the same way. The Factor Sensitivity Report considers change in only one attribute at a time, i.e., takes all other attribute levels to be that specified in the "base case" scenario, i.e., that described in Exhibit 2.

Question 4.   Based on the Factor Level Sensitivity, what attributes are most important to consumers? Does the factor level sensitivity report give any insight into the segmentation of the marketplace?

Question 5.   What are the key leverage points for Emergent?

Question 6.   Emergent does not have the resources required to improve its product line breadth in the short term. Second, it believes its margins are just barely adequate now so it would not look too favorably on anything like a price cut unless it gave big return. Nevertheless, it would like to improve its market share position. Without any cost data, you can't get too precise on this but what general directions would you suggest Emergent pursue? What market share gain could they expect?

Question 7.   If Emergent follows your strategy and gains share, who would it hurt? Can you tell anything about this from either the perceptual map or the factor level sensitivity?

John Morton provided Emergent with the Strategic Industry Model to allow it to simulate any environment it wished. This allowed Emergent to examine the impact of simultaneously changing many variables. Results of Emergent's first run are in Exhibit 5.

Question 8.   How does this "hands-on" capability help Emergent? What insights do you get from Exhibit 5?

Question 9.   What other scenarios would you like to simulate?

Question 10.   For what types of products and situations do you see this type of analysis exemplified by the Strategic Industry Model most useful?

Exhibit 5. *Example of results of Emergent attribute level changes*

Report: Demand Share   **Sorted by:**   Order of Base Case
Title: Emergent changes; moves into the strategic group
Date: Friday 10/25/91 - 16:25:29

Run description

Customer selected

All segments included

Resulting number of customers: 225

Product market changes

Added products:

Deleted products:

Changed products:

Emergent

| Hardware service | From | 3.20 | To | 2.00 |
| Support response | From | 1.60 | To | 1.20 |

(continued)

Exhibit 5 (continued)

Warranty (months)	From	9.00	To	24.00	
Financing avail	From	2.00	To	4.00	
Time to market	From	−1.00	To	4.00	

Key

CUR RUN	Calculated Demand Share, Current Run
BASE	Base Case Demand Share Market Unchanged
DIF	Difference between RUN and BASE

Name	Cur Run	Base	Dif
Alliance	12.5	12.9	−0.4
Beta	10.8	11.1	−0.3
CPS	12.1	12.5	−0.4
DIS	10.1	10.4	−0.3
Emergent	10.3	7.5	2.8
Attwood	8.6	8.9	−0.3
Penucchini	7.8	8.0	−0.2
Stobart	9.3	9.6	−0.3
Cheong	4.6	4.7	−0.1
Kojima	6.9	7.1	−0.2
Clones	7.0	7.2	−0.2

PART 3

Formulating the Market Introduction Strategy

INTRODUCTION

Part 2 dealt with the question "should we invest the development dollars necessary to turn this idea into an operating product or service?" Those ideas receiving a "yes" vote at this stage can be further tested prior to actual market introduction. Consumers being able to see, touch, use, or consume the product/service can provide valuable data in making the go/no go decision on market introduction and also in determining the best supporting marketing mix for the product launch. Part 3 deals with this stage of the development and testing process.

Part 2's research procedures (concept testing, perceptual mapping, and conjoint analysis) are applicable to a broad variety of product types—ranging from lo-cal peanut butter to condominiums to lift trucks. The tools of Part 3, in contrast, are more particular to either consumer or industrial goods contexts. Thus, we begin with two notes to introduce the research procedures: "Researching and Monitoring Consumer Markets" and "Industrial Market Research: Beta Test Site Management."

"Researching and Monitoring Consumer Markets" describes two tools: pre-test market models and electronic monitoring using scanner systems. The pre-test methodology has been widely used since its inception in the 1970s. It structures a situation in which consumers indicate their interest in trying a new product, and after trial use their interest in a repeat purchase. A particular model of this type, ASSESSOR, is the primary research tool in the first case in Part 3, Johnson Wax: Enhance. Electronic monitoring began with the BehaviorScan system in the late 1970s and represents an effective mechanism for monitoring purchase activity at the household level. The General Mills Yoplait Yogurt case poses the problem of developing the most effective research program when both a pre-test model and a mini-market test are possibilities.

The major technologies for consumer goods do not carry over into the industrial sphere due to the nature of the typical purchase process. In industrial settings, the common interaction with potential customers prior to product launch is a beta test in which a customer uses a product which has passed laboratory tests in a real world setting. The "Industrial Market Research: Beta Test Site Management" note describes and sets out guidelines for effective beta tests. Based on an analysis of over 20 beta site programs, the note sets out the full range of purposes that a beta can serve. The Cumberland Metals case then presents the results from a two-site beta test as input to development of the introductory marketing plan.

Collectively, the materials of Part 3 provide a broad overview of the process of moving from a product to market launch. In some cases, the "big bet" is the marketing expense which has yet to be incurred at this stage. In those cases, testing is extensive and has input to a go/no go decision. In other cases, the "big bet" was the product development expense. Nevertheless, the procedures of this part play a crucial role in setting the final design and indicating the optimal marketing plan.

5 _NOTE_

Researching and Monitoring Consumer Markets

Robert J. Dolan

Once a concept becomes an actual product or service, a different set of research tools provide useful input to a go/no go decision on a full market introduction and/or the optimal supporting marketing mix. For example, a product use test places the product in cooperating consumers' homes and measures their reaction. Two major developments in consumer product research are: (i) purchase stimulation procedures for pre-market introduction testing; and (ii) electronic monitoring of consumer purchases by scanners in supermarkets.

Professor Robert J. Dolan prepared this note as a basis for class discussion. It is based in part on two earlier notes, Pre-Test Market Models (9-588-052) and the Marketing Information Industry (9-588-027).

The impetus to the development of purchase simulation test was the high cost of test marketing (about $2 million) coupled with the fact that 50% of products test marketed were diagnosed as "No Go's" for full market introduction. This indicated the need for a "finer screen" than product use tests to weed out failures prior to the test market stage. Efforts to produce a useful intermediate step between the use test and a test market began in the early 1970s. By the mid-1980s, there were over a dozen different models which simulated actual customer buying behavior and estimated sales or market share. (See Shocker and Hall, 1986 for details.) Hundreds of applications have established the predictive accuracy of these methods.

Electronic monitoring of households' purchases began in 1978 with Information Resources, Inc.'s introduction of BehaviorScan. BehaviorScan concentrated on several small self-contained trading areas. IRI supplied all supermarkets with scanning equipment for checkout counters in return for access to the data. IRI also recruited a panel of households who received scannable ID cards to be shown each time they made a purchase. In BehaviorScan markets, IRI was also able to control panelists' exposure to media ads and promotions. Electronic monitoring has grown from a few isolated markets to nationwide capability with the development of services by IRI and Nielsen, the largest market research firm in the country.

Effective utilization of these services can be key in sorting winners from losers, and providing diagnostic information to maximize new produce performance. This note does not attempt to provide details on each service available. Rather, we seek to develop an understanding of the general approaches and knowledge of the strengths and limitations of each. We begin with purchase simulation models and focus on the two leading types of models, BASES II and ASSESSOR. Then, we describe the services of IRI and Nielsen for electronic monitoring and set out their utility.

For many products, a simple "hierarchy-of-effects" model has proven a good description of consumers' purchase activity. This model posits that a purchase phenomenon has three stages.

Stage 1: Consumers become **aware** of the product through media advertising or a promotion

Stage 2: Given awareness, some are sufficiently interested in the new brand to make a **trial** purchase

Stage 3: Given the trial, some like the brand well enough to **repeat** purchase and devote some proportion of their future category purchases to the new brand.

Figure 1. *Simple hierarchy model and typical major influences*

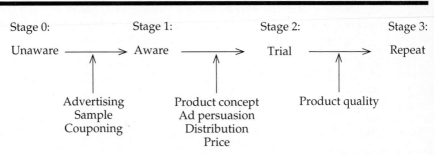

As shown in Fig. 1, different marketing factors influence consumer movement from one stage to the next.

This hierarchy structure disaggregates the big problem of predicting sales into three smaller problems. In the long run, sales come largely from regular users of a brand. The hierarchy framework takes:

Probability of being a regular user = Probability of being aware of product X
Probability of trail given aware X
Probability of regular use given trial

This awareness→trial→repeat is the common core of all nondurable goods models. (Similar type models, but with more complex purchase processes have recently been developed for consumer durables, e.g., automobiles in Hauser, Urban, and Roberts (1990).) While the models for nondurables share the core logic, estimation methods for the three key probabilities differ. One leading model, BASES II is based on survey data; another, ASSESSOR, is based on a simulation of a store setting.

BASES II

BASES II is part of a family of models developed by SAMI/Burke beginning in 1978. The BASES family accommodates testing from product ideas before they take physical form to ideas relating to products which have been on the market for some time. BASES' client test is both extensive and impressive including, e.g., Carnation, Colgate-Palmolive, Frito-Lay, Gillette, Nestlé, and Procter & Gamble. As of December 1986, BASES had been used to test 1,167 products and 2,424 concepts in the

U.S. market alone. BASES I is similar to a traditional concept test. The key difference is SAMI/Burke's extensive database of previous test results serving as valuable benchmarks to calibrate the concept scores.

The typical research process for BASES II is as follows:

Step 1: Shopping mall intercept interviews are done at four or more geographically dispersed cities; respondents are not screened for category usage since the intent is to provide a volume rather than market share estimate.

Step 2: Respondents are exposed to a concept and asked a standard set of questions, e.g., like/dislike, perceived value for money, purchase intention.

Step 3: Those expressing a positive purchase intention are given some of the product to use at home.

Step 4: After several weeks, users are called on the telephone to obtain "after-use" measures similar to the "before-use" measures obtained in Step 2.

SAMI/Burke has not published details of the BASES II estimating procedures but Fig. 2 shows the conceptual structure of the model.

The awareness → trial → repeat core runs down the center of the figure. Figure 2 depicts the role of SAMI/Burke's previous experience with BASES. On the right-hand side, there are three key influences.

1. Category Norms
2. Concept Tables
3. After-Use Tables

The category norms help in the estimation of the consumer awareness achieved by a given marketing plan. Second, the "concept tables" are used to convert the collected buying intentions data into a trial estimate. A SAMI/Burke brochure states ". . . BASES has developed an extensive database which includes the results of thousands of tests conducted in nearly every product category. BASES can apply this database to help put your forecasts in perspective." The after-use tables are used similarly to convert intentions to repeat rates. The collected data on (i) stated buying intentions; (ii) like/dislike scores; and (iii) perceived price/value are adjusted and combined with other factors to yield an estimated repeat rate. BASES II's heavy reliance on data from other similar product introductions to calibrate buying intentions data is a distinguishing characteristic. In principle, SAMI/Burke is relying on fundamental stable laws of the marketplace. Through extensive data collection and analysis, SAMI/Burke has evidently discovered some key regularities.

Figure 2. Bases II conceptual structure

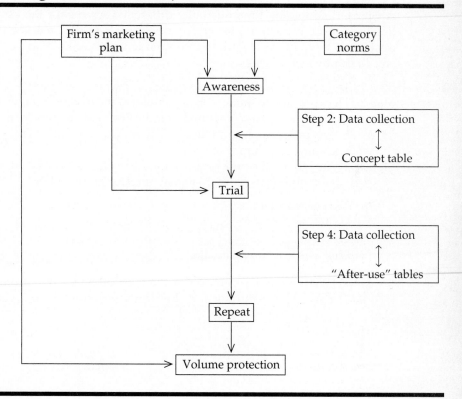

This use of data from other tests to aid in calibration is not universally hailed. NEWS, a similarly structured model developed by BBDO, also employs survey data but rejects other products' experience. Pringle, Wilson, and Brody (1982) state the NEWS philosophy as ". . . forecasts are based solely on input data derived specifically for the new brand under investigation . . . even a few waves of consumer research data collected for the new brand will lead to more insight and thus better new product decisions than will data collected on other brands . . . NEWS was designed to avoid projections based on aggregate new product data that may yield 'average' responses to marketplace stimuli."

ASSESSOR

ASSESSOR adopted a fundamentally different approach to the estimation task. It compresses in time and space the new product market introduction. In a typical test, a group of respondents is recruited and escorted to a nearby facility where:

Step 1: They are exposed to an advertisement for the new brand.

Step 2: They proceed to mock store setup where the new brand is available for sale as well as competing brands. Respondents receive a small amount of money and may purchase whatever brands they wish, keeping any money left over.

Step 3: Those buying the new product are called after a 2–3 week time period and offered a chance to repeat purchase the product.

In short, the sequence is:

Market share estimates can then be made based on the data from the trail and repeat opportunities and the firm's introductory marketing plan.

The model is:

The purchase opportunity in the simulated store measures the proportion of consumers who try under the conditions of forced awareness and product availability. This trial is downwardly adjusted based on management expectation of the awareness and distribution levels generated by the marketing plan. Any expected incremental trial from sampling is added to the trial figure to yield an estimate of T.

S, commonly referred to as the repeat rate, is more than the percentage of people who repeat when they are given the opportunity to do so over the phone in the post-use survey. More precisely, S is the "share or subsequent purchases" made by triers. Those who repeat on the first opportunity may switch to another brand the next time. Similarly, those who do not repurchase, in Step 3's phone interview perhaps would if given another opportunity later. Thus, S is computed based on: (i) the observed repurchase rate from Step 3; and (ii) some post-use preference data. Multiplying S times T gives the estimated market share.

ASSESSOR builds in a validity check by also estimating share on the basis of collected preference data. Before the simulated shopping trip and in the post-use telephone interview, respondents are asked to indicate their preferences for brands they know. They do this by allocating 11 points or "chips" between pairs of brands they are familiar with. For example, in the candy category, if one is familiar with Milky Way (MW), Three Musketeers (TM), Snickers (S), and Almond Joy (AJ), he or she would be asked to indicate relative preference for the six pairs: MW-TM, MW-S, MW-AJ, TM-S, TM-AJ, S-AJ dividing 11 points between the brands in each pair.

These data along with the trial-repeat observations collected through the trial and repeat purchase opportunities allow ASSESSOR to develop two distinct estimates of share. As Silk and Urban (1975) (developers of ASSESSOR) put it, ". . . agreement between the two market share predictions is not a built-in or guaranteed feature of these approaches and hence it is possible to make a meaningful check for convergence here. Finding that the two models do yield outputs that are in close agreement can serve to strengthen confidence in the prediction. In contrast, divergent forecasts trigger a search for the evaluation of possible sources of errors or bias that might account for discrepancy." (Details of the estimation procedure based on preference data are in Silk and Urban [1975].)

HOW WELL DO THEY WORK?

The above has set out the structure and inherent limitations of the models. A natural question is do these models, in fact, produce sales estimates which later "come true" in the real world?

This is not as simple a question as it might first seem. Between the time of the test and the real world experience, things can change, e.g., competitive offerings, consumer attitudes toward product attributes or toward spending money, or the firm's marketing plan for the product. Thus, a naive companion of the test estimate vs. real world may not be appropriate. Nonetheless, firms have attempted to accumulate data on the performance.

A 1986 SAMI/Burke brochure provides the following on BASES performance: ". . . we have established a validation database of over 200 cases. Based on our validation in the 1980s, 90% of our forecasts (sales volume, as well as trial and repeat rates) were within 20% of actual volume, and over half were within 10%."

Pringle, Wilson, and Brody (1982) report data on 22 applications of NEWS with a market share prediction and comparable market data later available. The error size ranged from −5.8 to +1.4 share points. The average "predictive error," defined as the absolute size of the difference between predicted and actual divided by actual was 18.5%.

ASSESSOR's developers report an extensive validation attempt covering 215 ASSESSOR studies (Urban and Katz [1983]). Predicted market shares were known and actual performance in a real test market was solicited from clients via a mail questionnaire. Eighty-one questionnaires were returned yielding 44 cases where test market results were available. The data revealed a tendency to overestimate share. The average test market share was 7.16 share points, with a mean difference from actual of .61, and mean absolute difference of 1.54. Thus the "predictive error" is $1.54/7.16 = 21.5\%$. These figures apply to "unadjusted data." In a number of cases, it was known that the awareness and distribution levels projected by management and used in deriving the ASSESSOR estimate were not achieved. Adjusting the estimates to reflect this reduced the mean difference to −0.1, the mean absolute difference to .83, and associated error "predictive error" percentage to 11.59%.

Diagnostic capability is an important complement to predictive ability. Because of the trial-repeat structure of each model, a low market share prediction can be traced to either low trial, low repeat, or both helping the marketer pinpoint the problem areas of the marketing plan. Secondly, data are collected to consumer's perceptions of the brand, advertising copy, etc., so the **why** behind the trial and repeat can be understood.

The predictive and diagnostic abilities of these models, their timeliness, and relatively low cost have made models of this type a staple in the marketing research tool list of most leading package goods companies. Recently, efforts have begun to extend these methods to consumer durable and industrial goods. For example, Hauser, Urban, and Roberts (1990) describe work at General Motors to forecast automobile model sales prior to launch. This work demonstrates both the opportunity and challenges in modeling more complex consumer decision making situations.

The second part of this note considers the monitoring of product performance when it has been introduced to the market in either a test market or rollout situation.

ELECTRONIC MONITORING

When the product is first on the market—either in a test market or roll-out situation—the manager needs timely data on sales performance, purchase profiles, and purchaser motivators. As recently as 1980, it was impossible to obtain the desired data in a timely manner. Sales performance was tracked by warehouse withdrawals, manual field audits, and some consumer panels. Each had major drawbacks. Brand managers' needs, technological advances in computers and telecommunications, and several firms' heavy investment in developing data collection systems have radically changed the situation.

The two major data providers are A.C. Nielsen (founded in 1923, now a division of Dun and Bradstreet) and Information Resources, Inc. Each now presents itself as a "single-source provider" for all data which a client might need. Their paths to the current status were quite different however. Nielsen started as a manual retail store audit service while IRI had its roots in BehaviorScan, an electronic test market service.

As a manual audit operation, Nielsen maintained a large field staff which visited 1,300 food outlets on a bi-monthly basis. During a store visit, a rep noted the current inventory, shipments received since the last audit, and shelf price items. The major problem with this system was the time lag from actual purchase to reporting to a client. The two-month reporting interval plus six-week lag due to data processing made the data 10 weeks old, on average, as it first became available to the client.

Nielsen's investment in scanners and electronic monitoring led to the SCANTRACK system which monitors 3,000 stores in 50 major metropolitan markets on a weekly basis. Forty-three of the 50 largest consumer packaged goods firms in the United States use SCANTRACK.

To provide data on who is buying, Nielsen developed the companion SCANTRACK National Electronic Panel with over 15,000 households. Each household has a hand-held scanning device at home which is to be scanned across the UPC codes on all items purchased. Data are electronically transmitted to Nielsen. To provide a test market capability, Nielsen has also developed extensive panels on a local level.

Nielsen also provides SCANFACT software to help clients make decisions utilizing SCANTRACK information. It integrates information from five databases: (1) store sales data; (2) store environmental data (e.g., display, ads, prices); (3) coupon distribution and redemption; (4) TV commercial viewing; and (5) household purchasing response. SCAN-FACT includes a variety of modules, e.g., SCANPRO to assess promotional effectiveness and AD PRO for advertising effectiveness. Nielsen provides retailers with Spaceman shelf management software to analyze scanner data to improve space utilization. System software cost can range between $500 and $10,000 depending on the information to be processed; customization is also possible. System education for both manufacturers and retail clients is available at training centers.

IRI, Nielsen's major competitor in this market, was founded in 1978 primarily as a test marketing company. By 1983, it was being referred to as "The New Magician of Market Research" as well as being included in *Inc.* magazine's list of fastest growing public companies.

IRI and, in particular, its product, BehaviorScan, grew out of the questions:

1. Is there a way to use in-store scanners to record a household's purchasing unobtrusively to overcome both the accuracy and participation problems of panels in which consumers had to record their purchases manually?
2. Is there a way to create custom panels for each client, i.e., let the client specify what characteristics Panel A and B should match on and then sort households into one panel or the other for that particular client's tests?

BehaviorScan solved these problems by: (i) equipping all grocery stores in a market with scanners (at a cost of about $2 million per market in its first small markets) and minicomputers to store the data; (ii) giving all panelists a scannable ID card to show when making purchases; (iii) developing an electronic device which allowed it to cut in test advertisement over cable TV lines to individual households as desired. Through this system, IRI is able to send, for example, two ads to the Smith household on a given evening and then monitor if the Smiths buy the advertised product over the next week.

Because of the relatively unobtrusive data collection, BehaviorScan achieved 70% panel participation rates and attracted the major consumer packaged goods firm as clients. Clients bought the exclusive right to do experiments in a category for a two year period. By 1984, BehaviorScan had expanded from two markets to eight. BehaviorScan represented new levels in timeliness and accuracy of data at the individual household level. By 1984, IRI revenues were $35.8 million, $27.6 million of which was from selling BehaviorScan services.

IRI's other product was the *Marketing Fact Book* which reported activity on all items scanned. A firm need not be doing experiments on new products to purchase the *Fact Book* with its quarterly reports. The *Fact Book* reported share of category, percent of households purchasing, average price paid, percentage volume associated with any trade deal, manufacturer coupon, etc. Aside from its limited geographic scope, it was similar to the tracking information provided by Nielsen. While IRI was widely acclaimed as the most innovative market research company in years, there were two major limitations in 1984. First, IRI was commonly held to be much better at data collection than at data analysis, i.e., the transformation of data to answers to management questions. The 1985 acquisition of Management Decision Systems, a leading company in marketing software and services for marketing analysis modeling addressed this. IRI's chairman and founder said, "IRI is the pioneer in using electronic data—bringing critical marketing information quickly into the hands of those who need it. But marketers don't want just raw data. They want answers to cause-and-effect marketing questions. . . . The merger of IRI and MDS will give marketers what they've always wanted—fingertip access to data only one day old and the powerful analytical tools to turn those data into answers." IRI's second limitation was that when it tried to sell *Marketing Fact Book*, the lack of national projectability of the BehaviorScan markets became a significant issue. Initial efforts to resolve this took the form of adding two large test cities in 1986, and the development of 12 metropolitan area sampling pods—two each in New York City, Los Angeles, and Chicago and one each in the next six largest metropolitan areas. These efforts to move to a **national** tracking service culminated in the InfoScan service introduced in July 1986, with billing in company brochures as "One single source database combining total store sales, with individual household purchase information."

An outgrowth of the *Marketing Fact Book*, InfoScan put together three kinds of information in one integrated package: (i) household level purchase data; (ii) national market information; and (iii) data such as coupons, price changes, spending, and store displays. Information was collected on a weekly basis and delivered to the client every four weeks in an integrated fashion. (Some limited reports were available 8–10 days after the week's close with "FlashScan" service.) With InfoScan, IRI moved from a primarily test market company with database sidelights to full product line company.

InfoScan consisted of 2,700 participating supermarkets in 66 local markets with data from an aggregate panel of 60,000 households. IRI has leveraged InfoScan to expand its service offerings. In an alliance announced in late 1990 with Burke, customers can be offered InfoScan information as an input to BASES.

Like Nielsen, IRI also provides analysis software variety of application modules. These include Data Server—the communication software designed to get the information in front of the manager, SalesPartner—a sales management "expert" system designed for use by both manufacturers and retailers, and CoverStory—an easy to use package that creates summary reports. Also, similar to Nielsen's Spaceman, IRI's Apollo shelf management software was sold to retailers. Overall, the decision support software portion of IRI's business was expected to become a greater part of the company's business.

Adding to the technological expertise provided by Management Decision Systems, IRI acquired Industry Systems Development, Inc. in 1988 and Javelin Software Corp. in 1989.

These technological and modeling developments have pushed consumer marketing into a new age. The manager must understand the power available in the extensive market data, have command of the process of converting the raw data into useful information, and be able to integrate that information with other factors bearing on the marketing decisions.

REFERENCES

Hauser, J., G. Urban, and J. Roberts, "Prelaunch Forecasting of Automobiles," *Management Science* (April 1990), pp. 401–420.

Pringle, L. G., R. D. Wilson, and E. I. Brody, "NEWS: A Decision-Oriented Model for New Product Analysis and Forecasting," *Management Science*, (Winter 1982),Vol. 1, No. 1, pp. 1–30.

Shocker, A. D., and W. G. Hall, "Pretest Market Models: A Critical Evaluation," *Journal of Product Innovation Management* (1986), 3, pp. 86–107.

Silk, A. J., and G. L. Urban, "Pretest Market Evaluation of New Packaged Goods: A Model and Measurement Methodology," *Journal of Marketing Research* (May 1978), pp. 171–191.

Urban, G. L., and G. M. Katz, "Pretest Market Models: Validation and Managerial Implications," *Journal of Marketing Research* (August 1983), pp. 221–234.

6 _NOTE_

Industrial Market Research:
Beta Test Site Management

Robert J. Dolan

INTRODUCTION

The new product development process for a 50 cent candy bar and that for
a $500,000 piece of computer hardware are the same—or so some text-
books say. In each situation, the manufacturer is advised to proceed
through a number of sequential steps: Idea Generation→Initial
Screening→Concept Testing→Product Use Testing→Market Testing→
Introduction. In practice, however, the processes are quite different.
Somewhat ironically, the process for the candy bar entry would likely fol-

Professor Robert J. Dolan prepared this note as the basis for class discussion.

Copyright © 1991 by the President and Fellows of Harvard College. Harvard Business
School case 592-010.

low the suggested model more closely and have a more scientific, rigorous appearance.[1]

This is because candy bar buyers:

- are numerous and easy-to-identify
- all use the candy bar for the same basic purpose
- follow a short decision making process in purchasing
- likely decide whether or not to buy a bar on their own
- can easily articulate whether they like the bar or not after use
- need only a short time to use up the bar and become a candidate for repeat purchase

In contrast, possible adopters of the $500,000 computer system may be few in number and hard-to-find, vary in the intended application of the system, have a decision-making process characterized by broad participation by individuals across the company and long gestation time, and take a long time in deciding how well the product fits their needs.

These contrasts in buyer behavior cause significant differences in the effective implementation of the steps of the development process. The product use and market test phases for a candy bar would commonly involve large samples, rigorous statistical analysis and carefully designed market experiments. The same phases for computers will usually find a handful of "respondents"—not selected with statistical analysis in mind. This handful is the vendor's "Beta Test"[2] sites.

Cooper's (1979) survey shows that money invested in the Beta Test phase of the new product development process is one of the key differentiators between industrial product successes and failures. The frequent use of beta programs suggests their importance. However, there are no well-articulated guidelines for management of such tests. In practice, beta site selection and management seem *ad hoc* at many firms—driven by convenience rather than recognition of the trade-offs involved. This lack of effective management leads Elmer (1989) to refer to beta site testing as "an informal method that's really not research" and to suggest prototype-testing research as a way to avoid the "significant potential marketing hazards" of beta testing.

The purpose of this note is to set out guidelines for maximizing the value of a beta test program. We begin by identifying the variety of relationships between vendors and sites. Based on an analysis of over 20

---

[1]See, for example, a description of the likely processes to be followed in "Concept Testing" (HBS case No. 590-063) and "Note on Pre-Test Markets" (HBS case No. 588-052).

[2]Alpha Testing refers to the prior usage of in-house product testing.

beta test programs, we then set out the major benefits and costs to both vendors and test sites. Having established potential costs and benefits, we then provide management guidelines for effective practice. The small sample sizes inherent in beta test programs and the multiplicity of purposes possibly served preclude reducing beta site management to a simple formula. However, specific prescriptions of value can be made.

Briefly stated, our guidance on effective beta management is this:

1. Carefully define the purpose of the program. In the second section, we set out and illustrate five major purposes of Beta Testing. Clarity in purpose aids in determining the number of sites required, the desired characteristics of sites, the length of the test, and data collection methods.
2. Design the testing program to guard against the significant threats to validity of a program. Central here is that beta sites are usually few in number and selected purposively by the firm rather than randomly. Section 3 provides the major issues to be considered in this.
3. Understand and manage the sites' motivation for participating in the test. This can help in recruiting sites and designing the program to be implemented. This is the subject of Section 4.

Section 5 provides a summary and conclusions.

BETA TEST PURPOSES

By definition, a beta test is "a real world test of a system after it has passed all its laboratory tests" (Sweetland [1988]). Implicit in this definition is the fact that this test precedes the general availability of the product. An example of a basic function check of a system is Accu-Chek's testing of its electronic shelf pricing system for grocery stores (Discount Merchandising, 1989). The 90-day test provided Accu-Chek:

1. Validation of the basic concept of 1/2 inch electronic labels changed by handheld computers replacing manual systems.
2. Diagnostic information on specific aspects of the program.
   Specifically, Accu-Chek obtained information pertaining to four constituent groups:
   (i) Its *own field force* found that the labels were not easily installed; (ii) the size and position of the labels were not appealing to *consumers*; (iii) *shelf-stockers* found the labels hung over too far making item placement difficult; and (iv) *store management's* experience with the test system raised accuracy and security concerns which had to be overcome before large scale adoption would be achieved.

Figure A shows this function and diagnostic check at the center of a beta site purpose diagram. While this purpose is at the heart of most test programs, important supplementary purposes are also served as indicated. As shown, the three major purposes served are:

1. **Product**
   - Basic Function Check
   - Refinement of Core Product Design
   - Added Features Desired in Core Product
2. **Augmented Product Design**
   A. Support Features
      - Training Required
      - Documentation Adequacy
      - Other Features

Figure A. *Beta test purposes*

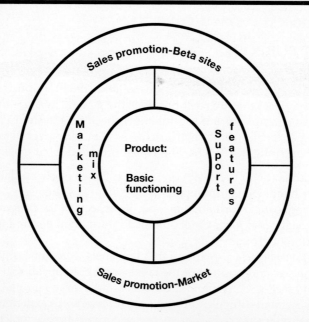

    B. Marketing Mix to Support Product Introduction, esp.
- Positioning
- Pricing

3. Sales Promotion
    A. To Beta Sites
- Develop Account Relationship
- Trial Path to Purchase

    B. To General Market
- Publicity/Credibility from Passing Test
- Reference Accounts/Demo Sites
- Equivalent to Pre-Announcement

In addition to the data on the core product, a beta program can test and refine augmentation of the core. For example, in the software industry the core product becomes commodity-like after a short time and hence support programs are key. For example, Lotus' agreements on support, connectivity, communication between vendor and user were arrived at after "extensive beta testing of various arrangements" (Bender [1986]).

Beta programs can also provide input to determining the appropriate marketing mix to support the product. Especially useful is testing to permit the calculation of the economic-value-to-the-customer, a key input to product pricing. (See Forbis and Mehta [1981] for details.) For example, the Cumberland Metals Industries case (1980) reports the field testing of a new type of pile driver pads. Via collection of data on pile driving efficiency in the two site-test, the company was able to calculate precisely the value of the pads to the customer. This would be the upper-bound on what any individual would pay. Systematic analysis of the variance in the value can be the key to market segmentation, product positioning, and target market selection issues.

Finally, the outer ring of Fig. A shows beta's use as a sales promotion device—to beta sites themselves and the market more generally. Xerox recently used 26 sites as betas for its $220,000 Docutech Production Publisher (Feder [1990]). While Xerox's usual practice was to beta at five or six sites, the quintupling of the number of sites was due to the fact that "the company used the new product as a tool for building closer relationships with key customers." These closer relationships achieved through beta testing can result in sales as effectively as the beta test is a trial run for the test site. For example, the first four U.S. based purchasers of Elran Technologies' ACE artificial intelligence software—AT&T, Pennwalt, General Dynamics, and Unisys—were all beta sites originally (Stein [1989]).

Betas can have a market impact for the system more generally as a successful beta program reduces the uncertainty about the product in the eyes of potential adopters. For example, Data Communications (1987) labelled AT&T the "League Leader" as it "moved to nail down a significant piece of business by passing initial beta tests. . . at General Electric Corp." Beta test results are news in the high technology area and can generate invaluable publicity as in a *Computerworld* article headlined "First Beta Test User Lauds Kontact for 'Smarts'." The first paragraph of the article read: "The first beta test use of Mitel Corp's $4000 executive workstation said it has more 'smarts' than the Northern Telecom, Inc. Displayphone and is more 'truly' an executive workstation than the more expensive Xerox Corp. 8010 Star" (Hoard [1983]).

Beta test sites can be useful to the general market as reference accounts or demo sites for potential adopters. For example, Feredata sold their data base machine to National Resource Management, an oil and gas company in Dallas, based on a demo at Wells Fargo Bank. NRM Management commented "We are impressed that Feredata took us to see the system at Wells Fargo. They [the bank] have different applications but the same type of thing, high level inquiry" (Myers [1985]). The Apparel Technology Center was set up in Raleigh, N.C. to act as a Beta Test site for advanced apparel technology and to document performance of systems for reference by member companies (Fortress [1988]). Easingwood and Beard (1989) suggest that using a prestigious firm as a beta is a good way to "legitimize" a product, which is important for very new/complex products.

Beta testing with Morgan Guaranty and Manufacturers Hanover has led to the establishment of Light Signatures as the standard of the industry in stock certificate fraud detection (Crane [1988]). Light Signatures' system takes a fiber fingerprint of a stock certificate. Testing with Morgan and Manufacturers (and improving the system based on that test) facilitated obtaining the commitment of 25 major security processors, getting banknote companies to design their documents in a way compatible with the system, and gaining the endorsement of the Securities Transfer Association.

Finally, Rabino and Moore (1989) position beta programs not only as serving the above purposes, but also note their signaling properties, i.e., they "serve the important function of alerting selected customers to an imminent product launch." Later, this "plays a critical role in enhancing product awareness as information about technical aspects begins to leak out and rumors are generated by the press."

In summary, beta site testing serves a multiplicity of purposes, not just as a "checking-out" of the functioning of the product as many propose. It is important, however, to give explicit priority to the desired purposes. The purpose to be served determines the type of site desired (e.g., "representative" for purpose 1, "large account" for purpose 3a, and "prestigious" for purpose 3b), number of sites (e.g. "few" for purpose 1's basic function check, "many" for purpose 2b (due to segmentation) and for purpose 3), the data collected from the site, and the agreement about confidentiality of results. Since different purposes lead to vastly different optimal designs, it is crucial to have these set prior to the start of the test.

THREATS TO TEST VALUE

There are four major issues to consider in designing a valid test:

1. Selecting the Proper Sites
2. Timing the Test at the Right Stage of the Product Development Cycle
3. Managing Account Relationships
4. Managing the Information Flow from the Sites

Due to the cost of managing a beta site, it is typical that few are chosen. The danger in using a small sample is well-illustrated by Jaben's [1987] discussion of banks as beta sites, "One software development company, for example, chose only one beta site to test a new product. To please that bank, the developer made several changes. The only problem was, that particular bank was not representative of the industry, and the product became so customized that it could not be marketed to other financial institutions."

While most firms do protect against this type of situation by using more than one site, it is crucial in segmented markets to understand (through other research) the variation in customers' requirements and evaluation criteria. Beta sites should be representative of the product's key target markets and be firms which will push the product to its useful limit in the test.

The second major issue is properly trading off the issues involved in timing of the beta test. One argument is to push the test toward the early stages of the new product development process where the results of the test are most easily incorporated into the design of the product. On the other hand, the argument is not to jeopardize an account relationship by sending out a product with lots of "bugs" in it as a beta. The need to make this decision reinforces the major point of the last section, i.e., be explicit about the goals of the beta test. When Westinghouse was offered a chance to beta IBM's 3090 scientific processing capability, its computer center director assessed the likely impact of a Westinghouse test on product design to be "about zero" (Stamps [1986]). IBM was testing late in the process, apparently after much in-house testing, and the design was reasonably fixed. On the other hand, Jenkins [1988] reports that "performance issues they discovered in beta test" led to delays in Lotus shipping Release 3.0 of 1-2-3. One software industry consultant lays some of the blame for "vaporware" on the lateness of actual customer contact in the development process.

Third, there are account relationship issues not directly related to product performance. In the course of a beta test, a customer relationship may be built or it may be destroyed. The vendor has information needs which the tester can find intrusive. For example, if the vendor is using the beta for the purpose of doing an economic-value-to-the-customer calculation, the vendor must understand the economics of the tester's business to translate product performance into dollar returns. Similarly, assessing product performance may require more than unobtrusive measures, e.g. it may involve survey work with a wide variety of people within the tester's organization.

Account relationship considerations extend to non-sites as well. Frequently (for reasons to be detailed in the next section), potential testers view being a beta site as a great advantage. Hence, not being considered or selected can upset potential customers.

Finally, one must manage the information flow from a beta site. Non-disclosure agreements have grown increasingly difficult to work out and thus general publicity and information to competitors can flow from beta sites. For example, the headline on *Computerworld*'s (Korzeniowski [1984]) article on CIGNA's beta testing of Lotus' Symphony was "Symphony gets mixed reviews from beta test site" and included CIGNA's judgment that "it is difficult to master, does not easily integrate data and lacks the versatility of stand-alone packages." Similarly, the *Computerworld* article (Hoard [1983]) on Chase Manhattan "the first U.S. beta test site to go public with its Wangnet experience" had Chase's vice president of telecommunications strategy describing Wang as having been pushed "into a future for which it was not entirely prepared," noting "there have been a series of delays. . . . In the overall, Wang never even could have made the original dates, and "Wang has a lot of work to do with its operating system." Whatever Wang learned from the test, one has to wonder how it could be enough to net out positively over this kind of publicity.

While non-disclosure agreements have historically functioned reasonably well in non-technology laden environments, now the number of interconnects with a multiplicity of vendors makes this unworkable generally. Consequently, one must be aware that the fact that one is testing and the general nature of the results of those tests are not secret for long.

THE TEST SITE INTERESTS

An effective beta test requires close cooperation from the test sites. Gaining this participation and cooperation requires understanding a site's motive for being part of a test. Firms consider and sometimes even compete to be part of a beta test program in order to:

1. get experience with newest technology ahead of competitors.
2. have the opportunity to influence product design to yield a product which better fits the firm's particular needs.
3. have the added attention of vendor personnel in learning how to use the new technology.
4. develop a relationship with the vendor in anticipation of preferential treatment such as price breaks.
5. enhance their reputation as a pioneer, on the forefront of technology.

The most common reason to seek experience as a beta site is to be first with new technology. The University of Pennsylvania Library was a beta site for a do-it-yourself online search system from Telebase Systems (Fayen [1988]) because previous experience with similar systems indicated a latent constituent need which could be satisfied with an upgraded system. Gillette approached Digital Equipment to become a beta site for an office automation and communications software package. Gillette's director of MIS commented:

> *We begged them [to allow Gillette to be a beta site.] They had a system that no one else had that solved our particular need at the time" (Alper [1986]). Alper also reports General Electric approaching Coefficient Systems to beta their product. In this situation, General Electric did achieve the second benefit noted above as it explained its later adoption of the Coefficient Systems' product by saying: "We had tested their software. . . . As a matter of fact, they took most of the suggestions we gave them and incorporated them into the next version of the product."*

It is clear from these first two benefits sought by test sites that vendor and test site interests do not always perfectly align themselves with one another. A site may wish a long test period to keep the product from general availability to competitors. More importantly, though, the sites do want customization. This places a heavy burden on the vendor to make sure that these benefits are widely sought by the market.

Important secondary benefits #3, 4, 5 provide added impetus. Stamps (1986) reports that some firms try to develop a reputation as a beta tester in order to attract the top technical personnel in the computer industry.

Understanding these inducements is necessary if the firm is to overcome the perceived barriers to being a test site. The President of Remington Shavers and Knives is not atypical in his view: "I don't like being a beta site . . ." *(Chain Store Age Executive, 1990).*

The most common concerns are:

1. the benefits to the test site are all uncertain. The product may never come to market or the test may reveal that it is not very well suited to the purpose of the tester.
2. if the function being performed by the beta system is a critical one for the tester's operation, a parallel system may have to be run because the beta system cannot be relied upon to do the job with the required accuracy.
3. the participation does involve a time commitment in learning how to use the system and provide the desired information to the vendor.

Explicit awareness of these potential barriers and attractions to being part of a beta program is very useful in terms of constructing a test so that the desired type of site is willing to be part of the program.

SUMMARY

Beta tests are a staple of industrial new product development. Their effective execution can be crucial to the proper design and ultimate market success of product. This note has set out explicitly the vendor and test site perspectives on beta programs. The purpose of the test—which can vary markedly from one situation to the next—drives the optimal program design and thus must be set clearly. The incentives presented by the vendor yield certain participation and cooperation levels from potential sites programs. The relationship of the elements is as follows:

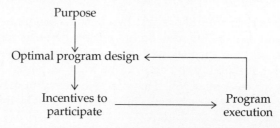

Many beta programs yield substantially less benefit (and in some cases have a negative net impact) to vendors than could be obtained. This note argues for more systematic setting of priorities on purposes, guarding against threats to validity and better understanding of test site motivations as a path to greater contribution from this stage of the new product development process.

REFERENCES

Alper, A., "Do Benchmarks Measure Up?" *Computerworld* (June 8, 1987), pp. 57, 64–65.

Alper, A., "Beta Sites: Pioneer Users Take Risks to Grab Technical Edge," *Computerworld* (August 25, 1986), pp. 1, 15.

Bender, E., "Software Hits, Lower Profits," *Computerworld* (May 12, 1986), pp. 35, 44.

Cooper, R. G., "Identifying Industrial New Product Success: Project Newprod," *Industrial Marketing Management* (1979), Vol. 8, pp. 124–135.

Crane, T. C., "Shedding Light on Certificate Fraud," *ABA Banking Journal* (May 1988), pp. 22, 25.

Cumberland Metal Industries (Boston, Mass.: Harvard Business School Case Services, 9-580-104, 1980).

Easingwood, C., and C. Beard, "High Technology Launch Strategies in the U.K.," *Industrial Marketing Management* (1989), Vol. 18, pp. 125–138.

Elmer, J. B., "Software Developers Can Benefit from Prototype-testing Research," *Marketing News* (January 1989), pp. 5, 6.

Fayen, E. G., "The Answer Machine and Direct Connect: Do-It-Yourself Searching in Libraries," *Online* (September 1988), pp. 13–16, 19–21.

Feder, B. J., "A Copier That Does a Lot More," *The New York Times* (October 3, 1990), pp. 1, D8.

Forbis, J.L., and N.T. Mehta, "Value Based Strategies for Industrial Products," *Business Horizons* (May–June 1981), pp. 32–42.

Fortess, F., "Squaring Off with the Competition," *Bobbin* (May 1988), pp. 104–106, 108, 110.

Hoard, B., ". . . But Beta Test Site Encounters Rough Seas," *Computerworld* (May 16, 1983), p. 7.

Hoard, B., "First Beta Test User Lauds Kontact for 'Smarts'," *Computerworld* (January 24, 1983), p. 13.

Jaben, J., "Banks as Beta Sites," *United States Banker* (December 1987), pp. 31, 33–34.

Jenkins, A., "Long Overdue—The Reasons Behind Vaporware," *Computerworld* (October 5, 1988), pp. 11–13.

Korzeniowski, P., "Symphony Gets Mixed Reviews from Beta Test Site," *Computerworld* (August 13, 1984), p. 6.

Myers, E., "Database Machines Take Off," *Datamation* (May 15, 1985), pp. 53–54, 58, 63.

"POS Flexibility Keep Remington Sharp," *Chain Store Age Executive* (July 1990), pp. 49–50.

Rabino, S., and T. E. Moore, "Managing New-Product Announcements in the Computer Industry," *Industrial Marketing Management* (1989), Vol. 18, pp. 35–43.

Stamps, D., "Beta Site Politics," *Datamation* (April 1, 1986), pp. 62–63, 66, 70.

Stein, J., "An Author's ACE in the Hole?" *Computerworld* (June 5, 1989), p. 104.

Sweetland, J. G., "Beta Tests and End-User Surveys: Are They Valid?" *Database* (February 1988), pp. 27–32.

"Technology Hits Shelf Pricing," *Discount Merchandising* (September 1989), pp. 72–74.

"Timeplex's Link/100 Draws Mixed Industry Response," *Data Communications* (August 1987), pp. 85, 86, 88, 90.

7 CASE

Johnson Wax: Enhance (A)

Darral G. Clarke

INSTANT HAIR CONDITIONER

In April 1979, John Sherman, product development manager for S. C. Johnson & Company, was facing a decision on the future of Enhance, a new instant hair conditioner. Designed as a companion product to Agree, the company's first hair-care product, development of Enhance had been under way for about a year and a half.

During the development process, Enhance had been tested against the leading existing products through blind comparisons and had

This case was prepared by Associate Professor Darral G. Clarke as the basis for class discussion rather than to illustrate either effective or ineffective handling of an administrative situation. This revision is by Professor Robert J. Dolan.

undergone a pre-test-market testing procedure called ASSESSOR. The results of these tests would need to play a significant role in Sherman's recommendations, because previous experience had convinced top management that such research was valuable. In fact, the company had performed a number of ASSESSOR or similar analyses in the past, and top management had on occasion seemed anxious to skip the test market and push for introduction when the ASSESSOR results were favorable.

John Sherman's task was to recommend the next steps for Enhance. While his experience and intuitive judgment would be valued, he knew the managerial climate at S. C. Johnson would require marketing research substantiation for his recommendations.

S. C. JOHNSON & COMPANY

S. C. Johnson & Company, headquartered in Racine, Wisconsin, was founded in 1886 as a manufacturer of parquet flooring. It was incorporated as S. C. Johnson & Son, Inc. and was familiarly known throughout the world as "Johnson Wax." A privately held corporation, Johnson Wax did not publicly report sales or earnings. Still, it was recognized as one of the world's leading manufacturers of products for home, auto and personal care, for commercial maintenance and industrial markets, and for outdoor recreation and leisure-time activities. Johnson Wax and its subsidiaries employed more than 13,000 people worldwide.

The buildings that served as international headquarters had been designed by Frank Lloyd Wright. They had won numerous architectural awards, and were listed in the National Register of Historic Places. U.S. manufacturing operations were conducted at the company's Waxdale, Wisconsin manufacturing plant, about eight miles west of Racine. This plant encompassed more than 1.9 million square feet of floor space and was one of the largest and most modern facilities of its kind in the world.

Johnson Wax maintained sales offices and sales and distribution centers in 20 major U.S. metropolitan areas.

Johnson Wax Associates, Inc. (JWA) was a group of nine associated companies that manufactured and marketed products for leisure-time activities and outdoor recreation. JWA products were distributed nationally and overseas to wholesalers and retailers through a system of manufacturers' representatives and factory salesmen.

The first Johnson Wax overseas subsidiary was established in England, in 1914. In 1979, Johnson Wax had subsidiaries in 45 countries.

The Johnson Wax consumer product line consisted of some of the best-known brands in household, automobile and personal-care products: Brite, Future, Glo-Coat, and Klear floor waxes; Jubilee and Pledge furniture polish, Rain Barrel Fabric Softener, Shout Stain Remover, Glory Carpet Cleaner, Glade Air Freshener, J-Wax auto care products, Raid insecticide, and Off insect repellent.

The Johnson Wax Innochem Division manufactured and distributed a complete line of heavy-duty polishes, cleaners, insecticides and disinfectants for use by commercial and institutional customers and a specialty line of chemicals.

The U.S. consumer products were distributed to supermarkets and drug, discount, and variety outlets through the company's own national sales force. Innochem commercial products distribution was handled through a separate sales force and through a network of more than 400 distributors nationally. Warehouse and distribution facilities were shared by the Innochem and Consumer Products Divisions.

NEW-PRODUCT DEVELOPMENT AT JOHNSON WAX

Development of these numerous product lines over the years had given Johnson Wax considerable experience in new-product evaluation and introduction. New product ideas came from laboratory research, marketing research, and customer contact. The product development process at Johnson Wax was fairly standard: ideas went through various commercial feasibility studies, performance tests against competitive products, and test markets before national introduction or rollout.

In recent years developing a new consumer product had become so expensive that Johnson Wax, like other manufacturers, had sought ways to reduce the cost. One solution was the pre-test-market test. One source[1] estimated the expected benefit from a $50,000 pretest to be in excess of $1 million. Before the Enhance pretest, Johnson Wax had performed many such pretests, most of them ASSESSORS.

---

[1]Glen L. Urban and John R. Hauser, *Design and Marketing of New Products* (Englewood Cliffs, NJ: Prentice-Hall, Inc., 1980), pp. 52–59. The cost of a 9-month, two-market test market was estimated at about $1MM. The expected savings of ASSESSOR, although also $1MM, are computed from a Bayesian analysis involving: 1) costs of ASSESSOR, test markets, and national introduction; 2) probabilities of success at various stages of the new-product introduction process.

THE HAIR CONDITIONING MARKET

During the 1970s, both the variety and the number of hair-care products and brands had increased drastically. Shampoos to combat dandruff were introduced; others were custom-formulated for use on dry, normal, or oily hair. During the same period, new products were introduced that would "condition" hair as well as clean it. According to one manufacturer:

> *A good creme rinse conditioner can help combat many hair problems. Hair can be easily damaged when it is combed following a shampoo, since hair is weakest when wet. Washing and towel-drying hair tend to tangle it, making it susceptible to breakage during combing. A creme rinse conditioner helps prevent this type of damage because it helps prevent tangles and makes for easy wet-combing. Creme rinse and conditioners also make hair feel softer; add to its bounce, shine, and body; and help prevent the buildup of static electricity that causes hair to be "flyaway."*

There were two types of hair conditioners:

- *Instant conditioners*, which were usually left on the hair for one to five minutes before being rinsed off.
- *Therapeutic conditioners*, which generally remained on the hair from five to twenty minutes before rinsing.

The term "creme rinse" was still used occasionally for conditioners that stressed easier combing and manageability. Gradually, the term was being replaced by "instant conditioner." Hair conditioner sales had grown dramatically during the 1970s, spurred by new-product introductions and increased use, especially among young women.

The major instant hair conditioner brands and their market shares in 1978 were Johnson's Agree (15.2%), Wella Balsam (4.7%), Clairol Condition (9.9%), Flex (13.4%), Tame (5.4%), and Sassoon.

Manufacturers' sales were as follows:

Manufacturers' sales ($ millions)		
Year	Total conditioner	Instant conditioner
1975	$132	$116
1976	160	141
1977	200	176
1978	230	202

Instant conditioners were sold in a variety of packages, but generally in either clear or opaque plastic bottles, often with nozzle tops. Popular sizes were 8-, 12-, and 16-ounce bottles. Retail margins generally ranged between 30 and 38%.

AGREE

In June 1977, Johnson Wax entered the hair-care market with Agree Creme Rinse and Conditioner, soon followed by Agree Shampoo. At that time some creme rinses and conditioners included oil in their formulation. Agree's selling proposition was that the addition of this oil, especially for people with oily hair, caused the hair to look oily, greasy, and limp soon after shampooing. A technological breakthrough by Johnson Wax enabled it to produce a virtually oil-free product (Agree) which helped "stop the greasies." According to Johnson Wax promotional material:

> *Agree has exceptional detangling properties making the hair easier to wet-comb. It is pleasantly scented and leaves the hair feeling clean, with healthy shine, bounce, and body. Agree contains no harsh or harmful ingredients and is pH balanced to be compatible with the natural pH of hair and scalp.*

Agree had fared well in product comparison tests and an ASSESSOR pre-test-market test. By 1978, Agree had a 4.5% share of the shampoo market and 15.2% share of the conditioner market.

ENHANCE PRODUCT DEVELOPMENT

Agree's early success created optimism and euphoria at Johnson Wax. Gaining a foothold in the attractive conditioner market offered an opportunity to expand the conditioner product line and subsequently make greater inroads on the even larger shampoo market.

Management felt Agree was successful largely because it solved a specific hair problem for a segment of the market. They also felt that it would be desirable to offer another personal-care product line. Enhance was conceived as an instant hair conditioner targeted toward women 25–45 years old with dry hair, and was formulated to appeal to that audience. Blind paired comparisons were run against Revlon's Flex.

The study, conceived by John Sherman and Neil Ford, of the marketing research department, was summarized as follows:

> *The purpose of the study was to determine the preference levels for Enhance, both overall and on specific performance attributes, versus those of Flex, the leading instant hair conditioner. A panel of 400 hair conditioner users was pre-selected by telephone. Each received both Enhance and Flex, blind-labeled and*

in identical nonidentifiable packages and, following proper rotations, used first one for three weeks, and the other for an identical period. At the end of the six-week usage period, respondents were interviewed regarding their preferences and behavior regarding the test products. A key part of the analysis was to determine preferences of women with specific hair care problems relevant to Enhance strategy and positioning.

A digest of the results appears in Exhibits 1 and 2. The conclusions drawn by Ford in an August 1978 report to Sherman were that:

Differences between the two products are not great, but where they exist, they tend to be focused on the problems Enhance wishes to address and on the women to whom the brand will be targeted. While work should continue to improve the product, it is suitable for use in ASSESSOR in its current state and, if needs be, for use in test-market introduction.

THE ASSESSOR PRE-TEST MARKET

Following the blind comparison tests, further work on product formulation, product positioning, packaging, and advertising copy produced an introductory marketing plan. Advertising copy presented Enhance as a solution to the dry and damaged hair problem. Enhance samples were produced in "regular" and "extra conditioning" formulas.

When the marketing plan was agreed upon and samples were available, an ASSESSOR pre-test-market procedure was arranged. The primary objectives were to estimate the ongoing market share of Enhance and determine consumer reaction to the product. Two independent techniques were used to arrive at a market share prediction one year after introduction. The observed trial and repeat levels were used to make one share prediction. Another was made from estimates of brand preference calculated from the respondents' perception of, and preference for, the attributes of Enhance and the existing brands. Additional qualitative and quantitative information gathered during the laboratory phase, and again after use, added support for the primary conclusions of the ASSESSOR study.

ASSESSOR,[2] developed in 1973 by Management Decision Systems (MDS), of Waltham, Massachusetts, was one of a number of commercial simulated test-market procedures. The first was the Yankelovich

---

[2]More detailed descriptions of ASSESSOR may be found in the appendix to this case and in Alvin J. Silk and Glen L. Urban, "Pre-Test-Market Evaluation of New Packaged Goods: A Model and Measurement Methodology," *Journal of Marketing Research* (May 1978), Vol. XV, pp. 171–191.

Exhibit 1. Blind use test results

Incidence of problems

	All Women	25–29	30–34	35 or Older
Dry/damage problems	53%	55%	53%	46%
Split ends	34	42	35	29
Dryness	32	29	35	31
Brittle/breaking	12	13	17	9
Damaged hair	13	10	18	11
Dull/limp problems	65%	64%	68%	58%
Hard to manage	38	32	42	39
Dull/no shine	24	16	21	30
Fine/limp hair	44	45	39	46

Each respondent was screened for the presence of any of these seven hair problems. The seven problems, in turn, were subjectively grouped into those to do with "dry/damage" and those to do with "dull/limp."

Overall preference

	(BASE)	Prefer Enhance	Prefer Flex	No difference
All users	(320)	48%	44%	8%
By age				
Under 35	(166)	46	47	7
35 or over	(154)	50	40	10
By hair type				
Oily	(94)	51	45	4
Normal	(154)	44	47	9
Dry	(72)	53*	35	12
By hair quality				
Dry/damaged – net	(168)	50*	40	10
Fine/limp – net	(208)	49*	43	8

* Significant at 90% confidence level.

Laboratory Test Market, begun in 1968. Elrick and Lavidges' COMP, National Purchase Diary's ESP, and Burke Marketing Research's BASES followed, and by 1979, nearly 1,400 applications of these models had been completed.

Exhibit 2. **Blind use test results (continued)**

Preference on specific attributes

	Prefer Enhance	Prefer Flex	No difference
Fragrance			
In bottle	27%	32%	41%
While using	34	37	29
After dry	28	28	44
Feels cleaner			
While using	18	17	65
When dry	26[*]	19	55
Next day	26	22	52
Conditioning			
Conditioning	28	24	48
Softer	31	26	43
Body	31	32	37
More manageable	32	30	38
Better shine	14	16	70
Relieves dryness	(22)	15	63
Combing			
Easy to comb	22	20	58
Tangle free	16	16	68
Use/application			
Applies evenly	(30)	14	56
Penetrates better	(28)	18	54
Rinses out easier	22	21	57
Product			
Better color	4	6	90
Better consistency	27	29	44
BASE: 320 Users			

( ) Significant at 95% C.L.
[*] Significant at 90% C.L.

The Enhance ASSESSOR consisted of a laboratory and a callback phase. During the laboratory *phase,* women were intercepted in shopping malls and asked if they would participate in a test market. Those who were willing and were found to be in the target segment went through a five-step procedure, as follows:

1: An *Initial Questionnaire* was used to determine the brands about which the respondent could provide meaningful information. This list of brands, called the respondent's "evoked set," included brands used recently or ever, and brands that would, or would not, be considered on the next purchase occasion.

2: The *Preference Questionnaire* was customized for each respondent to include only those brands in her evoked set. The respondent was asked to allocate 11 imaginary chips between each pair of brands in her evoked set. These allocations were used to calculate the strength of preference for each brand in each respondent's evoked set. If there were N brands, the respondent was asked to give allocations for each of the $N(N–1)/2$ pairs.

3: *Advertising Recall* was measured after the respondent was shown commercials for six creme rinse/conditioning products: Tame, Agree, Flex, Condition, Wella Balsam, and Enhance.

4: *Laboratory Purchasing* took place in a simulated store where the respondent was given a $2.25 certificate. If she wanted to buy more than $2.25 in merchandise, she was asked to pay the difference. Respondents who did not purchase Enhance were given a package of Enhance as a gift. Half the nonpurchasers received a 2 oz. container, the other half received an 8 oz. container. A limited number of those who did not purchase the test product were asked a few additional questions probing their impressions of Enhance and reasons for not purchasing it.

5: *Brand Ratings.* Respondents were then asked to rate several of their evoked brands on how well they performed on 22 product attributes. Enhance was also rated on these attributes. These ratings, since the respondent had not used Enhance, were based on perceptions created through advertising, price, and packaging. A 7-point rating scale was used.

The *callback phase* was designed to collect information about after-use preferences, repeat purchase rate, and diagnostics concerning product performance. Only those respondents who indicated they had used Enhance were asked to complete the interview. Callback interviews were conducted four weeks after the laboratory interview.

The field research was conducted in three markets—Atlanta, Chicago, and Denver—beginning September 25, 1978, with callback interviews approximately four weeks later. A total of 387 interviews were conducted with users of creme rinse/conditioning products. Respondents included 120 users of Agree creme rinse, a disproportionate number, in order to better determine Enhance's effect on Agree.

ASSESSOR RESULTS

ASSESSOR provided results in eight major areas of interest: (1) market structure, (2) advertising recall, (3) trial, (4) repeat purchase, (5) product acceptance, (6) market share prediction, (7) cannibalization, and (8) sampling response.

1. *Market Structure.* During the laboratory phase of the fieldwork, respondents were asked to rate several of their evoked brands as well as their "ideal" brand on 22 attributes. These brand ratings were used as inputs to factor analysis[3], a data-reduction technique used for grouping similar attributes into underlying factors or dimensions. From this analysis, four basic perceptual dimensions, or factors, emerged:

Factor	Relative importance	Attributes combined to form the factor
Conditioning	33%	Nourishes dry hair
		Restores moisture
		Keeps control of split ends
		Makes dry hair healthy looking
		Conditions hair
		Helps keep hair from breaking
		Penetrates hair
Clean	27%	Leaves hair free of residue/flakes
		Leaves hair grease- and oil-free
		Leaves hair clean looking
		Rinses out easily/completely
Manageability/effects	23%	Makes hair more manageable
		Leaves hair shiny/lustrous
		Leaves hair soft and silky
		Gives hair body and fullness
Fragrance	17%	Has pleasant fragrance while using
		Leaves hair with nice fragrance

Besides identifying the possible factors underlying the instant conditioner market, factor analysis provided a graphic representation of the

---

[3]See Appendix A for description of factor analysis procedure.

consumer's positioning of the brands in a "perceptual map." This was done by using pairs of factors as axes and assigning each brand a "factor score" that served as a coordinate on each axis. Using these coordinates, a brand was assigned a position on the perceptual map. MDS produced perceptual maps for a number of market segments. The maps for the total market are shown in Exhibit 3. (Maps including the fragrance factor are not presented.)

MDS's report concluded that, in terms of market structure,

> . . .*The fact that all four dimensions are important to all consumers' segments considered in the study suggests that being strongly positioned on only one dimension may not be sufficient to capture a significant portion of the market.*
>
> *Agree and Breck Creme Rinse have achieved the "clean" position, while Clairol Condition has succeeded in differentiating itself as the "conditioning" brand. Wella Balsam, based on these maps, appears to have virtually no image, and thus might be vulnerable to a new entry. Sassoon, a relatively new brand, appears to be enjoying a very strong positive image.*

2. *Advertising Recall.* Unaided advertising recall provided a measure of how well an ad broke through the clutter of competitive advertising. Total unaided recall for Enhance was 76%, about average for ASSESSOR-

Exhibit 3. ASSESSOR results

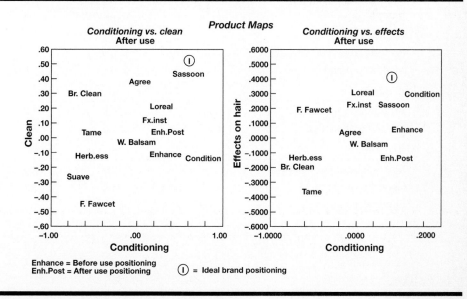

Enhance = Before use positioning
Enh.Post = After use positioning   ① = Ideal brand positioning

tested products, but somewhat lower than for other Johnson Wax products subjected to ASSESSOR tests. Unaided recall did not differ across hair type segments.

Among those who recalled the Enhance ad, almost 50% recalled that Enhance was "for dry hair." "Conditions" and "penetrates" received somewhat lower playback. Exhibit 4 summarizes the copy-point recall results.

Exhibit 4. ASSESSOR results

Copy point recall

	Overall	Buyer	Nonbuyer
For dry hair			
Good for dry hair	46.8%	50.0%	46.1%
Nourishes hair	33.1	37.9	32.0
Prevents dry hair	5.4	1.7	6.2
Doesn't leave hair dry	.7	0.0	.8
Conditions	20.4%	27.6%	18.7%
Conditions hair	8.0	17.2	5.8
Good for damaged hair	5.4	5.2	5.4
Repairs hair	4.0	6.9	3.3
For brittle hair	3.3	1.7	3.7
Protects from heat damage	.7	0.0	.8
Mends split ends	.7	0.0	.8
Penetrates	19.7%	31.0%	17.0%
Penetrates hair	19.7	31.0	17.0
Doesn't just coat hair	3.3	8.6	2.1
Manageability	11.4%	17.2%	10.0%
Makes hair more manageable	7.7	12.1	6.6
Good for limp hair	3.3	3.4	3.3
Eliminates tangles	.7	1.7	.4
Texture of hair	6.4%	5.2%	6.6%
Gives hair more body/bounce	4.3	1.7	5.0
Leaves hair soft	2.0	3.4	1.7
Base:	(299)	(58)	(241)

3. *Trial Estimation.* Store setups had been designed to reflect local conditions and simulate the anticipated competitive environment. Enhance was available in two sizes for both regular and extra conditioning formulations. Enhance had one facing for each size and formulation, and was featured in the middle of the middle shelf. In all, 24 shampoos and conditioners were represented in 60 facings. Enhance was offered in 8 and 16 ounce sizes at $1.31 and $1.94 respectively. Agree was offered in 8 or 12 ounce sizes at $1.31 and $1.67. Flex was offered only in the 16 ounce size at the same price as Agree. Enhance prices were very similar to those of Breck, Wella Balsam, and Tame.

Trial was measured as a percentage of total laboratory purchasing. Of the 387 respondents, 307 (79%) made a purchase in the store. Enhance's trial rate was 23%. Agree had achieved an overall trial rate of 33% in its ASSESSOR test. For purposes of comparison, Exhibit 5 shows trial rates for other ASSESSOR-tested products, both within and outside the health and beauty aids category.

4. *Repeat Purchase Estimation.* Repeat purchase and product acceptance were determined through telephone callback interviews four weeks after the laboratory interviews. Since all respondents who had not purchased

Exhibit 5.

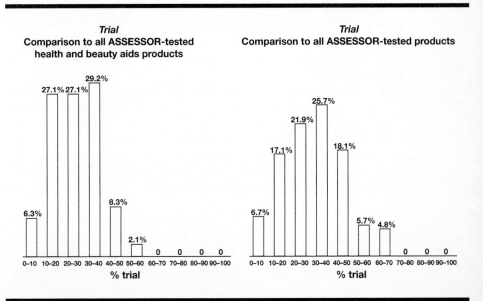

Trial
Comparison to all ASSESSOR-tested health and beauty aids products

Trial
Comparison to all ASSESSOR-tested products

Enhance were given samples, after-use data were potentially available for all respondents. Those who had not used Enhance were not asked to complete the phone interview. Telephone callbacks were completed with 215 respondents (55% of all laboratory respondents). This was lower than most ASSESSOR callback completion rates. Of those people with whom callback interviews were *not* completed, 23% (42 people) indicated they had not used Enhance because it was specifically formulated for dry hair.

During the callback interviews, respondents were again asked to compare Enhance with other brands in their evoked sets. This information was used to see whether use altered Enhance's position in the market structure (Enh. Post in Exhibit 3).

Respondents were also given the opportunity to purchase another bottle of Enhance at the prices found in the laboratory store. Those who decided to repurchase, plus those who said without prompting that their next conditioner purchase would be Enhance, were classified as repeaters. Repeat rates were as follows:

	Enhance	Agree
Repeat among buyers in laboratory	60%	78%
Repeat among nonbuyers (who received sample)	43	63

72% of those repeating purchased Enhance's "Extra Conditioning Formula" and 64% purchased the 16 ounce size.

The repeat purchase rates of other ASSESSOR-tested products are found in Exhibit 6.

5. *Product Acceptance.* During the callback interview the respondent was asked what she liked best about Enhance. Surprisingly, manageability, not conditioning, was mentioned most frequently, even though it was not considered a main copy point. Those who made a repeat purchase were even more likely than nonrepeaters to mention manageability. Open ended likes and dislikes for Enhance are found in Exhibit 7. Exhibit 8 presents after-use preferences and comparisons with users' favorite brands.

6. *Market Share Prediction.* A major feature that differentiated ASSESSOR from other pretest market procedures was the use of two convergent methods to predict market share. Market share was estimated separately with a "trial and repeat" model and a "preference" model.

Exhibit 6.

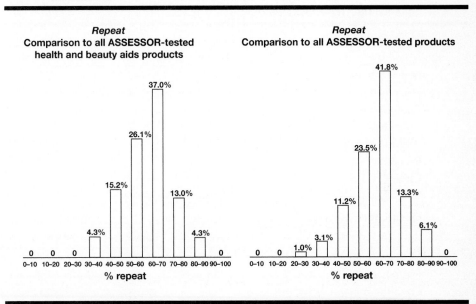

Repeat
Comparison to all ASSESSOR-tested health and beauty aids products

Repeat
Comparison to all ASSESSOR-tested products

TRIAL AND REPEAT MODEL

The trial and repeat model used the purchase information gathered during laboratory shopping and follow-up interview repeat measurements. The formula used was

$$M = TS$$

where   M   =   market share
         T   =   the ultimate cumulative trial rate (penetration or trial)
         S   =   the ultimate repeat purchase rate among those buyers who have ever made a trial purchase of the brand (retention)

Retention (S) was a function of the initial repeat purchase rate and the rate at which previous triers returned to Enhance after buying another product (called switchback). The relationship is explained in Appendix A.

As mentioned before, Enhance obtained a laboratory trial of 23%, and a repeat rate of 60%. Measured through a series of callback interviews, the

Exhibit 7. ASSESSOR *results open-ended likes and dislikes for enhance (multiple mentions)*

Open-Ended Likes

	Overall	Repeaters	Nonrepeaters
Manageability	42%	48%	37%
Fragrance	21	14	27
Conditioning	11	12	10
Consistency	7	7	6
Application/ease of use	7	6	7
Penetrates	6	5	7
Clean	5	7	4
Base	(215)	(102)	(13)

Open-Ended Dislikes

	Overall	Repeaters	Nonrepeaters
Manageability	24%	9%	38%
Fragrance	16	7	25
Conditioning	11	8	13
Consistency	1	3	0
Application/ease of use	1	1	1
Nothing Disliked	59	74	46
Base	(215)	(102)	(113)

switchback rate was 16%. Retention was calculated to be 28.6%. Since these estimates were achieved in an environment in which every respondent was aware of Enhance advertising, and Enhance was always available, corrections had to be made to adjust these laboratory measurements to actual market conditions. Market trial was estimated by

$$T = FKD + CU - \{(FKD) \times (CU)\}$$

where F = the trial rate in the ASSESSOR test—the trial rate that would ultimately occur if all consumers were aware of the advertising.

K = the long-run probability that a consumer will become aware of Enhance.

D = the proportion of retail outlets that will ultimately carry Enhance.

C = the proportion of the target market that receives samples.

Exhibit 8. **ASSESSOR** *results*

After-use preferences

	% Prefer Enhance[*]				
	1st	2nd	3rd	4th	(Base)
Dry hair	38	32	17	7	(93)
Oily hair	22	34	20	15	(41)
Normal	23	34	19	12	(69)
Total sample	28	33	19	11	(215)
Total sample (Agree)	54	26	12	2	(279)

Comparison to Regular Brand

	Among triers		Among nontriers	
	Enhance (%)	Agree (%)	Enhance (%)	Agree (%)
Much better	30	44	14	35
A little better	24	25	21	22
About the same	26	13	37	21
A little poorer	14	12	16	13
Much poorer	6	5	12	8
(Base)	(50)	(76)	(165)	(203)

[*] To be read, of the 93 respondents with dry hair, 38% rated Enhance as their favorite brand, for 32% it was their second choice, etc.

U = the proportion of those receiving samples that will use them.

Using CU to estimate the trial resulting from sampling would overstate the extent of sampling trial, since some trial would have resulted from advertising even without sampling. This "overlap" trial ((FKD) × (CU)) would be double-counted, and must therefore be subtracted from the sample-induced trial rate.

The market share estimates for Enhance depended not only on data obtained from the ASSESSOR test, but also on John Sherman's estimates of what advertising awareness and distribution levels would be realized for Enhance. Sherman had decided to initially use the advertising awareness and distribution levels realized for Agree:

awareness 70%

distribution 85%

Exhibit 9. ASSESSOR *results*

Market share prediction trial/repeat model

	Enhance	Agree
1. Trial	23%	33%
2. Awareness from Advertising	.70	.70
3. Distribution	.85	.85
4. Net cumulative trial [(1) × (2) × (3)]	13.7%	19.6%
5. Repeat	.60	.78
6. Switchback	.16	.15
7. Share of triers' choices (retention) $\left[\dfrac{6}{1 + (6) - (5)}\right]$	28.6%	41%
8. Base share [(4) × (7)]	3.9%	8.1

Preference Model

	Enhance	Agree
9. Share for Enhance if everyone evokes it	27.5%	42.0%
10. Estimated penetration [equal to (4)]	.14	.20
11. Base share	3.8%	8.4%

Using these values, and ignoring sampling for the moment, market share was predicted by the trial/repeat model at 3.9%. Sherman's computations of Enhance market share, together with those for Agree, are found in Exhibit 9.

PREFERENCE MODEL ESTIMATES OF SHARE

The preference model market share prediction was based on the respondents' answers to the questions about product attributes and the degree to which they perceived these attributes to be present in competing brands. The preference model predicted that Enhance would attain a 27.5% share of those consumers in whose evoked sets it appeared. Using the penetration rate found in the laboratory phase of the ASSESSOR study (14%), MDS obtained a base market share estimate of 3.8% (see Exhibit 9).

7. *Cannibalization.* An estimate of the cannibalization of Agree's share was also computed from the ASSESSOR results by computing Enhance's share separately for Agree users. This analysis demonstrated that Enhance would draw less than proportionately from Agree, with only a

share of 2.4% among Agree users. This indicated that Agree would lose less than half a share point to Enhance.

More detailed analysis indicated that Enhance would draw more than proportionately to share from Wella Balsam, proportionately to share from Flex and Sassoon, and less than proportionately from Agree, L'Oreal, and Clairol Condition.

8. *Incremental Share from Sampling.* The incremental share that might be expected from sampling could be estimated, since those respondents who had not chosen Enhance had been given a sample of the product at the end of the initial ASSESSOR interview. Their use and acceptance levels were determined during the callback interview.

The effects of sampling were evaluated by first determining the incremental trial rate that would result from sampling. Of those using samples, a certain percentage (equal to net cumulative trial) would have tried the product anyway; the remainder were new triers due to sampling. (See formula on page 248.) These incremental triers would now follow the normal switching process, and their long-run share potential could be estimated like that for the advertising induced triers. These calculations, found in Exhibit 10, estimated or incremental 2% share from a 35 million sample drop. Considering the effect of sampling, market share was estimated at 5.8% by the preference model and 5.9% by the trial/repeat model.

Exhibit 10. *ASSESSOR results: estimated incremental share from sampling for 35 million sample drop with 90% delivery*

Enhance vs. Agree

1. Number of samples delivered [35M × .9]	31.5M
2. % hitting target group	80%
3. % used[*]	60%
4. Number of samples used [(1) × (2) × (3)]	15.12M
5. Percent using samples[*] [(4)÷60MM Households]	25%
6. Overlap [(5) × Trial Rate Advertising (line 4, Ex.9)]	3%
7. Net incremental trial [(5) − (6)]	22%
8. First repeat[*] (repeat among nonbuyers)	43%
9. Share of triers' choices[**] (retention)	22%
10. Incremental share from sampling [(7) × (8) × (9)]	2.0%

[*] Measured through ASSESSOR callbacks.
[**] Calculated from formula (1+SB − R) where SB is given in line 6 of Exhibit 9 and R is line 8 of this exhibit.

VOLUME PREDICTIONS

As a final step in the evaluation of Enhance's success potential, it was necessary to convert the share estimates into dollar sales projections. Doing this required a number of additional facts and adjustments. The 1979 volume of instant hair conditioner sales was projected to be $250 million. To find the volume that would result from a given Enhance share, it would be necessary to adjust the share for price and frequency-of-use differences between Enhance and the average for the category.

A use adjustment based on expected source of volume and frequency of use, indicated that Enhance's frequency of use would be about .9 times the category average. The tested Enhance prices and share of sales accounted for by the two sizes resulted in a price adjustment of 1.04. Multiplying these two adjustment factors resulted in a factor of 0.94 to be used to convert unit market share to dollar share.

Volume was then predicted, according to the two models, as follows:

	Trial/repeat model	Preference model
Manufacturer's Category		
Volume	$250MM	$250MM
Enhance Unit Share	3.90%	3.80%
Enhance Dollar Share		
(Unit Share * .94)	3.66%	3.57%%
Enhance Sales	$9.15MM	$8.93MM
Additional Sales From Promotion		
Promotion Unit Share	2.0	
Promotion Dollar Share	1.88	
Enhance Sales	4.7MM	$4.7MM
Total Sales	$13.85MM	$13.63MM

RECOMMENDATIONS

MDS, as a result of the ASSESSOR study, was not encouraging about Enhance's prospects. It also thought sampling would not be successful for Enhance. Johnson Wax management had set a target market share of 10%.[4]

---

[4]As a privately held corporation, Johnson Wax did not report financial data publicly. Manufacturers of health and beauty aids in general held cost data close to their chests. Exhibit 11 displays some approximate information on industry cost structure. The data are included for discussion purposes only and should not be considered indicative of Enhance's actual cost structure.

Exhibit 11. *Approximate health and beauty aid industry cost structures* (indexed to suggested retail price)*

Suggested Retail Price	100
Expected Shelf Price (Large 16 oz.)	83
(Small 8 oz.)	73
Manufacturer's Selling Price	56
Cost of Goods Sold	21%

* These data are not supplied by the Johnson Wax Company, and are not known to be indicative of its actual costs. They are thought to reflect the average market cost structure closely enough to be helpful in the case discussion.

John Sherman knew, however, that the final recommendations were his to make. He could recommend that Enhance be abandoned; reformulated; and/or retested; or that a national rollout begin. The final decision lay somewhere higher up in the organization, but his recommendations would be considered carefully.

APPENDIX A MARKET SHARE PREDICTION MODELS

The market share prediction in ASSESSOR was calculated from two independent models.

1. The trial and repeat model was based on:
   - trial (measured in the laboratory store), repeat (measured in the callback interview), switchback (measured in multiple callbacks).
2. The preference model was based on:
   - after-use preferences for the test product (callback), the relationship between preferences and pur chasing behavior in the specific market (laboratory).

A convergence between the predictions of these two models serves to increase confidence in the final market share prediction.

TRIAL AND REPEAT MODEL

The target market for the product is represented by the respondents chosen in the ASSESSOR test. In the test procedure, some respondents buy Enhance in the laboratory store. The proportion of buyers provides an estimate of trial, which must be corrected for probable awareness and availability in the actual marketplace. This corrected trial level is used to estimate the *cumulative* penetration the test product will achieve in the real market. Once cumulative penetration has been estimated, it is necessary to estimate the number of purchases that will be generated on an ongoing basis. This is called "retention," and is a function of the amount of brand switching that will occur.

At any given time, t, the purchasers of instant hair conditioners could be segmented into two groups—those who bought Enhance last time and those who didn't. What could happen at time t + 1 is illustrated on the next page. Of those who bought Enhance at time t (X), some will also buy it at t + 1, their next purchase occasion (R), whereas others will buy a competitive brand (X − R). At t + 1 some of those who had bought Enhance before t, but didn't buy it at t, will switch back (SB). Others will continue to purchase a competing brand.

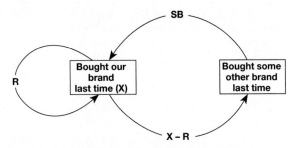

The customers who repeat plus those who don't repeat must equal 100% of those who bought the Enhance at their last purchase occasion. Similarly, switchback plus nonswitchback must equal 100% of those who bought Enhance at some time in the past, but not on the last purchase occasion. This is illustrated below.

Assume 100 consumers have tried Enhance. If the repeat rate is 81%[*] and the switchback rate 20%,[*] then on successive purchase occasions we would expect to observe the following:

Purchase cycle	Eligible to repeat	=	Repeat (R)	+	Do not repeat	Eligible to switchback	= Switchback (SB)	+	Do not switchback
1st	100.0		81.0		19.0	—	—		—
2nd	81.0		65.6		15.4	19.0	3.8		15.2
3rd	69.4		56.2		13.2	30.6	6.1		24.5
4th	62.3		50.5		11.8	37.7	7.5		30.2
5th	58.0		47.0		11.0	42.0	8.4		33.6
6th	55.4		44.9		10.5	44.6	8.9		35.7
7th	53.8		etc.		etc.	46.2	etc.		etc.

Now compute the percentage of triers who have purchased Enhance in any past period that will purchase it in the present period:

Purchase cycle	Buy enhance (R+SB)	Buy other brands
1st	81.0%	19.0%
2nd	69.4	30.6
3rd	62.3	37.7
4th	58.0	42.0
5th	55.4	44.6
6th	53.8	46.2
7th	52.8	47.2

---

[*]These values are used for illustration only.

Notice how the percentage of triers who will repurchase Enhance on a given occasion varies from the previous period value less and less as the number of purchase occasions increases. In fact, if we continued this sequence indefinitely, we would finally arrive at 51.3%, and this value would be called the retention rate. The value at which this process finally stabilizes is determined completely by the repeat rate and the switchback rate, so it is not necessary to calculate retention this way. This illustration is an example of what is called a two-stage Markov process. It is not critical to know any more about a two-stage Markov process to understand ASSESSOR than the formula for the final retention rate, or

$$S = \frac{SB}{1 + SB - R} .^*$$

We can compute retention quite simply by using this equation. If, for example, R = .50 and SB = .20, what would the retention rate be? We might also note that in our example, after only seven purchase occasions, we were getting quite close to .513.

The last step in the calculation is to compute market share as the product of penetration (the percentage who will try the product) and retention (the share of ongoing purchases by those who have tried the product).

Market share = penetration × retention.

To summarize, the procedure used to predict market share with the trial and repeat model is:

1. Measure trial in the laboratory.
2. Multiply this trial rate by expected awareness and availability to compute penetration in a nonlaboratory situation.
3. Measure repeat and switchback in the callback phase.
4. Use Markov formula to compute retention.
5. Multiply penetration by retention to get market share.

PREFERENCE MODEL

The preference model for predicting market share is considerably more sophisticated in its derivation than is the trial and repeat model, and much of the detail is beyond the scope of this case. Those interested are directed to the Silk and Urban article referenced earlier.

An overview of the process is as follows:

---

*SB and R are expected to be decimal fractions, i.e., .3 instead of 30%.

ANALYSIS OF EXISTING BRANDS

1. From a respondent's chip allocations, described on page 241, a preference score V(j) is computed for each brand (j). These preference scores are computed using a technique borrowed from mathematical psychology.
2. The next step is to use these estimated brand-preference scores to compute the probability of a brand j being purchased by a respondent, P(j). The conversion formula is

$$P(j) = \frac{\hat{V}(j)^\beta}{\Sigma_k [\hat{V}(k)]^\beta}$$

where the summation is over the j brands in the respondent's evoked set.

These steps are taken to estimate the probability of purchase for the brands that existed in the market before Enhance was introduced. In this formulation, β is an estimate of the degree of brand loyalty in the market.

3. The chip allocation procedure is repeated during the callback phase of the ASSESSOR process. β is assumed to remain unchanged with the introduction and trial of Enhance, so the following equation estimates the probability that a consumer would choose Enhance after having tried it.

$$L(i) = \frac{A(i)^\beta}{A(i)^\beta + \Sigma_k (A(k))^\beta}$$

where $A(i)$ = estimated preference of the consumer for Enhance after having tried it.

$A(k)$ = estimated preference of the consumer for brand k after having tried Enhance.

$\hat{\beta}$ = a parameter to be estimated.

Summation is over the brands in the consumer's evoked set.

These predicted brand preferences are computed for each consumer separately and are conditional on the evoked set of the consumer. Expected market shares could be computed for the brands by aggregating the individual brand preferences and multiplying by the proportion of consumers who would include Enhance in their evoked sets.

$$M(j) = E(j) \frac{\sum_{k=1}^{N} L_k(j)}{N}$$

where $M(j)$ = expected market share for brand j.

$E(j)$ = proportion of consumers for whom brand j will be in their evoked set.

$L_k(j)$ = predicted probability of purchase of brand j by consumer k.

N = number of consumers.

FACTOR ANALYSIS AND MARKET MAPS

Exhibit 3 displayed graphic representations of the relative location of existing and "ideal" brands. They were drawn using a technique called factor analysis. What follows is an intuitive idea of what factor analysis seeks to do and how these "maps" are drawn.

Suppose we had a set of six questions about the attributes of instant hair conditioners like these:

BRAND: _____

Please rate the above brand of creme rinse, hair conditioner, or balsam conditioning product on each of the items below. The *best possible rating* you can give is a 7, the *poorest possible* rating is a 1. Circle *one* number for each item listed. Even if you have never used the product yourself, we would like your impression of what it is like based on what you have seen or heard.

	Best possible rating					Poorest possible rating
1. Nourishes dry hair	7	6	5	4	3	2	1
2. Leaves hair free of residue, film, and flakes	7	6	5	4	3	2	1
3. Gives hair body and fullness	7	6	5	4	3	2	1
4. Rinses out easily/completely	7	6	5	4	3	2	1
5. Restores moisture	7	6	5	4	3	2	1
6. Keeps control of split ends	7	6	5	4	3	2	1
7. Leaves hair feeling soft and silky	7	6	5	4	3	2	1

Each respondent would answer these questions about Enhance and the other brands in her evoked set. We would like to see whether there are consistent patterns of response to these questions, e.g., questions 1 and 5 both seem to have something to do with moisture, so we might expect a respondent to give a brand either high or low ratings on both questions. The degree to which questions are answered in similar ways is measured by a number called the "correlation coefficient."

The correlation coefficient simply measures the extent to which two questions are answered above or below their respective averages. If every respondent in this test gave higher than average responses to two questions, the correlation coefficient for those two questions would be 1. If every respondent's answer to one question was higher than the average response while the answer to the other question was always lower than the average, the correlation coefficient for the two questions would be −1. Correlation coefficients are always between these two extreme values. A correlation coefficient of 0 would mean there was no consistent pattern of response for the two questions.

Exhibit A1 is a display of correlation coefficients for the responses to the seven questions presented above.

If we look at the correlations between the responses to the seven questions, we can see that some of them seem to be related, e.g., responses to questions 1, 5 and 6 seem to go together; 2 and 4; and 3 and 7 go together. Let's rewrite Exhibit A1 grouping these questions together.

As you examine Exhibit A2, notice how we have three blocks of questions and in each block the correlations between responses to the questions are high, while the correlations between responses to questions in different blocks are low. Suppose we had a set of three uncorrelated variables. Their correlation array would look like this:

$$
\begin{array}{ccc}
1. & & \\
0 & 1. & \\
0 & 0 & 1.
\end{array}
$$

Exhibit A1. *Hypothetical correlation between responses to selected questions**

Question #	1	2	3	4	5	6	7
1	1.						
2	.2	1.					
3	.1	−.1	1.				
4	−.3	.9	−.1	1.			
5	.8	−.2	.2	−.2	1.		
6	.7	−.1	.1	−.1	.9	1.	
7	.2	−.1	.8	.2	.1	.3	1.

*These are not the real correlations, but have been designed to illustrate a point.

259

Question#		f_1			f_2		f_3	
		1	5	6	2	4	3	7
	1	1.						
f_1	5	.8	1.					
	6	.7	.9	1.				
f_2	2	.2	.2	.1	1.			
	4	−.3	−.2	−.1	.9	1.		
f_3	3	.1	.2	.1	−.1	−.1	1	
	7	.2	.1	.3	−.1	.2	.8	1

That is what Exhibit A2 looks like if you look just at the blocks and not the individual questions. If we considered each block to represent a variable, we would have a new set of variables called factors: factor 1 would consist of questions 1, 5 and 6; factor 2 would consist of questions 2 and 4; and factor 3 would consist of questions 3 and 7.

What are these new variables? We have to name them ourselves, but their properties are given by the questions that define them. On page 11 of the case, factor 1 was called "conditioning"; factor 2—"cleaning"; and factor 3—"manageability/effects."

This exercise has been quite simplistic; the groupings were clear from the start. This isn't always the case. Frequently many questions are asked to explore consumers' perceptions of products and the underlying dimensions of the market are by no means obvious. Or perhaps a manager would just like to see whether his/her perception of the market is backed up by objective measurement. In either of these situations, factor analysis is very helpful.

What does factor analysis do? It finds the subgrouping of a large set of variables in which the original variables are highly correlated within the subgroup, or factor, and least correlated between factors.

How are graphs like those in Exhibit 3 drawn? That's fairly easy. Each of the original questions (variables) has a coefficient, a_i, that relates it to the factor to which it belongs, much like a regression coefficient. So we can write:

$$f_1 = a_o + a_1v_1 + a_2v_{22} + \text{---} + a_kv_k.$$

If we take the mean score attributed to each question for a given brand, we can use this equation to compute what is called the factor score f_1 for that brand. If we have three factors, we can compute three factor scores for each brand. Using these three factor scores, we can locate the brand in a three-dimensional space where each dimension represents a factor. This is how the graphs in Exhibit 3 were drawn.

7 CASE

Johnson Wax: Enhance (B)

Darral Clarke

Katherine Thompson had been the Enhance product manager at Johnson Wax (JW) for about three months in January 1982. Enhance, an instant hair conditioner, wasn't doing as well as had been expected. September/October 1981 market share was only 4.2% and, although it had been increasing slowly, it was far below the projected 8.8%.

In the fall of 1978, an ASSESSOR test of Enhance had resulted in a share prediction of about 5.9%, much lower than the 10% called for in the marketing plan.[1] Targeting Enhance to women with dry hair prob-

---

[1]See Johnson Wax: Enhance (A). HBS Case Services #9-583-046.

This case was prepared by Associate Professor Darral Clarke as a basis for class discussion rather than to illustrate either effective or ineffective handling of an administrative situation.

Copyright © 1983 by the President and Fellows of Harvard College. Harvard Business School case 9-584-009.

lems had restricted both trial and repeat purchases. Using the results of this ASSESSOR test, a new product position had been developed to appeal to a broader segment of instant conditioner users. Concurrent with efforts to develop a broader product position, R&D had modified the formula to improve its fragrance and increase its conditioning effect.

Enhance had been subjected to a second ASSESSOR test during January 1980. The result of this test was a projected market share of 8.8%, of which 1.9% would result from a 35 million-unit sampling program. Since the 8.8% share projection was a substantial improvement over the initial projection, and close to the original target of 10%, the decision was made to skip the test market that normally would have been the next step.

Enhance "went national" in September 1980, but by mid-May 1981, results were lagging far behind projections. Tracking studies done three and six months after the introduction showed disappointing awareness, trial, and use figures.

Katherine Thompson faced the problem of getting Enhance on track or making a very convincing statement recommending the product be dropped.

PRODUCT MODIFICATION

The forecast trial, repeat, and market share for Enhance in the initial ASSESSOR had been substantially lower than those attained by Agree, Johnson Wax's successful hair shampoo and conditioner product line. It was these results that led Johnson Wax to reformulate the product and broaden the target market. Katherine Thompson explained the new Enhance product position as follows:

> *Women want to look nice—but they start at different places. Some women have oily hair and need more powerful cleaning from a product—Agree was designed for them. Other women have dry hair and need a different kind of product—Enhance was supposed to be for them. The original positioning for Enhance may have been too therapeutic. With the new positioning for Enhance we've tried to serve up the damaged hair problem in a more palatable way and stress the benefits more than the problem. Our new product position is stated on the label, ". . . hair can become overworked—overworked from blow dryers, hot rollers, curling irons, perms and even brushing. It can lose its natural moisturizers. Enhance actually puts moisturizers back to leave your hair full of body and manageable again. Enhance normal formula is specially formulated to*

penetrate your hair. It makes hair soft, smooth, shiny and healthy looking. And because Enhance is 98.75% oil-free, your hair is left with a clean feeling."[2]

New advertisements had been produced as the product position was developed and the new product formulations were completed.

BLIND COMPARISONS

Two new formulas were produced in addition to the original Enhance: the first differed only in fragrance, while the second included the new fragrance and a small amount of mineral oil. These three formulations were then tested in a blind use test.

METHODOLOGY   The product was placed with a total of 1,200 women between 18 and 45 years of age who had used a conditioner in the past month. Three panels of 400 women each were balanced on four key demographic characteristics and were reasonably representative of most housewives.

Each respondent received a pair of products in blind-labeled bottles identified only as hair conditioner. Labels gave only order of use and directions pertinent to using the product. Following proper rotation, each respondent used first one product for two weeks and then the second product for a second two-week period. Respondents were asked not to use other conditioner products during the test, but otherwise to follow their normal hair-care routine. Telephone callbacks were made at the end of the four-week use period to determine preferences and reasons for them. In addition to the overall preferences, diagnostic information and demographics were collected.

Results of overall preference tests were as follows:

	Original Enhance formula vs. New formula (without mineral oil)	Flex vs. New formula (without mineral oil)	Flex vs. New formula & Mineral oil
Base	318	303	307
	%	%	%
Prefer New Formula	53	52	57
Prefer Other	46	47	42
No Preference	1	1	1

---

[2]Enhance label.

The new Enhance formula plus mineral oil was significantly preferred over Flex overall. It was also significantly preferred over Flex on the key attributes of fragrance, clean feel when dry, softness, and rinsing out.

On the basis of these results, a decision was made to further modify the product to produce Enhance formulations for normal, dry, and oily hair, and to test them using ASSESSOR. Enhance was priced at $1.59 for the 8-ounce and $2.39 for the 16-ounce size, roughly the same as Silkience, Gillette's new conditioner. In the original Fall 1978 ASSESSOR, prices were $1.31 and $1.94 for the 8 and 16 ounce sizes, respectively.

THE SECOND ENHANCE ASSESSOR TEST[3]

The second Enhance ASSESSOR test began in Atlanta and Chicago on January 30, 1980 and continued for about four weeks. During the laboratory phase of the test, 301 women, aged 18–44, who were hair-conditioner users with no prior ASSESSOR participation or connection with the Johnson Wax Company, took part in the study. The procedure for the new Enhance ASSESSOR was the same as had been used in the initial Enhance test and for Agree:

1. An initial screening interview to determine category use and demographics, and to provide a measurement of brand knowledge and perceptions before the ASSESSOR test began.
2. Exposure to advertising for established brands, as well as Enhance.
3. Measurement of reactions to advertising.
4. Shopping in a simulated store environment for instant hair conditioner.
5. Home use of the new brand.
6. Post-usage telephone interview and repeat purchase opportunity.

Using the data gathered in these various steps, MDS[4] supplied Johnson Wax with information and analysis relevant to advertising and brand awareness, trial, repeat, market-share prediction, and response to sampling programs. Market share was estimated by two procedures:

1. One market-share prediction was made from the observed shopping behavior and the repeat purchase level measured during the callback interviews. This share estimate was called the *trial/repeat share.*

---

[3]Discussions of ASSESSOR are found in HBS Case Services #9-582-141, Johnson Wax: Enhance (A); and Alvin J. Silk, and Glen L. Urban, "Pre-test-Market Evaluation of New Packaged Goods: A Model and Measurement Methodology," *Journal of Marketing Research,* Vol. XV (May 1978), pp. 171–191.

[4]Management Decision Systems, the consulting firm that designed and executed the ASSESSOR test.

2. A second market-share prediction was made by measuring the attributes consumers indicated were important and their perceptions of the degree to which various brands exhibited those attributes. This share estimate was called the *preference share*.

The results of the ASSESSOR test are found in Exhibits 1–9. The marketing research department summarized these results as follows:

  I. *Advertising Recall* (see Exhibit 1)
  - Advertising recall indicated that JW had succeeded in producing a less therapeutic brand image for Enhance and in stressing conditioning and reducing the "for dry hair" image.
  - Advertising copy stressed Enhance's conditioning and help for damaged hair. Enhance triers exhibited significantly higher unaided recall of these themes than nonbuyers (60% vs. 42%).
 II. *Market Structure*
  - Factor analysis indicated four basic dimensions of consumer perception—conditions, fragrance, cleans, and protects. The cleans and conditions dimensions are relatively more important to the consumer. After exposure to Enhance advertising, but before use, respondents gave Enhance a strong conditions perception, average protects perception, weak cleans perception, and virtually no fragrance perception. (See Exhibits 2 and 3.)
III. *Trial*
  - Enhance's overall trial rate was somewhat above average—32%. This represented a significant improvement over the initial ASSESSOR level of 23%. (See Exhibit 4.)
  - Trial for Enhance was split evenly between the 8-ounce and the 16-ounce sizes. Interestingly, trial was not skewed toward the dry formula. Half of all triers purchased the normal formula, one-quarter purchased the dry and oily hair formulas, respectively.
  - Enhance trial came disproportionately from Agree and Silkience users. There were not enough respondents, however, to determine cannibalization potential accurately.
IV. *Repeat*
  - The repeat rate for Enhance among triers was an above-average 72%. This was substantially better than the initial ASSESSOR's 60% repeat rate, but marginally lower than that for Agree. The repeat rate among nontriers was only 43%, identical to the initial ASSESSOR result.
  - After-use reaction to Enhance indicated that conditioning and fragrance were the most liked features. Repeaters mentioned liking the conditioning features of manageability and body more than

Exhibit 1. *ASSESSOR results: Copy point recall*

	Overall	Buyer	Nonbuyer
Conditions	47.6%	59.9%	42.3%
For overworked hair/over processed	15.0	22.8	11.5
Conditions damaged hair	8.0	8.8	7.7
Repairs damaged hair	7.5	12.3	5.4
Helps damaged hair from dryer	5.9	5.3	6.2
Helps damaged hair from rollers	5.3	5.3	5.4
Helps damaged hair from perms	5.3	5.3	6.2
Helps damaged hair from coloring	3.2	1.8	3.8
Restores dried-out hair	2.7	1.8	3.1
Protects hair against damage	2.7	0.0	3.8
Abuse can damage hair/for abused hair	2.7	5.3	1.5
Conditions (unspecified)	2.1	5.3	.8
Other effects on hair	17.6%	19.3%	16.9%
Makes hair shine	6.4	8.8	5.4
Beautiful hair-glamour-natural beauty	4.3	3.5	2.3
Enhances hair	2.7	3.5	2.3
For dry hair	16.6%	17.5%	16.2%
Designed to restore moisture/moisturizer	13.9	14.0	13.8
Fights dry hair	2.7	3.5	2.3
Texture of hair	13.9%	12.3%	14.6%
Gives hair body-fuller-bounce	10.7	10.5	10.8
Makes hair soft	3.7	1.8	4.6
Manageability	7.0%	7.0%	6.9%
Makes hair more manageable	4.8	3.5	5.4
Miscellaneous			
Don't remember	5.9	1.8	7.7
Nothing	5.3	5.3	5.4
Clean feel—not oily/greasy	2.7	3.5	2.3
New product	2.1	2.5	1.5
Ad was interesting	2.1	1.8	2.3
Base:	(187)	(57)	(130)

Exhibit 2. ASSESSOR results: Perceptual dimensions

Factor	Importance to buyer	Importance to nonbuyer	Attributes combined to form factor
Cleans	35%	36%	Leaves hair free of residue Rinses out easily, completely Leaves hair grease and oil-free Leaves hair clean-looking
Conditions	29%	34%	Makes hair more manageable Conditions hair Gives hair body and fullness Penetrates hair Restores moisture Moisturizes hair Leaves hair feeling soft and silky Leaves hair shiny, lustrous
Protects	28%	18%	Keeps hair from breaking Helps eliminate flyaway/static Helps control split ends Moisturizes hair Restores moisture
Fragrance	17%	11%	Leaves hair with pleasant fragrance Has a pleasant fragrance while using

did the nonrepeaters. Primary dislikes were not enough conditioning and hair not staying clean long enough. (See Exhibit 5.)

- "Comparison to regular brand" and "Intent to repurchase" were not improved over the levels measured in the first ASSESSOR. (See Exhibits 6 and 7.)
- Enhance's after-use position is:
  - close to, but slightly downscale from, Sassoon and Silkience on conditioning and cleans.
  - only moderately stronger than the average of other creme rinse/conditioner brands in conditioning and protection.
  - stronger than the majority of other brands, but not significantly better, on fragrance and clean feel. (See Exhibit 3.)

V. *Share Prediction*
- Based on the assumptions of 70% brand awareness and 85% ACV[5] distribution at end of the first year, Enhance is expected to obtain a 6.9% unit share from advertising. (See Exhibit 8.)

---

[5]All Category Volume — a distribution coverage measure.

Exhibit 3. ASSESSOR results: perceptual maps

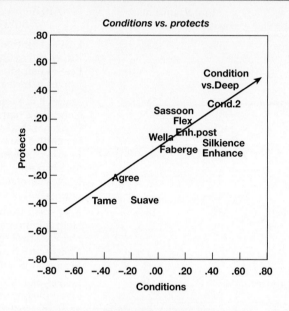

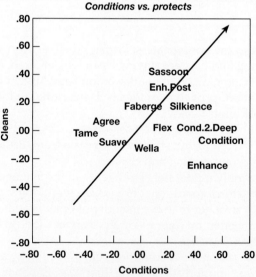

Note: The map locations of Silkience and
Enh.Post were so close they overlaped.

Exhibit 4. ASSESSOR results: Source of trial

Type purchased on trial	
Overall trial	32%
Type	% purchased on trial
Normal	52%
Oily	24
Dry	24
(Base)	(83)

Size purchased on trial	
Size	% purchased on trial
8-ounce	48%
16-ounce	52

Source of trial		
Brand last purchased	Buyer	Nonbuyer
Agree	18.1%	11.5%
Silkience	18.1	9.6
Wella Balsam	6.0	13.8
Flex		
Instant	8.4	9.6
Rinse	1.2	1.4
Sassoon	4.8	8.3
Condition II	4.8	6.4
Faberge Organic	6.0	4.1
Tame	4.8	4.1
Condition	2.4	4.6
Instant Condition	3.6	2.8
Suave	6.0	1.4
L'Oreal	2.4	2.8
(Base)	(83)	(218)

- Enhance's final market-share forecast also depended on the level of sampling that was chosen. Since the ASSESSOR forecasts were based on volume measurements and most of the available category data was based on dollar sales, it was necessary to convert the volume-share forecast to a dollar-share forecast. This was done using a usage adjustment factor and a price adjustment factor. (See Exhibit 9.)

Exhibit 5. ASSESSOR *results: Repeat rates*

	Among buyers	Among nonbuyers
Enhance (Final ASSESSOR)	72%	43%
Enhance (Initial ASSESSOR)	60%	43%
Agree	78%	63%

Brand last purchased
(repeaters vs. nonrepeaters)

	Repeaters	Nonrepeaters
Agree	17.4	14.7
Silkience	9.8	25.3
Wella Balsam	7.6	8.0
Flex		
Instant	8.7	8.0
Rinse	–	1.3
Sassoon	8.7	12.0
Condition II	6.5	1.3
Faberge Organic	6.5	5.3
Tame	5.4	4.0
Condition	3.3	1.3
Instant Condition	3.3	–
Suave	6.5	–
L'Oreal	2.2	2.7
(Base)	(92)	(75)

Exhibit 6. ASSESSOR *results: Comparison to regular brand*

	Among Buyers		
	Final ASSESSOR (%)	Initial ASSESSOR (%)	Agree (%)
Much better	25	30	44
A little better	31	24	25
About the same	24	26	13
A little poorer	15	14	12
Somewhat poorer	6	6	5
(Base)	(68)	(50)	(76)

(continued)

Exhibit 6 (continued)

	Among nonbuyers		
	Final ASSESSOR (%)	Initial ASSESSOR (%)	Agree (%)
Much better	15	14	35
A little better	19	21	22
About the same	34	37	21
A little poorer	19	16	13
Somewhat poorer	12	12	8
(Base)	(99)	(165)	(203)

	After-use preferences		
After-use preference for test brand	Final ASSESSOR %	Initial ASSESSOR %	Agree %
First	31	28	54
Second	35	33	26
Third	16	19	12
Fourth	9	11	2

THE DECISION TO GO NATIONAL

The projected market share for Enhance depended on the sampling program for it. For example, combining the unit market-share forecast of 6.9% from advertising with a 1.6% market share response from a 30 million-unit sample drop resulted in a forecast unit market share of 8.5% and factory sales of $20.2 million (see Exhibit 9). This forecast was close enough to the original market share target of 10% that, when it became available in June 1980, the decision was made to skip the test market and introduce Enhance nationally. Major factors in this decision were:

1. The laboratory people thought they had done as much to the basic formulation as they could, and the Enhance ASSESSOR showed that the reformulation of the product and the revised product position had increased the share prediction by more than 50%. Management thought that, all things considered, Enhance was about as good as it could be.

Exhibit 7. *ASSESSOR results: Intent to repurchase*

	Among buyers		
	Final ASSESSOR (%)	Initial ASSESSOR (%)	Agree (%)
Definitely	38	46	53
Probably	44	32	28
Might	7	10	9
Probably not	7	8	5
Definitely not	3	4	5
(Base)	(68)	(50)	(76)
	Among nonbuyers		
	Final ASSESSOR (%)	Initial ASSESSOR (%)	Agree (%)
Definitely	15	19	40
Probably	43	37	32
Might	23	20	16
Probably not	8	13	2
Definitely not	10	10	9
(Base)	(99)	(165)	(203)

Exhibit 8. *Base share projection—Comparison with past studies*

	Final ASSESSOR	Initial ASSESSOR	Agree
Laboratory trial	32%	23%	33%
Awareness[*]	70%	70%	70%
Distribution[*]	85%	85%	85%
Net cum trial	18.9%	13.7%	19.6%
Retention	36.4%	28.6%	42.1%
(Share of trier's choices)			
Base share	6.9%	3.9%	8.3%

(continued)

Exhibit 8 (continued)

		Base market sensitivity analysis		
			Awareness	
		60%	65%	70%
	75%	5.2%	5.7%	6.1%
Distribution	80%	5.6%	6.1%	6.5%
	85%	5.9%	6.4%	6.9%

*Managerial estimates.

2. Previous experience with ASSESSOR left doubts about how much more would be learned in a test market.
3. Management had confidence that the marketing organization could implement the marketing plan and make the product successful.
4. Gillette's introduction of Silkience and Agree's slipping share made it appear that entry would only become more difficult as time passed.
5. A great deal of the unique selling advantage a conditioner product had to offer was the positioning. Soon after Agree had been introduced, four other brands for oily hair were introduced. If a test market were run, the positioning could be stolen.

Exhibit 9. 1981 dollar volume prediction for various sampling levels

	Number of Samples				
	No Sampling	10MM	20MM	30MM	35MM
Base share from advertising	6.9%	6.9%	6.9%	6.9%	6.9%
+					
Incremental share from sampling		0.5%	1.1%	1.6%	1.9%
=					
Market share	6.9%	7.4%	8.0%	8.5%	8.9%
×					
Usage adjustment	0.9	0.9	0.9	0.9	0.9
×					
Price adjustment	1.04	1.04	1.04	1.04	1.04
×					
Category volume	$313MM	$313MM	$313MM	$313MM	$313MM
=					
Factory sales	$20.2MM	$21.7MM	$23.4MM	$25.0MM	$26.2MM

6. The cost of a 9-month test in two markets was estimated to be $1MM:

Store audits	$350,000
Product costs	150,000
Media costs	150,000
Commercial production	100,000
Attitude studies	50,000
Consumer research	120,000
Samples & sample study	80,000
Total	$1,000,000

The ASSESSOR study had cost about $250,000, including $200,000 for producing commercials, supplying product and packaging, and $50,000 paid to MDS. A regional introduction of a new product like Enhance would generally cost between $5–$8 million, and a national introduction was often a $35 million commitment. Product sales would reduce the net outlay for the regional and national introduction and, to some extent, for the test market, but introducing a new consumer product was a major undertaking for any company.

ENHANCE INTRODUCTION

Enhance Instant Conditioner was shipped for national distribution during the summer of 1980. Advertising began the first week of September—$2.72 million in 1980, and $4.5 million planned for 1981—and a 30 million-unit sample drop (3/4 ounce pouch in a Donnelley co-op mailing) took place the week of October 13, 1980. The market into which Enhance was launched was dynamic. Twenty-one new brands—including Gillette's Silkience, a substantial competitor backed by $6 million in media advertising in 1979—had been introduced since the ASSESSOR. The shares of the established brands had declined, and the brands included in the second ASSESSOR test accounted for only 75% of category sales in 1980. Dollar sales and market shares of the leading brands in 1980 were estimated by one national service as follows:

Manufacturer sales		
Brand	Company	$ Million
Flex	Revlon	$42
Silkience	Gillette	29
Agree	Johnson Wax	27

(continued)

Brand	Company	$ Million
Sassoon	Vidal Sassoon	19
Clairol Condition	Bristol-Myers	13
Tame	Gillette	12
All other		143
Total		295

The market was forecast to reach $397 million in 1980 dollars by 1985, a real growth rate of 6% per year. Instant hair conditioners were estimated by JW to be used in a majority of U.S. households, and penetration was growing slowly. Industry advertising expenditures in 1979 had been $33.8 million, and would surpass $38 million in 1980 (based on expenditure levels in the first nine months).

	Advertising expenditures	
	$ Thousands	
Brand	*1980 (9 mos.)*	*1979 (12 mos.)*
Silkience	$ 4,830	$ 6,063
Revlon Flex	3,372	3,008
Vidal Sassoon	3,127	2,876
Clairol Condition Beauty Pack	2,917	1,850
Alberto VO5 Hot Oil	2,880	3,112
Agree	2,798	4,036
Wella Balsam	2,503	3,079
Condition II	955	512
Clairol Small Miracle	856	
Others	4,290	9,249
	$28,528	$33,785

Retail share data on the instant conditioner market were incomplete, but indicated considerable turmoil. New brands had been introduced, and older brands had lost share or been withdrawn from the market. See Exhibit 10.

SAMPLING EFFECTIVENESS STUDY

A study to measure the effect of the 30 million-unit sample drop was undertaken in October 1980. The results were to be used to validate the ASSESSOR estimate of Enhance's sampling contribution. The study was

Exhibit 10. Hair conditioner shares

	1972	1973	1974	1975	1976	1977	1978	1979	1980	1981
Long & Silky	3.7	3.6	3.7	4.0	3.4	2.1	1.4	NA	NA	NA
Clairol Condition	13.0	14.7	15.5	15.2	15.2	14.3	9.9	10.2	9.5	8.8
Herbal Essence	NA	3.2	4.5	4.6	2.9	1.9	NA	NA	NA	NA
Wella Balsam	NA	NA	4.8	5.1	5.5	4.9	4.7	4.0	3.5	NA
Flex	NA	NA	NA	16.1	10.5	11.0	13.4	12.0	10.2	10.3
Tame	NA	NA	NA	12.3	10.2	6.7	5.4	5.1	3.9	2.6
Breck	NA	NA	NA	7.1	10.6	7.0	5.4	NA	NA	NA
Agree	NA	NA	NA	NA	NA	NA	15.2	11.9	8.4	6.0
Enhance	NA	NA	NA	NA	NA	NA	NA	NA	2.7*	4.1

NA = Not available either because the product was not marketed or because there were no clients for the data.
*6 months only.

performed by National Family Opinion (NFO), one of the largest survey houses in the United States.

Telephone interviews with 2,000 women who had used a creme rinse/conditioner during the past four weeks were conducted October 3–10, 1980 to determine the brand last purchased and which other brands had been purchased during the previous six months. Half of these women received a 3/4 oz. sample during the last three weeks of October. About eight weeks later, repeat interviews were conducted to determine brand use. The results of this test were as follows. Note that the control group did not receive the sample so is used as a measure of false reporting. These reports are subtracted from the Test numbers to generate the Net numbers.

	Test		Control		Net
	Number	%	Number	%	
Interviewed	510	100	506	100	
Reported Receiving Sample	158	31	40	7.9	23%
Reported Using Sample	63	12.4	16	3.2	9.2
Reported Purchasing Enhance	31	6.1	10	2.0	4.1

- The net difference in Enhance use due to sampling was significant at the 90% confidence level.
- Only 23% of those surveyed remembered receiving the sample, compared to the managerial assumption of 48% in the ASSESSOR.
- Only 40% of those receiving a sample had used it, compared to the 60% managerial assumption in ASSESSOR.
- The incremental share from sampling in the Enhance ASSESSOR had been predicted to be 1.9% based on a 35 million sample unit drop. The findings of the sampling effectiveness study indicated only a 0.4% incremental share. A revised best estimate based on the results of both studies indicated an incremental share from sampling of 0.9% (see Exhibit 11). This revision was partly due to JWC's changing the size of the sample to 3/4 ounce and cutting the mailing to 30 million units.

ENHANCE TRACKING STUDIES

To monitor the progress of Enhance, a series of tracking studies, similar to previous studies done for Agree, were performed during December

Exhibit 11. *Enhance sampling effectiveness[a]*

Assumptions		ASSESSOR 2 oz.	Sample effectiveness Study 3/4 oz.	Revised best Estimate 3/4 oz.
	Method of Delivery	Direct Mail	Co-op Mailing	
	Number of Samples	35MM	30MM	30MM
	Delivered	90%[b]		
	Hitting target group	80%[b]		
(1)	Received by target group	72%	23%	
(2)	Used/received	60%[b]	40%	
(1)x(2)	Percent of Samples Used	43%	9.2%	22%
(3)	Number of Samples Used	15.1MM	2.8MM	6.6MM
(3)÷60MM	Percent of Category Users Using Samples	25.2%	4.6%	11%
	Incremental Trial	20.4%	3.9%	9.2%
	First repeat	43.0%	48.0%	45.0%
	Retention	21.9%	23.5%	22.5%
(3)	Incremental Share	1.9%	0.4%	0.9%
(4)	Base Share	6.9%	6.9%	6.9%
(3)+(4)	Share Prediction	8.8%	7.3%	7.8%

[a]Assuming 60MM households and 16% switchback.
[b]Managerial estimate in the ASSESSOR study.

1980 and March 1981 to measure advertising and brand awareness, and trial and repeat rates. Each study consisted of telephone interviews within a national probability sample of 1,000 women, at least 14 years old, who had used a creme rinse/conditioner during the past four weeks. The sample included a quota of 145 Enhance buyers. Interviews were conducted throughout the day to obtain interviews with both working and nonworking women. Exhibit 12 summarizes the results of this test. At the end of six months, Enhance had not yet achieved the same level of trial (17%) as Agree had achieved at four months (18%). Conversion (ever used/brand awareness) had not increased in the three months between the studies. "Recent use" divided by "ever used" dropped from 63% to 39% (see Exhibits 13–15).

Exhibit 12. *Tracking studies results*

	Enhance—key measures			
	Agree 4 Months National 6/77	Enhance 3 Months National 12/80	Enhance 6 Months National 3/81	Silkience 9 Months National 11/79
Base	800	1006	752	1003
	%	%	%	%
Brand Awareness	60 —s—	51 —s—	63	64
Unaided	NA	9	7 —s—	10
Aided	NA	42 —s—	55	54
Conversion (Ever Used/ Brand Awareness)	30	28	27 —s—	30
Ever Used	18 —s—	14	17	19
Used Last	NA	4	4	5
Past 4 Week Use	NA	9	7	9
Past 4 Week Use/ Ever Used	NA	63 —s—	39	47
Advertising Awareness	NA	23 —s—	30 —s—	44

s = measures which significantly different from one another at 95% confidence level.

THE CURRENT SITUATION

The arrival of the most recent market share reports showed that Enhance's share for July/August 1981, the end of its first year, was only 3.7% compared with the ASSESSOR forecast of 8.8%. The March/April share had been only 3.2%. The news prompted Katherine Thompson to review her marketing program yet again.

> The problem facing me now is to determine and correct what is keeping Enhance's share low. There is a big temptation in this market, with so many brands appealing to so many different segments, to throw your hands in the air and say, "It's just too complicated to understand." But I don't think it really is. Most women want their hair to look nice, but have one or two problems they need to overcome.

> When I look at our sales force reports and other data, I see some problems. Our sales force is stretched very thin. There are 400 good people in that sales force, but they were primarily trained in the supermarket class of trade. Since a large percentage of hair-care products are sold by drug and mass merchandisers,

Exhibit 13. *Tracking studies results—awareness*

	Nov. 77	Oct. 78	Nov. 79	Dec. 80	Mar. 81
Brand awareness					
Base	771 %	748 %	1,003 %	1,006 %	752 %
Enhance	–	–	–	51 —s—	63
Agree	68[*]	86	90	92	92
Breck	97	95	96	97	96
Condition	–	–	94	93	92
Flex	68	80	82	85	87
Jhirmack	–	–	–	39 —s—	56
Sassoon	–	–	67 —s—	78	83
Silkience	–	–	64 —s—	90	91
Tame	91	90	93	91	91
Wella Balsam	92	92	98	98	97
Advertising awareness					
Enhance				23 —s—	30
Agree				60	60
Flex			39	45	46
Silkience			44 —s—	72	73

[*]First shipment 1/77; ads began 2/77.
s = measures which are significantly different from each other at 95% confidence level.

when Agree came along they had to start visiting a whole new class of trade in addition to the old one they knew. Unless we were terribly overstaffed before, this increase in the number of calls has to hurt somewhere. And it would be a miracle if they were as good in the new class of trade as they were in the old one, even with the good training we gave them.

With both Enhance and Agree, maybe we've stretched them a bit too far. I'm not sure we have all sizes in each store we cover, or that our shelf space is ideal, or whether we get our share of end aisle displays. Some reports imply that some retailers may be "making margin" on us by pricing Enhance higher than our competition. Our advertising hasn't been nearly as effective as we had planned and, as a result, awareness and trial are low. I'm sure that Enhance is sound! It's just our execution of the marketing plan that is keeping us from reaching our targets!

Exhibit 14. **Tracking studies results—*ever used***

	Nov. 1979		Dec. 1980		Mar. 1981
Base	1,003		1,006		752
	%		%		%
Enhance	–		14		17
Agree	53		53		52
Breck	56		54		54
Condition	50		52	—s—	58
Flex	50	—s—	55		53
Jhirmack	–		14*		15
Sassoon	24	—s—	29		32
Silkience	19	—s—	44	—s—	50
Tame	59		58		58
Wella Balsam	62		61	—s—	56

*Jhirmack is also used in beauty salons—about 4% of the 14% is accounted for by salon use.
s = measures which are significantly different from one another at 95% confidence level.

Thompson didn't face an immediate deadline in making a decision about Enhance's future, but brand reviews and the planning process would certainly raise some very difficult questions. She resolved to begin her analysis now so that she would be ready for the review.

Exhibit 15. **Past four-week use**

	Nov. 1979		Dec. 1980		Mar. 1981
Base	1,003		1,006		752
	%		%		%
Enhance	–				9
	7				
Agree	15	—s—	10		11
Breck	8	—s—	5		4
Condition	14		15		18
Flex	15	—s—	18		15
Jhirmack	–		5		5
Sassoon	9		10		11
Silkience	9	—s—	19		19
Tame	10	—s—	7		8
Wella Balsam	13	—s—	11		13

s = measures which are significantly different from one another at 95% confidence level.

8 CASE

Cumberland Metal Industries:
Engineered Products
Division, 1980

Benson P. Shapiro
Jeffrey J. Sherman

Robert Minicucci,[1] vice president of the Engineered Products Division of Cumberland Metal Industries (CMI), and Thomas Simpson, group manager of the Mechanical Products Group, had spent the entire Wednesday (January 2, 1980) reviewing a new product CMI was about to introduce. (See Exhibit 1 for organization charts.) The room was silent, and as he watched the waning rays of the sun filtering through the window, Minicucci pondered all that had been said. Turning toward Simpson, he paused before speaking.

---

[1]Pronounced Minikuchi.

Research Assistant Jeffrey J. Sherman prepared this case under the supervision of Professor Benson P. Shapiro as a basis for class discussion rather than to illustrate either effective or ineffective handling of an administrative situation. It was made possible by a company that prefers to remain anonymous. All data have been disguised.

Exhibit 1. Engineered products division organization chart

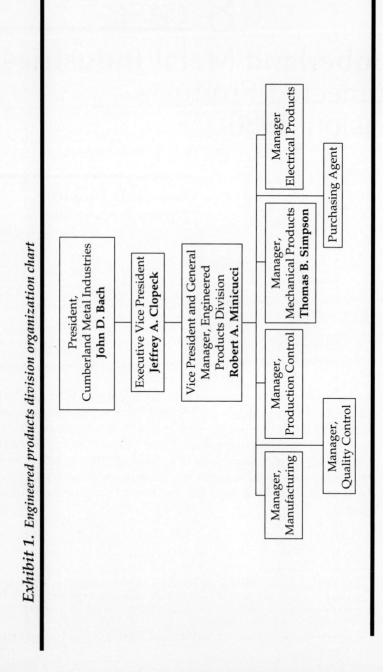

Exhibit 1 (continued). Mechanical products group organization chart

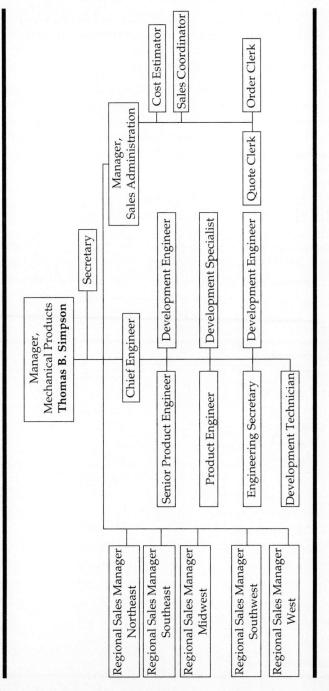

Curled metal cushion pads seem to have more potential than any product we've ever introduced. A successful market introduction could as much as double the sales of this company, as well as compensate for the decline of some existing lines. It almost looks too good to be true.

Simpson responded, "The people at Colerick Foundation Company are pressing us to sell to them. Since they did the original test, they've been anxious to buy more. I promised to contact them by the end of the week."

"Fair enough," Minicucci said, "but talk to me before you call them. The way we price this could have a significant impact on everything else we do with it."

THE COMPANY

Cumberland Metal Industries was one of the largest manufacturers of curled metal products in the country, having grown from $250,000 in sales in 1963 to over $18,500,000 by 1979. (Exhibit 2 shows CMI's income statement.) It originally custom fabricated components for chemical

Exhibit 2. **Income statement**

December 31	1979	1978
Net sales	$18,524,428	$20,465,057
Costs and expenses:		
Cost of sales	11,254,927	11,759,681
Selling expenses	2,976,396	2,711,320
General and administrative expenses	2,204,291	2,362,528
	16,435,614	16,833,529
Income from operations	2,088,814	3,631,528
Other income (expense):		
Dividend income	208,952	—
Interest income	72,966	186,611
Interest expense	(40,636)	(31,376)
	241,282	155,235
Income before income taxes	2,330,096	3,786,763
Provision for income taxes:	1,168,830	1,893,282
Net income	1,161,266	1,893,481
Net income per share	$1.39	$2.16

process filtration and other highly technical applications. Company philosophy soon evolved from selling the metal as a finished product to selling products that used it as a raw material.

The company's big boost came with the introduction of exhaust gas recirculation (EGR) valves on U.S. automobiles. Both the Ford and Chrysler valve designs required a high temperature seal to hold the elements in place and prevent the escape of very hot exhaust gases. Cumberland developed a product that sold under the trademark *Slip-Seal*. Because it could meet the demanding specifications of the automakers, the product captured a very large percentage of the available business, and the company grew quite rapidly through the mid-1970s. Company management was not sanguine about maintaining its 80% market share over the long term, however, and moved to diversify away from a total reliance on the product and industry. Thus, when a sales representative from Houston approached CMI with a new application for curled metal technology, management examined it closely.

THE PRODUCT

BACKGROUND

The product that Minicucci and Simpson were talking about was a cushion pad, an integral part of the process for driving piles.[2] Pile driving was generally done with a large crane, to which a diesel or steam hammer inside a set of leads was attached. The leads were suspended over the pile for direction and support. The hammer drove the pile from the top of the leads to a sufficient depth in the ground (see Exhibit 3).

The cushion pads prevented the shock of the hammer from damaging hammer or pile. They sat in a circular "helmet" placed over the top of the pile and were stacked to keep air from coming between striker plate and ram, as shown in Exhibit 3. Of equal importance, the pads effectively transmitted energy from the hammer to the pile. A good cushion pad had to be able to transmit force without creating heat, and still remain resilient enough to prevent shock. With an ineffective pad, energy transmitted from the hammer would be given off as heat, and the pile could start to vibrate and possibly crack.

---

[2]Piles were heavy beams of wood, concrete, steel, or a composite material which were pushed into the ground as support for a building, bridge, or other structure. They were necessary where the geological composition could shift under the weight of an unsupported structure.

Exhibit 3. Typical steam- or air-operated pile driver with helmet and cushion pad

Steam or Air Cylinder

Guide Rods, or "Leads"

Rising and Falling Weight (Ram)

Piledriver Ram Point

Piledriver Base

Striker Plate

CMI Cushion Pads

Helmet (or Cap Block)

Pile

A schematic diagram of typical pile driver

Pile hammer inside leads driving a steel H-beam into the ground

CMI pile-driving pad in position in helmet

Close-up of hammer driving pile (most of the pile is already in the ground)

Despite the importance of these pads to the pile-driving process, little attention had been paid to them by most of the industry. Originally, hardwood blocks had been used. Although their cushioning was adequate, availability was a problem and performance was poor. Constant pounding quickly destroyed the wood's resiliency, heat built up, and the wood often ignited. The blocks had to be replaced frequently.

Most of the industry had shifted to asbestos pads (normally 1/4-inch thick) which were used most often and seemed to perform adequately, or stacks of alternate layers of 1/2-inch-thick aluminum plate and 1-inch-thick micarta slabs. (These were not fabricated, but simply pieces of micarta and aluminum cut to specific dimensions.) Both pads came in a variety of standard diameters, the most common being 11 1/2 inches. Diameter was determined by the size of the helmet, which varied with the size of the pile.

CURLED METAL AND THE CMI CUSHION PAD

Curled metal was a continuous metal wire that had been flattened and then wound into tight, continuous ringlets. These allowed the metal to stretch in both length and width and gave it three-dimensional resiliency. Because it could be made of various metals (such as copper, monel, and stainless steel), curled metal could be made to withstand almost any temperature or chemical. Stacking many layers could produce a shock mount, an airflow corrector, or a highly efficient filter. Tightly compressed curled metal could produce the Slip-Seal for exhaust systems applications or, when calendered and wound around an axis, a cushion pad for pile driving.[3]

Cumberland purchased the wire from outside vendors and performed the flattening and curling operations in-house. The CMI pad started with curled metal calendered to about one-inch thick and wound tightly around the center of a flat, metallic disk until the desired diameter had been reached. A similar disk was placed on top, with soldered tabs folded down to hold it all together. The entire structure was then coated with polyvinyl chloride to enhance its appearance and disguise the contents (see Exhibit 4).[4]

---

[3]In calendering, curled metal ringlets were compressed between rollers to make a smooth, tight band.

[4]The managers at CMI were concerned that other manufacturers might discover this new application for curled metal and enter the business before CMI could get patent protection. The company had a number of competitors, most of whom were substantially smaller than CMI and none of whom had shown a strong interest or competence in technical, market, or product development.

Exhibit 4. Close-up of CMI curled metal cushion pad for pile driving

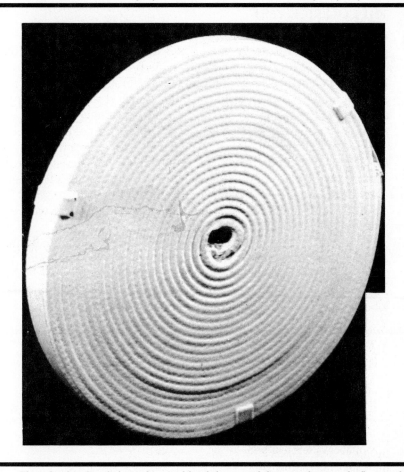

The calendered curled metal is would tightly around the central point of a flat metal-lic disk. (The disk is on the back side of the pad from this view.) Soldered tabs secure the curled metal to the disk. The entire structure is coated with polyvinylchloride.

The advantage of this manufacturing process was that any diameter pad, from the standard minimum of 11 1/2 inches to over 30 inches for a custom-designed application, could be produced from the same band of curled metal.

COMPARATIVE PERFORMANCE

THE COLERICK TEST

After struggling to find a responsible contractor to use the product and monitor its performance, CMI persuaded Colerick Foundation Company of Baltimore, Maryland, to try its pads on a papermill expansion in Newark, Delaware. The job required 300 55-foot piles driven 50 feet into the ground. The piles were 10-inch and 14-inch steel H-beams; both used an 11 1/2-inch helmet and, thus, 11 1/2-inch cushion pads. The total contractor revenue from the job was $75,000 ($5 per foot of pile driven).

Colerick drove a number of piles using the conventional 1/4-inch-thick asbestos cushion pads to determine their characteristics for the job. Eighteen were placed in the helmet and driven until they lost resiliency. Pads were added, and driving continued until a complete set of 24 were sitting in the helmet. After these were spent, the entire set was removed and the cycle repeated.

The rest of the job used the CMI pads. Four were initially installed and driven until 46 piles had been placed. One pad was added and the driving continued for 184 more piles. Another pad was placed in the helmet, and the job was completed. Comparable performances for the entire job were extrapolated as follows:

		Asbestos	CMI
1.	Feet driven per hour while pile driver was at work (does not consider downtime)	150	200
2.	Piles driven per set of pads	15	300
3.	Number of pads per set	24	6
4.	Number of sets required	20	1
5.	Number of set changes	20	1
6.	Time required for change per set (minutes)	20	4
7.	Colerick cost per set	$50	N/C[a]

[a]N/C = not charged

Although the CMI pads drove piles 33% faster than the asbestos and lasted for the entire job, Simpson felt these results were unusual. He believed that curled metal set life of 10 times more than asbestos and a performance increase of 20% were probably more reasonable, because he was uncertain that the CMI pads in larger sizes would perform as well.

TABLE A   Equipment rental, labor, and overhead costs

	Per standard		Per hour	Average cost per real hour[a]
	Month	Week		
1. Diesel hammer	$4,500–7,200	$1,500–2,400	$62.50–100.00	$34
2. Crane	8,000–10,000	2,667–3,334	111.00–140.00	52
3. Leads @ $20 per foot per month (assume 70 feet)	1,400	467	19.44	8
4. Labor[b]—three laborers @ $6-$8 per hour each			18.00–24.00	21
▪ 1 crane operator			8.00–12.00	10
▪ 1 foreman			12.00–14.00	13
5. Overhead[c] (office, trucks, oil/gas, tools, etc.)			100.00	100

Casewriter's note: Please use average cost per real hour in all calculations, for uniformity in class discussion.

[a]These costs were calculated from a rounded midpoint of the estimates. Hammer, crane, and lead costs were obtained by dividing standard monthly costs by 4.33 weeks per month and 40 hours per week.

[b]Labor was paid on a 40-hour week, and a 4.33-week month. One-shift operation (40 hours per week) was standard in the industry.

[c]Most contractors calculated overhead on the basis of "working" hours, not standard hours.

INDUSTRY PRACTICE

Industry sources indicated that as many as 75% of pile-driving contractors owned their hammers, and most owned at least one crane and set of leads. To determine the contractors' cost of doing business, CMI studied expenses of small contractors who rented equipment for pile-driving jobs. These numbers were readily available and avoided the problem of allocating the cost of a purchased crane or hammer to a particular job.

Standard industry practice for equipment rental used a three-week month and a three-day workweek.[5] There was no explanation for this, other than tradition, but most equipment renters set their rates this way. The cost of renting the necessary equipment and the labor cost for a job similar to that performed by Colerick were estimated as shown in Table A.

---

[5]This means that a contractor who rented equipment for one calendar month was charged only the "three-week" price, but had the equipment for the whole calendar month. The same was true of the "three-day week." Contractors generally tried to use the equipment for as much time per week or per month as possible. Thus, they rented it on a "three-week" month, but used it on a "4.33-week" month.

Exhibit 5. Curled metal cushion pad standard sizes

Diameter (inches)	Thickness (inches)	Weight (pounds)
11.5	1	15.5
14	1	23
17.5	1	36
19	1	48
23	1	64
30	1	110

Hidden costs also played an important role. For every hour actually spent driving piles, a contractor could spend 20 to 40 minutes moving the crane into position. Another 10% to 15% was added to cover scheduling delays, mistakes, and other unavoidable problems. Thus, the real cost per hour was substantially more than the initial figures showed. Reducing the driving time or pad changing time did not usually affect the time lost on delays and moving.

All these figures were based on a job that utilized 55-foot piles and 11 1/2-inch pads. Although this was a common size, much larger jobs requiring substantial bigger material were frequent. A stack of 11 1/2-inch asbestos pads weighed between 30 and 40 pounds; the 30-inch size could weigh seven to eight times more. Each 11 1/2-inch CMI pad weighed 15 1/2 pounds. The bigger sizes, being much more difficult to handle, could contribute significantly to unproductive time on a job. (See Exhibit 5.)

Most contracts were awarded on a revenue-per-foot basis. Thus, contractors bid by estimating the amount of time it would take to drive the specified piles the distance required by the architectural engineers. After totalling costs and adding a percentage for profit, they submitted figures broken down into dollars per foot. The cost depended on the size of the piles and the type of soil to be penetrated. The $5 per foot that Colerick charged was not atypical, but prices could be considerably greater.

TEST RESULTS

The management of CMI was extremely pleased by how well its cushion pads had performed. Not only had they lasted the entire job, eliminating the downtime required for changeover, but other advantages had become apparent. For example, after 500 feet of driving, the average temperature was between 600°F and 700°F, which created great difficulty when they had to be replaced. The crew handling them was endangered, and substantial time was wasted waiting for them to cool. (This accounted for a major portion of the time lost to changeovers.)

The CMI pads, in contrast, never went above 250°F and could be handled almost immediately with protective gloves. This indicated that substantial energy lost in heat by the asbestos pads was being used more efficiently to drive the piles with CMI pads. In addition, the outstanding resiliency of the CMI product seemed to account for a 33% faster driving time, which translated into significant savings.

In talking with construction site personnel, CMI researchers also found that most were becoming wary of the asbestos pads' well-publicized health dangers. Many had expressed a desire to use some other material and were pleased that the new pads contained no asbestos.

The CMI management was quite happy with these results; Colerick was ecstatic. Understandably, Colerick became quite anxious to buy more pads and began pressing Tom Simpson to quote prices.

A SECOND TEST

To confirm the results from the Colerick test, CMI asked Fazio Construction to try the pads on a job in New Brighton, Pennsylvania. This job required 300 45-foot concrete piles to be driven 40 feet into the ground. Asbestos pads (11 1/2 inches) were again used for comparison. Total job revenue was $108,000, or $9 per foot, and Fazio would have paid $40 for each set of 12 asbestos pads used. The results from this test are shown as follows:

	Asbestos	CMI
1. Feet driven per hour while pile driver was at work (does not consider downtime)	160	200
2. Piles driven per set of pads	6	300
3. Number of pads per set	12	5
4. Number of sets required	50	1
5. Number of set changes	50	1
6. Time required for change per set (minutes)	20	4
7. Fazio cost per set	$40	N/C[a]

[a]N/C = not charged

THE MARKET

PROJECTED SIZE

There were virtually no statistics from which a potential U.S. market for cushion pads could be determined, so Simpson had to make several assumptions based on the information he could gather. A 1977 report by *Construction Engineering* magazine estimated that approximately 13,000 pile hammers were owned by companies directly involved in pile driving. Industry sources estimated that another 6,500 to 13,000 were leased. He assumed that this total of 19,500 to 26,000 hammers would operate about 25 weeks per year (because of seasonality) and that they would be used 30 hours per week (because of moving time, repairs, scheduling problems, and other factors).

Simpson further assumed that an average actual driving figure (including time to change pads and so on) for most jobs was 20 feet per hour, which amounted to between 290 million and 390 million feet of piles driven annually. To be conservative, he also assumed that a set of curled metal pads (four initially installed, plus two added after the originals lost some resiliency) would drive 10,000 feet.

PURCHASE INFLUENCES

In the pile-driving business, as in other parts of the construction industry, a number of entities participated in purchases. The CMI management was able to identify six types of influences.

1. *Pile hammer manufacturers.* A number of manufacturers sold hammers in the United States, although many were imported from Western Europe and Japan. The leading domestic producer in 1979 was Vulcan Iron Works of New Orleans, whose Model #1 had become the standard used by architectural engineers specifying equipment for a job. Simpson did not feel these manufacturers would purchase a large dollar volume of cushion pads, but they could be very influential in recommendations.
2. *Architectural/consulting engineers.* Pile driving required significant expertise in determining the needs of a construction project. Thorough stress analysis and other mathematical analyses were necessary. Because of the risks in building the expensive projects usually supported by piles, the industry looked to architectural/consulting engineers as the ultimate authorities on all aspects of the business. Consequently, these firms were very detailed in specifying the materials and techniques to be used on a project. They always specified

hammers and frequently mentioned pads. The CMI management felt that, although no sales would come from these people, they could be one of the most important purchase influences.

3. *Soil consultants.* These consultants were similar to the architectural/consulting engineers, but were consulted only on extraordinary conditions.

4. *Pile hammer distributing/renting companies.* This group was an important influence because it provided pads to the contractors. In fact, renting companies often included the first set of pads free. CMI management felt that these companies would handle the cushion pads they could most easily sell and might even hesitate to provide pads that enabled a contractor to return equipment faster.

5. *Engineering/construction contractors.* The contracting portion of the industry was divided among large international firms and smaller independents. The former almost always participated in the bigger, more sophisticated jobs. Companies like Conmaco and Raymond International not only contracted to drive piles, but also designed jobs, specified material, and even manufactured their own equipment. It was clear to Simpson that if he was to succeed in getting CMI pads used on bigger, complex construction projects, CMI would have to solicit this group actively on a very sophisticated level.

6. *Independent pile-driving contractors.* These contractors represented the "frontline buying influence." The primary objective was to make money. They were very knowledgeable about the practical aspects of pile driving, but not very sophisticated.

No national industry associations influenced this business, but some regional organizations played a minor part. Contractors and others talked freely, although few were willing to reveal competitive secrets. The company was unsure how important word-of-mouth communication would be. Very little was published about the pile-driving industry, although construction-oriented magazines like *Louisiana Contractor* occasionally reported on pile-driving contractors and their jobs. These magazines featured advertising by suppliers to the trade, mostly equipment dealers and supply houses. One industry supplier, Associated Pile and Fitting Corporation, sponsored professional-level "Piletalk" seminars in various cities, bringing designers, contractors, and equipment developers together "to discuss practical aspects of installation of driven piles."

Another potential influence was Professor R. Stephen McCormack of Pennsylvania A&M University. He had established a department to study pile driving and had become a respected authority on its theoretical aspects. Sophisticated engineering/construction firms and many architectural consultants were familiar with his work and helped support it. Cumberland management felt that his endorsement of the operational performance of CMI cushion pads would greatly enhance industry acceptance. The company submitted the pads for testing by Dr. McCormack in the fall of 1979, and although the final results were not yet available, he had expressed considerable enthusiasm. Final results were expected by early 1980.

COMPETITIVE PRODUCTS AND CHANNELS OF DISTRIBUTION

The pile-driving industry had paid very little attention to cushion pads before CMI's involvement. Everyone used them and took them for granted, but no one attempted to promote pads. No manufacturers dominated the business. In fact, most pads came unbranded, having been cut from larger pieces of asbestos or micarta by small, anonymous job shops.

Distribution of pads was also ambiguous. Hammer sales and rental outlets provided them, heavy construction supply houses carried them, pile manufacturers sometimes offered them, and a miscellaneous assortment of other outlets occasionally sold them as a service.[6] The smaller pads sold for $2 to $3 each; larger ones sold for between $5 and $10. Three dollars each was typical for 11 1/2-inch pads. The profit margin for a distributor was usually adequate—in the area of 30% to 40%—but the dollar profit did not compare well with that of other equipment lines. Most outlets carried pads as a necessary part of the business, but none featured them as a work-saving tool.

The CMI management felt it could be totally flexible in establishing an organization to approach the market. It toyed with the idea of a direct sales force and its own distribution outlets, but eventually began to settle on signing construction-oriented manufacturers' representatives,[7] who would sell to a variety of distributors and supply houses. The company feared an uphill struggle to convince the sales and distribution channels that there really was a market for the new pad. Management expected considerable difficulty in finding outlets willing to devote the attention necessary for success, but it also felt that once the initial barriers had

---

[6] Supply houses were "hardware stores" for contractors and carried a general line of products, including lubricants, work gloves, and maintenance supplies. Distributors, in contrast, tended to be more equipment oriented and to sell a narrower line of merchandise.

[7] Manufacturers' representatives were agents (sometimes single people, sometimes organizations) who sold noncompeting products for commission. They typically did *not* take title to the merchandise and did *not* extend credit.

been penetrated, most of the marketplace would be anxious to handle the product.

THE PRICING DECISION

Simpson had projected cost data developed by his manufacturing engineers. Exhibit 6 shows two sets of numbers: one utilized existing equipment; the other reflected the purchase of $50,000 of permanent tooling. In both cases, the estimated volume was 250 cushion pads per month. Additional equipment could be added at a cost of $75,000 per 250 pads per month of capacity, including permanent tooling like that which could be purchased for $50,000.

Both sets of numbers were based on the assumption that only one pad size would be manufactured; in other words, the numbers in the 11 1/2-inch size were based on manufacturing only this size for a year. This

Exhibit 6. *Two sets of projected manufacturing costs*

	Size					
	11 1/2"	14"	17 1/2"	19"	23"	30"
Estimates per pad with existing equipment						
Variable:						
Material	$15.64	$20.57	$31.81	$40.39	$53.16	$95.69
Labor	28.80	33.07	50.02	57.07	69.16	118.36
Total variable	44.44	53.64	81.83	97.46	122.32	214.05
Fixed factory overhead:						
@ 360% direct labor	103.68	119.05	180.07	205.45	248.98	426.10
Total manufacturing cost	$148.12	$172.69	$261.90	$302.91	$371.30	$640.15
Estimates with purchase of $50,000 of permanent tooling						
Variable:						
Material	$15.64	$20.57	$31.81	$40.39	$53.16	$95.69
Labor	11.64	15.25	21.85	26.95	30.57	56.09
Total variable	27.28	35.82	53.66	67.34	83.73	151.78
Fixed factory overhead						
@ 360% direct labor	41.90	54.90	78.66	97.02	110.05	201.92
Total manufacturing cost	$69.18	$90.72	$132.32	$164.36	$193.78	$353.70

Note: Estimated volume was 250 cushion pads per month.

was done because CMI had no idea of the potential sales mix among product sizes. Management knew that 11 1/2 inches was the most popular size, but the information available on popularity of the other sizes was vague. CMI accounting personnel believed these numbers would not vary dramatically with a mix of sizes.

Corporate management usually burdened CMI products with a charge equal to 360% of direct labor to cover the overhead of its large engineering staff. Simpson was uncertain how this would apply to the new product, because little engineering had been done and excess capacity was to be used initially for manufacturing. Although it was allocated on a variable basis, he thought he might consider the overhead "fixed" for his analysis. Corporate management expected a contribution margin after all manufacturing costs of 40% to 50% of selling price.

Simpson was enthusiastic about the potential success of this new product. The Engineered Products Division was particularly pleased to offer something with such high dollar potential, especially since in the past, a "large customer" of the division had purchased only about $10,000 per year.

He was still uncertain how to market the pads and how to reach the various purchase influences. Advertising and promotion also concerned him because there were no precedents for this product or market.

For the moment, however, Simpson's primary consideration was pricing. He had promised to call Colerick Foundation Company by the end of the week, and Minicucci was anxious to review his decision with him. He hoped other prospects would be calling as soon as word about the pads' test performance got around.

9 *CASE*

General Mills, Inc.: Yoplait Custard-Style Yogurt (A)

John A. Quelch
John Teopaco

In June 1980, Bruce Becker, Director of New Business Development at Yoplait USA, a Consumer Foods Group subsidiary of General Mills, Inc., was deciding on how to proceed with a new product, Custard-Style Yogurt. The product was the first in Yoplait's product line expansion program, and test results to date were encouraging. Yoplait's original product line had been introduced into 60% of the United States—the Midwest and West—during the previous two years, and had become the

Research Assistant John Teopaco prepared this case under the supervision of Professor John A. Quelch as the basis for class discussion rather than to illustrate either effective or ineffective handling of an administrative situation.

number two yogurt brand nationally. General Mills management was very pleased with Yoplait Original-Style's success, but they were also eager to introduce new products to capitalize on Yoplait's momentum and to preempt competition.

Management attention was focused on Custard-Style Yogurt, identified early on as the most promising line extension. Consumer product testing results had been positive, but Becker realized that he needed test market data for a more reliable measure of Custard-Style's potential. He was considering the following options: a simulated test market, a "mini-market" test and a regular test market. Given unlimited time, Becker would have considered doing all three, but under pressure to roll out Custard-Style as soon as possible, he had to select one or two test approaches to conduct in sequence or at the same time. In preparing for any test, Becker knew that there were still several marketing issues that needed resolution such as Custard-Style's positioning, pricing and final product specifications.

COMPANY BACKGROUND

In 1928, James Ford Bell, president of the Washburn Crosby Company, incorporated several flour millers to form the world's largest grain processor, General Mills, Inc. Gold Medal Flour, General Mills' original product, was still a major brand in 1980, but, by then, General Mills had expanded into other consumer foods and nonfood categories.

Total company sales for fiscal year 1980 (ending May 25, 1980) were $4.17 billion with net earnings of $170.0 million. Fiscal 1980 was the fourteenth successive year of sales increase and the eighteenth consecutive year of gain in earnings. Advertising expenditures increased 13% in 1980 to $213.1 million.

General Mills comprised five major operating groups—Consumer Foods, Restaurants (e.g., Red Lobster Inns, York Steak House), Creative Products (e.g., Parker Brothers, Star Wars toys), Fashion (e.g., Izod/Lacoste shirts, Monet jewelry) and Specialty Retailing (e.g., Pennsylvania House furniture). Consumer Foods was the largest group with 1980 sales of $2.2 billion and operating profits of $210.5 million (53% of total company sales and operating profits). The group marketed products such as Cheerios and Wheaties breakfast cereals, Nature Valley Granola Bars, Gold Medal Flour, Hamburger Helper Dinner Mixes, Betty Crocker Desserts, Gorton's Frozen Fish products and Yoplait Yogurt.

PRODUCT MANAGEMENT AT GENERAL MILLS

General Mills established its product management system more than twenty years ago. Under this system, responsibility for every General Mills brand was assigned to a product manager. By placing one person in charge of a brand's overall performance in the market-place, General Mills tried to ensure that every brand was managed as if it were a small company, rather than part of a large bureaucracy. It was the product manager's duty to be wholly knowledgeable about all issues involving his or her brand—from product ingredients to media planning.

General Mills recruited MBAs for its product management training program. They began as marketing assistants working under the supervision of a product manager. After about a year, they were promoted to assistant product manager. Approximately two years later, the successful assistant product manager was promoted to product manager.

General Mills took pride in several distinctive features of its product management system. The organization had fewer levels than most large consumer goods companies. Product managers reported to marketing directors (each responsible for a group of brands) who, in turn, reported to division general managers.[1] Unlike other packaged goods companies, General Mills did not have senior product managers or group product managers between the product managers and the marketing directors, nor were there business unit managers between the marketing directors and division general managers. General Mills believed that a flat organizational structure and an emphasis on verbal rather than written communications promoted more efficient decision making and greater breadth of responsibility for entry-level managers.

A second distinctive feature of General Mills' product management system was the systematic rotation of junior marketing personnel not only among brands at different stages of development, but also across divisions. For example, a marketing assistant on Cheerios might be promoted to assistant product manager on new products—Betty Crocker desserts—and later be reassigned to an established frozen foods brand.

---

[1]There were six division general managers within the Consumer Foods operating group. Each division had its own marketing research organization, but shared an 800-person national sales force. In addition, division general managers did not control plants dedicated to manufacturing their products but, rather, purchased manufacturing services from the Packaged Foods Operations Division.

Career development was further helped by General Mills' mix of small and large brands. According to one marketing director:

> *A small brand would have only one marketing assistant reporting to a product manager. He or she can take a cut at everything and develop considerable breadth. On a large brand, each of several marketing assistants might be given a specific functional responsibility on a six-month rotational basis. In this kind of job, an individual can develop depth of expertise.*

General Mills felt that a series of assignments on diverse brands of varying sizes enriched the manager's learning experience and prepared him or her for general management.

YOPLAIT USA

In October 1977, General Mills acquired the rights to market Yoplait products in the United States from Sodima, a French dairy cooperative. General Mills was interested in entering the yogurt market, but without any dairy experience, the company decided to enter via acquisition instead of internal development. Sodima had been licensing its technology around the world since the late 1960s, and in the United States, it began by licensing the rights to Yoplait Yogurt to Michigan Brand Cottage Cheese, a regional dairy company. The company sold Yoplait Original-Style Yogurt in five flavors in Michigan, Indiana and Ohio. Annual sales were about $10 million. Upon taking over the rights to the Yoplait name, General Mills also bought Michigan Brand's yogurt manufacturing plant.

General Mills integrated the Yoplait acquisition into its operations by forming Yoplait USA as a subsidiary of the Consumer Foods Group. At 33 years of age, Stephen Rothschild, formerly a marketing director in the New Business Division, was made president of Yoplait USA.[2] Rothschild believed that Yoplait required a nontraditional type of management. Yogurt was different from the standard General Mills product—it was refrigerated and had only a 30-day shelf life; Production could not build up inventory. This required greater coordination with Distribution and Sales and quick decision making in day-to-day operations.

Recruiting from various parts of the General Mills organization, Rothschild assembled an entrepreneurial management team of individu-

---

[2] General Mills typically maintained a New Business Division, investigating new product opportunities in categories in which the company did not yet compete.

Exhibit 1. *Yoplait USA organizational structure*

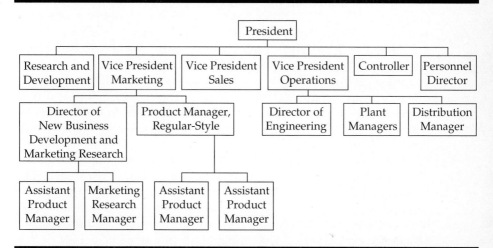

als who were looking for a challenge and who wanted to "do something different." As Bruce Becker observed, "The appeal was the opportunity to deal with the total business. The team was highly self-motivated. Being located in a building outside corporate headquarters, we built up a strong camaraderie. Sometimes, we spent weekends in the pilot plant making yogurt."

Exhibit 1 shows Yoplait USA's organizational structure in 1980. With a background in marketing research, Becker assumed responsibilities for new product development and marketing research. He had an assistant product manager who worked on new products. A three-person brand group managed regular-style yogurt and, along with Becker's group, reported to the Vice President of Marketing.

THE YOGURT MARKET

Yogurt was produced by inoculating milk with bacteria. After multiplying in the milk, the bacteria consumed the milk's sugar lactose and replaced it with acids. The acids curdled the milk, giving yogurt its thick consistency and tart flavor.

When General Mills began rolling out Yoplait regular-style yogurt to the West Coast in late 1978, the yogurt market comprised three product segments: sundae-style (53% of yogurt volume), Swiss-style (37%) and plain (9%). Sundae-style yogurts such as Dannon contained fruit on the bottom of the cup which was stirred up prior to eating. Swiss-style contained fruit mixed in or blended throughout the yogurt, while plain yogurt contained no fruit. All three types had a thick consistency.

Yoplait Original-Style Yogurt was all natural and had fruit mixed throughout. Yoplait was differentiated by its French origin (all other yogurts were American), its unique, reverse-cone, plastic package very different from the traditional, cylindrical, waxed paper cup, and most especially, by its creamy, smooth texture as opposed to the thicker consistency of sundae-style and Swiss-style yogurts. Yoplait also was less tart than other yogurts.

The total U.S. refrigerated yogurt market in 1980 was estimated at 87 million cases (12 8-oz. cups/case) or $425 million in retail sales. This represented annual consumption of five cups per capita compared to 45 cups per capita in France. Unit volume had not changed from the previous year, but over the last ten years category volume had increased at an average annual rate of 13%, roughly trebling since 1970. However, in 1980, 45% of Americans still had not tried yogurt and only 25% of households were buying yogurt in any two-month period. Ten percent of the population accounted for three-quarters of all yogurt consumption. Advertising media spending for yogurt in 1980 was estimated at $18 million.

The yogurt market was fragmented and highly regional, partly because regional dairies used surplus milk to manufacture either yogurt or cottage cheese. There was no nationally distributed brand in 1980 although Dannon, the number one brand with a 24% unit market share and availability in two-thirds of the country, was expected to be national within two years, along with Yoplait. Private label, accounting for 26% of yogurt volume nationwide, made it difficult for new national brands to obtain shelf space without heavy dealing (especially in the East) and without convincing the trade that the total category would expand in size.

Exhibit 2 lists market shares and yogurt per capita consumption indexes (PCI) for key markets. In Southern California, Yoplait was the leading brand with a 25.2% market share followed by Knudsen with 20.6% and Jersey Maid with 11.3%. In metro New York, on the other hand, Dannon was the leader with 41.0% of the market followed by Colombo with 12.6% and Breyers with 11.5%. Category development, as measured by a market's per capita consumption of yogurt relative to the national average, also varied greatly by region. Southern California was highly developed with a 252 PCI whereas Carolina/Virginia was underdeveloped with a 40 PCI.

Exhibit 2. *Yogurt per capita indexes (PCI) and unit market shares (February/March 1980)*

Market	% of U.S. population	PCI	Leading brands' market shares	
Southern California	6.4%	252	Yoplait	25.2%
			Knudsen	20.6
			Jersey Maid	11.3
			Johnston's	6.1
			Private label	27.7
Northern California	4.1	220	Yoplait	20.5
			Knudsen	15.1
			Crystal	5.8
			Private label	47.7
Pacific Northwest	3.4	132	Yoplait	19.5
			Yami	10.4
			Private label	57.5
Minnesota/Iowa	3.0	55	Dannon	25.3
			Yoplait	20.8
			Slim 'n Trim	10.6
			Gaymont	6.0
			Private label	0
Metro Chicago	3.5	96	Dannon	54.8
			Yoplait	18.9
			Private label	17.9
Metro New York	7.1	192	Dannon	41.0%
			Colombo	12.6
			Breyers	11.5
			Light 'n Lively	9.3
			La Yogurt	7.3
			Private label	9.1
Baltimore/Washington	3.4	82	Dannon	30.8
			Breyers	10.2
			Light 'n Lively	7.1
			Private label	40.4
Carolina/Virginia	6.6	40	Dannon	29.6
			Light 'n Lively	18.6
			Breyers	12.5
			Pet	7.0
			Private label	27.1

The yogurt market was expected to become highly competitive with the growing involvement of sophisticated marketers. Dannon was owned by Beatrice Foods, Breyers and Light 'n Lively by Kraft, Inc., and Borden yogurt by Borden, Inc. The market was becoming increasingly segmented as the various brands attempted to carve out market niches through a variety of product positionings. Dannon's strategy was to offer nutrition and value; Breyers was positioned as superior tasting natural yogurt; Light 'n Lively also emphasized taste and naturalness, but was targeted at light users and nonusers of yogurt; Borden was positioned as the all-natural American yogurt and capitalized on the company's heritage as a dairy products leader; New Country claimed fewer calories and full taste. Yoplait regular-style was positioned as a premium, all-natural French yogurt with a smooth, creamy texture. Johanna Farms had a strong presence in metropolitan New York with La Yogurt, a Yoplait-type product that emphasized superior taste, claiming that it was yogurt made the French way—all natural fruit blended with yogurt to produce a creamy, smooth texture. Exhibit 3 summarizes competitive positionings, advertising expenditures and geographic coverage.

Competitors also differed in their distribution systems. Using a fleet of leased trucks, Dannon delivered its yogurt direct to supermarkets where the drivers stocked the shelves. Dannon's shelf life was limited to 17 days. Inventory control and shelf space management were, therefore, extremely important. However, some major supermarket chains, especially in the West, disliked store door delivery and wanted Dannon to ship to their refrigerated warehouses. Yoplait and most other yogurt producers, except for some regional dairies, shipped to chain warehouses rather than using store door delivery. Yoplait had experimented with store door delivery in Chicago, but the test proved uneconomical. The chains objected to the loss of control, there was union opposition, and out-of-stocks were frequent on the most popular flavors.

CONSUMER ATTITUDES AND USAGE

A Gallup national survey of yogurt users showed that the yogurt user group stopped growing in 1979—32% of adults had eaten refrigerated yogurt in the past four weeks, the same as in 1978. Little or no growth was anticipated in the near term because the number of people who expected to eat yogurt in the next four weeks grew only 2%:

	Among all respondents		
	1977	1978	1979
Have eaten yogurt in past 4 weeks	28%	32%	32%
Expect to eat yogurt in next 4 weeks	32	36	38

Exhibit 3. Yogurt brands geographic coverages, positionings, and media expenditures (fiscal year 1980)

Brand	Parent company	% U.S. coverage	Positioning/strategy	Estimated media expenditures (000)	% Change vs. previous year
Yoplait	General Mills, Inc.	60%	All-natural, premium quality, creamy French yogurt	$3,150	+90%
Dannon	Beatrice Foods	66	Nutrition/value reassurance	6,500	+110
Breyers	Kraft, Inc.	54	Superior tasting, natural yogurt	2,800	+15
Light 'n Lively	Kraft, Inc.	48	Good taste, natural reassurance	2,700	+50
Borden	Borden, Inc.	45	Good tasting, all-natural American yogurt/Borden heritage	660	+15
Knudsen	Knudsen Co.	14	Nutrition/taste/leadership	810	+15
Colombo	Colombo Co.	21	Product reassurance/all-natural	600	+50
La Yogurt	Johanna Farms	NA	Superior taste because of fruit and French recipe/natural reassurance	NA	NA

Current users ate yogurt primarily for taste, followed by nutrition and dietary considerations. The biggest changes since the survey began in 1977 were the decreases in use for dietary reasons and as a lunch or meal substitute. This reflected the growing recognition of yogurt as a high calorie product:

Reasons for usage	Among respondents expecting to use yogurt in next 4 weeks		
	1977	1978	1979
Like the taste	51%	57%	54%
Nutritious	21	17	21
Nonfattening/dietary	20	14	13
Eat for lunch/meal	12	5	4

In terms of usage occasion, yogurt continued to be eaten most often at lunchtime, but this occasion continued to decline significantly. "Evening snack" and "between meals" were the next most important usage occasions:

Have eaten yogurt at:	Have eaten yogurt in past 4 weeks and intend to use in next 4 weeks		
	1977	1978	1979
Lunchtime	62%	56%	51%
Evening snack	32	30	36
Between meals	31	34	34
Dessert	18	14	14
With dinner	12	14	12

Among those who ate yogurt at lunch, for the first time since 1977, more consumers ate yogurt with other foods than by itself:

Ate yogurt:	Among respondents who ate yogurt at lunch		
	1977	1978	1979
By itself	50%	46%	40%
With other foods	38	37	47

On a national basis, Dannon scored highest on unaided brand awareness, followed by Light 'n Lively and Yoplait. Yoplait moved up from fifth place in 1978, passing Breyers and Borden. In its two major markets, the Midwest and West, Yoplait had the second highest unaided awareness:

	Unaided brand awareness—1979		
	U.S.	Midwest	West
Yoplait	12%	28%	13%
Dannon	47	68	2
Light 'n Lively	13	11	0
Knudsen	6	0	28
Breyers	8	3	1

Dannon was the brand eaten most often on a national basis. No other brand was mentioned by more than 5% of respondents. Regionally, Yoplait was the second most frequently consumed brand in the Midwest, and third in the West:

	Brand eaten most often—1979		
	U.S.	Midwest	West
Yoplait	4%	8%	6%
Dannon	41	51	0
Light 'n Lively	3	1	0
Knudsen	5	0	21
Breyers	3	1	1
Lucerne	3	2	8

Respondents who were aware of both Yoplait and Dannon rated the two brands along several product attributes. Dannon was rated superior to Yoplait on nine attributes including overall quality, overall taste and texture:

	% Rating excellent—1979[3]	
	Yoplait	Dannon
Overall quality	17%	31%
Overall taste	17	35
Fruit flavor	17	37
Texture	14	28

---

[3]Dannon's earlier market introduction meant that it had achieved a higher trial rate than Yoplait at the time of the Gallup survey.

| | % Rating excellent—1979 | |
	Yoplait	Dannon
Amount of fruit	13	23
Overall appearance	16	27
Appeal to entire family	8	21
Container	11	18
Value	10	18

A demographic analysis of respondents who indicated that they would be likely to eat yogurt in the next four weeks showed that the characteristics of those who would be relatively more inclined to eat yogurt were college educated, female, young (18–34 years) or old (63+ years), living in metropolitan areas in the West and East, and concerned with weight and diet. Children's usage declined from 1978 to 1979. In 1978, 32% of families with children reported child consumption of yogurt, versus 25% in 1979. The predominant usage occasions for children were as a between-meal and after-school snack (56% of yogurt-eating children) and as an evening snack (46%).

YOGURT MOTIVATION STUDY

As a result of the unexpected decline in yogurt usage in 1979, General Mills conducted an in-depth qualitative research study involving 30 focus groups nationwide to identify the underlying motivations of yogurt usage. The major change that had taken place in the yogurt category was the shift from meal to snack as the primary usage occasion. This was a result of consumers realizing that fruit yogurt was high in calories and that yogurt was not filling enough to replace a meal. The shift towards a snack orientation resulted in a decline in consumption among both regular/traditional and new users of yogurt. Yogurt was increasingly viewed as a treat rather than a staple by the health and diet conscious and by ethnic traditionalists. In its new role as a snack, yogurt was in competition with other snacks which were mostly shelf-stable, easier to keep in inventory in the home, and often cheaper.

The reduction in yogurt purchases by regular user households had a secondary effect among marginal users—members of regular user households for whom yogurt was not specifically purchased, but who, on occasion, ate the product because it was available. Marginal users' consumption declined with the reduction in yogurt inventory kept by regular users. Regular/traditional yogurt users continued to be an important market segment, but new users had passed them in number. New users were more likely to view yogurt consumption as an indulgence and treat it primarily as a snack. Total yogurt consumption was down because the volume accounted for by new users did not make up for the lost volume from regular/traditional users. The study forecast that long-term yogurt volume would erode substantially unless the category was able to reestablish a strong, heavy user base.

The shift to a snack orientation resulted in a proliferation of new, taste-oriented yogurts and taste improvements among existing brands. In spite of such efforts, hard-core nonusers were not expected to be converted. It was believed that they would always hold a negative taste perception for yogurt. However, improved flavor was expected to increase yogurt's appeal among children. Its foreign taste had dissuaded many children from eating yogurt. The study concluded that price would play a more important role in yogurt purchase behavior. As a meal, yogurt was inexpensive, but not as a snack.

In mature yogurt markets, consumers perceived Dannon as being synonymous with yogurt. The reason was not that Dannon was their regular brand, but that Dannon had been on the market the longest. Most yogurt users had tried the brand. Yoplait was perceived as a high-quality, premium-priced brand. Yoplait's primary positive attribute was its flavor; many preferred its less tart taste. But Yoplait's thinner consistency typically determined a consumer's acceptance or rejection of the brand. Many disliked it, but everyone considered the texture to be unique. The research indicated that Yoplait's thinner texture would continue to limit the scope of its appeal.

YOPLAIT USA OPERATIONS AND STRATEGY

Yoplait had three yogurt plants in California, Michigan and Texas. They made yogurt with freeze-dried yogurt cultures imported from France. Yogurt's production process began with raw milk in a base formula that was heat treated and inoculated with bacteria culture. The product was fermented in tanks and collected, and afterwards, fruit was added. The yogurt was packaged and refrigerated. Sodima worked closely with General Mills in developing Yoplait USA's technical expertise. A Sodima engineer worked at Yoplait USA for two years to help in product development.

At the time of the General Mills acquisition, Yoplait was sold through brokers, but by 1980, it was sold in almost all markets by the General Mills sales force who handled all Consumer Foods Group products.

Stephen Rothschild had committed to four 5-year goals when he assumed Yoplait USA's presidency: (1) national distribution, (2) $100 million in sales, (3) 20% market share, and (4) profitability. His first priority was to expand Yoplait Original-Style to the entire country within three years, but he also identified early on that the major growth opportunity lay in additional product lines. To this end, the New Business Development Group was formed in July 1978. As a starting point, Yoplait USA looked to Sodima, who had many products, such as soft cheeses, refrigerated desserts and different types of yogurt, for new product ideas.

CUSTARD-STYLE'S PRODUCT DEVELOPMENT

The New Business Development Group's charter was to make Yoplait USA a multiproduct company. The group decided initially to focus its new product exploration on the refrigerated yogurt category, including new forms of yogurt and yogurt-based products. Becker and his staff held idea generation sessions with their advertising agency and research and development personnel which resulted in 26 product concepts considered suitable for testing.

The first screening was a concept test (no actual products were presented to respondents) to measure the incremental volume that each potential new product would add to the existing Yoplait line. To pass the screening, a concept had to be in the top quartile in anticipated unit purchases for both the total Yoplait line and the test product line only. The concept also had to be in the top 50% in anticipated retail dollar sales for both the total Yoplait line and the new line only. Out of the 26 product concepts tested, seven met these criteria. Based on further analysis of the results, the New Business Development Group decided to give top development priority to Custard-Style.

The key issue in Custard-Style's early development was defining the yogurt's consistency or texture. Yoplait USA started with prototypes similar to Sodima's set-style yogurt which had a firm texture. But as Yoplait USA's R&D director said, "We had to Americanize the French product from ingredients, texture and flavor standpoints." A completely new flavoring system had to be developed to meet U.S. consumer tastes. In France, "nature identical" ingredients—artificial ingredients that had the same chemical structure as their natural counterparts—could legally be called "natural." In the United States, an all-natural claim had to be based on truly natural or nonartificial ingredients.

Hundreds of prototypes were developed in the search for a viable set-style formula, including formulations with varying levels of fat, different types of fruit and fruit flavors, colors, mouthfeel, textures and fermentation processes. The yogurt could be either fermented in vats or in individual cups. Vat fermentation required less capital investment, lower labor costs and could be integrated more easily with current Yoplait operations, but it produced an inferior yogurt texture. Fermentation in the cup, the French method of set-style production, produced the proper custard-like texture. Custard-Style Yogurt required a firm texture that produced a clean cut when sliced with a spoon. The texture had to be smooth and creamy, yet firm and thick like fine, French custard. It could not be lumpy, gelatinous or watery.

Due to the great number of prototypes developed, all could not be consumer tested. Members of the project team met in biweekly R&D review meetings and monthly new business review meetings. On these occasions, they sampled prototypes and used their collective judgment to screen and provide direction for future product development.

Aside from the product formulation, there were several other issues that had to be addressed, including packaging, size, positioning and name. The team tackled these issues with the aid of consumer research. Focus group research indicated that the key appeal of the concept was its custard-like texture. The concept conveyed a smooth, creamy, thick and rich-tasting yogurt. Anticipated usage varied among consumers—many expected the same usage as for other yogurts; some thought a dessert orientation more appropriate due to Custard-Style's richness and creaminess; those with younger children indicated usage as a snack.

MARKETING ISSUES

Concept testing and product prototype testing in focus groups had shown Custard-Style Yogurt to be a potentially viable addition to the Yoplait line. Yoplait management, however, was still faced with several fundamental issues such as product positioning, name, packaging type and size. The research pointed to the custard-like texture as a potential basis for positioning, but the New Business Development Group wondered whether texture, as opposed to taste, was sufficiently significant and communicable to be the key selling point.

There was also the question of whether the new yogurt should be positioned as a meal substitute, a snack, or a dessert. Some Yoplait executives argued that a new usage occasion positioning such a dessert might be more effective and help to increase category usage. A snack positioning was also being considered, offering Custard-Style Yogurt as an alternative to snacks such as potato chips, cookies, and ice cream. Aside from usage occasion positionings, Becker and the advertising agency also were looking at the overall quality of Custard-Style as a possible basis for positioning. Some of the positioning ideas included "the elegant/highest quality yogurt—the Haagen-Dazs of yogurts"; "the superior tasting yogurt—the gourmet's yogurt"; and "the yogurt for nonyogurt eaters."

When Yoplait regular-style yogurt was first introduced in the U.S.A., many consumers could not remember or pronounce the name, but they remembered the unique, conical, plastic cup. For Custard-Style's packaging, Becker was faced with the decision of using the same Vercon (the name of the manufacturer) cup, capitalizing on its high recognition, or of using a different design such as a traditional straight cup to reduce cannibalization of regular-style.

Becker also had to decide between a 4-oz. and a 6-oz. size. Most yogurt brands were sold in 8-oz. packages, while regular Yoplait was sold in a 6-oz. size, positioning it more as a snack than a meal substitute. Since Custard-Style Yogurt was very filling, a 4-oz. size seemed adequate. A 4-oz size, the standard serving size for pudding, would be compatible with a dessert positioning, and a small size would be a way to keep the unit price down. Finally, a 4-oz. size would be more appropriate for children and would reduce waste, an important point for Yoplait because its cup was not recappable with its aluminum foil cover. Tooling for a 4-oz. cup would require $75,000 in capital investment.

The New Business Development Group and the advertising agency were exploring two directions in developing a product name: linking the name to Yoplait and developing a name that was totally unrelated in sound or spelling to Yoplait, but used a "from the maker of Yoplait" tag. In exploring the first option, some of the names proposed so far were Yoclaire and Yofleur. Examples in the second category were Crème de Yogourt and Yogourt Classique. The term "custard style" could not be trademarked because it was too generic.

Becker and the R&D team members were also deciding on the appropriate fat level for Custard-Style Yogurt. Regular Yoplait was a full-fat formulation. Full-fat provided a better eating experience. Low-fat (less than 2% fat) was lower in calories and healthier. Some project team members argued for the low-fat option to develop a further difference between Custard-Style and regular Yoplait.

CONCEPT FULFILLMENT TEST

Faced with various alternative product formulations (low-fat vs. full-fat), positionings (dessert vs. snack), packages (Vercon vs. traditional) and sizes (4 oz. vs. 6 oz.), the New Business Development Group conducted a concept fulfillment test to determine which "mix" was the best for Custard-Style Yogurt. Seven product/positioning/package/cup size "mixes" plus the regular Yoplait concept (as control) were developed for an in-home concept fulfillment test.[4]

Interviewers screened random supermarket shoppers for interest in purchasing one of the seven concepts based on exposure to a concept board such as that shown in Exhibit 4. They gave interested respondents two cups of the strawberry product corresponding to the concept for which they were screened. Three days later, the respondent was interviewed by phone. Results indicated that, on the basis of sales volume potential, the dessert/full-fat/traditional cup/4-oz. product mix (48.8 volume index) and the snack/full-fat/Vercon/6-oz. mix (47.2 volume index) were virtually tied as the top alternatives. In terms of delivered profit margins, the latter scored highest (60.4 delivered margin index) with the former (50.3 delivered margin index) taking second place. Two different package configurations, the regular Vercon cup and the traditional cup, were compared using the snack positioning, full-fat formulation and 4-oz. size. The Vercon cup scored significantly higher than the traditional cup.

The winning Custard-Style alternative (snack positioning/full-fat product/Vercon cup/6-oz. size) was estimated to add 36% in incremental volume to the total Yoplait line. This was based on the assumption that Custard-Style's volume relative to regular Yoplait's was the ratio of their volume indexes from the test: 47.2 Custard-Style/66.7 regular Yoplait= 71% of regular Yoplait's volume. It was assumed further that Custard-Style would have only 75% of regular Yoplait's distribution level, and that one-third of Custard-Style's volume would be cannibalization of regular Yoplait's volume (or, two-thirds of Custard-Style's volume would be incremental). This resulted in incremental volume from Custard-Style equal to 36% of regular Yoplait volume (71% x 75%x 2/3). The study forecast further that, if Custard-Style were introduced as the lead item in non-Yoplait markets, it would generate 17% more volume than Original-Style. Custard-Style seemed more likely than Original-Style to attract light users and nonusers.

Diagnostic information from the test pointed to potential improvements for the winning Custard-Style prototype—more fruit, sweeter,

---

[4]The regular Yoplait concept was tested in markets where it had not yet been introduced, so there was no bias as a result of in-market experience.

Exhibit 4. *Concept fulfillment test—Custard-Style yogurt concept board*

Introducing New Custard-Style Yogurt from Yoplait—
A New Kind of Yogurt Made Especially for Dessert

Now, you can have a delicious tasting dessert with the richness and creaminess of the finest French custards, yet it has the lightness, nutrition and lower calories of yogurt.

Yoplait Custard-Style Yogurt has a unique texture that is firm, but smooth and creamy—just like custard—and it's blended throughout with 100% natural real fruit purée to give you the same delicious natural fruit taste in every spoonful.

It's available in strawberry, raspberry, blueberry, lemon, and plain.

Nothing artificial is added and it contains active yogurt cultures.

It comes in an individual 4 oz. cup that is just the right size for dessert. One cup contains only 120 calories and costs 35¢.

more natural, stronger fruit flavor, and more color. The product received high scores on texture attributes:

Product attribute	Custard-style satisfaction level
Amount of fruit	30%
Naturalness of fruit taste	47
Strength of fruit flavor	49

(continued)

Appearance	51
Color	54
Overall flavor	56
Sweetness/tartness	58
Calories	58
Texture/heaviness	63
Amount of product	72
Consistency	74
Smoothness/creaminess	76

CREATIVE GROUP INTERVIEWS

Custard-Style Yogurt's 36% incremental volume potential seemed quite promising to the new business group. Becker wanted some marketplace experience to confirm Custard-Style's viability. He also needed further insights on possible positionings as a basis for developing advertising concepts. The New Business Development Group and the advertising agency decided to conduct group interviews with yogurt users and nonusers to aid in creative development. Respondents were shown headline descriptions and given product samples of Custard-Style.

The interviews confirmed earlier research findings that texture was the main difference between Custard-Style and other yogurts. The research showed, however, that yogurt nonusers would be difficult to convert. Several nonusers thought that the Custard-Style Yogurt was bitter, sour and tangy. However, some yogurt users thought that the product would appeal to members of their families who did not eat yogurt because Custard-Style sounded less "yogurty." Custard-Style's retail price (45¢) was a purchase barrier to the more casual users who bought the less expensive store brands. On the other hand, many name brand (e.g., Dannon) yogurt users liked the Custard-Style concept. The product was viewed as more dessert-oriented than most yogurts because of its custard-like connotations. None of the respondents were concerned about the absence of fruit pieces—they were more concerned about a natural fruit taste. Yogurt users said the product tasted like yogurt with virtually no fruit flavor.

VOLUME ESTIMATION OPTIONS

By June 1980, nearly two years after its formation, the New Business Development Group felt ready to test market Custard-Style Yogurt.

Concept testing and consumer evaluations had indicated the potential viability of the product, and management now wanted a more "scientific" sales volume estimate to help in planning production requirements. They also needed a reliable measure of Custard-Style's cannibalization of regular Yoplait.

Becker's first decision was whether to conduct a test market simulation, such as BASES, before a field test market, or to go directly to a field test market. BASES, a sales estimation technique for new products, was a service offered by Burke Marketing Services, Inc. BASES's major advantages over a test market were its low cost ($29,000) and fast results (12 weeks). Other General Mills divisions had used BASES before but Yoplait USA did not. As Becker explained, "We weren't sure how relevant the Betty Crocker Division's experience with BASES was to a radically different category such as refrigerated yogurt. Also, we considered ourselves to be an entrepreneurial team. I wondered if we were researching ourselves to death. We were rolling out regular Yoplait quite successfully without a whole lot of industry data and primary research. Aside from that, the research we had done on Custard-Style had consistently indicated that it was a winner. We had the unshakable belief that Custard-Style was the way to go."

The BASES test that Yoplait was considering combined a concept test and a home-use test to provide year one and year two sales volume estimates. Finished commercials and packaging were not required. BASES allowed for simulation of the sales effects of key marketing variables before major resources were committed. The methodology required a shopping mall intercept of up to 300 shoppers in each of at least four geographically dispersed cities. Respondents were screened for purchase interest in the product concept. Test product was placed with interested respondents and their reactions were obtained through telephone callback. Key after-use measures provided inputs to the BASES estimating model, including buying intentions, intended frequency and quantity of repurchase, price/value assessments and other diagnostics. Secondary model inputs were provided by the client, including estimates of distribution build, media weights, trade and consumer promotion plans, size of the target market and consumption indices. The BASES model could evaluate alternative marketing scenarios by varying media weight, distribution build, and sales promotion expenditures, and by analyzing the impact of these adjustments on trial rates, repeat rates, total sales volume and cannibalization.

BASES claimed advantages over other simulated test markets. First, it was less expensive than some because it did not require the use of a finished commercial for the test product. Second, it forecast sales volume rather than market share and was, therefore, more suitable for test products in new or underdeveloped categories. Third, the model was dynamic and could therefore take into account the timing of proposed marketing expenditures. BASES claimed that 35% of validated test cases forecast sales that were no more than 5% different from actual market results; another 31% of test cases had an error range of 5–10%.

If Becker decided on a field test of Custard-Style, he had the option of a full-scale test market or a "mini-market." A full-scale test meant marketing the test product in two to four nationally representative markets through normal distribution channels with the General Mills sales force selling the test product to the trade. The results would have great credibility because the test would replicate actual roll-out conditions. "Ideally, yes, a full-scale test was the sophisticated thing to do. But, again, Yoplait USA was still a "start-up" company. I didn't have much money for research; we were on a shoestring budget. A full-scale test market would cost $1,700,000 and would take a year to give a proper reading." Becker was also concerned about giving competition an opportunity to size up Yoplait's actions and to retaliate accordingly.

An alternative to a full-scale field test market was a mini-market test. The New Business Development Group was considering the LaCrosse/Eau Claire market in western Wisconsin because it was close to General Mills headquarters in Minneapolis and it was already a strong Yoplait market which would permit a good measure of cannibalization. The area was upscale and had above-average quality stores and dairy sections. The group felt that the market would provide a "clean" reading of test results. A mini-market test had the advantage over BASES of true marketplace experience, and yet at $200,000, it cost significantly less than a full-scale test market. A mini-market test was limited in that trade reaction to Custard-Style could not be evaluated since distribution was "forced" or controlled by the marketing research firm hired to administer the test. Given the extensive regional differences in the yogurt market, a La Crosse/Eau Claire test could not provide a national sales estimate for Custard-Style, nor a nationally projectable estimate of regular Yoplait cannibalization. A mini-market test would take 20 weeks.

CONCLUSION

Bruce Becker had to decide what research step to take next—a BASES test, a full-scale test market or a mini-market test. Aside from what was best from a market research standpoint, there were production considerations that bore on this decision. Yoplait's plants could not yet produce Custard-Style Yogurt. All prototype production had been done in General Mills' R&D technical center. A full-scale test would require tooling up one of the existing Yoplait plants for Custard-Style production whereas a mini-market test's more limited requirements could be accommodated by production at the General Mills' technical center where the pilot plant was one-tenth the scale of a full plant. Becker realized that capacity had to be managed properly in the scale-up from a pilot plant to full-scale production and that product quality had to be maintained in the scale-up process.

Becker continued to wrestle with the details of questions associated with Custard-Style Yogurt's marketing mix. The snack positioning/ Vercon cup/6-oz. size alternative in the concept fulfillment test seemed to be a convincing winner in terms of delivered margins, but the dessert positioning/traditional cup/4-oz. alternative was equally promising in terms of volume potential. In support of the latter, creative group interviews indicated that a major appeal of Custard-Style was its "unyogurty" and dessert-like connotations.

Yoplait Custard-Style Yogurt was the name favored by many Yoplait executives because custard accurately described the product's texture, and because the name built on the Yoplait brand name. On the other hand, a name such as Yoclaire gave the product a greater individual identity, and potentially could offer more incremental volume than a name that was shared with regular Yoplait.

Pricing was an area that had not been considered an issue. Custard-Style Yogurt had the same, basic cost structure as Original-Style, and the New Business Development Group operated under the assumption that the Custard-Style line would be priced the same as Yoplait Original-Style. The most recent financial analysis which assumed that Custard-Style would be available in six flavors (strawberry, raspberry, blueberry, lemon, vanilla and plain), and produced in two plants, showed that Custard-Style had a delivered margin over variable costs comparable to Yoplait Original-Style.

Becker had to decide whether to resolve these marketing program issues before the next phase of research and test one concept, or test several alternatives.

9 *CASE*

General Mills, Inc.: Yoplait Custard-Style Yogurt (B)

John A. Quelch
John Teopaco

Bruce Becker, director of New Business Development at Yoplait USA, decided in June 1980 to put new Yoplait Custard-Style yogurt in a 6 oz. Vercon cup into a "mini-market" test. Results were positive. The test showed that, on a national basis, total Yoplait volume would more than double (+107%) with the addition of Custard-Style. To obtain a more nationally representative volume estimate, a BASES volume test was conducted next. The test forecast that total Yoplait volume would grow by 43% with Custard-Style. Becker now was convinced that Yoplait

Research Assistant John Teopaco prepared this case under the supervision of Professor John A. Quelch as the basis for class discussion rather than to illustrate either effective or ineffective handling of an administrative situation. Proprietary data have been disguised.

Custard-Style Yogurt was a winner, and ready for roll-out. However, details of the introductory marketing program still had to be decided along with level of support that should be placed behind Custard-Style, relative to Original-Style Yogurt. In addition, some members of Yoplait management still favored putting Custard-Style into a full-scale test market first before deciding on a national roll-out.

"MINI-MARKET" TEST

By June 1980, Custard-Style Yogurt had been in development for nearly two years. Numerous consumer tests had shown consistently that the product had high potential. When the time came for test market confirmation, the New Business Development Group was faced with a slim budget, production capacity limitations, and the pressure to introduce Yoplait's first new product as soon as possible. As a result, Bruce Becker opted for a mini-market test in the Eau Claire/La Crosse, Wisconsin ADI market instead of a full-scale test market.[1]

The New Business Development Group realized that the results of a limited test market in Wisconsin could not be projected nationally because the U.S. yogurt market was highly regional. On the other hand, the test was easily managed due to the small size of the market and its proximity to Minneapolis, the location of General Mills headquarters.

METHODOLOGY   The test involved 22 stores, lasted 20 weeks and cost about $150,000. After a pretest audit to establish market shares and case movement, Yoplait Custard-Style was placed in all the stores priced the same as Original-Style at 49¢ per cup. Weekly store audits were conducted for sales and share information during the entire test period by an outside market research firm.

To supply the test market, approximately 200 twelve-cup cases per week were produced in a pilot plant at the General Mills R&D Technical Center. Becker commented:

> The mini-market was very much a self-managed test. But with our limited production experience and capacity, we had to choose a test market that was close by because we would be shuttling product back and forth. We couldn't find a refrigerated warehouse to serve as an inventory drop-off, so we bought a walk-

---

[1]An Area of Dominant Influence (ADI) was a geographical market defined primarily by the range of VHF television signals.

in cooler and installed it in a mini-warehouse. On some days, we drove the truck down ourselves.

Becker acknowledged the unsophisticated nature of the mini-market test. But in spite of the limitations, he and his staff attempted to make the results as valid as possible. Their objective was to replicate a realistic national marketing program.

MARKETING VARIABLES The marketing support behind Custard-Style consisted of radio and newspaper advertising, product sampling, and trade deals. Radio was used instead of television in order to control costs and minimize wasted impressions. Radio media weight was adjusted upwards to compensate for the absence of television's visual dimension. A total of 500 gross rating points of radio advertising targeted at women over 18, and 12 newspaper insertions (six each in Eau Claire and La Crosse newspapers) were used in the test. The advertising copy, known as the Fourchette campaign, emphasized the Frenchness, thickness, and everyday use of Yoplait Custard-Style and had been selected over an execution that conveys a more gourmet, dessert image. Exhibit 1 presents a newspaper advertisement from the campaign. The total media plan was the equivalent of a national spending plan of $5.7 million.

Product sampling was a major consumer promotion tactic used by Yoplait for generating trial. In the mini-market, Yoplait management followed Original-Style's strategy of in-store consumer sampling in nine stores at an average of two days per store. Sampling took place during the first seven weeks of the test. Given a sampling cost of 48¢ per unit, the mini-market's national equivalent sampling plan was $800,000.

Three trade deals were offered during the test, each lasting six weeks. Average Custard-Style volume in stores that accepted one or more deals was 52% higher than in those that accepted none. The test's national equivalent trade promotion plan was $900,000.

SHARE AND VOLUME RESULTS The mini-market test forecast sustainable market shares of 23.1% for Custard-Style, and 24.9% for Original-Style. The addition of Custard-Style resulted in a total Yoplait share of 48.0%, up 21.4 points from Yoplait Original-Style's 26.6% pretest market share. Custard-Style gained share mainly from Dannon, the number one brand, and Gaymont, a major regional brand. Exhibit 2 presents the mini-market test share and volume results.

Average category weekly sales, excluding sampling store volume during sampling weeks, increased 26% with the introduction of Custard-Style. Yoplait Original-Style volume increased 18%, while Dannon and

Exhibit 1. Mini-market test print advertisement

Exhibit 2. **Mini-market test share and volume results share of sales**

	Pretest	Sustaining estimate[a]	Change from pretest
Yoplait Custard-Style	—	23.1	+23.1
Yoplait Original-Style	26.6	24.9	−1.7
Total Yoplait	26.6	48.0	+21.4
Dannon	38.2	21.8	−16.4
Gaymont	10.7	6.0	−4.7
Old Home	10.8	10.7	−0.1
Slim 'n Trim	10.9	9.2	−1.7
All Others	2.7	4.1	+1.4

[a]Average rolling 4-week share for weeks 11-20 (after Custard-Style sampling was completed).

Weekly equivalent[a] case volume/store

	Pretest	Sustaining weekly volume	% Change vs. pretest
Yoplait Custard-Style	—	12.1	
Yoplait Original-Style	11.0	13.0	+ 18.2
Total Yoplait	11.0	25.1	+128.2
Dannon	15.8	11.4	− 27.9
Gaymont	4.4	3.1	− 29.6
Old Home	4.5	5.6	+ 24.4
Slim 'n Trim	4.5	4.8	+ 6.7
All Others	1.1	2.2	+100.0
Total Category	41.1	52.2	26.0%

[a]One equivalent case = 12 single-serving cups, 6 oz. or 8 oz.

Gaymont declined. In test market stores, an average of 6.8 (out of 10) flavors of Original-Style and 5.3 (out of 6) flavors of Custard-Style were on the shelves at the end of the test period.

Custard-Style volume potential was calculated using the sustainable share estimates under two category volume scenarios: no change and a 26% category growth with Custard-Style. The estimation procedure assumed national distribution of 80% ACV (all-commodity volume), similar to that achieved by Original-Style Yogurt. With no category growth, Custard-Style would deliver 87% of Original-Style's current national volume potential, and 109% with category growth. Total Yoplait volume would be up to 227% of Original-Style's national volume projection. Exhibit 3 details the volume estimation methodology.

% of Yoplait Original-Style's national volume potential	Minimum (no market growth)	Maximum (26% market growth)
Yoplait Custard-Style	87%	109%
Yoplait Original-Style	94	118
Total Yoplait	181%	227%

Exhibit 3. Mini-market volume estimate methodology (unadjusted)

I. Custard-Style

$$\text{Custard-Style National Vol.} = \frac{\text{Custard-Style share in test market} \times \text{Test period category vol. in test market}}{\text{Yoplait share before test period} \times \text{Pretest category vol. in test market}} \times \text{Current Yopliat projected national volume}$$

A) Assuming no market growth

Test period category volume = pretest category volume

$$= \frac{23.1 \times \text{Test category volume}}{26.6 \times \text{Pretest Category Volume}} \times \text{Current Yoplait projected national volume}$$

= .87 current Yoplait projected national volume

B) Assuming 26% market growth

Test period category volume = 1.26 pretest category volume

$$= \frac{23.1 \times 1.26 \times \text{Pretest category volume}}{26.6 \times \text{Pretest Category Volume}} \times \text{Current Yoplait projected national volume}$$

= 1.09 current Yoplait projected national volume

Pretest plans assumed that, on the average, 75% of the Custard-Style line would be in stock. In the test, 89% were stocked. Volume potential estimates were adjusted downward to reflect the pretest assumption. Exhibit 4 details the adjusted volume estimation methodology. On an adjusted basis, Custard-Style volume would be 73–92% of

---

Exhibit 4. *Mini-market volume estimate methodology (adjusted)*

I. Custard-Style

$$\text{Custard-Style National Volume} = \frac{\begin{array}{c}[(\% \text{ line adjustment})^a \text{ (C-S test market share)} \\ (\text{market growth factor})(\text{Total Mkt. Pre})] \\ + \\ [1-\% \text{ line adjustment}^b](\text{C-S pretest share}) \\ (\text{Total mkt. pre})]\end{array}}{(\text{Yoplait pretest share})(\text{Total Mkt. Pre})} \times \begin{array}{c}\text{current} \\ \text{Yoplait} \\ \text{projected} \\ \text{national} \\ \text{volume}\end{array}$$

A) Assuming no market growth

Test period category volume = pretest category volume

$$= \frac{\begin{array}{c}(75/89)(23.1)(1.00)(\text{Total Mkt. Pre.}) \\ + \\ (14/89)(0)(\text{Total Mkt. Pre.})\end{array}}{26.6 \text{ (Total Market Pre)}} \times \begin{array}{c}\text{current Yoplait projected} \\ \text{national volume}\end{array}$$

= .73 current Yoplait projected national volume

B) Assuming 26% market growth

Test period category volume = 1.26 × pretest category volume

$$= \frac{\begin{array}{c}(75/89)(23.1)(1.26)(\text{Total Mkt. Pre.}) \\ + \\ (14/89)(0)(\text{Total Mkt. Pre.})\end{array}}{26.6 \text{ (Total Market Pre)}} \times \begin{array}{c}\text{current Yoplait projected} \\ \text{national volume}\end{array}$$

= .92 current Yoplait projected national volume

---

[a]Adjustments made for the percent of the Custard-Style line in stock. In the test market 89% of Custard-Style flavors were stocked on average. 75% of Custard-Style flavors in stock was anticipated for national introduction. Yoplait Original-Style percent flavors in stock for the test was equivalent to current national levels and, therefore, required no adjustment.

[b]Adjustment to reflect Yoplait regular performance if fewer Custard-Style flavors stocked (75% vs. 89%).

Original-Style's national potential, and total Yoplait volume would be 168–207%.

% of Yoplait Original-Style's national volume potential	Minimum (no market growth)	Maximum (26% market growth)
Yoplait Custard-Style	73%	92%
Yoplait Original-Style	95	115
Total Yoplait	168%	207%

CONSUMER DYNAMICS STUDY In addition to the weekly store audit, a yogurt consumer dynamics study was conducted during the test. The research consisted of three waves of a supermarket intercept study, each conducted over three consecutive weekends (3–5 weeks, 9–11 weeks, and 15–17 weeks after the start of advertising). Interviewers, stationed in the yogurt section of each store, recorded consumers' yogurt purchases by brand. Each yogurt shopper was then asked questions about trial and repeat and future purchase interest. Waves 2 and 3 included a telephone follow-up interview of Yoplait Custard-Style, Original-Style, and Dannon purchasers. Respondents were asked questions on products likes, dislikes, and usage.

Custard-Style trial among yogurt buyers increased with each wave of the study, and, by the third wave (35%), was approaching Original-Style's trial level (36%) and that of all competitors except Dannon

Exhibit 5. *Mini-market consumer dynamics study Yoplait Custard-Style trial*

	% of Yogurt buyers		
	Wave I	Wave II	Wave III
Yoplait Custard-Style	25%	31%	35%
Yoplait Original-Style	34	34	36
Dannon	68	66	63
Old Home	18	20	19
Gaymont	21	22	21

(63%). Exhibit 5 reports trial levels by wave. Repeat intention for Custard-Style nearly equalled Original-Style's and Dannon's, and exceeded Gaymont's and Old Home's. The percentage of Custard-Style triers who actually repeated consistently increased throughout the study; all depth of repeat categories (percent of triers who made one through ten or more repeat purchases) showed steady growth, indicating strong consumer satisfaction.

Of those who used any Yoplait product, 20% were exclusive Custard-Style users, 20% were exclusive Original-Style users, and 60% used both. Custard-Style users were primarily past buyers of Original-Style and Dannon:

Source of Custard-Style buyers as of wave 3		
Past buyers of:	Trial	Repeat
Yoplait	38%	41%
Dannon	33	27
Gaymont	4	5
Old Home	8	7
All Other	17	21
	100%	100%

By wave 3, 91% of Original-Style and 63% of Dannon buyers had tried Custard-Style, versus 35% of Gaymont and 37% of Old Home buyers.

The number of Custard-Style units bought per buying occasion by repeaters (1.7) was about the same as the number of Original-Style (1.6) and Dannon (1.8) units, but more than the number of Old Home (1.1) and Gaymont (1.1) units bought by these brands' repeaters. This suggested to Becker that Custard-Style buyers were mainstream yogurt consumers. Of the total yogurt purchases made by Custard-Style buyers, 70-80% were of Custard-Style, about the same level as for Original-Style and Dannon. This indicated that Custard-Style would not be merely a secondary brand among its consumers.

Among Custard-Style acceptors, the most often mentioned reasons for repeat purchasing were "flavor" (33%), "natural fruit flavor" (23%), "firm, thick texture" (22%), and "smooth, creamy texture" (16%). Custard-Style rejecters' most frequently mentioned reasons for not repeating were "too custardy/don't like custard" (21%), "too thick/too firm" (18%), "don't like texture" (18%), and "no fruit/no chunks of fruit"

(16%). Acceptors indicated that they would eat Custard-Style on the same occasions as other yogurts:

	Breakfast	Lunch	Dinner	Morning snack	Afternoon snack	Evening snack
% of Custard-Style uses	14.1%	21.1%	9.7%	10.1%	22.4%	21.2%
% of other yogurt uses	15.3	22.3	8.6	9.2	21.9	21.9

No unusual competitive responses were observed during the mini-market test. Dannon was preoccupied with penetrating the West Coast market and with testing a new product of its own, Melangé, which appeared to be positioned against Original-Style.

By any standards, the mini-market test results were encouraging. The estimated doubling of total Yoplait volume with the addition of Custard-Style was considered by Becker and his group to be outstanding. Some Yoplait executives, however, were skeptical, claiming that the test results could not be used to project Custard-Style's performance in regions with different market structures at different stages of yogurt market development. In short, the test was too localized. Management wanted national and regional estimates of Custard-Style's volume potential, and its impact on Original-Style's volume before making a decision on Custard-Style's introduction, and the associated plant investment. To address these concerns, a BASES simulated test market was conducted.

BASES TEST

METHODOLOGY   The BASES test was conducted in twelve geographically dispersed cities, distributed equally among three regions.[2] Two hundred respondents were interviewed in each region. An additional 200 interviews were conducted in Minneapolis/St. Paul to compare results with those of the La Crosse/Eau Claire mini-market test. Respondents qualified if they were female heads of household at least 18

---

[2]East—Boston, Buffalo, Cleveland, Hartford; Midwest—Minneapolis, Chicago, St. Louis, Milwaukee; West—Los Angeles, San Francisco, Portland, Phoenix.

years old, and were the principal household shoppers. Current users and nonusers of yogurt were included in the sample.

Qualified respondents were shown a color print advertisement with a picture of the Custard-Style product, a concept statement and the price (53¢). They were asked questions on purchase intent, like/dislikes of the concept, price/value evaluation and past category usage. Respondents who indicated that they definitely or probably would buy Yoplait Custard-Style Yogurt took home as many cups as they would buy at trial. (All flavors were available except for plain.) After two weeks, participants responded again to the same set of questions asked before the in-home use test.

In addition to the consumer test results, Yoplait provided the following inputs to the BASES volume estimation model: target market, consumption indexes for each city, seasonality indexes, year one distribution and out-of-stock estimates by flavor and marketing expenditures for each quarter of the first two years following launch.

MARKETING VARIABLES   Three national spending plans were simulated by the BASES model: high (Plan A), medium (Plan B), and low (Plan C). Plan A assumed that Custard-Style would be supported at 100% of the media spending level used in the Yoplait Original-Style introductory plan. Plan B represented 50% of Original-Style media spending while Plan C assumed a lower spending level. The plans assumed that two-thirds of expenditures would be made during the first half of any year, and that 70% of media spending would be on television advertising.

	Year 1 (000)			Year 2 (000)		
Promotion	Plan A (High)	Plan B (Medium)	Plan C (Low)	Plan A (High)	Plan B (Medium)	Plan C (Low)
Media	$9,200	$4,600	$3,700	$6,100	$3,050	$2,380
Consumer	2,300	700	700	—	—	—
Trade	1,000	700	700	1,250	950	920
Total	$12,500	$6,000	$5,100	$7,350	$4,000	$3,300

VOLUME RESULTS   Yoplait management established, on the basis of economic analysis, two performance criteria for Custard-Style: it had to provide at least 40% incremental volume to the total Yoplait line, and its sales volume had to be at least 60% of Original-Style's under Plan B.

The BASES results showed that with the medium plan, Custard-Style would deliver 3.5 million cases (12-pack) in Year 2. The BASES model forecast that total Yoplait volume would grow by 43%:

Custard-Style national estimates			
	Plan A (High)	Plan B (Medium)	Plan C (Low)
Year 1 trial	14.9%	10.5%	9.1%
Repeat (measured)	38.7%	38.8%	38.6%
Year 1 volume (12-unit cases)	4.4MM	3.2MM	3.0MM
Year 2 volume	4.8MM	3.5MM	3.3MM
Year 2—% incremental volume	57%	43%	41%

Custard-Style volume seemed somewhat sensitive to spending. Under Plan A, at twice the media dollars of Plan B, Year 2 volume was 34% higher, whereas under the low-spending Plan C, volume was only 5% lower than Plan B's.

Custard-Style's performance varied by region. Sales were strongest in the West, although lower than Original-Style's. The East showed larger than expected sales:

Regional volume indexes: Plan B/Year 2				
	West	Midwest	East	Total U.S.
Custard-Style	180	88	120	100
Original Style	190	82	98	100

There was no significant regional variation in each flavor's expected share of Year 1 Yoplait Custard-Style volume. Average flavor splits were:

Strawberry	28%	Vanilla	25%
Raspberry	18	Plain	9
Blueberry	13	Lemon	7

POTENTIAL STEAL   On a national basis, the BASES model estimated that 22% of Custard-Style volume would be at the expense of Original-Style. Regionally, potential steal varied widely with the Midwest showing the highest level (28%).

The greatest competitive source of Custard-Style volume was Dannon (22%) in the East, Yoplait Original-Style (28%) in the Midwest, and Knudsen (18%) in the West:

Sources of Custard-Style volume

	West	Midwest	East	Total U.S.
Total new yogurt purchases	51%	51%	49%	50%
Steal from yogurt:	49	49	51	50
Dannon	8	15	22	15
Yoplait Original-Style	13	28	14	22
Knudsen	18	0	0	6
All others	10	6	15	6

COMPARISON TO MINI-MARKET   BASES estimates based on the responses of the 200 interviewees in Minneapolis/St. Paul, a similar competitive environment to La Crosse/Eau Claire, were very similar to those from the mini-market. Assuming 80% Custard-Style ACV (all-commodity volume) distribution (Yoplait Original-Style distribution level in the Twin Cities), BASES estimated Custard-Style's volume at 97% of Original-Style's. Assuming 90% ACV distribution, Custard-Style volume was forecast at 110% of Original-Style's. The mini-market test, which forecast 26% category growth following Custard-Style's introduction, had estimated a Custard-Style volume of 109% of Original-Style's. This forecast was based on 89% of the line being stocked on average as observed in the mini-market.

ADDITIONAL FINDINGS   Exhibit 6 presents additional findings from the BASES interviews. After exposure to the concept, about 40% of the respondents said that they definitely or probably would buy Custard-Style. Among triers, 68% expressed continued purchase intent. These purchase intent levels met the norms for successful, new refrigerated products. Custard-Style's price/value rating (3.6 on 5-pt. scale) equalled the refrigerated product's norm, while its "liking" rating 95.6 on a 9-pt. scale) was close to the norm (5.5).

Before trying Custard-Style, taste/flavor (particularly the variety of flavors), texture/consistency ("creamy, thick, smooth") and health/nutrition were the most frequently mentioned reasons for liking the concept. After use, taste and texture reasons again were cited most often, but few mentioned the health benefits of Custard-Style. Taste was the most frequently mentioned reason for not liking Custard-Style, both before and after use. After trying the product, some commented on the absence of fruit pieces. Price was the second most often mentioned reason for disliking Custard-Style before trial, but after use, its share of mentions was much lower.

Exhibit 6. *Additional findings from BASES test*

	Total U.S.	West	Midwest	East
Purchase intent—% "Definitely/Probably Would Buy"				
Before use	41%	42%	39%	42%
After use	68	67	66	69
Norms: Before use— 40%; after use—65%.				
Price/value—5-point scale				
Before use	3.7	3.6	3.7	3.8
After use	3.6	3.6	3.5	3.7
Norms: After use—3.6.				
Liking rating—9 point scale				
Before use	5.2	5.3	5.1	5.2
After use	5.6	5.5	5.5	5.7
Norms: After use—5.5.				
Product vs. expectations				
Better than expected	58%	56%	54%	64%
About the same	28	29	28	25
Worse than expected	13	14	16	10
Don't know	1	1	2	1

ALTERNATIVE SPENDING LEVELS   In addition to the three marketing spending levels used in the first BASES analysis, two additional sets of media and consumer promotion spending levels were simulated later. The objective was to determine the optimal allocation of incremental spending. One alternative Plan (A Media/B Promotion) used the original Plan A's high-level media spending and Plan B's low-level consumer promotion spending. The other new Plan (B Media/A Promotion) used low-level media and high-level promotion spending:

		A Media/B Promo	B Media/A Promo
Year 1:	Media	$9,200	$4,600
	Consumer promotion	700	2,300
Year 2:	Media	6,100	3,050
	Consumer promotion	0	0

For planning purposes, Yoplait management considered the original Plan B (B Media/B Promotion) as Custard-Style's base support level. Based on this, the new simulation results indicated that incremental spending in consumer promotion was more efficient than incremental media spending. The B Media/A Promotion plan resulted in the lowest cost per incremental case:

Alternate plan	Incremental spending vs. Plan B	Incremental cases vs. Plan B	Cost/ incremental case
B Media/A Promotion	$1,600,000	455,000	$3.52
A Media/B Promotion	4,000,000	694,000	6.61
A Media/A Promotion	6,200,000	1,190,000	5.19

Exhibit 7 shows the performance results of Custard-Style under the new alternate plans.

COPY TESTING

The BASES test results confirmed the New Business Development Group's conclusion from the mini-market that Custard-Style had high volume potential. They began preparation for the new product's launch by next developing and testing four television commercial executions: (1) Custard-Style only with a Yoplait tag and no celebrity (Police execution); (2) Custard-Style only with a Yoplait tag and a celebrity (Sanford execution); (3) integrated Custard-Style and Original-Style without celebrities (Secretaries execution); and (4) integrated Custard-Style and Original-Style with celebrities (LaSorda/Brothers execution). Several executives argued strongly that Custard-Style advertising should be clearly distinguishable by consumers from the Original-Style campaign.

METHODOLOGY   After a series of focus groups, a four-panel advertising copy test with 300 respondents per panel was conducted in nine geographically dispersed cities. In each panel, 150 respondents were selected from established Yoplait West Coast markets which were also Knudsen yogurt markets, and 150 were selected from other established Yoplait markets which were also Dannon markets. Respondents were female shoppers, aged 18–60, who had purchased yogurt two or more times in the previous three months.

Exhibit 7. BASES alternative spending plan simulations (in millions)

	Plan A Media/Plan B Promotion					Plan B Media/Plan A Promotion				
	West	Midwest	East	Remaining U.S.	Total U.S.	West	Midwest	East	Remaining U.S.	Total U.S.
Year 1 consumer volume (in cases of 12)	1,194	315	1,625	270	3,904	1,015	880	1,445	325	3,665
Year 2 consumer volume	1,206	812	1,940	300	4,258	1,100	855	1,502	401	3,858

	Plan B Media/Plan B Promotion					Plan A Media/Plan A Promotion				
	West	Midwest	East	Remaining U.S.	Total U.S.	West	Midwest	East	Remaining U.S.	Total U.S.
Year 1 consumer volume (in cases of 12)	940	705	1,305	260	3,210	1,260	935	1,805	400	4,400
Year 2 consumer volume	945	720	1,530	320	3,515	1,290	940	2,105	435	4,770

Each respondent viewed a prerecorded videotape which contained the following: the Yoplait Original-Style Jack Klugman commercial (see Exhibit 8),[3] a Knudsen (West Coast market) or Dannon (all other markets) commercial and one of the four alternative Custard-Style commercials. After viewing the tape, the respondent was asked abut her likelihood of buying different brands of yogurt. From the responses, share scores were calculated and weighted according to each respondent's past category usage. Regional share scores were combined on the basis of each region's share of total category volume.

Finally, a subsample of 100 respondents per panel was re-exposed to the Custard-Style test commercial, and asked a series of communication/comprehension diagnostic questions.

The four test commercials showed different people discovering the characteristics of Yoplait Custard-Style. One focused on two female secretaries, a second on a group of police officers. A third featured baseball coach Tommy LaSorda and popular psychologist Dr. Joyce Brothers, while the fourth featured television personality Isabel Sanford. The Sanford commercial is shown in Exhibit 9.

RESULTS   Yoplait management had decided that the commercial that received the highest postviewing share would be recommended for introductory Custard-Style copy. These criteria were to be applied separately to Knudsen markets and Dannon markets.

In both Knudsen and Dannon markets, the Isabel Sanford commercial scored highest. (See Exhibit 9 for the Sanford commercial storyboard.)

	Custard-Style post shares		
	Total U.S.	Knudsen markets	Dannon markets
Sanford	21.8%	23.6%	21.0%
Secretaries	19.0	16.4	20.1
LaSorda/Brothers	18.7	18.6	19.5
Police	16.4	19.8	15.3

Note: The Sanford advertisement scored significantly better than the other executions at the 0.8 confidence level in Knudsen markets, and in aggregate, but not in Dannon markets.

---

[3] A series of celebrity spokesperson commercials which emphasized Yoplait's heritage as the yogurt of France.

Exhibit 8. Yoplait Original-Style television commerical

ANNCR: The yogurt of France is called Yoplait.

Some Americans don't know about it... yet.

But what happens when Americans get their first taste of Yoplait...

they'll think...it's different...it's creamy, smooth,

all natural yogurt...with real fruit.

It's just amazing what happens when a real American gets a little taste of French culture.

JACK KLUGMAN: Ce Yogurt Yoplait est fantastique,

merveilleux , sensationnel, cremeux... (HE CONTINUES UNDER V.O. ANNCR)

ANNCR: Yoplait Yogurt. Get a little taste of French culture.
JACK KLUGMAN: ...naturel.

Exhibit 9. *Isabel Sanford Custard-Style television commercial*

ANNCR: Yoplait, the yogurt of France introduces a second yogurt,

ISABEL: Custard style???

ANNCR: And when Americans get their first taste,

ISABEL: With a fork?

ANNCR: they'll think it's different.

ANNCR: Wholesome, with real fruit pureed throughout, but very different,

because new Yoplait Custard Style is thick.

ANNCR: So thick, you can eat it with

ISABEL: Un "fourchette!"

ANNCR: New Yoplait Custard Style, so thick you can eat it with a...

fourchette. But please, eat Yoplait original with a....

cuillere.

| | Total Yoplait post shares | | |
Commercials	Total U.S.	Knudsen markets	Dannon markets
Sanford	43.7%	48.7%	41.6%
Police	38.5	46.9	35.2
Secretaries	38.0	44.9	35.0
LaSorda/Brothers	37.0	44.9	33.7

Note: Sanford execution scored significantly higher (at 0.8 confidence internal) in total U.S. and in Dannon markets, but not in Knudsen markets.

In general, diagnostic results for the four Custard-Style commercials were very similar. Exhibit 10 shows communication results from the test. The Sanford and Police commercials (Custard-Style-only executions) communicated best Custard-Style's thickness. They were less effective than the integrated commercials in communicating that Custard-Style was a new type/style of yogurt. The Custard-Style-only commercials also deemphasized the product's "Frenchness." In the Knudsen markets, the Sanford commercial communicated "better taste" most effectively. Otherwise, there were no significant differences in the pulling power of the four executions between Knudsen and Dannon markets.

On brand recall, the Sanford commercial scored highest with 90% of respondents remembering the Yoplait Custard-Style name (and variations). Brand recall was better for the Sanford commercial than for the other alternatives in both Knudsen and Dannon markets.

CONCLUSION

By February 1981, Becker and the New Business Development Group were ready to introduce Yoplait Custard-Style Yogurt in six flavors. Consumer product testing, the mini-market test and BASES test results all showed Custard-Style to be a highly viable product that would not steal significantly from Original-Style volume. In addition, they now believed they had a television commercial that could support strongly Custard-Style's introduction.

As the national launch decision approached, there was increasing debate over where Custard-Style should be rolled out first. In the BASES test, Custard-Style sales were strongest in the West, but sales in the East were greater than expected (based on Original-Style volume). Becker believed that Custard-Style should be introduced first in markets such as the West, where Yoplait was strongest. But some executives contended

Exhibit 10. *Custard-Style test communication results*

1. Main idea—% indicating

	Commercials			
	Sanford	LaSorda/ Brothers	Secretaries	Police
New type	16.4%	19.0%	21.5%	12.5%
Thicker	19.8	10.2	14.2	21.7
Frenchness	1.7	7.1	6.0	3.0

2. What's new or different

	Sanford	LaSorda/ Brothers	Secretaries	Police
New style/type	7.4%	11.2%	12.8%	10.2%
Thicker	15.7	12.6	12.8	14.6
Frenchness/classy	11.8	13.9	13.2	12.2
Casting/type of people	4.1	6.8	2.6	3.1

3. Everything seen or heard

	Sanford	LaSorda/ Brothers	Secretaries	Police
Two types	13.7%	12.2%	14.8%	11.8%
Eat with fork (thick)	26.5	19.0	21.9	24.4
Casting (celebrities)	31.2	32.0	30.7	31.2
Fruit in yogurt	4.7	3.8	2.4	1.7

4. Advantages over other yogurts

	Sanford	LaSorda/ Brothers	Secretaries	Police
Two styles/better	11.1%	11.2%	13.2%	9.5%
Thicker/creamier	13.4	9.8	16.5	12.9

5. Brand recall

	Sanford	LaSorda/ Brothers	Secretaries	Police
Yoplait Custard-Style	87.2%	80.2%	82.4%	82.0%
Variations	3.0	2.4	2.1	2.0
Total	90.2%	82.6%	84.5%	84.0%

that Custard-Style provided an opportunity for establishing Yoplait in the East where it had been weak, and unable to break Dannon's dominance. They advocated an Eastern introduction. A third alternative was to launch Custard-Style as Yoplait's lead product in new markets such as those in the West which neither Original-Style Yoplait nor Dannon had yet penetrated.

As Becker considered these options, he wondered how the sales force and trade would react to each. The trade regarded yogurt as a difficult category to manage, given the proliferation of brands and flavors. In some areas of the country, continuous trade deals were almost mandatory to secure shelf space. At the same time, Yoplait's sales force and brokers had been under pressure to secure distribution for more Original-Style flavors. Some Yoplait executives believed the sales force would welcome Custard-Style as "genuine product news." Others felt that the introduction of Custard-Style would give them an excuse for not meeting flavor distribution goals for Original-Style.

Another issue related to the roll-out plan was the appropriate balance of advertising and promotion support to be placed behind Custard-Style and Original-Style, particularly in those regions where both would be distributed. Becker believed Custard-Style had the potential to be a major new product introduction. Since both Custard-Style and Original-Style would carry the Yoplait name and be sold in similar packages, he argued that the weight of support should be placed behind Custard-Style and that this would maintain awareness and distribution of Original-Style. The brand manager on Original-Style argued against this approach. Indeed, he proposed that Custard-Style, once launched, should be managed within his brand group as a line extension to ensure the integration of Custard-Style and Original-Style marketing programs.

Finally, Becker believed that although Custard-Style offered significant, incremental volume potential, it should be priced the same as Original-Style (54¢ suggested retail price). According to him, a price differential would cause consumer and sales force confusion, and be hard to explain to the trade. A member of the new business group felt, however, that Custard-Style could be positioned as Yoplait's premium product, and priced higher than Original-Style. He pointed to the limited steal level from Original-Style as an indication that consumers perceived the two products differently.

Becker had to decide on an introductory program for Custard-Style to recommend to Stephen Rothschild. He proposed Salt Lake City for the launch because it was an established market where Yoplait was the share leader (22%). Yoplait sales for fiscal year 1981 were up 32% over the previous year. The Salt Lake market was well managed and served by highly committed salespeople.

Becker's Salt Lake City marketing program was based on a national equivalent spending plan of $4.7 million consisting of the following:

Advertising	650 television GRPs (annual, in four flights)	$3.2 million
	50 radio GRPs (introductory)	
	3 full-page newspaper free-standing inserts with coupons	
Consumer promotion	12 weeks of in-store trial demonstrations	$0.9 million
Trade promotion	7 weeks normal volume on introductory deal @ $.60/case	$0.6 million

Becker was confident that he could convince Rothschild and other key Yoplait executives that Custard-Style was a major new product opportunity worthy of substantial investment.

PART 4
Managing the Dynamics of Product Line Evolution

INTRODUCTION

The introduction to Part 1 began by characterizing new product development as "imperative" due to a simple fact: things change. Customer wants, competitive products, and enabling technologies change rendering existing products unwanted or presenting opportunity for developing superior price/performance products. The firm best positioned to respond to changes, create changes, and manage product evolution is the long-term winner.

While market evolution has been a part of previous parts, this final part has an explicit focus on it. It begins with "The House of Quality" article reprinted from *Harvard Business Review*. This article describes a process of interfunctional coordination known as Quality Functional Deployment (QFD), which brings together current market data and engineering data in such a way that general managers are able "to discover strategic opportunities." Our focus in Parts 1–3 has been on obtaining insightful data on the market; this QFD process shows how that data must be integrated with technological possibility data.

The final case in the book, Barco Projection Systems, presents a market leader whose reaction to a new technological opportunity in the form of a superior tube component was ". . . engineers had considered incorporating the tube in the BD700 data projector, but had decided against the idea because it involved redesigning the shape of the projector's chassis and sourcing a new lens to match." The case asks how Barco should respond to the "shock" of Sony developing a projector based on the new tube which outperformed others on brightness, image quality, and resolution—all things that would benefit a customer.

To market leaders, the status quo is good—something to be preserved. Everyone else, though, has an incentive to change the game. This part considers how to bring the market and technological data together in a timely way and explores how a market leader can preserve its position in a changing market.

7 <u>NOTE</u>

The House of Quality

John R. Hauser
Don Clausing

Digital Equipment, Hewlett-Packard, AT&T, and ITT are getting started with it. Ford and General Motors use it—at Ford alone there are more than 50 applications. The "house of quality," the basic design tool of the management approach known as quality function deployment (QFD), originated in 1972 at Mitsubishi's Kobe shipyard site. Toyota and its suppliers then developed it in numerous ways. The house of quality has been used successfully by Japanese manufacturers of consumer electron-

John R. Hauser, at the Harvard Business School as a Marvin Bower fellow during the current acade-mic year, is professor of management science at MIT's Sloan School of Management. He is the author, with Glen L. Urban, of Design & Marketing of New Products *(Prentice-Hall, 1980). Don Clausing is Bernard M. Gordon Adjunct Professor of Engineering Innovation and Practice at MIT. Previously he worked for Xerox Corporation. He introduced QFD to Ford and its supplier compa-nies in 1984.*

ics, home appliances, clothing, integrated circuits, synthetic rubber, construction equipment, and agricultural engines. Japanese designers use it for services like swimming schools and retail outlets and even for planning apartment layouts.

A set of planning and communication routines, quality function deployment focuses and coordinates skills within an organization, first to design, then to manufacture and market goods that customers want to purchase and will continue to purchase. The foundation of the house of quality is the belief that products should be designed to reflect customers' desires and tastes—so marketing people, design engineers, and manufacturing staff must work closely together from the time a product is first conceived.

The house of quality is a kind of conceptual map that provides the means for interfunctional planning and communications. People with different problems and responsibilities can thrash out design priorities while referring to patterns of evidence on the house's grid.

WHAT'S SO HARD ABOUT DESIGN

David Garvin points out that there are many dimensions to what a consumer means by quality and that it is a major challenge to design products that satisfy all of these at once.[1] Strategic quality management means more than avoiding repairs for consumers. It means that companies learn from customer experience and reconcile what they want with what engineers can reasonably build.

Before the industrial revolution, producers were close to their customers. Marketing, engineering, and manufacturing were integrated—in the same individual. If a knight wanted armor, he talked directly to the armorer, who translated the knight's desires into a product. The two might discuss the material—plate rather than chain armor—and details like fluted surfaces for greater bending strength. Then the armorer would design the production process. For strength—who knows why?—he cooled the steel plates in the urine of a black goat. As for a production plan, he arose with the cock's crow to light the forge fire so that it would be hot enough by midday.

Today's fiefdoms are mainly inside corporations. Marketing people have their domain, engineers theirs. Customer surveys will find their way onto designers' desks, and R&D plans reach manufacturing engineers. But usually, managerial functions remain disconnected, producing

---

[1]David A. Garvin, "Competing on the Eight Dimensions of Quality," HBR
November–December 1987, p. 101.

a costly and demoralizing environment in which product quality and the quality of the production process itself suffer.

Top executives are learning that the use of interfunctional teams benefits design. But if top management *could* get marketing, designing, and manufacturing executives to sit down together, what should these people talk about? How could they get their meeting off the ground? This is where the house of quality comes in.

Consider the location of an emergency brake lever in one American sporty car. Placing it on the left between the seat and the door solved an engineering problem. But it also guaranteed that women in skirts could not get in and out gracefully. Even if the system were to last a lifetime, would it satisfy customers?

In contrast, Toyota improved its rust prevention record from one of the worst in the world to one of the best by coordinating design and production decisions to focus on this customer concern. Using the house of quality, designers broke down "body durability" into 53 items covering everything from climate to modes of operation. They obtained customer evaluations and ran experiments on nearly every detail of production, from pump operation to temperature control and coating composition. Decisions on sheet metal details, coating materials, and baking temperatures were all focused on those aspects of rust prevention most important to customers.

Today, with marketing techniques so much more sophisticated than ever before, companies can measure, track, and compare customers' perceptions of products with remarkable accuracy; all companies have opportunities to compete on quality. And costs certainly justify an emphasis on quality design. By looking first at customer needs, then designing across corporate functions, manufacturers can reduce prelaunch time and after-launch tinkering.

Exhibit 1 compares startup and reproduction costs at Toyota Auto Body in 1977, before QFD, to those costs in 1984, when QFD was well under way. House of quality meetings early on reduced costs by more than 60%. Exhibit 2 reinforces this evidence by comparing the number of design changes at a Japanese auto manufacturer using QFD with changes at a U.S. automaker. The Japanese design was essentially frozen before the first car came off the assembly line, while the U.S. company was still revamping months later.

BUILDING THE HOUSE

There is nothing mysterious about the house of quality. There is nothing particularly difficult about it either, but it does require some effort to get

Exhibit 1. **Startup and preproduction costs at Toyota Auto Body before and after** QFD *Source: Lawrence P. Sullivan, "Quality Function Deployment," Quality Progress, June 1986, p. 39. © 1986 American Society for Quality Control. Reprinted by permission.*

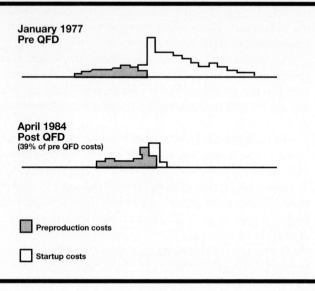

used to its conventions. Eventually one's eye can bounce knowingly around the house as it would over a roadmap or a navigation chart. We have seen some applications that started with more than 100 customer requirements and more than 130 engineering considerations. A fraction of one subchart, in this case for the door of an automobile, illustrates the house's basic concept well. We've reproduced this subchart portion in the illustration "House of Quality," and we'll discuss each section step-by-step.

What do customers want? The house of quality begins with the customer, whose requirements are called customer attributes (CAs)—phrases customers use to describe products and product characteristics (see Exhibit 3). We've listed a few here; a typical application would have 30 to 100 CAs. A car door is "easy to close" or "stays open on a hill"; "doesn't leak in rain" or allows "no (or little) road noise." Some Japanese companies simply place their products in public areas and encourage potential customers to examine them, while design team members listen and note what people say. Usually, however, more formal market research is called for, via focus groups, indepth qualitative interviews, and other techniques.

Exhibit 2. *Japanese automaker with QFD made fewer changes than U.S. company without QFD* *Source: Lawrence P. Sullivan, "Quality Function Deployment,"* Quality Progress, *June 1986, p. 39. © 1986 American Society for Quality Control. Reprinted by permission.*

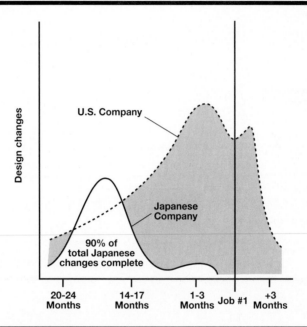

CAs are often grouped into bundles of attributes that represent an overall customer concern, like "open-close" or "isolation." The Toyota rust-prevention study used eight levels of bundles to get from the total car down to the car body. Usually the project team groups CAs by consensus, but some companies are experimenting with state-of-the-art research techniques that derive groupings directly from customers' responses (and thus avoid arguments in team meetings).

CAs are generally reproduced in the customers' own words. Experienced users of the house of quality try to preserve customers' phrases and even clichés—knowing that they will be translated simultaneously by product planners, design engineers, manufacturing engineers, and salespeople. Of course, this raises the problem of interpretation: What does a customer really mean by "quiet" or "easy"? Still, designers' words and inferences may correspond even less to customers'

Exhibit 3. Customer attributes and bundles of CAs for a car door

PRIMARY	SECONDARY	TERTIARY
	EASY TO OPEN AND CLOSE DOOR	Easy to close from the outside Stays open on a hill Easy to open from the outside Doesn't kick back Easy to close from inside Easy to open from inside
Good operation and use	ISOLATION	Doesn't leak in rain No road noise Doesn't leak in car wash No wind noise Doesn't drip water or snow when open Dosen't rattle
	ARM REST	Soft, comfortable in right position
	INTERIOR TRIM	Material won't fade Attractive (nonplastic look)
Good appearance	CLEAN	Easy to clean No grease from door
	FIT	Uniform gaps between matching panels

actual views and can therefore mislead teams into tackling problems customers consider unimportant.

Not all customers are end users, by the way. CAs can include the demands of regulators ("safe in a side collision"), the needs of retailers ("easy to display"), the requirements of vendors ("satisfy assembly and service organization"), and so forth.

Are all preferences equally important? Imagine a good door, one that is easy to close and has power windows that operate quickly. There is a problem, however. Rapid operation calls for a bigger motor, which makes the door heavier and, possibly, harder to close. Sometimes a creative solution can be found that satisfies all needs. Usually, however, designers have to trade off one benefit against another.

To bring the customer's voice to such deliberations, house of quality measures the relative importance to the customer of all CAs. Weightings are based on team members' direct experience with customers or on surveys. Some innovative businesses are using statistical techniques that allow customers to state their preferences with respect to existing and hypothetical products. Other companies use "revealed preference techniques," which judge consumer tastes by their actions as well as by their words—an approach that is more expensive and difficult to perform but yields more accurate answers. (Consumers say that avoiding sugar in cereals is important, but do their actions reflect their claims?)

Weightings are displayed in the house next to each CA—usually in terms of percentages, a complete list totaling 100% (see Exhibit 4).

Will delivering perceived needs yield a competitive advantage? Companies that want to match or exceed their competition must first know where they stand relative to it. So on the right side of the house, opposite the CAs, we list customer evaluations of competitive cars matched to "our own" (see Exhibit 5).

Ideally, these evaluations are based on scientific surveys of customers. If various customer segments evaluate products differently—luxury vs. economy car buyers, for example—product-planning team members get assessments for each segment.

Comparison with the competition, of course, can identify opportunities for improvement. Take our car door, for example. With respect to "stays open on a hill," every car is weak, so we could gain an advantage here. But if we looked at "no road noise" for the same automobiles, we would see that we already have an advantage, which is important to maintain.

Marketing professionals will recognize the right-hand side of Exhibit 5 as a "perceptual map." Perceptual maps based on bundles of CAs are often used to identify strategic positioning of a product or product line. This section of the house of quality provides a natural link from product concept to a company's strategic vision.

How can we change the product? The marketing domain tells us what to do, the engineering domain tells us how to do it. Now we need to describe the product in the language of the engineer. Along the top of the

Exhibit 4. *Relative-importanced weights of customer attributes*

Bundles	Customer attributes	Relative importance
EASY TO OPEN AND CLOSE DOOR	Easy to close from outside	7
	Stays open on a hill	5
ISOLATION	Doesn't leak in rain	3
	No road noise	2
	A complete list totals 100%	

Exhibit 5. Customers' evaluations of competitive products

BUNDLES	CUSTOMER ATTRIBUTES	RELATIVE IMPORTANCE	CUSTOMER PERCEPTIONS
EASY TO OPEN AND CLOSE DOOR	Easy to close from outside	7	
	Stays open on a hill	5	
ISOLATION	Doesn't leak in rain	3	
	No road noise	2	

Worst 1   2   3   4   5   Best

OUR CAR DOOR
COMPETITOR A'S
COMPETITOR B'S

house of quality, the design team lists those engineering characteristics (ECs) that are likely to affect one or more of the customer attributes (see Exhibit 6). The negative sign on "energy to close door" means engineers hope to reduce the energy required. If a standard engineering characteristic affects no CA, it may be redundant to the EC list on the house, or the team may have missed a customer attribute. A CA unaffected by any EC, on the other hand, presents opportunities to expand a car's physical properties.

Any EC may affect more than one CA. The resistance of the door seal affects three of the four customer attributes shown in Exhibit 6—and others shown later.

Engineering characteristics should describe the product in measurable terms and should directly affect customer perceptions. The weight of the door will be *felt* by the customer and is therefore a relevant EC. By contrast, the thickness of the sheet metal is a part characteristic that the customer is unlikely to perceive directly. It affects customers only by influencing the weight of the door and other engineering characteristics, like "resistance to deformation in a crash."

In many Japanese projects, the interfunctional team begins with the CAs and generates measurable characteristics for each, like foot-pounds

Exhibit 6. Engineering characteristics tell how to change the product

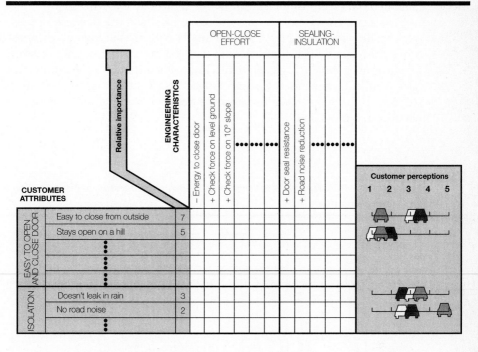

OUR CAR

A'S CAR

B'S CAR

of energy required to close the door. Teams should avoid ambiguity in interpretation of ECs or hasty justification of current quality control measurement practices. This is a time for systematic, patient analysis of each characteristic, for brainstorming. Vagueness will eventually yield indifference to things customers need. Characteristics that are trivial will make the team lose sight of the overall design and stifle creativity.

How much do engineers influence customer-perceived qualities? The interfunctional team now fills in the body of the house, the "relationship matrix," indicating how much each engineering characteristic affects each customer attribute. The team seeks consensus on these evaluations, basing them on expert engineering experience, customer responses, and tabulated data from statistical studies or controlled experiments.

The team uses numbers or symbols to establish the strength of these relationships (see Exhibit 7). Any symbols will do; the idea is to choose those that work best. Some teams use red symbols for relationships based on experiments and statistics and pencil marks for relationships based on judgment or intuition. Others use numbers from statistical studies. In our house, we use check marks for positive and crosses for negative relationships.

Exhibit 7. **Relationship matrix shows how engineering decisions affect** *customer perceptions*

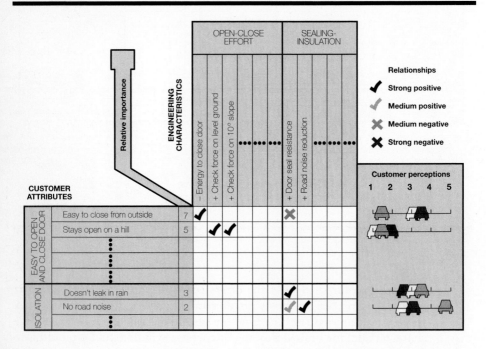

Once the team has identified the voice of the customer and linked it to engineering characteristics, it adds objective measures at the bottom of the house beneath the ECs to which they pertain (see Exhibit 8). When objective measures are known, the team can eventually move to establish target values—ideal new measures for each EC in a redesigned product. If the team did its homework when it first identified the ECs, tests to measure benchmark values should be easy to complete. Engineers determine the relevant units of measurement—foot-pounds, decibels, etc.

Exhibit 8. *Objective measures evaluate competitive products*

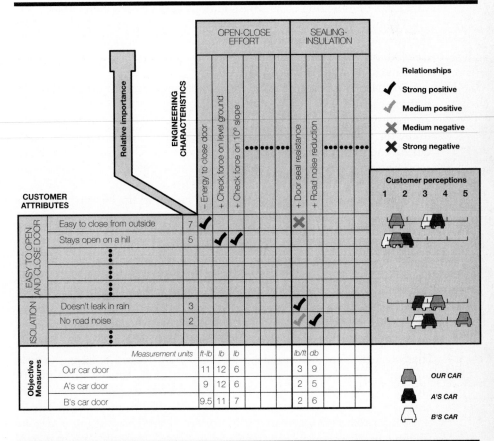

Incidentally, if customer evaluations of CAs do not correspond to objective measures of related ECs—if, for example, the door requiring the least energy to open is perceived as "hardest to open"—then perhaps the measures are faulty or the car is suffering from an image problem that is skewing consumer perceptions.

How does one engineering change affect other characteristics? An engineer's change of the gear ratio on a car window may make the window motor smaller but the window go up more slowly. And if the engineer enlarges or strengthens the mechanism, the door probably will be heavier, harder to open, or may be less prone to remain open on a slope. Of course, there might be an entirely new mechanism that improves all relevant CAs. Engineering is creative solutions and a balancing of objectives.

The house of quality's distinctive roof matrix helps engineers specify the various engineering features that have to be improved collaterally (see Exhibit 9). To improve the window motor, you may have to improve the hinges, weather stripping, and a range of other ECs.

Sometimes one targeted feature impairs so many others that the team decides to leave it alone. The roof matrix also facilitates necessary engineering trade-offs. The foot-pounds of energy needed to close the door, for example, are shown in negative relation to "door seal resistance" and "road noise reduction." In many ways, the roof contains the most critical information for engineers because they use it to balance the trade-offs when addressing customer benefits.

Incidentally, we have been talking so far about the basics, but design teams often want to ruminate on other information. In other words, they custom-build their houses. To the column of CAs, teams may add other columns for histories of customer complaints. To the ECs, a team may add the costs of servicing these complaints. Some applications add data from the sales force to the CA list to represent strategic marketing decisions. Or engineers may add a row that indicates the degree of technical difficulty, showing in their own terms how hard or easy it is to make a change.

Some users of the house impute relative weights to the engineering characteristics. They'll establish that the energy needed to close the door is roughly twice as important to consider as, say, "check force on 10° slope." By comparing weighted characteristics to actual component costs, creative design teams set priorities for improving components. Such information is particularly important when cost cutting is a goal. (Exhibit 10 includes rows for technical difficulty, imputed importance of ECs, and estimated costs.)

There are no hard-and-fast rules. The symbols, lines, and configurations that work for the particular team are the ones it should use.

Exhibit 9. Roof matrix facilitates engineering creativity

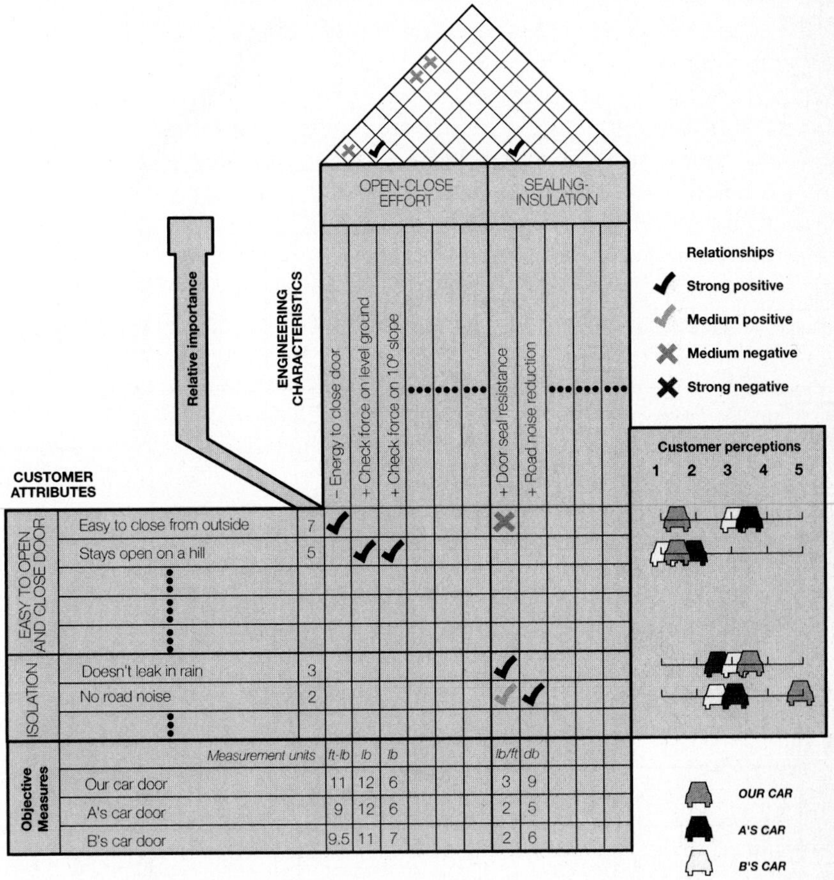

USING THE HOUSE

How does the house lead to the bottom line? There is no cookbook procedure, but the house helps the team to set targets, which are, in fact, entered on the bottom line of the house. For engineers it is a way to summarize basic data in usable form. For marketing executives it represents the customer's voice. General managers use it to discover strategic opportunities. Indeed, the house encourages all of these groups to work together to understand one another's priorities and goals.

Exhibit 10. House of quality

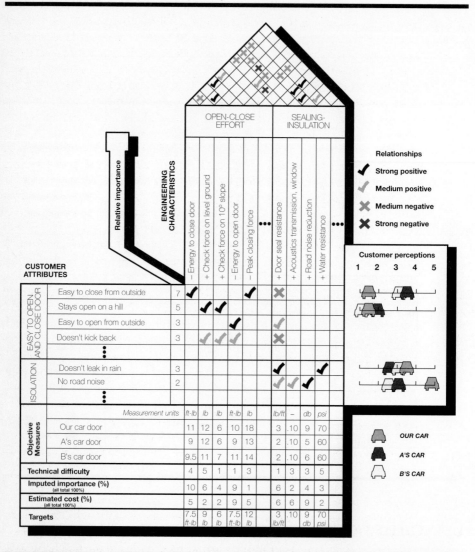

The house relieves no one of the responsibility of making tough decisions. It does provide the means for all participants to debate priorities.

Let's run through a couple of hypothetical situations to see how a design team uses the house. Look at Exhibit 10. Notice that our doors are much more difficult to close from the outside than those on competitors' cars. We decide to look further because our marketing data say this customer attribute is important. From the central matrix, the body of the house, we identify the ECs that affect this customer attribute: energy to close door, peak closing force, and door seal resistance. Our engineers judge the energy to close the door and the peak closing force as good candidates for improvement together because they are strongly, positively related to the consumer's desire to close the door easily. They determine to consider all the engineering ramifications of door closing.

Next, in the roof of the house, we identify which other ECs might be affected by changing the door closing energy. Door opening energy and peak closing force are positively related, but other ECs (check force on level ground, door seals, window acoustic transmission, road noise reduction) are bound to be changed in the process and are negatively related. It is not an easy decision. But with objective measures of competitors' doors, customer perceptions, and considering information on cost and technical difficulty, we—marketing people, engineers, and top managers—decide that the benefits outweigh the costs. A new door closing target is set for our door—7.5 foot-pounds of energy. This target, noted on the very bottom of the house directly below the relevant EC, establishes the goal to have the door "easiest to close."

Look now at the customer attribute "no road noise" and its relationship to the acoustic transmission of the window. The "road noise" CA is only mildly important to customers, and its relationship to the specifications of the window is not strong. Window design will help only so much to keep things quiet. Decreasing the acoustic transmission usually makes the window heavier. Examining the roof of the house, we see that more weight would have a negative impact on ECs (open-close energy, check forces, etc.) that, in turn, are strongly related to CAs that are more important to the customer than quiet ("easy to close," "stays open on a hill"). Finally, marketing data show that we already do well on road noise; customers perceive our car as better than competitors'.

In this case, the team decides not to tamper with the window's transmission of sound. Our target stays equal to our current acoustic values.

In setting targets, it is worth noting that the team should emphasize customer-satisfaction values and not emphasize tolerances. Do not specify "between 6 and 8 foot-pounds," but rather say, "7.5 foot-pounds." This may seem a small matter, but it is important. The rhetoric of tolerances encourages drift toward the least costly end of the specification limit and does not reward designs and components whose engineering values closely attain a specific customer-satisfaction target.

THE HOUSES BEYOND

The principles underlying the house of quality apply to any effort to establish clear relations between manufacturing functions and customer satisfaction that are not easy to visualize. Suppose that our team decides that doors closing easily is a critical attribute and that a relevant engineering characteristic is closing energy. Setting a target value for closing energy gives us a goal, but it does not give us a door. To get a door, we need the right parts (frame, sheet metal, weather stripping, hinges, etc.), the right processes to manufacture the parts and assemble the product, and the right production plan to get it built.

If our team is truly interfunctional, we can eventually take the "hows" from our house of quality and make them the "whats" of another house, one mainly concerned with detailed product design. Engineering characteristics like foot-pounds of closing energy can become the rows in a parts deployment house, while parts characteristics—like hinge properties or the thickness of the weather stripping—become the columns (see Exhibit 11).

This process continues to a third and fourth phase as the "hows" of one stage become the "whats" of the next. Weather-stripping thickness—a "how" in the parts house—becomes a "what" in a process planning house. Important process operations, like "rpm of the extruder producing the weather stripping" become the "hows." In the last phase, production planning, the key process operations, like "rpm of the extruder," become the "whats," and production requirements—knob controls, operator training, maintenance—become the "hows."

Exhibit 11. **Linked houses convey the customer's voice through to manufacturing** Source: *Modified from a figure supplied by the American Supplier Institute, Inc., Dearborn, Michigan.*

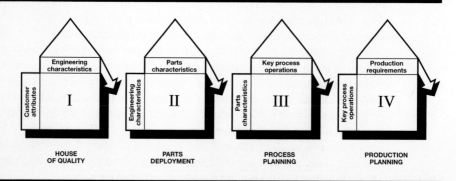

| HOUSE OF QUALITY | PARTS DEPLOYMENT | PROCESS PLANNING | PRODUCTION PLANNING |

These four linked houses implicitly convey the voice of the customer through to manufacturing. A control knob setting of 3.6 gives an extruder speed of 100 rpm; this helps give a reproducible diameter for the weather-stripping bulb, which gives good sealing without excessive door-closing force. This feature aims to satisfy the customer's need for a dry, quiet car with an easy-to-close door.

None of this is simple. An elegant idea ultimately decays into process, and processes will be confounding as long as human beings are involved. But that is no excuse to hold back. If a technique like house of quality can help break down functional barriers and encourage teamwork, serious efforts to implement it will be many times rewarded.

What is also not simple is developing an organization capable of absorbing elegant ideas. The principal benefit of the house of quality is quality in-house. It gets people thinking in the right directions and thinking together. For most U.S. companies, this alone amounts to a quiet revolution.

10 CASE

Barco Projection Systems (A):
Worldwide Niche Marketing

Rowland T. Moriarty
Krista McQuade

On Saturday morning, September 23, 1989, Erik Dejonghe, Frans Claerbout, and Bernard Dursin met to draft a crucial presentation that Dejonghe was scheduled to make to the Barco N.V. board of directors on the following Monday. As the senior vice president and chief operating officer (COO) of Barco N.V., with responsibility for Barco's Projection Systems division (BPS), Dejonghe had to respond to the recent move of a BPS competitor that threatened the heart of the division's sales.

Research Associate Krista McQuade prepared this case under the supervision of Professor Rowland T. Moriarty as the basis for class discussion rather than to illustrate either effective or ineffective handling of an administrative situation. The data contained in this case have been adapted and are not useful for research purposes. Historical information has been condensed.

Copyright © 1991 by the President and Fellows of Harvard College. Harvard Business School case N9-591-133.

Claerbout, the general manager of BPS, and Dursin, in charge of managing Barco's distribution subsidiaries and coordinating the worldwide marketing of projectors, had both worked closely with Dejonghe to formulate the company's options.

One month earlier, the Sony Corporation surprised BPS and the rest of the industry with the unveiling of its 1270 "superdata" projector at the SiGgraph trade show in Boston. Sony's product had seized first place at SiGgraph as the industry's highest performing projector from BPS and its BG400 projector. More damaging still, the 1270 was rumored to be priced 20%–40% below the established market price in its performance class. The industry saw the 1270's positioning as an attempt to widen the market through lower prices. For BPS—a small, batch manufacturer—the 1270's combination of low-price and high-performance threatened to collapse its traditional market segmentation, and to bring prices down to untenable levels. Dejonghe estimated that BPS stood to lose as much as 75% of its forecasted 1990 profits.

Sony's introduction of the 1270 had been timed to prevent competitive response; the industry's most important trade show, Infocomm, was scheduled to take place in the United States in January. Major customers, industry analysts, and dealers would be there, and BPS' performance would determine its sales for the rest of the year. Dejonghe, Claerbout, and Dursin had sketched out their pricing and product development options, and they weighed each one carefully as they plotted BPS' strategy for the following months.

BARCO'S PROJECTION SYSTEMS DIVISION

Barco Projection Systems (BPS) was the second largest division of the Barco N.V. group, with 350 employees, and turnover of 1.39 billion Bfr ($35 million)[1] in 1988 (Exhibit 1). Headquartered at Kuurne, Belgium, 15 km from Barco's main facilities at Kortrijk, the division had been formed in the early 1980s as a result of Barco's interest in the emerging technology of video projection. Throughout the 1980s, the division had grown rapidly. In 1988 it represented 23% of Barco N.V.'s turnover of 5.98 billion Bfr ($150 million).

---

[1]For this case, one U.S. dollar is equal to 40 Belgian francs (Bfr). The actual value of the dollar was extremely volatile during the historical period covered.

Exhibit 1. Key BPS financial data, 1988–1989 (in millions of Bfr)
Source: BPS

	1988 Bfr	$US	1989e Bfr	$US
Turnover[a]	1,387	34.7	1,983	49.6
Direct production costs	772	19.3	815	20.4
Total production overhead	40	1.0	45	1.1
Marketing and R&D	130	3.3	170	4.3
Depreciation and charges	138	3.5	329	8.2
Income before taxes	307	7.7	624	15.6

[a]In addition to sales of video, data, and graphics projectors, BPS turnover recorded sales of projector accessories. In 1988, this category amounted to 168.5 million Bfr ($4.2 million); in 1989 it was 239.3 million Bfr ($6 million).

BACKGROUND: BARCO N.V.

Barco N.V. began operations in 1934 as a producer of radio broadcast receivers. In 1948, it built its first television (TV) receiver, and from then on, consumer TV formed the bulk of its sales. As a small company, Barco was able to compete successfully by carving out a market on the basis of its R&D strength and product quality. From 1955 to 1975, the company grew rapidly and expanded into broadcast monitors and professional video equipment. At the end of the 1970s, however, during the global recession that followed the 1977 oil supply shock, demand for Barco's consumer products sagged. In response, the company redefined its focus from consumer to industrial markets. In 1989, Hugo Vandamme, Barco's president and CEO, looked back on that period:

> We knew that as a small, batch manufacturer we could not have continued to survive in markets for consumer products. Instead, we redrew our strategy to try and focus on top-of-the-line products in niche markets. In one instance, in 1983, we went as far as to say "no" to a customer asking for 15,000 computer monitors. We were able to turn that order down because we had spread our operations out and become involved in other markets. We had set out with a clear vision of who we wanted to be, how we wanted to operate, and where we wanted to compete. Vision is what counts.

The company's strategy throughout the 1980s consisted of three key elements. First, Barco committed itself to becoming a leader in a variety of distinct, but complementary, niche markets. The company entered a new activity only if it had an in-depth knowledge of the market and the technology involved, and if it could be among the top three manufacturers.

The second element of Barco's strategy was a strong commitment to research and development; throughout the 1980s, between 8% and 10% of its annual turnover and 15% of the company's employees were dedicated to R&D. And third, in addition to growth in its businesses, the company sought a growing presence in international markets in sales, product development, and production. In 1988, Barco launched a global expansion campaign for acquisitions and joint ventures abroad. Three major acquisitions in the first half of 1989 totalled 4.4 billion Bfr ($110 million). In that same year, Barco reorganized its operations into seven, autonomous divisions, each with its own research, product development, production, marketing, and sales.

In 1989, with 2,400 employees, Barco N.V. was positioned as one of the top three worldwide manufacturers in each of its product lines: automated production control systems, graphic arts, computer-aided design, and industrial projection. As a result of the company's early 1989 acquisitions and expanding sales in several key markets, turnover was expected to grow 50% in 1989. A number of international awards testified to Barco's technological lead in several fields. In 1988, for example, the company received the international Emmy Award for its studio monitors. The year after, BPS won the Hi-Vi Silver Award in Japan, given for the product contributing the most to electronic visualization technology.

BPS ORGANIZATION WITHIN BARCO N.V.

As part of the divisionalization of Barco N.V.'s operations in 1989, President Hugo Vandamme and Senior Vice President Erik Dejonghe divided responsibility for products between them; BPS reported to the latter. Dejonghe, who assumed his current position at the time of reorganization, was part of the team that propelled Barco's industrial projection activities throughout the 1980s. Joining Barco in the early 1980s, as the product and project manager for special activities, he was promoted in 1983 to president of the division that fabricated TVs and large screen projectors. Frans Claerbout was head of the R&D department for that division, while Bernard Dursin was in charge of its marketing and sales. Dejonghe, Claerbout, and Dursin worked closely together on projectors throughout the 1980s.

In 1989, Claerbout was promoted to vice president of Barco N.V. and was named general manager of BPS. Dursin, also named a Barco N.V. vice president, became the general manager of Barco International, a group that managed the marketing of certain Barco product lines worldwide, including projectors. Claerbout's and Dursin's offices remained within shouting distance of one another, however, and they continued to collaborate on projectors. Dursin continued to manage relations with the division's distributors, and, in addition, he played a leading role in setting the prices for projectors worldwide. Three regional marketing managers, who reported directly to Claerbout, were responsible for sales support to all of the division's distributors. Camiel Derijcke replaced Claerbout in 1989 as the chief engineer in charge of product development at BPS, however Claerbout continued to make the final decisions. (See Exhibit 2 for BPS' organization chart.)

BPS PRODUCTS

BPS designed, manufactured, and marketed sophisticated video projectors for industrial applications. Unlike movie projectors, which operated by shining white light through an image recorded on celluloid film, video projectors recreated an image electronically. Barco's projectors could be connected to TVs, VCRs, and most recently to computers. They were used to project images and information stored in these media onto large screens, for large-audience viewing (see Exhibit 3 for a diagram of the unit). BPS did not invent video projection, but throughout the 1980s, it played a key role in the development of niche market applications for the technology. By 1989, BPS had developed three lines of projectors: video, data, and graphics.

All of BPS' projectors were based on the same design concept, and comprised three major components—tubes (3), lenses (3), and electronics. The division's product line was built primarily around a 7" tube. BPS' strength had traditionally been in electronics; given the same lens and tube combination, BPS was able to achieve measurably better performance in each of the main areas of evaluation than its competition. In 1989, the most important considerations in evaluating the performance of an industrial projector were brightness (measured in lumens), image quality, and resolution. A projector's three components worked together to provide particular results. In general, the tubes, lenses, and electronics represented 15%, 20%, and 50% of the projector's cost structure, respectively. The housing and mechanics represented an additional 15%.

What differentiated BPS' product lines was *scan rate*, or scanning frequency, which measured the speed at which a projector was able to read and process incoming electronic signals. BPS used scan rate to segment its markets; as the sophistication of the application for BPS projectors increased, scan rate increased. BPS' *video* projectors were designed for

Exhibit 2. The management of Barco Projection Systems, 1989

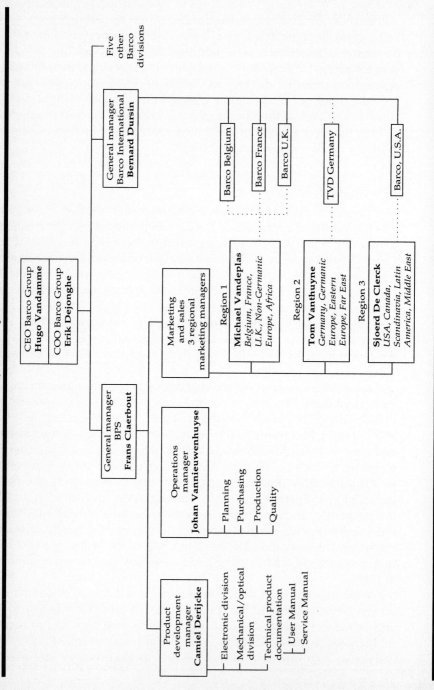

Note: Non wholly-owned distributors not shown here reported jointly to Barco International and the appropriate regional marketing manager.

Exhibit 3. *Projector diagram*

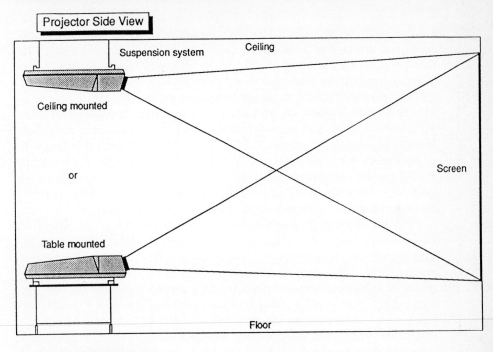

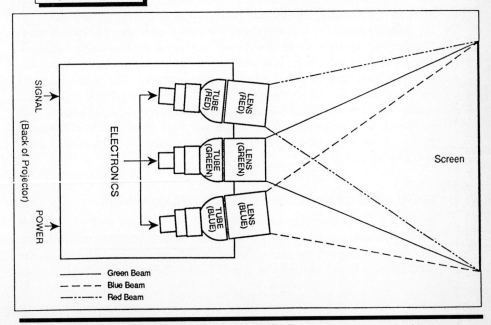

Note: A projector functioned in three stages. First, the information contained in an electronic signal was split into its color (red, green, blue) content. Then, each color's information was redrawn by the electrons of the projector's tubes, one for each color. Finally, the three resulting images were passed through magnifying lenses and projected in sync onto the screen for a full-color image.

compatibility with standard video sources, such as broadcast TV and VCR, and scanned at 16 kilohertz (kHz), or 16,000 lines per second.[2] Its *data* projectors scanned at 16 kHz to 45 kHz, and were capable of displaying input from personal computers as well as video sources. Its *graphics* projectors, BPS' most sophisticated products, scanned from 16 kHz to well above 64 kHz, and accepted input from the powerful computer-aided design and manufacturing (CAD/CAM) systems, as well as from video and data sources. A projector needed to match the scan rate of its source for a clear picture to result; Barco's graphics projectors would not be compatible with any computer scanning higher than 64 kHz. BPS was continually upgrading the scan rates of its most sophisticated projector line to match advances in computer technology.

In 1989, BPS had well-established sales for its video and data lines in a variety of entertainment, training, and presentation markets. Board rooms, training centers, discotheques, classrooms, airplanes, and betting shops around the world had all installed Barco projectors. The monthly sales log of one of BPS' European distributors, for example, listed the sale of four data projectors to the Commission of the European Economic Community (E.E.C.) for video conferencing, five video projectors to a chain of holiday resorts for entertainment rooms, and five data projectors to Groupe Bull, a large French computer company, for training centers. IBM had been one of BPS' best customers throughout the 1980s, having decided in 1984 to equip all of its U.S. training centers with Barco projectors.

In addition, BPS was pursuing a number of more specialized markets for its projection technology, such as process control and simulation. Data and graphics projectors were used for these specialized applications. In 1989, BPS installed a series of projectors in the process control room of the U.S. Union Pacific Railroad, which displayed more than 23,000 km of track on a 200 foot-wide screen. Barco projectors could also be found at the process control centers for the English Channel Chunnel project, in factories, and in flight simulation rooms for military and aerospace applications.

EVOLUTION OF BPS' PRODUCT LINES AND MARKETS

Barco N.V.'s involvement in projection systems began in 1981, when it developed a video projector for showing motion pictures in airplanes. The projector, called the BarcoVision 1 (BV1), was priced at 450,000 Bfr ($11,250), and sold strongly in the U.S. and European markets. As the

---

[2]16 kHz = 30 frames of information per second × 533.3 lines per frame

company began to investigate other applications for its technology, Dejonghe, Claerbout, and Dursin presented their views on the future of projection to Barco's board of directors. They believed the company could pursue one of three directions: 1) it could downgrade its technology to suit consumer video applications, 2) it could upgrade its technology for long-distance, high-performance video projection, 3) or, it could enter the untested market for computer applications.

In their presentation to the board, Dejonghe, Claerbout, and Dursin related discussions of a possible computer-compatible projector that they had had with one BV1 customer, IBM. Developing the computer application, they learned, was feasible, but scan rates would have to be increased to match a computer's faster electronics. Moreover, the projector would have to be designed with enough flexibility to be used by computer companies with different standard scanning frequencies. But Dejonghe and the others felt that the complexity of the application would work to Barco's advantage, keeping larger firms out of the market. They also thought it had the potential to expand projection markets significantly. The board voted to follow their suggestion, and made Dejonghe the new president of the TV and projector division.

In 1983, the sales of that division at Barco were split 80%–20% between TV and projectors. Dejonghe set out to reverse that ratio. By the end of 1983, BPS had introduced the BarcoData 1 (BD1)—the first computer-compatible projector on the marketplace. Priced at 540,000 Bfr ($13,500), the BD1 was able to scan to 18 kHz, and was immediately successful in corporate presentation markets, as well as others. In 1984, BPS introduced two more projectors—the BV2 (395,000 Bfr, $9,875) and the BD2 (590,000 Bfr, $14,750), which incorporated engineering advances that permitted higher scan rates, and thus broader compatibility. From 1984 on, BPS' video and data lines continued to evolve, keeping pace with breakthroughs in design, improved components, and, in the case of data projectors, with ever-changing computer technology. In 1986, BPS began work on a graphics application for its technology.

BPS developed its graphics projectors to handle input from CAD/CAM sources, which required the upgrading of a data projector's scanning frequency to 64 kHz and above. (BPS' most powerful data projector at that time, the BD3, scanned up to 32 kHz). Dejonghe recalled how the division's market segmentation scheme was formalized:

> *I remember the meeting when we decided to create a graphics segment of the marketplace for a machine scanning at 64 kHz and above. Limiting the scan rate on our data projectors would frustrate some end-users. Our plan was to respond to that frustration by offering a graphics projector. We could have made it one machine, but we could not have sold it for the highest price.*

Dejonghe, Claerbout, and Dursin decided to limit video-only projectors to a scan rate of 16 kHz; data projectors to a scanning range of 16 kHz to 45 kHz; and graphics projectors, their newest line, to a scanning range of 16 kHz to 64 kHz and above. In June 1987, BPS introduced its first graphics projector, the BarcoGraphics 400 (BG400), for 1 million Bfr ($25,000). The BG400 was the industry's most sophisticated high-end projector, scanning at up to 72 kHz. By 1989, the price of the BG400 had come down to 960,000 Bfr ($24,000). (Exhibit 4 displays a time chart of BPS' product evolution.)

By September 1989, BPS was looking toward its next generation of product introductions—digitally controlled projectors. Currently, all adjustments to the settings of a BPS projector were carried out manually. The new projectors would incorporate digital technology to allow a projector's mechanisms to be controlled by a hand-held remote-control unit. BPS planned to introduce the technology into the data segment of its marketplace first, and then into its graphics and video segments. BPS engineers had reached the beta test point for its first digital data projector, to be called the BD700, and were completing all modifications. The BD700, to be priced at 640,000 Bfr ($16,000), was scheduled for full production and delivery in October 1989.

Frans Claerbout summed up the forces driving the evolution of Barco's projection product line throughout the 1980s as 1) the constant search for the best possible image, 2) flexibility towards inputs, and 3) increasing user-friendliness. Product evolution, he explained, was "more a result of engineering solutions to problems that arose, than of a specific development plan." Barco's competition in industrial projection had adopted its practice of segmenting its markets by scanning frequency. Video, data, and graphics had become the standard terms for each market by 1989.

PROJECTOR MARKETS

Through 1994, the worldwide market for projectors was expected to grow 8.5% per year. Growth rates for the video, data, and graphics segments of the market, however, varied widely (see Table A).

The largest market for industrial projectors in 1989, across all segments, was North America, with 50% of total unit sales. Western Europe and the Far Eastern market followed, with 36% and 12%, respectively, of total unit sales. The five-year annual market growth predicted for these regions was 9%, 11.5%, and 18%.

Exhibit 4. *BPS product evolution, 1982–1989* *Source: BPS*

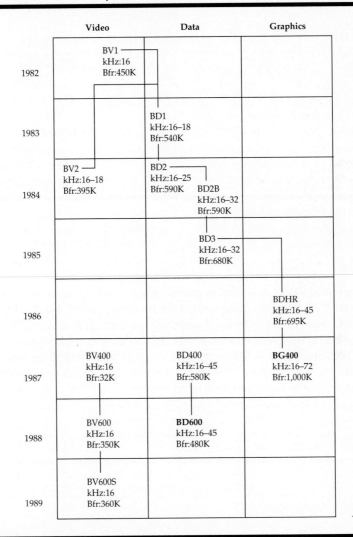

Note: This diagram contains principal 7" projector introductions only; modifications and special-application projectors are not included.

TABLE A   The worldwide market for industrial projectors, 1988

	% units	Predicted growth 1989–1994[a]	Price range
Video	63%	.8%	200,000–280,000 Bfr ($5,000–$7,000)
Data	33%	12.3%	320,000–600,000 Bfr ($8,000–$15,000)
Graphics	4%	40.2%	800,000–960,000 Bfr ($20,000–$24,000)
Total	100%	8.5%	200,000–960,000 Bfr ($5,000–$24,000)

[a]Estimated average annual growth

BPS IN 1989

In September 1989, the data segment of the marketplace represented the heart of BPS' sales for both units and revenues (see Table B). The video segment was moving toward commodity, and BPS was concentrating less and less of its effort in this area. In the high end of the marketplace, BPS was the acknowledged technological leader. BPS estimated its worldwide market share, based on the total number of units sold, at 8% in video, 23% in data, and 55% in graphics.

TABLE B   BPS sales by segment, 1988[a]

	% units	% revenues	% margins
Video	35	23	20
Data	53	54	51
% BD600 of total data	79	67	NA
Graphics	12	23	29
% BG400 of total graphics	85	80	NA
Total	100	100	100

[a]Includes sales to captive BPS distributors.

Exhibit 5. *Barco's product positioning, August 1989 (pre-Siggraph)*

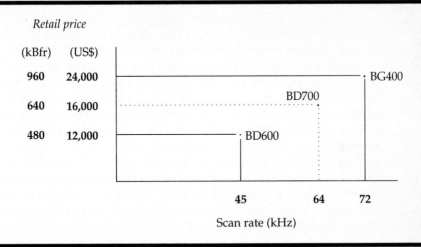

Through 1994, BPS predicted that its video, data, and graphics unit sales would grow 1.4%, 12.3%, and 25% respectively per year. It anticipated that the worldwide market for industrial projection would continue to expand for at least five more years before being superseded by new technologies. In 1989, the division's principal products were the BD600, which scanned to 45 kHz, and the BG400, which scanned to 72 kHz. The two projectors sold in 1989 for 480,000 Bfr ($12,000) and 960,000 Bfr ($24,000), respectively (Exhibit 5). BPS' main line of video projectors sold for 280,000 Bfr ($7,000). BPS sold 4,400 units in all three categories in 1988.

DISTRIBUTION

In 1989, BPS had a two-step distribution system with 45 distributors and approximately 400 dealers worldwide.[3] The division owned four of its distributors—in Belgium, France, the United Kingdom, and the United States—while the other 41 operated independently, but were Barco-exclusive for projectors. Fully-owned distributors represented 61% of BPS' total unit sales, 61% of its revenues, and 59% of its margins. By individual product, they represented 57% of unit sales, 53% of revenues, and

---

[3]BPS could only estimate the number of dealers that carried its products worldwide, since most independent distributors were reluctant to disclose exact figures.

50% of margins for video projection; 61% of units, 60% of revenues, and 57% of margins for data projection; and 75% of units, 71% of revenues, and 70% of margins for graphics projection.

BPS started selling its video projectors in Europe and the United States in 1982, through Barco's video distribution network. When the division entered the data projection market in the mid-1980s, these distributors had been required to invest in training and to add technical personnel. In Belgium, BPS had always handled its own distribution. In the United States, Barco had established a wholly-owned distribution subsidiary in 1986 after the insolvency of its distributor. In France, a key market where the distributor had not kept up with the necessary investment, BPS had acquired its operations in 1988.

In Germany, a market which represented 5%, 9%, and 12% of video, data, and graphics unit sales respectively in 1988, the owner had consistently refused a BPS offer of purchase. In 1989, he had three years remaining in his contract with BPS. Regional Marketing Manager Tom Vanthuyne explained why he would have preferred to own the German distributor:

> *Independent distributors tend to think short term. They are not willing to invest in advertising, or to broaden the number of dealers they work through because they want the margins themselves—for example, they prefer going direct on large accounts. When does it make sense to buy? Until now, we've done it when there were problems in our key markets. In the case of my German distributor, although it is doing OK, it is not making as much money for Barco as it is for itself. That market could be bigger; recently we lost a deal of 600 video units simply because our distributor there was not prepared to cut its margins.*

For each product, BPS established a distributor price in Belgian francs. The distributors, in turn, set their own price to dealers. On average, prices in the United States were a consistent 15% lower than in Europe. The typical pricing relation approach appears in Table C.

TABLE C   BPS' pricing index

	List price	Actual price	Comments
BPS	100	100	41% direct cost, 59% gross margin
Distributor	142	142	30% margin, 12% import duties and freight
Dealer	204	173–184	List price calculated with 30% margin Street price incorporates discounts of 10%–15%

Dealers carrying Barco projectors ranged from "box" dealers to systems dealers. The box dealer, normally found in large cities, sold projectors on the basis of cost alone, providing no service or expertise. Twenty percent of BPS' dealers were "box", while 90% of box sales were video projectors. Systems dealers, at the other extreme, had the know-how to integrate and install packages of equipment according to the end-user's individual needs. Often these systems involved more than one brand of equipment. Given the complexity of Barco projectors—particularly its data and graphics models—80% of the company's dealers were the systems-type.

Projector dealers typically carried three manufacturers' projectors, selecting a line for the low, middle, and high ends of the market, although these could overlap. In addition, projector dealers rounded out their sales with other audio-visual equipment such as overhead projectors, lighting, screens, and consumer electronics. A typical dealer in the United States had turnover ranging from 120 million Bfr ($3 million) to 800 million Bfr ($20 million). About 8%–10% came from after-sales service.

Although a dealer's ideal margin on projectors was 30%, fierce competition resulted more often in margins of 15% to 20%, and occasionally a dealer would go as low as 5% to preserve a customer. Dealer overhead, however, averaged greater than 5%. Margins on service were higher, typically 25% to 35%, and sometimes as high as 70%. Dealers processed information from manufacturers, held vendor fairs and training sessions, and sent mailings. Barco's dealers were required to attend sales and technical courses given by the distributor, and to hire a certain number of Barco-approved technicians. In return, BPS promised price protection for unsold units at a time of a price drop, and stable pricing between the time of the first customer contact and the final order, generally a period of three to six months.

Barco projectors had a reputation among dealers for the highest quality final image and excellent reliability once fully installed. Dealers complained, however, that the machines were unnecessarily complex—designed to win awards, and not be friendly to the end-user. They frequently encountered complications in installing the equipment. End-users, too, often found BPS' control panels and instructions too complExhibit BPS' engineers contended that many of the problems arose when the instruction manual was disregarded.

The typical end user purchased a new projector every five years. With an eye to ever-increasing computer scan rates, customers tended to purchase more performance in a projector than they needed.

COMPETITION

In 1989, three companies competed with Barco in the data and graphics segments of the market for industrial projection: Sony, Electrohome, and NEC. Several other firms, including Panasonic, Mitsubishi, and General Electric, competed primarily in the video and low-scanning data segments of the marketplace, and were not considered major competitors to BPS. In data projection, Sony held the largest percentage of the marketplace, followed by Barco, Electrohome, and NEC. In graphics, BPS was in first place with 55% of the market. BPS' only major competition in the graphics segment was Electrohome, with 44% (see Table D). Exhibit 6 lists the products of each major competitor.

SONY

The Sony Corporation, headquartered in Tokyo, Japan, was a diverse manufacturer of consumer electronics, with 1988 turnover of 460 billion Bfr ($11.5 billion). Industrial projectors were manufactured at its Sony Projectors division, and were estimated to represent 1% of the total company's turnover. Sony was the main player in the video segment of the projection marketplace, with 50% of all units sold. In data, too, Sony held 49% of total units sold; however, its most powerful projector in 1989, the 1031, scanned at 35 kHz. In 1988, the company's product mix was 66% video and 34% data, on a total of 15,000 units.

TABLE D   Market share of the major competitors, 1988 as % of total units sold[a]

		Barco	Sony	E.H.	NEC	Other
Europe	Data	35	35	8	6	16
	Graphics	55	–	43	–	2
N. America	Data	16	62	14	8	–
	Graphics	60	–	40	–	–
Far East	Data	15	30	7	23	25
	Graphics	15	–	80	–	5
Gen. total	Data	23	49	11	9	8
	Graphics	55	–	44	–	1
	TOTAL[b]	25	45	14	8	8

[a]To be read horizontally; "Barco held 35% of the market for data projectors in Europe, vs. Sony's 35%, Electrohome's 8%, etc."
[b]Omits video

Exhibit 6. Products of the major manufacturers, August 1989

Source: BPS

Manufacturer	Model	Scan rate (kHz)	Light output (lumens)	Resolution (# lines)	Retail price (Bfr)	(US$)
Barco	BD600	16–45	600	1,600	480,000	12,000
	BG400	16–72	400	2,000	960,000	24,000
Sony	VPH1031	16–35	300	1,100	420,000	10,500
Electrohome	ECP2000	16–36	400	1,280	344,000	8,600
	ECP3000	16–50	650	1,280	580,000	14,500
	ECP4000	16–70	650	1,280	960,000	24,000
NEC	DP1200	16–35	475	800	420,000	10,500
	GP3000	16–54	600	1,100	640,000	16,000

Note: Light output and resolution were used in addition to scan rate to measure a projector's performance on the world marketplace. Brightness increased with the number of lumens, however the human eye could discern only large increases; for example, the eye perceived a 1,000 lumen projector as 50% brighter than a 100 lumen projector. With resolution, the larger the number of lines, the better the quality of the final image. Barco believed that its projectors had the highest light output of all the competitors, however, due to differences in the standards used to calculate lumens, light output was difficult to compare between companies.

Typically, Sony projectors were positioned below Barco's in terms of performance (scan rate, brightness, image quality, and resolution), and were, on average, 15% lower in price. BPS guessed, in addition, that Sony had fewer engineers dedicated to projection than BPS. BPS expected Sony's next product introduction to be a higher-performance data projector, introduced in the fall of 1989, with an upper scanning limit between 46 kHz and 50 kHz. The division also expected Sony to enter the market with a graphics projector in late 1990.

Sony sold projectors through its network of captive commercial video distributors worldwide. In turn, these distributors worked with over 1,500 dealers across the globe. It was estimated that 50% of Sony's dealers were box dealers. Extensive dealer coverage—Sony had 500 dealers in the U.S. market versus BPS' 100—resulted in a low street price for Sony projectors. While dealers used 30% margins to figure list prices on both Sony and Barco projectors, Sony units were typically discounted 15% for the final sale, while Barco units were discounted 10%. Dealers tended to prefer to sell Barco, because they received not only a higher price, but a higher percentage of that price. In general, however, dealers did a higher volume in Sony. In 1989, few dealers could survive without the Sony volume; an estimated 80% to 90% of professional audiovisual dealers worldwide carried Sony video equipment. Among dealers, Sony had a reputation for reliability and low price.

SONY COMPONENTS AND BPS   Sony had entered industrial projection in 1985, with the 1020 video projector. Although it was slower than Barco's video projectors at that time, it had a sharper focus, indicating a better quality tube. Upon closer examination, BPS engineers found the tube, manufactured in-house at Sony Components, (a division of Sony Corporation), to be far superior in quality to Clinton's, BPS' U.S.-based supplier.

In late 1985, Frans Claerbout traveled to Japan to investigate the possibility of buying from Sony Components. The division, which remained independent from Sony Projectors up to the chairman's level, agreed to supply Barco, and six months later, the first Sony tube was introduced in the Barco Data 3 (BD3). Measured by lumens, Barco was able to achieve better brightness with Sony's tube than Sony itself. Barco terminated its supply relationship with Clinton, and Sony became its sole supplier. Claerbout commented on the relationship:

> Our relationship with Sony is a strange one. We are competitors with Sony projectors, yet we source from their in-house supplier. To obtain tubes that suit our needs, we share a certain amount of technical and developmental information with Sony Components, while they keep us abreast of their latest developments. The fact that we rely on them for an important component makes us vulnerable, but at the same time we think that they value our business because we bring their manufacturing costs down. I would say that over the course of our relationship with Sony Components, I think that they have treated us fairly.

In one instance in 1987, however, Sony introduced a video projector with a tube that Barco had not seen; BPS subsequently purchased the tube, which appeared in its BD600.

In 1989, BPS was actively seeking other tube suppliers. All other tubes available on the market were either inferior to Sony's, more expensive, or both. Many firms manufactured tubes suited to consumer video applications, including Hitachi, Toshiba, Thomson, and Philips, but only the Sony tube had the quality necessary for high-end video projection. Sony, Barco, and Electrohome all sourced tubes from Sony Components. To protect itself against a sudden supply freeze, BPS kept a three-month supply of tubes in-house, and two months of orders in transit from Sony.

BPS spent 90–100 million Bfr ($2.25 million to $2.5 million) annually for approximately 20,000 Sony tubes, which represented around one-fifth of Sony Component's projector tube business. One tube cost between 5,000 Bfr ($125) and 18,000 Bfr ($450), depending on size and quality, and

BPS negotiated continuously with Sony to get the prices down. Altogether, perhaps 35% of Sony Component's business was non-captive. Operations Manager Johan Vannieuwenhuyse observed: "Any time Sony wanted to squeeze us out, they could raise the price of their tubes. We would be dead in the water six months before finding another source. But I don't think they will. When we discuss other suppliers, we are taken seriously." Erik Dejonghe agreed:

> *Sony has told me that their ultimate goal is to be 50% an industrial supplier, and 50% a consumer supplier—not to beat Barco in projection. I am making a bet that they continue to supply us reliably. They need competition to survive, and we are the only competition on whom they make substantial amounts of money.*

In February 1989, Sony Components contacted BPS about a new 8" tube that it was developing. BPS received its first sample of the product in June, and its engineers were running tests on its performance capabilities. The face of the tube was square, rather than the conventional rectangular shape, and the product was significantly more costly than the 7" tubes that BPS was currently sourcing from Sony. BPS engineers had considered incorporating the new tube in the BD700 data projector, but had decided against the idea because it involved redesigning the shape of the projector's chassis, and sourcing a new lens to match.

OTHER COMPETITORS

ELECTROHOME   Electrohome was a privately-held Canadian electronics manufacturer, with 1988 turnover of 5.6 billion Bfr ($139.8 million). Industrial projectors were the most successful group in its Electronics division, which had turnover of 2.5 billion Bfr ($62.5 million) in 1988. Electrohome operated in the data and graphics segments of the marketplace only, and was BPS' largest competitor in graphics. In terms of unit sales, Electrohome was the third largest player, behind Sony and Barco, with 1,585 units sold in 1988. Its product mix was 73% data and 27% graphics. Worldwide, the company had an estimated 11% of total data units sold, and 44% of graphics units.

Electrohome was estimated to have comparable distribution strength to BPS, with close to 100 dealers in the U.S. market; 80% of Electrohome's dealers were systems specialists. Given the intense competition between BPS and Electrohome in graphics, it was rare to find the two manufacturers' products sold by the same dealer. In general, Electrohome's products were priced just below BPS'. Together with BPS, it was viewed as having higher quality projectors than Sony.

NEC   NEC was a major Japanese manufacturer of electronics, with 1988 turnover of 876 billion Bfr ($21.9 billion). The company sold video and data projectors, with a product mix divided 48% and 52% between the two. NEC had pioneered digital convergence technology in the marketplace, introducing a digital data projector in 1987 that became the market standard. The company had not captured as much market share as expected, however, in part due to its inefficient distribution network. Originally, NEC projectors had been sold through the company's well-established network of computer dealers. When sales proved disappointing, NEC granted an OEM agreement to the U.S.-based General Electric Corporation (GE). In 1988, the company sold 1,799 units through its own network, and another 1,200 through GE. The company was estimated to hold 4% of the video market worldwide, in terms of units, and 9% of the data market.

THE SONY 1270 INTRODUCTION

In August 1989, at the SiGgraph trade show in Boston, Sony previewed a projector whose performance shocked Barco and the rest of the industry. Introduced as a "superdata" projector, Sony's new model—the 1270— had the power to scan to 75kHz, placing it in a market for high-performance graphics applications that BPS could not enter. In addition, the 1270 featured the new 8" Sony tube, which gave it higher marks than the BG400 in brightness, image quality, and resolution. Price rumors at SiGgraph, however, placed the unit in BPS' data range, at 600,000 Bfr to 800,000 Bfr ($15,000 to $20,000). If these rumors proved true, such performance had never been available on the market for such a low price. Erik Dejonghe, Bernard Dursin, and Sjoerd de Clerck, the regional marketing manager for the United States, were the Barco representatives at SiGgraph that afternoon. Sjoerd de Clerck described the scene:

> Sony had chosen the U.S. market for its kick-off preview. They had one pre-production unit set up in a very small booth, and their presentation was quite low-key. But the 1270 was a show-stealer. It was a magnificent product. I spent two days at the booth, in a crowd of people, trying to find out as much as I could.

Dejonghe and the others were not so much surprised by a Sony introduction, as by the type of projector the 1270 turned out to be. There had been rumors, spread mostly by dealers, about an impending Sony introduction earlier in 1989. Erik Dejonghe explained:

> Barco had a pretty good idea that Sony was bringing out a new product, but we had expected it to be a direct competitor for the BD600. We thought it would be a 46–50 kHz machine, priced 10%–15% lower than ours. In response, we

*planned to introduce a 64 kHz digital upgrade of the BD600 (the BD700) by
October. We planned to maintain the 960,000 Bfr ($24,000) price tag on our
BG400 until we introduced a digital version (the BG800) in late 1990. Then,
we expected Sony to introduce a 75 kHz graphics projector in 1990, priced
somewhere near 800,000 Bfr ($20,000). All of our projections, however, were
based on the assumption that Sony would respect our "vision" of the marketplace. The 1270 did just the opposite. Its positioning threatened to take a lot of
money out of the industry.*

Sony had announced that it would begin a roll-out of the 1270 in its
major markets in November. The company planned the largest-ever publicity campaign in the history of its involvement in industrial projection;
for example 15,000 customers, dealers, and distributors had been invited
to the 1270's preview in France, and 5,000 to the preview in Belgium.
Regional Marketing Manager Michel Vandeplas commented:

> *It is obvious that Sony is not interested in competing with Barco and
> Electrohome for a few hundred projectors per year in the graphics segment.
> Instead, their aim is to reconquer our data and graphics markets, and, to do it,
> they need to break their market image as a mass producer of low-end products.*

Although the price reports on the projector could not be confirmed, confusion reigned in the marketplace. Dealers were panicked about the possibility of a low priced graphics projector from Sony, while Barco distributors
were anxious to know how Barco planned to react. In early September, in an
effort to calm the market, Barco had spread the word that it did not believe
the rumors about the low price of the 1270. Privately, however, BPS management was worried about the potential for significant erosion of its market share. On the plane ride home from Boston, Dejonghe calculated that
BPS stood to lose as much as 75% of its forecasted 1990 profits.

SATURDAY, SEPTEMBER 23, 1989

As Saturday morning turned into afternoon, Dejonghe, Claerbout, and
Dursin continued to weigh the options that confronted them. Mindful that
BPS risked losing up to 75% of its forecasted 1990 profits, they had yet to
reach agreement on the course to recommend to the board on Monday.

PRICING OPTIONS

Sony had targeted the U.S. and European markets with its 1270—markets which represented 83% of BPS graphics revenues and 91% of its
data revenues. In the month since SiGgraph, Dejonghe, Claerbout, and

Dursin had given considerable thought to the potential impact of the 1270 for the rest of 1989 (October, November, and December) and 1990. By their estimations, if the BG400's price remained unchanged and the 1270 was priced at 800,000 Bfr ($20,000), the BG400 could lose 30% of its market share, or 153.8 million Bfr ($3.85 million).[4] At 600,000 Bfr ($15,000), the Sony 1270 threatened to capture 60% of the BG400's market share, or 307.5 million Bfr ($7.69 million). In addition, at this lower price point, Dejonghe and the others were concerned that the 1270 would cause significant share erosion of the BD600, priced at 480,000 ($12,000).

How should the BG400 and the BD600 be priced in response to the Sony 1270? For each machine, there were the questions of how much, if any, of a price change to implement, which markets to lower prices in, and over what time frame. Dursin reported that BPS' German distributor was feeling the pressure of the 1270 most severely, and had been calling for a significant price decrease since SiGgraph. In early September, the president of the distributorship had declared:

> *The German market is the second largest consumer of BG400s in the world. Our dealers inform us that Sony is taking advance orders on its 1270 in Germany. We need to protect this market, and to do it, we need to drop the price on the projectors drastically and immediately.*

The French distributor, too, was experiencing market pressure to announce a price decrease on the BG400. In the U.S. market, however, the distributor was adamantly opposed to lowering the price. Regional Marketing Manager Sjoerd de Clerck had described the reasoning behind this opposition:

> *It goes without saying that Barco cannot win a price war against Sony. Lowering our price might drive Sony to lower theirs further, and we could not follow. We might never be able to recover our price positioning on graphics machines. In addition, a drastic price drop would damage our reputation among recent, and hopefully repeat, BPS customers. Our only option is to develop a competitive projector.*

Frans Claerbout was concerned about moving too quickly to lower the BG400 price—in markets where Sony was not coming out strongly, it

---

[4]BPS estimated that graphics sales for the last three months of 1989 would reach 106.7 million Bfr ($2.67 million), making the total for the year 426.8 million Bfr ($10.67 million). Assuming 25% growth for the following year, the 1990 graphics revenue estimate was 533.5 million Bfr ($13.34 million). The 15 month revenue estimate was thus 640.7 Bfr ($16.02 million), of which 80%, or 512.56 million Bfr ($12.8 million), could be assumed to be sales of the BG400. A 30% loss in sales of the BG400 would total 153.8 million Bfr ($3.85 million), while a 60% loss would total 307.5 million Bfr ($7.69 million).

would be the equivalent of giving away profit. He wanted to wait on confirmation of the Sony price before making any pricing decisions. In direct contrast, Dursin felt strongly that BPS should preempt the pricing of the 1270.

PRODUCT DEVELOPMENT OPTIONS

The team also had a series of product development options to consider in light of the Sony 1270 introduction. Early in 1989, BPS' development plan had been sketched out according to the division's expectations of increased competition in the data segment of the marketplace. The plan called for the introduction of the digital BD700 by October, followed by the development of the digital BG800 for a late 1990 introduction. Twenty-seven man months were required to complete the BD700 project, while 180 man months had already gone into the project. In addition, BPS engineers were working concurrently on four other projector-related projects.

BPS could continue along its development schedule as planned, introducing the BD700 on time in October for immediate production and delivery. The projector was BPS' first digital model, and also incorporated an improved generator and a scanning frequency of 64 kHz. Sales of the BD700 in 1990 were expected to show an increase of 25% in incremental sales over the forecasted revenue of the BD600, representing some 171.7 million Bfr ($4.3 million).[5] By September, BPS' German distributor and several others already had orders for the BD700, priced at 640,000 Bfr ($16,000), on their books. Claerbout understood the importance of the on-time completion of the BD700 project, for both his engineers' morale and his customers. At the same time, however, the BD700 would not beat the performance of the 1270 at Infocomm in January 1990.

Alternatively, BPS could use the advances made in the BD700 development as a springboard to a digital graphics projector. Dejonghe estimated that BPS engineers could develop a graphics version in two to three months, working from the BD700's chassis, tubes, and lenses, with the sole addition of higher scanning frequency to match that of the 1270. If this option were pursued, the introduction of the BD700 would have to

---

[5]Data revenues were predicted to reach 912.7 million Bfr ($22.8 million) in 1989, and, assuming 12.3% growth for the next year, 1,025 million Bfr ($25.6 million) in 1990. Sixty-seven percent, or 686.8 million Bfr ($17.2 million) in 1990, could be assumed to be sales of the BD600. The BD700 was expected to increase data sales 25% over the BD600, representing 171.7 million Bfr ($4.3 million).

be postponed until December, causing delay in the delivery of the projector to advance-order customers. Also, with BPS' standard 7" tube, the digital graphics projector would still be inferior to the 1270 in terms of light output, picture quality, and resolution.

BPS' third option was to turn immediately to the development of the BG800. As originally planned, it was to be a digital upgrade of the BG400. Faced with the threat from Sony, however, the BG800 now had to be designed to surpass the 1270's performance. This would require a scanning frequency well above that of the 1270's—at least 90 kHz—as well as the incorporation of the Sony 8" tube for the best possible performance. Dejonghe had received confirmation from Sony Components that it would be willing to start supplying the tube immediately. The 8" tube required a special lens, however, and BPS' traditional lens supplier, U.S. Precision Lens of Cincinnati (USPL), had no compatible product. Although in the past Barco and Sony sourced lenses from the same supplier, Sony had worked with a Japanese firm, Fujinon, to develop the lens that appeared in the 1270. Dejonghe was not sure that Fujinon would supply Barco as well.

Claerbout estimated that the development of the BG800 with at least 90 kHz of scanning frequency and new tubes would require at least 80 man-months. In addition, he felt strongly that the projector would have to be ready in time for Infocomm if it was to be effective against the 1270. Meeting that deadline would require the cessation of all other BPS development projects from October 1 on, including the BD700. He voiced a number of concerns about committing BPS' resources to such a drastic move:

> My engineers have been working overtime on the development of the BD700 since mid-summer. Now, we're considering a move that would require the indefinite postponement of the BD700 project, and an even greater commitment on their part. Overtime would be a given, but they'd also have to be willing to give up vacation days until Infocomm at least. We have the capability to produce a great machine, and a machine that is superior to the 1270. But the compression of its development could have repercussions on the quality of the final product. In addition, we don't know yet when the 1270 will actually hit the marketplace, how it will be priced, or how the customers will respond to it.

In addition to these considerations, Claerbout gave the BG800 only a 40% chance of making the Infocomm deadline.